T0223998

Thomas Plagemann   Vera Goebel (Eds.)

Interactive Distributed Multimedia Systems and Telecommunication Services

5th International Workshop, IDMS'98
Oslo, Norway, September 8-11, 1998
Proceedings

Springer

Series Editors

Gerhard Goos, Karlsruhe University, Germany
Juris Hartmanis, Cornell University, NY, USA
Jan van Leeuwen, Utrecht University, The Netherlands

Volume Editors

Thomas Plagemann
Vera Goebel
University of Oslo, UniK - Center for Technology at Kjeller
P.O. Box 70, Granaveien 33, N-2007 Kjeller, Norway
E-mail: {plageman,goebel}@unik.no

Cataloging-in-Publication data applied for

Die Deutsche Bibliothek - CIP-Einheitsaufnahme

**Interactive distributed multimedia systems and
telecommunication services** : 5th international workshop ;
proceedings / IDMS '98, Oslo, Norway, September 8 - 11, 1998.
Thomas Plagemann ; Vera Goebel (ed.). - Berlin ; Heidelberg ; New
York ; Barcelona ; Budapest ; Hong Kong ; London ; Milan ; Paris ;
Singapore ; Tokyo : Springer, 1998
   (Lecture notes in computer science ; Vol. 1483)
   ISBN 3-540-64955-7

CR Subject Classification (1991): H.5.1, C.2, H.4, H.5

ISSN 0302-9743
ISBN 3-540-64955-7 Springer-Verlag Berlin Heidelberg New York

© Springer-Verlag Berlin Heidelberg 1998
Printed in Germany

Typesetting: Camera-ready by author
SPIN 10638782   06/3142 – 5 4 3 2 1 0   Printed on acid-free paper

Lecture Notes in Computer Science 1483

Edited by G. Goos, J. Hartmanis and J. van Leeuwen

Springer

Berlin
Heidelberg
New York
Barcelona
Budapest
Hong Kong
London
Milan
Paris
Singapore
Tokyo

Preface

The area of interest of the International Workshop on Interactive Distributed Multimedia Systems and Telecommunication Services (IDMS) ranges from basic system technologies such as networking and operating system support to all kinds of teleservices and distributed multimedia applications. Technical solutions for telecommunications and distributed multimedia systems are merging, for example, the Internet protocol, middleware solutions and standards, and Qualiy-of-Service (QoS) play a key role in both areas. However, the range from basic system technologies to distributed multimedia applications and teleservices is still a broad area. We believe that it is important to understand the implications of multimedia applications and their requirements for middleware and basic system technology and vice versa. We are challenged to develop new and better suited solutions for all layers of distributed multimedia systems and telecommunication systems to meet the requirements of the future information society.

In the call for papers we invited contributions in this area in form of full papers and position papers. We attracted 68 submissions from Asia, Australia, Europe, North America, and South America; despite the fact that September 1998 is a very busy conference month. In cooperation with ACM Multimedia'98, we turned the potential problem of overlapping and conflicting interests into an advantage, by placing both events back-to-back and coordinating parts of the organization process.

The IDMS'98 program committee (PC) members and additional referees worked hard to review all submissions such that each contribution received at least three reviews. Based on the comments and recommendations in these reviews, the PC performed in the course of one week an online meeting over the Internet that was structured into two discussion and ballot phases. For this purpose, our local organization team integrated two isolated applications (from Brandenburg University of Technology at Cottbus, Germany and Darmstadt University of Technology, Germany) and extended them to a full conference organization tool. The resulting system, called *ConfMan*, combines World Wide Web and e-mail with a database system and enforces security, privacy, and integrity control for all data acquired during workshop organization, including comments and votes during the PC online meeting.

The final result from the discussions and ballots of the PC online meeting was a very uniform suggestion for the final program and for the best paper of IDMS'98. The additional task for us as program co-chairs was only to group the selected papers and structure them into sessions.

We are proud to present at IDMS'98 a high quality program with 23 full papers and seven position papers that discuss topics like: user aspects and Quality-of-Service, distributed multimedia applications, multimedia documents and authoring, platforms for collaborative systems, MPEG, coding for wireless and mobile environments, storage servers, flow control, and congestion control. The best paper of IDMS'98 is entitled *Single Pair of Buffers: Reducing Memory Requirements in VBR Media Servers* and is authored by A. Garcia-Martinez, J. Fernandez-Conde, and A. Vina. This selection is extended with two invited keynotes: D. Shepherd from Lancaster University (UK) will discuss *ATM, Reservations and IP - ATM, RIP?* and G. Parulkar from Washington University St. Louis (USA) will present *High Speed Packet Switching and QoS: (A) Guru's Perspective.*

We are confident that this technical program will enable IDMS'98 to follow the tradition of previously very successful IDMS workshops. We would like to express our deepest gratitude to R. Steinmetz and L. Wolf, who organized IDMS'97 in Darmstadt, Germany, and the organizers of the previous IDMS workshops for the honor and their confidence in us that allowed us to take over the responsibility for IDMS'98 in Oslo, Norway. The organization of IDMS'98 is an important milestone for us, because IDMS'98 takes place exactly four years after we started to create and build up a new research group in distributed multimedia systems at UniK - Center for Technology, University of Oslo.

Next years IDMS will be organized by M. Diaz, LAAS-CNRS, in Toulouse, France. We hope that we can pass at least part of all the help and support we received from the IDMS'97 organization team on to the organizers of IDMS'99.

We would like to acknowledge the cooperation with ACM and Gesellschaft für Informatik e.V. (GI), the technical co-sponsorship of IEEE, and the financial support from Den Norske Dataforening (DnD), Ericsson, the Norwegian Research Council, Telenor Research and Development, Thomson CF Norcom AS, and UniK - Center for Technology. Due to this support we are able to keep the fees of IDMS'98 affordable and to offer a very interesting technical and social program.

Finally, we would like to thank Hellfrid O. Newman as treasurer and Pål Halvorsen, Ketil Lund, and Nader Mirzadeh in local organization for their dedication and hard work that enabled us to make IDMS'98 a successful event.

June 1998   Thomas Plagemann and Vera Goebel

Welcome Address from the Royal Ministry of Education, Research and Church Affairs

To the Participants of the 5th International Workshop on Interactive Distributed Multimedia Systems and Telecommunication Services:

I am delighted to welcome the participants at the 5th International Workshop on Interactive Distributed Multimedia Systems and Telecommunication Services.

Throughout the world we see that plans are being developed and conferences are arranged to form and organize the information society. I am happy to see that the University of Oslo and the Center for Technology at Kjeller are hosting this international conference on multimedia technology and distributed multimedia applications.

I am very concerned about the new possibilities that we see in the use of digital media and global computer networks for creating new and flexible learning opportunities. We want to use these new opportunities actively in a lifelong learning perspective.

I send you my best wishes for a successful workshop and hope that this opportunity to present new interesting research results to a broad professional audience gives stimulus for collaboration and further progress in the field.

I wish all participants a pleasant stay in Oslo.

June 1998

Jon Lilletun
Minister of Education, Research and Church Affairs

Welcome by the Rector of the University of Oslo

On behalf of the University of Oslo, I heartly welcome all participants to IDMS'98. In a generation, computers have grown from curious devices to a ubiquitous technology of unprecedented power and influence. Information technology and multimedia content now link us across time and space in a manner that is revolutionizing the learning society and human organizations. The University of Oslo has over the last years initiated new research and education activities in areas of information technology. We experience new focus points with communication technology in natural sciences and broad new initiatives with interdisciplinary collaborations including natural sciences, humanity sciences, social sciences, educational sciences, and sciences of law. Distributed multimedia systems and telecommunication services have been one of the basic fields for this new collaboration effort.

I hope all participants will enjoy the workshop and the visit to our university.

June 1998   Lucy Smith
                                                   Rector of the University of Oslo

Welcome by the Faculty of Mathematics and Natural Sciences of the University of Oslo

We welcome all participants to IDMS'98. One of the most significant technology changes for the next decade is distributed computing and network technology that can handle and integrate all media data types into the global network. The title of the conference addresses distributed multimedia systems and telecommunication services as basic instruments for the implementation of information channels between the public information and knowledge providers, private companies and the customers. Our scientists work very hard to implement new and better technologies for multimedia applications. We experience rapid developments of new systems, services and applications, but the technology has clearly been limited by lack of functionality. In the future, we face a new technology push, and it is an expectation that the multimedia system area will give new perspectives to the global research, education and commercial activities.

We hope the workshop will be an inspiration for you all and provide opportunities for all and a pleasant time in Norway.

June 1998

Jan Trulsen, Dean
Rune Fløisbonn, Director of Faculty
Faculty of Mathematics and Natural Sciences
University of Oslo

Organization

Patronage

Rune Fløisbonn   University of Oslo, Norway

Program Co-Chairs

Vera Goebel   University of Oslo, Norway
Thomas Plagemann   University of Oslo, Norway

Program Commitee

Finn A. Aagesen   NTNU Trondheim, Norway
Hossam Afifi   ENST Bretagne, France
Ernst Biersack   Institut Eurécom, France
Gregor v. Bochmann   University of Montreal, Canada
Berthold Butscher   DeTeBerkom, Germany
Andrew T. Campbell   Columbia University of, USA
Samuel T. Chanson   Hong Kong University of S & T, Hong Kong
Luca Delgrossi   University Cattolica Piacenza, Italy
Michele Diaz   LAAS-CNRS, France
Frank Eliassen   University of Tromsø, Norway
Wolfgang Effelsberg   University of Mannheim, Germany
Domenico Ferrari   University Cattolica Piacenza, Italy
Jean-Pierre Hubaux   EPFL Lausanne, Switzerland
David Hutchison   Lancaster University, UK
Winfried Kalfa   TU Chemnitz, Germany
Thomas D. C. Little   Boston University, USA
Eckhard Moeller   GMD FOKUS, Germany
Kjersti Moldeklev   Telenor, Norway
Klara Nahrstedt   University of Illinois, USA
Gerald Neufeld   University of British Columbia, Canada
Guru Parulkar   Washington University St. Louis, USA
Bjørn Pehrson   KTH Stockholm, Sweden
Stephen Pink   SICS, Sweden
Bernhard Plattner   ETH Zurich, Switzerland
Hans Scholten   University of Twente, Netherlands
Ralf Steinmetz   GMD, Germany
Hiroshuda Tokuda   Keio University, Japan
Lars Wolf   TH Darmstadt, Germany
Martina Zitterbart   TU Braunschweig, Germany

Treasurer

Hellfrid O. Newman   UniK - Center for Technology at Kjeller, Norway

Local Organization

Pål Halvorsen   University of Oslo, Norway
Ketil Lund   University of Oslo, Norway
Nader Mirzadeh   University of Oslo, Norway

Referees

F. A. Aagesen
R. Ackermann
H. Afifi
G. Ahanger
O. Angin
S. Arbanowski
R. Baier
E. Biersack
G. v. Bochman
B. Butcher
A. T. Campbell
S. T. Chanson
M. Clarke
L. Delgrossi
M. Diaz
J. Dittrich
C. Edwards
W. Effelsberg
D. Elias
F. Eliassen
P. J. Emstad
G. Fankhauser
D. Ferrari
S. Fischer
S. Fischer
C. Fuhrhop
N. Georganas
W. Geyer
V. Goebel

C. Griwodz
P. Halvorsen
E. Hartley
B. E. Helvik
V. Hilt
K. Hofrichter
J.-P. Hubaux
D. Hutchison
J. Incera
W. Kalfa
M. Kouvanis
R. Krishnan
G. Kuehne
C. Kuhmuench
N. Lagha
R. Liao
R. Lienhart
M. Liepert
T. D. C. Little
K. Lund
L. Maknavicius
L. Mark
L. Mathy
H. d. Meer
S. v. d. Meer
N. Mirzadeh
E. Moeller
K. Moldeklev
K. Nahrsted

A. Narayanan
G. Neufeld
R. Noro
G. Parulkar
S. Pfeiffer
S. Pink
T. Plagemann
B. Plattner
J. Schmitt
H. Scholten
P. Schoo
D. Sisalem
B. Slagsvold
P. Spilling
R. Steinmetz
B. Stiller
N. Stol
Å. Sudbø
D. Venkatesh
D. Waddington
J. Werner
R. Wittmann
L. Wolf
V. Wuwongse
W. Yu
A. Zisowsky
M. Zitterbart

Supporting/Sponsoring Institutions

ACM SIGMM and SIGCOMM
DnD – Den Norske Dataforening
Gesellschaft für Informatik e.V.
IEEE Communications Society
NFR – Norwegian Research Council
UniK – Center for Technology at Kjeller

Supporting/Sponsoring Companies

Ericsson
Telenor – Research and Development
Thomson CF Norcom AS

Table of Contents

ATM, Reservation and IP
ATM, RIP?

Professor D. Shepherd

Distributed Multimedia Systems Group
Computing Department
Lancaster University, UK

Recent advances within IP have raised significant questions over the future of ATM. The only major advantage of ATM has been its ability to handle streamed multimedia traffic, however, even in this role ATM has been seen as too heavy-weight; the simple AAL (AAL5) has won the day - but this is little more than an admission that IP, or at least an IP like protocol, is what is needed.

The 'feature' of ATM that made it suitable for multimedia was reservation, but yet again IP has won the day by providing support for streaming via RSVP and differential services. The power of the new reservation functionality within IP is significantly better than that offered within ATM as it can provide a degree of fault tolerance through the use of soft-state; it can no longer even be argued that this is simply an add-on as IPv6 has the flow label and type-of-service fields as a fundamental part of the header.

Another problem with ATM is its poor support for multicast applications; simply duplicating cells, which seems almost an afterthought in any case, can hardly be considered sufficient for current, let alone developing, multimedia applications. If one looks at the capabilities of IP multicast and RSVP it is clear that support for the heterogeneity that must be inevitable within any real environment has been included in the basic design; anything less will simply force these issues to be addressed at a higher level creating unacceptable inefficiencies. Looking more closely at performance, it has long been argued that IP just can not be engineered to perform at high enough speeds to support the next generation of networks; again this has been shown to be a totally unfounded criticism, gigabit routers can be bought off the shelf today.

The final nail in the coffin of ATM must be the headlong rush to provide IP support on ATM systems, even the European Commission seems to have this view and has funded a number of major projects on this one issue alone. Sure, this must be seen as an admission of failure by the ATM community.

Professor Shepherd will elaborate on these points within his keynote address and outline what he sees as the future role of IP, and the systems that support it, within the distributed computing environments of tomorrow.

High Speed Packet Switching and QoS: (A) Guru's Perspective

Guru Parulkar

Applied Research Laboratory
Department of Computer Science
Washington University in St. Louis
St. Louis MO 63130
guru@arl.wustl.edu
http://www.arl.wustl.edu/~guru

The last decade has seen remarkable transformations throughout the data and telecommunications industries. The Internet has progressed from a tool for technical sophisticates to an important infrastructure for the global information based economy, and countries all over the world are moving quickly to deploy advanced network systems to exploit the benefits of online services. There are numerous studies that report on the tremendous growth of the Internet and related industries and their impact on various aspects of our lives. The basic conclusion of all these studies is that the Internet is growing and growing fast in terms of almost all possible metrics: number of users, hosts, networks, bits per second transmitted, services, and most importantly Internet companies and their revenues.

High speed packet switching and support for Quality of Service (QoS) are two key technologies for the emerging Internet infrastructure. Significant progress has been made in developing these technologies. However, there has been a lot of confusion and controversy about which technologies and in what form would have the most impact on the real commercial Internet and its applications. In this talk I will provide my own perspective on these issues (and aid to the ongoing confusion and debate!).

A Secure, Accountable, and Collaborative Whiteboard

Werner Geyer and Rüdiger Weis

Praktische Informatik IV
University of Mannheim, 68131 Mannheim, Germany
{geyer,rweis}@pi4.informatik.uni-mannheim.de

Abstract. This paper addresses the design issues and the security concept of the digital lecture board which is an enhanced whiteboard tailored to the specific needs of collaborative types of work, for instance, in computer–based distance education. The development of the digital lecture board emerged from our experiences with synchronous, computer-based distance education in the TeleTeaching projects of the University of Mannheim. For almost two years, we have been using video conferencing tools for transmitting lectures and seminars. These tools prove to be far from optimal for this purpose since they do not take into account the specific requirements of teaching. Security issues such as authentication, secure key exchange, and fast symmetric encryption are almost completely neglected, even though security is extremely important to allow for confidential, private sessions, and billing.

1 Introduction

Computer–based video conferencing is one of today's most exciting multimedia applications. Powerful hardware and advances in communication technology have enabled the synchronous transmission of audio and video even over low-bandwidth networks, such as ISDN, in an acceptable quality. Besides pure teleconferencing, these systems are employed in a variety of application fields such as distance education, teleconsulting, telemedicine, telecooperation etc. Most of these advanced application fields impose a high demand on additional functionality, which is not satisfied by existing video conferencing software. Specifically, most systems do not provide secure data delivery or accounting. Moreover, the systems are not tailored to their field of application, i.e. video conferencing systems are too limited in their functionality for these more advanced applications. This concerns specifically the support of collaborative types of work.

The shared whiteboard is often the core part of these systems since it is used to transmit additional contents (e.g. slides) besides audio and video. In this paper, we present a novel whiteboard – called *digital lecture board* (dlb) – which is being developed in the context of computer–based distance education, i.e. the whiteboard takes into account the specific requirements of synchronous teaching and learning in higher education, continuous education or corporate education [GeEf98]. The development of the dlb has been motivated by the experiences we gathered in the TeleTeaching projects of the University of Mannheim where, for almost two years, lectures and seminars have been transmitted using standard video conferencing tools [Ecea97].

In the first part of this paper, we discuss shortcomings of existing video conferencing tools and describe features, we had in mind while designing the digital lecture board. We then present our security concept which is a user–oriented approach taking into account the specific security requirements of different user groups. The last section covers implementation issues of the current prototype.

2   Related Work

Many existing video conferencing systems such as NetMeeting, CUSeeMe, ProShare, or PictureTel provide audio, video, application sharing, and standard whiteboard features but consider neither security issues nor the specific requirements of collaborative types of work, such as reference pointing, raising hands, forming work groups, controlling the course of instruction etc. The MBone tools vic (video conferencing tool), vat (visual audio tool), and wb (whiteboard) actually support security but only weak DES encryption [MaBr94]. Due to export limitations, the DES encryption cannot be used legally outside the US.

For the platform–independent whiteboard TeleDraw [TeDr98], which is being developed in the context of the MERCI project [MERCI98], it is planned to include MERCI security enhancements; the current version is still insecure. Since TeleDraw has been designed for video conferencing, it also does not consider requirements of collaborative work.

Security within the MERCI project is basically realized by the Secure Conferencing User Agent (SCUA), developed by GMD [Hiea96] . SCUA is an email–based approach which allows to initiate conferences securely using PEM (Privacy Enhanced Mail). For the actual transmission of data, SCUA relies on the built–in weak security mechanisms of the MBone tools. After key exchange, the tools have to be started with the session key as a parameter or the key has to be introduced by hand.

The following two projects focus on the specific needs of teleteaching but do not consider security issues: The "Authoring on the Fly" (AOF) concept [BaOt96] merges broadcasting of a lectures with authoring of CBT software. With AOF, lectures are transmitted by means of an extended whiteboard to a number of receivers. Interactivity is limited to audio and video, the whiteboard has no back channel. Thus, collaborative types of instruction are not supported.

The Interactive Remote Instruction (IRI) system developed at Old Dominion University [Maea96] is a very powerful, integrated teaching and learning environment. The system allows to view or make multimedia class presentations, to take notes in a notebook, and to interact via audio/video and shared tools. The system differs from ours in that IRI partly relies on analog transmission of NTSC video signals. Collaboration is limited to application sharing and the secure transmission of data is not supported.

3 The Digital Lecture Board

3.1 Motivation

The digital lecture board is being developed in the context of the TeleTeaching project of the University of Mannheim [Ecea97]. The project aims at an improvement in quality and quantity of teaching and learning by using multimedia technology and high speed networks for the distribution of lectures and seminars. We have implemented three different instructional settings which are characterized by their scope of distribution, interactivity, and individualization of the learning process. In the *Remote Lecture Room* (RLR) scenario, large lecture rooms, equipped with audio/video facilities, are connected via high speed networks, and courses are exchanged synchronously and interactively between participating institutions. *Remote Interactive Seminars* (RIS) describe a more interactive type of instruction. Small groups of participants are distributed across few seminar rooms which are also connected by a network. The focus of RIS is the cooperative, on-line construction and presentation of reports. The *Interactive Home Learning* (IHL) scenario aims at a maximization of the distribution degree of all class participants. Each students learns asynchronously as well as synchronously at home in front of his or her PC.

We use the Internet and the MBone video conferencing tools for remote lecturing. Observations, surveys, and interviews with the students and lecturers during the last two years indicate that these tools can provide satisfactory results if the lecturer adapts the layout of the lecture exactly to the limited features of these tools. But they are far from optimal for teleteaching since they have not been designed for this purpose. This concerns specifically the whiteboard, which can be considered to be a substitute for the traditional blackboard. Along with audio, the whiteboard is most important for conveying knowledge to distributed participants. In order to overcome the weaknesses of the whiteboard, we decided to develop the digital lecture board (dlb) which will better satisfy the needs of computer–based teaching and learning.

3.2 Functional Requirements

In this Section, we present, in more detail, the shortcomings of the existing MBone tools[1], and we discuss the most important features which we had in mind when designing the dlb.

Integrated User Interface. The MBone tools do not provide an integrated user interface. Teachers and students complained about many confusing windows and control panels which are not important for remote instruction but make it more difficult to operate the tools. Since computer–based distance education should not be restricted to computer experts, we find it especially important

---

[1] The described shortcomings more or less concern also other video conferencing systems such as NetMeeting, CuSeeMe etc.

that the dlb provides an easy–to–operate user interface which integrates also audio and video communication. In order to allow the interface to adapt to different instructional settings, it should be configurable.

Media Usage and Handling. One of the most limiting factors of the MBone whiteboard is media usage and handling: only postscript and plain ASCII text are supported as external input formats, and the later or joint editing of the built–in graphic and text objects is not possible. For instance it is not possible for a distributed group to create a common text or graphic, or to modify objects created by different participants. Since media are very important for a modern instruction, the dlb should support a variety of media formats (e.g. GIF, HTML, AIFF, MPEG etc.) as well as many built–in object types (e.g. lines, rectangles, circles, text etc.). Objects must be editable by every participant, and the dlb should provide functions like select, cut, copy, paste, group, raise, lower etc. similar to a word or graphic processing software.

Workspace Paradigm. The shared workspace of wb is limited to a two–layer concept with a postscript slide in the background and drawings and text in the foreground. It is, for instance, not possible to render two different postscript slides onto a single page so that results of two distributed work groups may be compared. Moreover, participants cannot have a private workspace where they can prepare materials, for instance, when doing on–line group work. Modern tele-cooperation software requires a more flexible workspace concept with multiple layers where arbitrary media objects (audio, video, images, animations etc.) can be displayed, grouped, raised, lowered etc. Single participants or small groups should be offered private workspaces (invisible to the rest of the whole group) in order to allow for modern types of instruction such as group work. The outcome of the group work can be transferred to the shared workspace so as to allow a wider discussion of the results.

Collaborative Services. Today's video conferencing systems suffer a lack of communication channels compared to the traditional face–to–face situation. Social protocols or rules, which control the human interaction and the course of instruction in a classroom, are not automatically available in a remote situation and are difficult to reproduce. These mechanisms include, for instance, raising hands, giving the right to talk or to write on the black board, setting up work groups, and reference pointing. Collaborative services provide mechanisms to support the communication of persons through computers and to increase social awareness. In this sense, collaborative services provide an electronic surrogate to compensate as far as possible for the lack of inter–personal communication channels. Basic services such as floor control, session control, telepointers, or voting should be supported by the dlb. Floor control realizes concurrency control for interactive, synchronous cooperation between people by using the metaphor of a *floor*. A floor is basically a temporary permission to access and manipulate shared resources (e.g. a shared drawing area). Session control denotes the administration of multiple sessions with its participants and media. Session control increases social awareness in distributed work groups because members gain knowledge of each other and their status in the session. A detailed analysis of collaborative requirements in teleteaching for the dlb can be found in [HiGe97].

Synchronized Recording and Playback of Sessions. The dlb should also provide the possibility to record a transmitted lecture or course including all media streams (audio, video, whiteboard actions and media, telepointers etc.). Students will then be able to retrieve the lecture in order to review certain topics, or the complete lecture if they have missed it. In order to achieve a synchronized recording, data has to be time–stamped. The data streams could then be recorded by existing systems like the VCRoD service (Video Conference Recording on Demand) [Holf97] . These systems rely on the Real–Time Transport Protocol RTP for synchronized recording [Schea96]. The current release of the MBone whiteboard wb does not implement the RTP standard.

Storage and Retrieval of Pages and Teaching Materials. Lectures or courses given with the computer need to be prepared in advance like any lecture, i.e. producing slides, images, animations etc. The preparation of materials with the MBone whiteboard is limited to a list of postscript files which can be imported by mouse click during a session. In order to allow for a better preparation of on–line lectures and for saving results after a lecture, the dlb should support storage and retrieval of pages and objects in a structured, standardized file format such as SGML. Moreover, it would also be desirable for the dlb to have access to a multimedia database which stores teaching and learning materials of teachers and students.

4   Secure Communication

The exponential growth of the Internet in recent years has fostered the importance of secure communication. Security has become a major research task in computer science. Especially for commercial applications, security in the Internet is a "conditio sine qua non".

4.1   State–of–the–Art

The well-known DES encryption algorithm, which was originally designed for confidential, not–classified data, is used in many applications today (e.g. electronic banking). The MBone whiteboard wb also relies on DES for encryption. The weaknesses of DES have been disclosed by several brute force attacks , which indicate that the key length for symmetrical algorithms should be at least 75–90 bits [Blea96].

DES was originally developed for the hardware of the seventies. Many multimedia applications today have high demands on performance, which cannot be satisfied by DES software encryption. In recent years, novel algorithms with better performance but similar to the DES scheme have been developed [Weis98]. Some of these algorithms are even specifically designed for fast software encryption on modern processor generations or for bulk encryption. Due to export restrictions of the US government, export versions of many software products have the DES encoding disabled. Hence, outside the US, the DES encryption feature of wb cannot be used. Moreover, the source code of wb is not publicly available which inhibits the evaluation or modification of the cryptographic implementation.

These security limitations of the MBone whiteboard have stimulated the integration of modern encryption algorithms into the digital lecture board in order to provide secure video conferencing with a powerful, collaborative whiteboard also outside the US.

4.2 Security Requirements

Besides the functional requirements described in Section 3.2, a secure digital lecture board has to satisfy the following security requirements:

- **Fast symmetric encryption** for the secure transmission of confidential whiteboard data. Data streams will be encrypted by the use of a session key.
- **Flexibility for different user groups** with different requirements concerning legal issues, costs, level of security, and performance.
- **Strong and flexible public key cryptography** allows for authentication and automated, secure exchange of session keys.
- **Light–weight payment protocols** are required for the automated billing of telecourses and teleseminars which are offered by educational institutes or by companies. Since the group of session participants may be rather large and the paid amounts rather small, we prefer light–weight protocols with minimal overhead.
- **New voting schemes** for light–weight and secure voting in a session. Voting as a collaborative service adds an additional communication channel to a distributed group which increases social awareness (see Chapter 3).

4.3 Security Concept

User–Orientated Cryptography. The digital lecture board dlb uses a flexible user–oriented security concept which can be adapted to different user requirements. Users may choose from predefined security profiles or even customize their own security requirements. The choice may be driven, for instance, by legal issues, costs, required level of security, and performance. We identify the following main profiles or user groups: *public research*, *financial services*, and *innovative companies*.

Since users who work in the *public research* often benefit from license–free employment of patented algorithms, we rely on the *IDEA* cipher [Lai92]. The algorithm has a strong mathematical foundation and possesses good resistance against differential cryptoanalysis. The key length of 128 bit immunizes against brute force attacks. IDEA was the preferred cipher in the PGP–Versions (Pretty Good Privacy) until 2.63. However, commercial users have to pay high license fees.

In the *financial services* business we find a strong preference for DES–based systems. Since DES has been cracked by brute force attacks, we suggest to use *Triple–DES, DESX* or *DES²X* in this application field. In addition to the fact that Triple–DES has a poor performance, it also does not provide the same high security level like IDEA. Recent work of Stefan Lucks showed that the effective key length for exhaustive search attacks can be reduced to 108 bits [Luck98a] while still being immune against brute force attacks. A cheaper method to avoid brute force attacks on DES is whitening. With one key–depended permutation before and after the DES encryption, exhaustive key search is provably not feasible. RSA Data Security Inc uses this procedure under the name DESX [KiRo96] in their toolkit BSAFE. In addition, we have implemented DES²X [Luck98b] which combines whitening and double encryption. It seems that DES²X is more secure and faster than Triple–DES.

For *innovative companies,* which are not afraid of new algorithms, we use the novel, license–free algorithm *CAST*. CAST is a very fast DES–like Substitution–Permutation Network cryptosystem designed by Carlisle Adams and Stafford Tavares. The system has rather good resistance to differential cryptoanalysis, linear cryptanalysis, and related–key cryptanalysis. The CAST–128 [RFC2144] implementation uses 128 bit keys. CAST possesses a number of other desirable cryptographic advantages compared to DES, e.g. no complementation property and an absence of weak and semi–weak keys. CAST is the preferred cipher in the PGP–Versions 5.x.

In addition to these predefined user profiles, we have implemented options for full compatibility to *PGP 2.63i*, *PGP 5.x* and *GPG* [Koch98]. GPG is a free PGP replacement which does not rely on patented algorithms. For users with low computing power, speed issues are most important. *Blowfish* [Schn94] is one of the fastest secure block ciphers which encrypts plaintext on 32–bit microprocessors at a rate of 26 block cycles per byte while being very compact. It was designed by Bruce Schneier with a variable key length up to 448 bit. We use a key length of 128 bit for the Open–PGP Blowfish–128 and 160 bit for GPG compatibility.

Table 1: Predefined Profiles.

Profile	Public key	Secret key	Hash
Public research	Rabin	IDEA	RIPEMD–160
Financial services	RSA	Triple–DES	RIPEMD–160
Innovative companies	Rabin	CAST	RIPEMD–160
PGP 2.63i	RSA	IDEA	MD5
PGP 5.x	DLP	CAST	SHA–1
GPG	DLP	Blowfish	RIPEMD–160

Automatic Key Exchange and Authentication. For authentication and to simplify the key exchange, we use asymmetric cryptography. In addition to *RSA*, we offer signature and key exchange procedures based on the *Discrete Logarithm Problem* (ElGamal/DSA) in order to avoid problems with US patents.

We have also included *Rabin's* scheme for key exchange and signatures. Rabin's scheme achieves security through the difficulty of finding square roots modulo a composite number, which is equivalent to factorization. Due to this fact, Rabin's scheme is *provably* at least as secure as RSA. Rabin encryption needs only one modular squaring which provides faster encryption than in RSA. After decryption of the session key, we get four possible results. Using a specific padding designed by Lucks and Weis, we can easily find the right result.

This Scheme improves cryptographic security and strengthens Rabin against several attacks [LuWe98a].

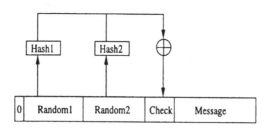

Fig. 1. Simple Scheme of redundant use of random oracles [LuWe98b].

As innovative, new procedure group, we further implement ElGamal and DSA procedures over *elliptic curves*. These cryptosystems are assumed to provide the same security as the discussed RSA scheme while operating with a shorter key length. This allows, for instance, for shorter signatures, reduced communication, less storage space, and faster computation.

4.4 Research Issues

Fast Multimedia Encryption. All presented algorithms are well tested and state–of–the–art in cryptography. But we are also developing new algorithms for fast software encryption of continuous multimedia streams. A very interesting idea is to use *Luby–Rackoff* [LuRa88] ciphers. These ciphers can operate very fast on large block sizes [Luck96a]. Anderson and Biham have proposed two fast block ciphers: *Lion* and *BEAR* [AnBi96]. The fastest new algorithm in this class is *BEAST* (Block Encryption Algorithm with Shortcut in the Third round) [Luck96b]. BEAST is assembled from key–dependent hash functions and a stream cipher and it is *provably* secure if these building blocks are secure. The performance is very good when operating on large blocks sizes. We have tested different versions of BEAST in a real application for the first time [WeLu98].

Light–weight Payment. Based on encrypted communication, it is rather easy to implement light–weight payment protocols. After the transmission of an electronic coin, the current session key – encrypted with the public key of the client (payer) – is transmitted. This method of separating encrypted multi-/broadcast transmission of the bulk data and the key transmission can be found in many distributed multimedia systems. Since for many information on the Internet only small and inexpensive payments are acceptable, some light–weight payment systems have been developed.

The *Payword* system proposed by Rivest and Shamir seems to be most suitable [RiSh96]. Payword uses the values of a hash chain as coins. This idea can be also found in the S/Key–protocol of Lamport [Lamp81]. The cost for the required calculations is very low. Even the frequently required verification of a payment needs only one hash. According to Rivest and Shamir, the calculation of a hash function is up to ten thousand times faster than public key operations. Therefore, we will rely on the payword scheme for billing multimedia applications.

Voting Schemes. The implementation of secure election and voting as a collaborative service is subject to current research. One idea is to build a "Virtual Hyde Park" where the participants can decide in a confidential vote who should manage the floor. So far, no light–weight, group–oriented, and secure voting schemes are known.

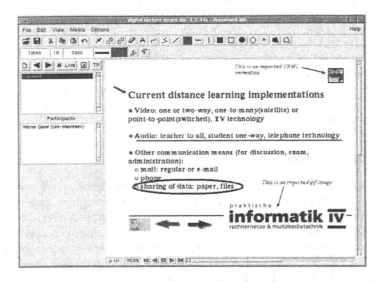

Fig. 2. User interface of the digital lecture board.

5 Implementation Issues

The prototype implementation of the digital lecture board includes already pretty much all of the features mentioned in Chapter 3 as well as the security concept described in Chapter 4. We do not have integrated audio and video communication yet; the interface to our VCRoD system is in preparation. For a high degree of portability, we implemented the prototype in C++ and the Tcl/Tk scripting language [Oust94], and we took great care to reuse only components which are available on all major platforms. Figure 2 shows a screen shot of dlb's user interface.

The security concept described above is integrated directly in the core part of the digital lecture board as indicated in Figure 3. We have implemented a security library, which includes the cryptographic algorithms and protocols discussed in the previous Chapter. The library provides full compatibility with the Open–PGP standard [OPGP97], i.e. dlb's RTP data packets are wrapped in OPGP packets. We then use either unreliable UDP connections (e.g. for telepointers) or reliable SMP connections to transmit the OPGP/RTP packets. SMP (scalable multicast protocol) is a reliable transport service which has been specifically developed for the dlb. Security functionality can be accessed and controlled through dlb's graphical user interface or via command line parameters.

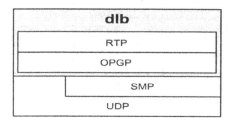

Fig. 3. Communication protocols.

6 Conclusion

Our experience with computer–based distance education indicates that standard video conferencing systems are far from optimal for collaborative types of instruction or work. Furthermore, they almost completely neglect security issues. As a consequence, we have developed the digital lecture board presented in this paper. The digital lecture board is an integrated, extended whiteboard tool which is tailored to the specific needs of computer–based distance education, but also integrates state–of–the–art security mechanisms. The digital lecture board can also be employed for high–secure video conferencing with extended demands on collaboration and media flexibility. Future research directions are distributed

VRML animations for the dlb, light–weight payment protocols and a novel secure voting scheme.

7 Acknowledgment

The authors would like to thank Prof. Dr. Wolfgang Effelsberg and Dr. Stefan Lucks for helpful comments and interesting discussions.

References

[AnBi96]   Anderson, R., Biham, E., "Two Practical and Provable Secure Blockciphers: BEAR and LION", Proc. Fast Software Encryption (ed. D. Gollmann), LNCS 1039, Springer, 1996.

[BaOt96]   Bacher, C., Ottmann, T., "Tools and Services for Authoring on the Fly", Proc. ED–MEDIA'96, Boston 1996.

[Blea96]   Blaze, M., Diffie, W., Rivest, R., Schneier, B., Shimomura, T., Thompson, E., Wiener, M., "Minimal Key Lengths for Symmetric Ciphers to Provide Adequate Commercial Security", a report by an ad hoc group of cryptographers and computer scientists , January 1996.

[Ecea97]   Eckert, A., Geyer, W., Effelsberg, W., "A Distance Learning System for Higher Education Based on Telecommunications and Multimedia – A Compound Organizational, Pedagogical, and Technical Approach", Proc. ED–MEDIA'97, Calgary, June 1997.

[GeEf98]   Geyer, W., Effelsberg, W., "The Digital Lecture Board – A Teaching and Learning Tool for Remote Instruction in Higher Education", accepted at ED–MEDIA'98, Freiburg, Germany, June 1998.

[Geea97]   Geyer, W., Eckert, A., Effelsberg, W. ,"Multimedia Technologie zur Unterstützung der Lehre an Hochschulen" (in German). To appear in: Multimediales Lernen in der beruflichen Bildung, Verlag BW, Nürnberg 1997.

[HiGe97]   Hilt, V., Geyer, W., "A Model for Collaborative Services in Distributed Learning Environments", Proc. of IDMS'97, Darmstadt, LNCS 1309, 1997, pp. 364 –375.

[Hiea96]   Hinsch, E., Jaegemann, A., Wang, L., "The Secure Conferencing User Agent – A Tool to Provide Secure Conferencing with MBONE Multimedia Conferencing Applications". Proc. IDMS'96, Berlin, LNCS 1045, 1996, pp. 131–142.

[Holf97]   Holfelder, W., "Interactive Remote Recording and Playback of Multicast Videoconferences", Proc. IDMS'97, Darmstadt, LNCS 1309, 1997.

[KiRo96]   Kilian, J., Rogaway, P., "How to protect DES against exhaustive key search", Proc. Advances in Cryptology–Crypto'96, Berlin, Springer, 1996.

[Koch98]   Koch, Werner, "GPG – The free PGP Replacement", 1998. http://www.d.shuttle.de/isil/gnupg.html

[Lai92]   X. Lai, "On the Design and Security of Blockciphers", ETH Series in Information Processing, v. 1, Hartmut–Gorre–Verlag, Konstanz, 1992.

[Lamp81]   Lamport, L., "Password Authentication with Insecure Communication", Communications of the ACM 24(11), November 1981.

[LuRa88]   Luby, M., Rackoff, C., "How to construct pseudorandom permutations from pseudo random functions", SIAM J. Computing, V17, N2, 1988.

[Luck96a]   Lucks, S., "Faster Luby–Rackoff ciphers", Proc. Fast Software Encryption (ed. D. Gollmann), LNCS 1039, Springer, 1996.

[Luck96b]   Lucks, S., "BEAST: A fast block cipher for arbitrary blocksize", (ed. Hoprster, P.), Proc. IFIP'96, Conference on Communication and Multimedia Security, Chapman & Hall, 1996, pp. 144-153.

[Luck98a]   Lucks, S., "Attacking Triple Encryption", Proc. Fast Software Encryption 5, 1998, (ed. S. Vaudenay), LNCS 1372, Springer, 1998.

[Luck98b]   Lucks, S., "On the Power of Whitening", Manuscript, Universtität Mannheim, Fakultät für Mathematik und Informatik, 1998.

[LuWe98a]   Lucks, S., Weis, R., "How to Encrypt with Rabin", Technical Report, Universtität Mannheim, Fakultät Mathematik und Informatik, 1998.

[LuWe98b]   Lucks, S., Weis, R., "Improced Security throw Redundant Random Oracle", Technical Report, Universtität Mannheim, Fakultät Mathematik und Informatik, 1998.

[MaBr94]   Macedonia, M.R., Brutzmann, D.P., "MBone Provides Audio and Video Across the Internet", IEEE Computer. 27(4), 1994.

[Maea96]   Maly, K., Wild, C., Overstreet, C., Abdel–Wahab, H., Gupta, A., Youssef, A., Stoica, E., Talla, R.,Prabhu, A., "Virtual Classrooms and Interactive Remote Instruction", International Journal of Innovations in Education", 34(1), 1996, pp. 44–51.

[MERCI98]   Multimedia European Research Conferencing Integration, Telematics for Research Project 1007, 1996-1998. http://www-mice.cs.ucl.ac.uk/mice/merci/

[OPGP97]   Callas, J., Donnerhacke, L., Finnley, H., "OP Formats – OpenPGP Message Format", Internet Draft, November 1997.

[Oust94]   Ousterhout, J. K., "Tcl and Tk Toolkit", Addison–Wesley, 1994.

[RFC2144]   Adams, C., "The CAST–128 Encryption Algorithm", May 1997.

[RiSh96]   Rivest, R., Shamir, A., "Payword and Micromint", to appear, http://theory.lcs.mit.edu/ rivest/RivestShamir-mpay.ps

[Schn94]   Schneier, B., "Description of a New Variable–Length Key, 64–Bit Block Cipher", Proc. Cambridge Security Workshop on Fast Software Encryption, LNCS 809, Springer, 1994, pp. 191–204.

[Schea96]   Schulzrinne, H., Casner, S., Frederick, R., Jacobsen, V. , "RTP: A Transport Protocol for Real–Time Applications", Internet RfC 1889, IETF, Audio–Video Transport Working Group, 1996.

[TeDr98]   Part of the Telematics for Research Project 1007 MERCI, 1996-1998. http://www.uni-stuttgart.de/Rus/Projects/MERCI/MERCI/TeleDraw/Info.html

[Weis98]   Weis, R., "Moderne Blockchiffrierer" (in German), in: "Kryptographie", Weka-Fachzeitschriften–Verlag, Poing, 1998.

[WeLu98]   Weis, R., Lucks,S., "Faster Software Encryption",Technical Report, Universtität Mannheim, Fakultät Mathematik und Informatik, 1998.

Mobile Guide –
Location-Aware Applications from the Lab to the Market

Tom Pfeifer, Thomas Magedanz, Stephan Hübener

Technical University of Berlin / GMD FOKUS,
Kaiserin-Augusta-Allee 31, D-10589 Berlin, Germany
Phone: +49-30-3463-7288, Fax: +49-30-3463-8000
pfeifer@fokus.gmd.de

Abstract: Location-Aware applications for supporting the mobile user have proven significant relevance for future telecommunication and computing. The paper evaluates the outcome of the labs and the requirements of commercial usage. Based on the state-of-the-art analysis and the business view, a system architecture is proposed from the technical perspective. The required support of heterogeneous resources leads to the necessity of an adequate middleware platform. Merging data from different sources and constraints in the transmission and presentation capabilities of the mobile side require sophisticated media scaling and conversion capabilities. The envisaged service architecture leads finally to the discussion of the prototype developed on our Mobile Guide test-bed.

Keywords: Location-Awareness, Mobility, Multimedia communication in distributed, heterogeneous networking and computing environments, Media Conversion, Multimedia Databases, Electronic Commerce.

1 Introduction

The rapid progress in the melting computing and telecommunication technologies enables new application scenarios within shorter and shorter periods of time. Mobile voice and data communication, localisation and positioning systems, portable devices, have not only become available for everybody, they have even reached a degree of miniaturisation that enables even further integration of complex systems to hand-held devices.

Communication technology comprises available systems such as GSM, DCS1800, DECT, as well as proposed systems such as wireless ATM and UMTS [1]. Positioning and localisation, scaling from global to in-house systems, is provided by miniature Global Positioning System (GPS) receivers as well as infrared tracking. Personal Digital Assistants (PDAs) are produced for various dedicated purposes and for general use with increased processing power, memory, presentation capabilities, and extendability by standardized expansion cards.

From the content point of view, platforms for electronic commerce and information currently establish themselves in the Internet. Future scenarios could be considered as virtual electronic marketplaces, where providers of services and consumers communicate and trade. However, applications are designed for mainstream stationary office use; only very few content providers will maintain dedicated tailored content considering the special requirements of mobile usage.

On the other hand, the majority of potential users demand to be supported in the way they are used to live and to do things. So, even in the new world of Electronic Commerce and Cyberspace, the old habits of the users need to be mapped to the capabilities of technology.

Within this context, GMD FOKUS and TU Berlin / OKS have established the Mobile Guide Project, focusing on the integration of state of the art mobile and localization technology with special consideration of content handling and adaptation. The project is based on sound experience within the institutes regarding electronic tracking, Personal Communication Support, filtering and dynamic conversion of communication media [19], middleware platforms [16], and Mobile Agents [14].

The experiments consider as the business case for Mobile Guide the support of travelling business men and tourists visiting foreign cities and having the need to be guided and to communicate, to book commercial services as car rentals, local travel, accommodation, to inform themselves about leisure entertainment, etc. Therefore, the system supports the major domains of location-aware, mobile computing, which are Navigation, Communication Services, Information services, and Electronic Commerce.

The basis for these services represent the information already available through internet services like WWW on the one hand, or databases inside a provider domain, which are filtered, converted, and/or combined in accord to the desired added value. Obviously navigation support and directory services are also offered by Mobile Guide. In addition Mobile Guide features location independent information services access as well as personalizable communication services (e.g. fax, email, (internet) telephony, etc.), access to service brokerage and electronic commerce.

This paper describes the Mobile Guide architecture, the potential application cases and the design of a prototype. In the following section, the paper provides a review of the state of the art in related technologies, regarding location awareness, mobile communication, distributed processing, and mobile computing technology. Based on a short discussion of the business view, we discuss the system architecture in general technical terms, the requirements of middleware platforms, the media adaptation, and the service architecture. Finally, the Mobile Guide system is introduced with descriptions of the hardware test-bed, the currently supported scenario, and the prototype implementation.

2 State of the Art

2.1 Related Work in Location Awareness

The emerging interest in location-aware, mobile computing has brought up several experimental platforms within the recent years, since the early 90s. Very active pools of research are grouped around Xerox PARC and Cambridge University, UK.

For location derivation, Olivetti Research and Cambridge University, UK, provided the nowadays classical approach of the Active Badge [4] infrared sensor system, sufficiently published, currently supported by the weight-measuring Active Floor [5], and the ORL ultrasonic location system [6]. While the floor measures the movement of people and carried objects, analysed by Markov Chains, the latter employs hardware attached to objects, transmitting ultrasonic pulses in specific directions, detected by a matrix of receivers mounted on the ceiling. It obtains a resolution of 10..15 cm.

B.N. Schilit and R. Want described experiments with PARCTab [7] PDAs and infrared communication and pioneered the Ubiquitous Computing Experiment at Xerox [8], where they discussed philosophical and design aspects of hand-held computing interfaces. They provided basic definitions and categorizations of context-aware applications [9], like proximate selection, automatic contextual reconfiguration, contextual information and commands, and context-triggered actions. With the Active Map Service (AMS) [10], they propose a hierarchical structure for the description of objects in relation to locations, such as rooms, floors, buildings, regions, and areas. They discuss the effects of bandwidth limitations in wireless scenarios.

S. Long discusses various aspects of context-aware applications [13] and describes an electronic guidebook experiment, employing GPS. She receives dedicated informa-

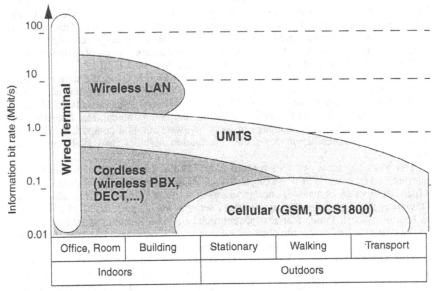

Fig. 1. Comparison of Wireless Transmission Capabilities (after [1])

tion, previously tailored to the requirements of the PDA, such as maps and routing facilities. The approach suffers from the bulkiness of the GPS receiver these days. She discusses the relationship of positioning and communication: PARCTab and Active Badge are found relying on the very close coupling of positioning and communication, as the beacon of mobile communication is used for location. If positioning comes from GPS as a provider of pure location data, a separate communication link is required if the stationary entity needs this knowledge for selection and preparation of content.

P.J. Brown uses prototype systems in Kent [12], based on the PARCTab PDA [7] and the HP Palmtop for local infrared communication, deriving location information from Active Badges and separate GPS receivers. He describes the context-aware application of "stick-e" notes, mapping the metaphor of PostIt notes into the electronic domain. The retrieval of previously produced notes is triggered by entering the same context by the same or a different person.

2.2 Mobile Communication

Various ongoing activities ensure that the user in the 21st century will have access to mobile broadband networking facilities, at any time and in any place [1]. Figure 1 provides a comparison of existing and proposed wireless communication technology. Hereby, UMTS will provide a generic core network comprising various radio access networks, either already existing (GSM, DECT), or specifically designed for UMTS, either terrestrial, or satellite based.

The solutions already in use still have strong limitations regarding bandwidth and QoS. Although the situation will improve with technology like wireless ATM, also in future the bandwidth will be magnitudes smaller than in wired networks. As a consequence, mobile information systems have to consider the necessity to receive content specifically tailored for this kind of application, or to adapt and scale the commonly used content for the specific limitations, i.e., to tailor it 'on the fly'.

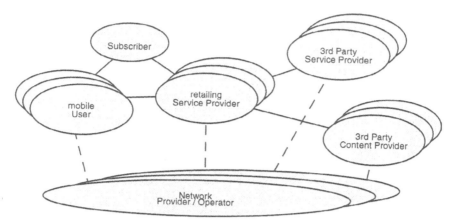

Fig. 2. Business Role model of mobile services

2.3 Distributed Object Technology, Platforms, Mobile Agents

The necessity of object oriented middleware platforms as a basis for future telecommunication, defining sets of principles and components supporting openness, flexibility, and programmability has gained general acceptance within the recent years. The Common Object Request Broker Architecture (CORBA) has been established as standard which enhances RPC based architectures by free and transparent distribution of service functionality.

Promising CORBA based technologies like the Telecommunication Information Network Architecture (TINA) [15], have been developed for the domain of fixed access networks and succeed their current evaluation for migration into mobile communication networks [3]. In the latter case, special consideration is dedicated to specific problems, which distinguish radio access from fixed networks, such as seamless handover.

The TANGRAM platform [16] prototypes and evaluates an environment supporting the object-oriented development of distributed multimedia applications based on the architectures developed by TINA-C. This platform suggest how to structure software for information networking. Its strength is the applicability for a wide range of telecommunication services and the independence of system and network technology. To enforce the approach taken in TINA-C, the concepts of abstract object-oriented frameworks are introduced and applied. Such frameworks can be a means to support the design and development of software sharing the advantages of object-orientation like reusability, scalability, and customizability.

The technology of Mobile Agents (MA) is currently overcoming the threshold from laboratory to its application within the telecommunication industry. It is today's current understanding that MA provide an important enhancement of distributed object technology. M. Breugst [14] discusses their influence on mobile communication and illustrates, how they can be used for the implementation of service control and mobility management functionalities. He describes an agent platform, Grasshopper, entirely implemented in JAVA on top of CORBA, developed in compliance to the OMG Mobile Agent System Interoperability Facility (MASIF).

2.4 Terminal Device Technology

One of the limiting factors of previous experiments, the bulkiness of the mobile hardware, has now been eliminated. PDAs provide nearly the same processing power

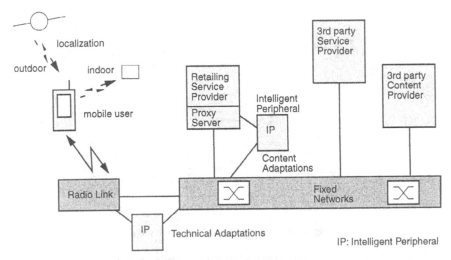

Fig. 3. Technical System Architecture

as modern notebook computers. Communication and localization devices are either integrated or delivered as a small PC card. This modularity and easy exchangeability of these devices is regarded as a feature, allowing the scalability of location-aware scenarios from global or metropolitan to in-house applications.

Some PDAs, such as the Nokia 9000i Communicator, already integrate GSM communication, so we expect to see this approach within other devices sooner or later. On the other hand, the Nokia concept is completely proprietary, not flexible like the open concept of the Apple Newton, regarding the operating system and the hardware support for two PC cards.

For communication, combined modem adaptors for GSM and plain old telephony are available as PC card for the connection to a mobile telephone. Nokia and Ericsson have announced a card with integrated transmitter and antenna for spring 1998, in form of a slim Nokia Wireless Data PC card (type II), and a thick PC card (type III) from Ericsson. For in-house connectivity, a WaveLAN card provides access to the wireless LAN. Alternatively, a DECT compliant communication device or infrared data transmission can be used for this purpose.

The other PC card slot is occupied with the localization equipment, which might be a GPS receiver. It differs from a standard card just by the hunchback of the antenna. As an alternative within buildings, this card could easily be replaced by an infrared transmitter compliant to the Active Badge system.

We believe that it is only a question of very short time in industrial development to have very compact devices for dedicated purposes.

3 System Architecture

3.1 Business View

The case studies evaluated in section 2 were focused on laboratory experiments, where content and adaptation services were concentrated on the same party, playing different roles. Today's situation in the Internet, on the other hand, is characterized by many parties involved, which lack classification into their roles. Approaches in Electronic Commerce now consider the division of labour between specialized parties, as illustrated in the Business Role Model in Figure 2.

Our model follows the ideas in UMTS [2], while it brings stronger focus to the variety of providers in a contract relationship to the user, and third party providers distinguished for services and content.

As depicted, the Network Operators provide mobile access networks as well as fixed network connections, interconnected by core and backbone networks.

The various service providers in direct relation to the user are subdivided in contractors for network services, information retailers, and parties providing commercial services. These service providers retail their own applications, additionally, they may add value to services and content from third party providers, e.g. by adapting public domain information and common services for the specific requirements of the mobile user.

While the user and the subscriber may be identical (e.g. individual user), this model covers also the case that e.g. a company subscribes services used by their employees.

3.2 General Technical Overview

When describing the system architecture, the business model from the previous section has to be mapped into more technical terms, which leads to Figure 3. Generic use of location-aware technology has to consider all degrees of coupling between localization and communication, i.e. the use of independently received position data (GPS), transmitted IDs (Active Badge), as well as beacon derived data (in-house infrared). Positioning methods employing data from cellular structures (e.g. GSM) are not discussed separately here, as the granularity of the cells is too coarse for the applications in mind. In consequence, the position data have to be transmitted from the mobile user to the retailer, hence making the latter role mandatory.

The mobile user is free to decide about the source of the received information. He may contact third parties directly for location independent purposes. When he needs the location awareness, and/or wants the data adapted to the specific needs, he contacts his retailer. The latter may provide service from his own databases, or collect information from the third parties.

Adaptation, scaling and conversion of data may be performed at different places in the scenario. Technical adaptations, such as simple stream format conversions, may be performed at the network level, in particular at the interface between fixed network and the radio access provider. More sophisticated conversion may be performed by the retailer, who knows the terminal profile of its customer in detail, or through a fourth party, specialized in this specific service. For the unit executing the conversion, the term of an Intelligent Peripheral (IP) [17] has been adopted from advanced concepts of Intelligent Networks (IN).

3.3 Distributed Processing Architecture

The main feature of employing a Distributed Processing Environment (DPE) is the provision of an abstraction from the complexity of the underlying structure of heterogeneous hardware platforms and the difficult networking functionality. The DPE spans all potential end user systems and provider systems. Having in mind the openness and heterogeneity of target environments, e.g. as envisaged in UMTS, the usage of a standardized platform, such as CORBA, is mandatory for interoperability between different providers and vendors.

On top of the DPE, cf. Figure 4, dedicated environments may be installed. As depicted, a Distributed Agent Environment (DAE) can be used for specific services, while other applications can avoid the agents and employ the DPE directly. Details of the DAE usage and functionality can be found in [14]. The usage of agents itself opens various interesting applications in electronic commerce and service brokerage.

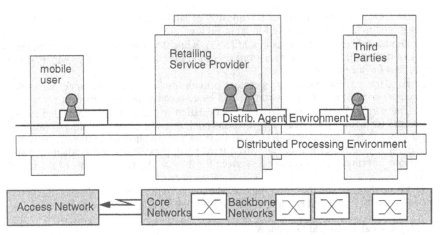

Fig. 4. Middleware architecture for distributed processing and agent support

3.4 Dynamic Content Adaptation by Media Conversion

Approaches discussed in the section of related work rely on data specifically tailored for the needs of location-aware PDA applications. The applications itself are either proprietarily designed, or employ the WWW browsing technology built into the PDA.

To restrict the scope of available information to previously tailored data limits the freedom of choice of the user and builds dependencies on specific content providers. Therefore, the goal of our research is the usage of content not specifically designed for the purpose of PDA technology and mobility. On the other hand, we cannot ignore the bandwidth limitations currently existing in mobile communication and the restricted presentation capabilities of hand-held devices for multimedia data.

We need capabilities to convert information from one carrying medium into another while maintaining the semantic; or to scale and adapt the information to the displayable resolution or transmittable volume. Within the context of Personal Communication Support, we have achieved this goal by providing a system for dynamic selection and allocation of suitable media converters from a large set of available modules, followed by their automatic configuration and chaining [19]. Our approach (Figure 5) goes far beyond the classical provision of pre-wired converters for dedicated purposes, as it allows flexible access to data of previously unknown type and characteristics.

This technology provides therefore a platform for easy definition and upload of filters for personal preferences, and common and personalized content filters.

While simple adaptations might be performed within the limited resources of the PDA, the more complex scenario of adaptation happens either within a proxy server in the provider environment, or as a third party service, or in case of format adaptation in the network layer. As depicted in Figure 3, the mobile entity might have unfiltered access to common resources like the WWW or various Electronic Commerce servers, and additionally the possibility to connect themselves to the personalized interface at the proxy provider.

In Figure 5, the mobile terminal delivers its location data as well as its wishes to the retailing provider, who searches the relevant information. He selects the content from third parties and finds that the data do not match the capabilities of the mobile user. Therefore, he sends the media requirements to the media adaptation service, where the Intelligent Resource Selector evaluates the conversion capabilities for the incoming media, selects the appropriate converters, configures a converter chain, and starts the

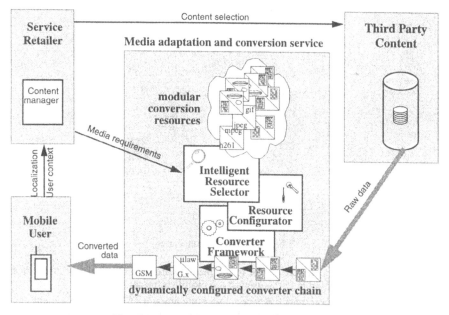

Fig. 5. Media Adaptation and Conversion Service

Job and Stream Control (Converter Framework) with the dynamically configured chain. The raw data from the content provider are finally converted and delivered to the mobile user.

3.5 Service Architecture

While the previous sub-sections discussed the technical preconditions, we will now classify the services that can be provided within the described environment. The possible scenarios share the basic capabilities of the system architecture. The services comprise

- navigation support,
- location dependent and location independent information access with user specific context selection,
- communication support,
- electronic commerce.

However, these list of services is open to any future extension by plugging components into the modular platform. The four "slices" in Figure 6 build the service architecture of our prototype Mobile Guide system, which each contains a number of exchangeable and expandible services and components for specific tasks. In combining currently available key technologies for mobile communication and distributed information processing the Mobile Guide system realizes a couple of value added services beneath a wireless internet access and an intelligent mobile computing device.

The slice of navigation support realises distinct components for localisation techniques and route planning services. The localisation includes components for outdoor localisation like GPS, cellular tracking, as well as components for in-house localisation using infrared systems. Specialized service providers for navigation support are part of the Mobile Guide infrastructure and feed the mobile terminals with location

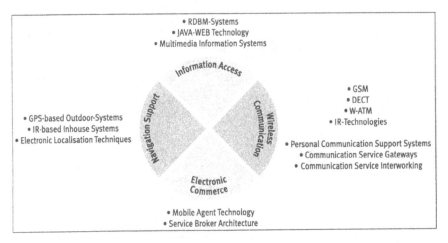

Fig. 6. Service Architecture

information. Also the components for route planning are provided by external service providers and are accessible to the user on the mobile terminal.

The second slice represents the access to a huge amount of location dependent and location independent information by the remote mobile user. Various services and technologies are necessary to realise the complex information structure behind the Mobile Guide system. The use of web technology in combination with state-of-the-art Java and CORBA components enables the composition of content tailored to the specific requirements of the mobile terminals. The data are retrieved from various information services like web contents, remote databases, Geographic Information Systems (GIS), or input from different commercial content providers like Pointcast or Marimba. The filtering, conversion, and processing of these information is the task of the Content Provider of the Mobile Guide system.

Realized inside the communication support of the Mobile Guide service architecture, there is a transparent access to various transport media for the mobile device as well as the access to a broad number of personal communication services for a single user. Therefore different wireless communication services for the data transmission between the mobile terminal and the content provider of the Mobile Guide system like GSM-Data, DECT, wATM, and UMTS communication are currently part of this service architecture block.

The personal communication services will be realized as embedded services inside the Mobile Guide service architecture. Depending on the type of the required service the communication will be transmitted via GSM/DECT-voice or will be routed through several gateways at the Mobile Guide service provider domain. These gateways include access to Internet Protocol services like e-mail, www, ftp as well as access to networks of third party service and network providers like ISDN, POTS, local PABX, paging and messaging services, etc. Also more enhanced services like internet telephony, video and audio conferencing will be integrated via appropriate gateways into the Mobile Guide service architecture [19].

The last section of the Mobile Guide service architecture represents the supported services for electronic commerce. This enables a user to participate from the possibilities of the upcoming electronic market, including services for electronic cash, accounting for enhanced communication services, booking and reservation services, electronic shopping, the subscription of mobile agent based services, etc.

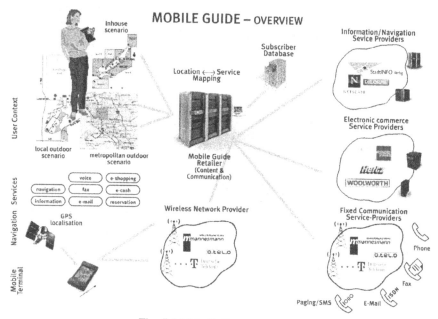

Fig. 7. Mobile Guide system overview

4 Mobile Guide System Overview

The Mobile Guide system is designed upon the state-of-the-art technologies (as discussed above) in the area of mobile computing devices, localisation techniques, wireless communication and information, and communication platforms realized through internet technologies like WWW, Java, CORBA, etc. The integration of these technologies and the open system architecture makes the Mobile Guide system flexible for future trends and developments in this area.

The distinct components of the Mobile Guide system combine these different technologies to enable the access to information sources and communication facilities in various scenarios. The mobile terminal is realised by an easy-to-use intelligent handheld PDA equipped with internal storage (for information caching) and exchangeable devices for wireless communication and localisation. Localisation information will be retrieved via GPS, infrared data or cellular tracking, according to the facilities available at the current location (in-house/outdoor usage). The wireless communication is currently realized through the access to GSM and will be extended to upcoming services like DECT, WATM, etc. Within the project, the development of UMTS is followed closely.

The application running on the mobile terminal needs to provide a generic access to a localized context of information depending on the user's current position. It will provide user selectable contexts related to the current location, e.g. shopping facilities, traffic information, points of interest. Among the information related to the special context of the location of the user the Mobile Guide system also offers a couple of location independent, generic services. These services enable a user to access personal communication services like fax, e-mail, etc. and generic services like a yellow page service or a search for topics and keywords. Also an intelligent route planning service (e. g. fastest way to airport, way to next letter box, next metro link to the Zoo) will be available as a basic service.

The information request containing the location information and the selected context is transmitted wireless to a dedicated service and content provider. This service combines different sources of information and communication services according to the requests of the mobile user, and transmits this information (e.g. a bitmapped image containing visual information, a list of choices, etc.) back to the mobile terminal.

4.1 Scenarios

A mobile information and communication system like the proposed Mobile Guide system is designed for scenarios, where location dependent up-to-date information is needed to satisfy the individual needs of a potential user in an easy and intuitive way. The system will be especially useful to visitors, foreigners and tourists inside one of the following scenarios:

- a city area:
  offering points of interest, shopping possibilities, public traffic, etc.,
  each topic may be enriched with additional services, like reserving cinema or theatre tickets, hotel reservation, booking sightseeing tours, or simply browsing through the daily offers of a restaurant or department store;
- a museum or exhibition area:
  providing guided tours, object specific information (by standing in front of one), links to related topics, etc.; here an interactive intelligent route planner, communication capabilities for visitor groups and a recorded tour will be additional services for this type of scenario;
- a fair or conference area:
  accessing schedules, theme and location specific information, etc.,
  also useful for this scenario will be the personalised handling of communication (e-mail, fax, messaging), a personal time planner with reminder functions and offers for evening events incl. restaurant reservation, etc.;
- an airport or railway station:
  presenting actual timetables, booking & reservation possibilities.
  This scenario may also contain similar services of the above scenarios, like shopping facilities, daily offers of shops and restaurants, etc.

Also an integration with existing enterprise in-house information, communication and access control systems will be a possible scenario for the Mobile Guide system, like an interactive shopping assistant inside a department store, or a guide to persons, events and locations inside an organisation.

4.2 Prototype

The Mobile Guide system architecture is divided into three major domains which are embedded into the underlying DPE Middleware Platform discussed before (Figure 4). These domains are represented through the mobile terminal, the communication and content server, and a variety of third party service and content providers.

Each of these domains follows a layering of components (Figure 8). In the bottom, the network access layer needs to support all involved wired and wireless networks permanently on the communication server domain for supporting multiple terminals. On the mobile side, these networks are used in a modular way, one at a time. The transport layer provides the unified access to the heterogeneous network components.

While the communication & content server domain needs Internet client services for collecting and combination of information, it also provides server services (HTTP, FTP, CORBA-layers, etc.) for the mobile terminals. Appropriate gateways forward the communication, or adapt them to the mobile requirements. The Service Management components handles subscription and accounting for a personalized use of the system. The Content Composer retrieves the demanded location-dependent information from

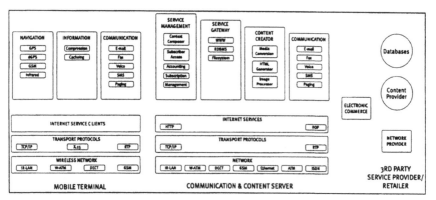

Fig. 8. Mobile Guide system architecture

different sources according to subscribed services. The service gateways provide access to information requests in local and remote databases and file systems as well as from the WWW and other internet based information systems. Inside the component of the Context Creator, the retrieved information is converted to the capabilities of the mobile device. This information processing includes dynamic media conversion and type conversion as well as dynamic page generation.

Based on the communication layers mentioned above the mobile terminal provides components for navigation support, information access, personal and data communication and a component for management of the terminal itself (e.g. software upgrade by download).

Inside the open and object oriented system design, all these components are realized as interchangeable modules, which can be combined according to the specific requirements of the mobile device, the customer and the service provider. This architecture makes it possible to exchange several components of the system (e.g. localisation techniques) or to use different types of terminals without the need to change major parts of the whole system.

4.3 Test-Bed

For our prototype test-bed (Figure 9), we use an Apple Newton MessagePad 2100 with 160 MHz RISC processing power, 8 MB RAM memory, and a 480x320 pixel greyscale pen-sensitive display. As one of the most important features, this device provides two PC cards slots for flexible expansion.

For the purpose of localisation one of these slots is used by a Centennial GPS card, which differs from a standard PC card just by the hunchback of the antenna. As an alternative within buildings, this card could easily be replaced by an infrared transmitter compliant to the Active Badge system, which is currently under development in our hardware department. In future, the infrared capabilities of the PDA itself could be used for this purpose, currently the heterogeneity of the infrared bearing layer hinders the immediate integration.

The wireless communication located in the other slot is currently based on GSM-technology for outdoor use or on a PC-Card based WaveLAN interface for indoor scenarios.

Based on this mobile terminal and the DPE environment described above we have established a small test-bed for an dedicated outdoor-scenario covering parts of the Berlin city area around the Kurfürstendamm and Wittenbergplatz (Figure 10). Inside the DPE middleware platform we realized a couple of services by example. One service provides shopping information of different department stores, which resides in a

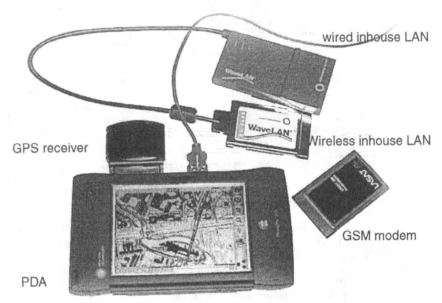

Fig. 9. Compact PDA with integrated, exchangeable positioning
and communication technology

local database maintained by the Content Server environment. The underlying map information is provided by an external CORBA-based Geographical Information Service (GIS) of Berlin's public transportation company (BVG) as a third party provider, which uses the same data also for tracking their GPS-equipped vehicle park.

This way, the latter example maps the location-aware systems of two providers together, considering the location of the user in relation to the location of the approaching bus.

The adaptation of the Grasshopper agent platform [14] is in progress for the integration of intelligent agent services for electronic commerce. Another service uses the databases of the BVG for up-to-date information about the public transport around the users current location. An alphabetical overview about currently available services is another service developed inside the prototype scenario.

5 Summary

Within this paper, we have discussed the state-of-the-art in location-aware mobile applications. We have proposed a system architecture fulfilling the requirements of upcoming Electronic Commerce scenarios, by introducing a middleware platform for distributed processing, enabling the 'plug-in' of modular services. Some of them can be based on Mobile Agents, currently under implementation. The prototype installation is already implemented in CORBA and provides the communication with third party services as well as media adaptation by dynamically generated converter chains.

References

[1] Swain, R.S.: Evolving the UMTS Vision. - Draft Paper from the ACTS Mobility, Personal & Wireless Communications Domain. December 1997. - http://www.infowin.org/ACTS/IENM/CONCERTATION/MOBILITY/
[2] ETSI DE/SMG-0102201U, Universal Mobile Telecommunications System (UMTS). Service Aspcts. Service Principles (UMTS 22.01). - Version 2.0.1, August 1996

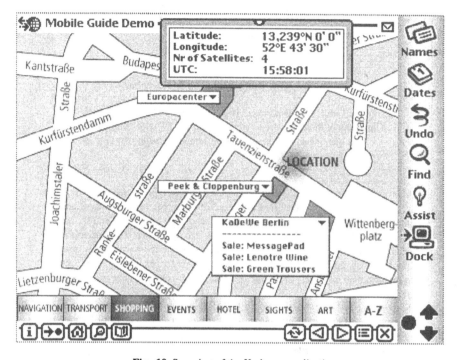

Fig. 10. Snapshot of the Kudamm application

[3] EURESCOM Project P608. TINA Concepts for Third Generation Mobile Systems. Deliverable 1 (public). Opportunities to utilise TINA concepts within UMTS standards and UMTS requirements on TINA. - Heidelberg, June 1997
[4] Harter, A; Hopper, A.: A Distributed Location System for the Active Office. - IEEE Network, 8(1994)1, Jan/Feb. 1994, IEEE Computer Society, pp. 62-70
[5] Addlesee, M.D.; Jones, A.; et al.: The ORL Active Floor. - IEEE Personal Communications; Vol. 4 (1997) 5; New York: IEEE, Oct. 1997, pp. 35-41
[6] Ward, A.; Jones, A.; Hopper, A.: A New Location Technique for the Active Office. - IEEE Personal Communications; Vol. 4 (1997) 5; New York: IEEE, Oct. 1997, pp. 42-47
[7] Schilit, B.N.; et al.: The PARCTab Mobile Computing System. - Technical Report CSL-93-20, Xerox Palo alto Research Center, December 1993
[8] Want, R.; Schilit, B.N.; et al.: The PARCTab Ubiquitous Computing Experiment. - Technical Report CSL-95-1, Xerox Palo Alto Research Center, March 1995
[9] Schilit, B.N.; Adams, N.; Want, R.: Context-Aware Computing Applications. - Proc. of the Workshop on Mobile Computing Systems and Applications, Santa Cruz, CA, Dec 1994, IEEE Computer Society, pp. 85-90
[10] Schilit, B.N.; Theimer, M.M.: Disseminating Active Map Information to Mobile Hosts. - IEEE Network, 8(1994)5, Sept/Oct. 1994, IEEE Computer Society, pp. 22-32
[11] Context-Aware Computing Applications. - Proc. of the Workshop on Mobile Computing Systems and Applications, Santa Cruz, CA, Dec 1994, IEEE Computer Society, pp. 85-90
[12] Brown, P.J.; Bovey, J.D.; Chen, X.: Context-Aware Applications: From the Laboratory to the Marketplace. - IEEE Personal Communications; Vol. 4 (1997) 5; New York: IEEE, Oct. 1997, pp. 58-64
[13] Long, S.; Kooper, R.; Abdowed, G.D.; Atkeson, C.G: Rapid Prototyping of Mobile Context-Aware Applications: The Cyberguide Case Study. - in Proc. 2nd ACM Intl. Conf. on Mobile Computing and Networking, MobiCom 1996.
[14] Breugst, M.; Hagen, L.; Magedanz, T.: Impacts of Mobile Agent Technology on Mobile Communication System Evolution. - to appear in: IEEE Personal Communications Magazine, Autumn 1998
[15] TINA-C Baseline. Service Architecture. Version 5.0, June 1997
[16] Eckert, K.-P.; Festini, M.; Schoo, P.; Schürmann, G. TANGRAM: Development of Object-Oriented Frameworks for TINA-C Based Multimedia Telecommunication Applications. - Proc. of the 3rd International Symposium on Autonomous Decentralized Systems: ISADS'97, Berlin, 9-11 April 1997
[17] Leconte, A.: Emerging Intelligent Peripherals (IP) Applications for IN. - Proc. of the 3rd Int. Conference on Intelligence in Networks, ICIN'94, Oct. 11-13, 1994, Bordeaux
[18] Pfeifer, T.; Popescu-Zeletin, R.: Generic Conversion of Communication Media for supporting Personal Mobility. - Proc. of the 3rd COST 237 Workshop on Multimedia Telecommunications and Applications, Barcelona, Nov. 25-27, 1996, publ: Lecture Notes on Computer Science Vol. 1185, Springer: Berlin 1996
[19] Pfeifer, T.; Magedanz, T.; Popescu-Zeletin, R.: Intelligent Handling of Communication Media, Proc. of 5th IEEE Workshop on Future Trends of Distributed Computing Systems (FTDCS'97), Tunis, Tunisia, Oct 29-31, 1997, pp. 144-151

Interactive Protocol Simulation Applets for Distance Education

Cora Burger, Kurt Rothermel, Rolf Mecklenburg

Institue of Parallel and Distributed High Performance Systems (IPVR),
University of Stuttgart, Breitwiesenstrae 20-22, D-70565 Stuttgart,
{caburger, mecklerf, rothermel}@informatik.uni-stuttgart.de

Abstract. Traditionally, education relies on lectures and on execercises. During lectures, information is transferred from teacher to learner via text, images and sometimes videos. But these communication media are mostly fix and do not allow manipulation. Exercises care for stepping into this breach. They take place in simulated or real environment and enable experimenting but can be far from lectures. Thus, learners have to stay in relatively close contact to tutors to be able to perform their exercises. In distance education, such closeness can not always be guaranteed.

To overcome this problem, the project HiSAP (Highly interactive Simulation of Algorithms and Protocols) introduces interactive simulation ap plets for lectures as well as exercises in the area of distributed system protocols. Such applets contain a suited model of certain learning material and provide a high level of interaction from changing the speed of the animation up to modifying the simulated material itself.

1 Introduction

Education is based on two complementary methods: On one hand, teachers transfer information to learners via books and lectures, on the other hand learners perform exercises while being supervised by teachers. During this process learners have to build an adequate mental model of the presented material. By using technical equipment for information exchange between teacher and learner, distance education is enabled. This new possibility of education is bearing advantages especially for life long learning, for inhabitants of secluded regions with bad infrastructure and for handicapped people but exhibits disadvantages too.

Main differences between traditional education and distance education concern kind and frequency of contact between teacher and learner. Direct vis a vis contact is is restricted or does not take place at all. Therefore, instead of the whole personality of teachers, only some features are transmitted and technical ways of information transfer are obtaining more importance. Because of the need for technical equipment, contacts are performed less frequently, thus forcing learners to become more autonomous.

Traditionally, information transfer during lectures relies on slides with text and images or on videos. If dynamic and complex processes like communication protocols of distributed systems have to be explained, videos are best suited but are rather seldomly used. Furthermore, presentation with all these media is fix. Only predefined processes can be shown, changes according to actual questions of learners are not possible. As a consequence, these fixed media are not suited to educate in a natural way by testing and playing. Therefore, they cannot be used for exercises resulting in the well known fact, that exercises are more or less far from lectures. To overcome this problem, learners are supervised and are staying in close contact to teachers. For distance education however, such closeness can not always be practised.

Another, more flexible mechanism, that is suited for lectures as well as for exercises, consists in animating and simulating learning material in visual form and allowing interactive influences. To abstract from details, the material is modeled first. This model can be simulated where behavior of simulation is similar to the one of the original. The model is composed of a number of components. Each of these component can be represented in visual form thus defining the visualization. Components of the model are either static or dynamic. Dynamic behavior is presented by means of animation.

There exist already approaches like [MH94], [BN96] and [EHS97] that enable animation, visualization and simulation of dynamic processes. Regarding their interactivity, parameters like speed, direction of animation and appearance of icons can be varied. But interactively changing the behavior of simulated processes themselves has not been studied extensively.

In the following sections we introduce an approach to use simulation applets with a high degree of interaction. To start with, we restricted to simulation of protocols in the area of networks, distributed systems and electronic commerce. Such protocols can be rather complex. Thus, they are suited to demonstrate the principle of our approach.

In Sec. 2 a model of interaction is proposed, which distinguishes between different degrees of interaction. To achieve all degrees of interaction, interactive simulation applets have to contain certain components. Sec. 3 focuses on definition and realization of these components. Production and usage of the interactive simulation applets for distance education are described in Sec. 4. Finally, Sec. 5 provides the reader with summary and outlook.

2   Interaction Model

As mentioned above, one of the best ways to get a deep understanding of a protocol, i.e. to establish a correct and adequate mental model of it, is to be able to "try it out". By playing with the protocol and doing some experiments with parts of it, the learner can identify important characteristics and dependencies in the way, the protocol works. If the learner is completely free in the way she is working with the protocol the best results will be achieved (of course there should be some guidance!).

A simple visualization and animation of a protocol usually provides users with a minimal set of operations for influencing the animation. These operations are mostly operations for manipulation the process of animation, i.e. stopping, step-by-step, speed of animation etc. To give the user complete control of the protocol, interaction has to be supported on different levels.

We distinguish three levels or modes of interactive control, a user can be provided with:

1. Control of animation
2. Control of visualization
3. Control of simulation

This three levels or modes of interaction will be examined more detailed in the following sections.

2.1 Control of Animation

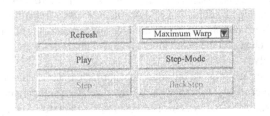

Fig. 1. Interface for Control of Animation

Every learner has individual characteristics regarding the perception of animated scenes, and these characteristics may change while learning different aspects or getting acquainted with a matter. There are e.g. preferences regarding the speed of animation. In a certain context, a step-by-step mode or reviewing of certain segments of the animation may be useful. All these operations, which deal only with the way the animation is presented (analogous to the way someone manipulates the presentation of a video) are subsumed under the term of *animation control*. Fig. 1 shows an interface for animation control.

2.2 Control of Visualization

This interactive mode can be characterized by the question: "What is visualized in what way?" It can refer to rather superficial aspects of the visualization like what icons to use for the presentation of visualization elements, but also to more important aspects as to placement of such elements and level of detail of the visualization. Depending on these parameters, the learner experiences different kinds of information regarding the overall behaviour and characteristics of an protocol.

Examples for different placement methods are the *time-sequence* method and one, we will for simplicity call the *animated-graph* method. Screenshots of these two methods displaying the simple Stop&Wait-Protocol are shown in Fig. 2.

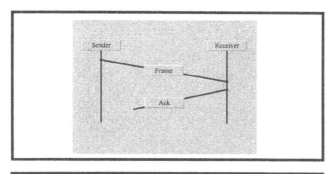

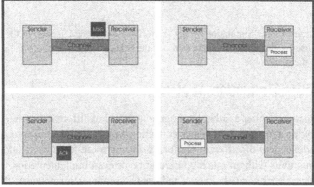

Fig. 2. Two Visualization Methods for Protocol Visualization: top) Time Sequence Diagram bottom) Animated Graph

2.3 Control of Simulation

Control of simulation encompasses two kinds of interaction. On one hand there is the pure interaction with the simulated and animated protocol, where the user gives input to the simulation and watches what is happening.

On the other hand, we introduce a manipulative mode of simulation control that is the most intriguing one. To gain full control over the animated simulation of a protocol, the learner has to have access to the simulation component and the underlying simulation model. By manipulating this simulation model, she can experiment with certain aspects of the protocol and derive an intimate understanding of the protocol. In this mode it is possible to change important parameters (e.g. the channel bandwidth) or change the protocol itself (e.g. remove or add a certain message). The animated simulation with this modified model shows the consequences of these changes, thus contributing to the creation of an adequate mental model of the protocol.

By actually changing the protocol in different aspects, the learner can experience the importance of data fields, input and output events, parameters etc. Fig. 3 shows such a kind of interaction, where the user wants to remove the field of sequence number from the data frame of the acknowledge message.

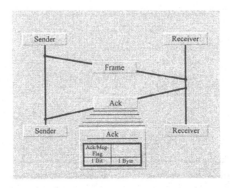

Fig. 3. Interaction with the Simulation Model in the Time-Sequence-Diagram of the Stop&Wait-Protocol. The user is just editing the data frame of the acknowledge message, which is sent from the receiver to the sender.

3   Interactive Simulation Applets

Distance education implies a rather heterogenous world of different computers and platforms. To provide a method for distance education we have to take this into account and try to stay independent of different platforms. Furthermore learners should be able to use educational units without much configuration or even implementation work. Since the Internet establishes a widely known and used communication network, this medium should be usable for the transfer of educational units. This suggests to use Java as a programming language and its construct of applets for such units.

That means, we developped applets, which show animated simulations of certain protocols and which establish the aforementioned interaction model. Such an interactive simulation applet has to contain components as shown in Figure 3. They define what is simulated and how it is visualized and animated.

Fig. 4 shows a very simplified view of the internal structure of such an interactive simulation applet.

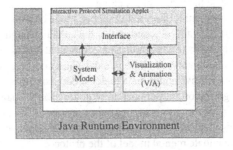

Fig. 4. Simplified view of the internal structure of an interactive simulation applet

The Simulation Model contains all necessary information regarding the protocol and is the base for simulation at runtime. Further components are responsible for the visualization of events and objects, for controlling the animation and for providing an interface to the environment. By making a sharp distinction between the simulation model of the protocol to be visualized and the component realizing this visualization the applet structure follows the well known MCV (Model-View-Controller) principle.

This structure is enhanced in Figure 4, which shows the internal structure of the interactive simulation applets, as we pursue it in our approach. In the following sections the shown components shall be discussed in more detail.

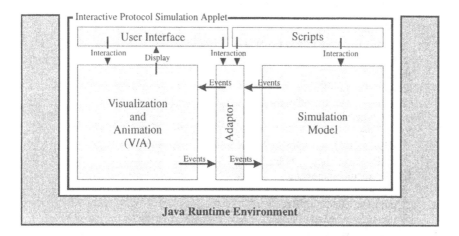

Fig. 5. Enhanced view of the internal structure of an interactive simulation applet

3.1 The Simulation Component

The core of the Simulation is, what we call the Simulation Model. This model represents the protocol to be simulated in a finite state automaton based form. It delivers information about the input and output events, states and state transitions, actions to be performed during a state transition etc. It also contains information about abstraction layers, so a learner does not have to deal always with finite state automatons, influencing parameters (e.g. channel characteristics) etc., but can start with a bird's-eye view on the whole system as shown in Fig. 2.

The use of abstraction layers is an important feature for the use of these applets in an educational environment. The material represented by the simulation model has to be presented to the learner in an appropriate way, which fits his current status of training. That means, that it is inapporiate to confront a learner the first time, she wants to get some information regarding the Stop&Wait-Protocol, with a detailed view of the corresponding finite state machines. The first presentation should be a rather simplified explanantion of the protocol and its basic functionality. Only by demand of the user a more and more detailed view ot the material should be provided.

Using our example of the Stop&Wait-Protocol, the Simulation Model has to contain information as shown in the following draft of such a model, the numbers indicating different abstraction layers:

0 StopWait:Protocol

```
1  "Sender":ProtocolComponent
     2  type=ProtocolEntity
     2  aSender:ProtocolComponent
          3  type=Automaton
          3  etc.
     2  aTimer:ProtocolComponent
          3  type=Automaton
          3  etc.
     2  inEvents=("Send", "Ack", "NAck")
     2  outEvents=("Msg", "RMsg", "Error")
1  "Receiver":ProtocolComponent
     2  type=ProtocolEntity
     2  aReceiver:ProtocolComponent
          3  type=Automaton
          3  etc.
     2  inEvents=("Msg", "RMsg", "Error")
     2  outEvents=("Ack", "NAck", "Notify")
1  "C1":ProtocolComponent
     2  type=BiChannel
     2  points=("Sender", "Receiver")
     2  messages=("Msg", "RMsg", "Ack", "NAck", "Error")
     2  influenceValue=lossRate:(1..100)
     2  influenceTarget=messages
     2  etc.
1  etc.
```

The FSA's implementing the two protocol entities are not refined in this exemplary Simulation Model.

3.2 The Visualization and Animation Component

The Visualization and Animation Component (from now on shortened as VA-Component) is responsible for displaying every information contained in the Simulation Component and to animate every event and action happening during the simulation process. What exactly is presented to the user via the User Interface is determined by the selections and interactions by the user or some previously recorded scripts (ref. Sec. 3.6).

We realized this component by creating a so called Visualization Toolkit, which is build up of visualization elements for every kind of information of the Simulation Model. The toolkit is implemented in Java following the Java Beans concepts. So you can find visualization elements as well for a process, as modelled in the time-sequence diagram, or for messages and the movement of messages, as shown in Figure 2.

The VA-Component is driven by the Simulation Model and interactions from the environment, either by a learner or some prescriptions kept in a file.

3.3 The Adaptor Component

The Adaptor Component realizes some kind of filtering mechanism between the VA-Component and the Simulation Component. It controls, what information is exchanged between these two components. For this control the Adaptor Component can be adjusted from the environment.

The name of this component derives from our approach to realize it using the Java Beans event model. The VA-Component and the Simulation Component communicate using events. They register themselves for a group of events fired by the other component.

Fig. 6 shows this relation in a schematic view.

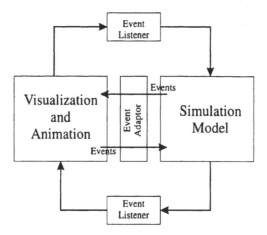

Fig. 6. Schematic view of the relation between VA-Component and Simulation Component following the Java Beans event model.

Since user's selection determines, what is to be displayed and how the simulation model is to be manipulated, the Adaptor Component is responsible for "masking", forwarding and firing certain events. If for instance the learner just wants to view the highest detail level of the protocol using the animated-graph method, the adaptor supresses all events concerning the visualization of state transitions or value changes. It just forwards all events regarding the transport of a message from one node to the other.

On the other hand, when the user chooses to change the characteristics of the communication channel by clicking on the channel visualization object and changing for instance the bandwith property in the detailed view of the channel, the corresponding events are interpreted by the Adaptor Component and then forwarded to the Simulation Comonent, maybe in addition to some other events fired by the Adaptor itself to achieve this change in the Simulation Model.

3.4 Cooperation of the VA-Component and the Simulation Model

Let us now have a more detailed look at the cooperation of the Simulation Model and the V/A-Component via the Adaptor. We strictly separate the objectives of these two components. That means, that for instance the Simulation Model provides information about all its elements, states and changes without caring, what is displayed by the V/A-Component and in what way.

Following the Java Beans approach, communication between these two components is established using events. Every component fires certain events at certain times, which are filtered and preprocessed by the Adaptor and then passed on to the appropriate component. We call events fired by the Simulation Model *simulation events*. In the same way V/A-Component events are called *visualization events*.

Simulation Events: On the side of the Simulation Model we have different kind of events, which are fired under different circumstances. We have to distinguish between simulation events regarding structural information (*structure events*) and simulation events regarding actions (*action events*).

Structural information is used by the V/A-Component to decide, what elements are needed to build up a visual representation of the protocol parties, their interconnections and the objects exchanged. For instance, there has to be a visual object for every communication partner, for the communication channel between them, the messages they exchange and so on. If the learner chooses to display the finite state machines of the protocol instances, the structural information says, what states are to be shown, what events may occur (generated by the automaton), what variables are needed and how they are initialized etc.

Structure events are always fired on request. That means, that every time the V/A-Component asks for structural information, the Simulation Model fires a shower of events regarding all aspects of structure. If the user has chosen to display a high abstraction level of the protocol, then all events ragarding the automaton structure are masked by the Adaptor.

Actions happen during a running simulation. Since a running simulation is driven by some finite state machines interoperating with one another and reacting to certain events (not simulation events!), all action simulation events are generated by these machines. We can subclassify these actions (and therefore the corresponding events) into state transitions, firing and processing of events and operation on variables.

Action events are fired without need for any request during a running simulation. The whole time, the simulations runs, the Simulation Model generates showers of action simulation events, which are again filtered and processed by the Adaptor Component.

Visualization Events: Visualization Events are generated by the V/A-Component due to some user interaction or some commands from the scripts driving the simulation and are directed to the Simulation Model. There are other user or script generated events, which stay in the V/A-Component where they control the animation process (interactive control of animation); these are no visualization events.

We distinguish between two kinds of visualization events: Visualization events regarding information (*information events*)and visualization events regarding mainpulation (*manipulation events*).

Information events are events which lead to structure events as a response. Those events are generated when the user (or a script) chooses for instance to "zoom" into or out of a certain visualization object or anything, which requires an update on the display of structural information.

Manipulation events are the means of establishing manipulative control of simulation. These events announce that the user wants to change the Simulation Model, for instance changing the fields of a message frame between two protocol parties.

The example of the Stop&Wait-Protocol: Let us have a look again at our Stop&-Wait-Protocol example. When intializing the applet, there is an automatically fired information event, which results in every ProtocolComponent of the Simulation Model firing a structure event. Let us also assume, that the current user is quite unexperienced and wants to see at first the general operation of the protocol.

When intializing the applet, there is an automtically fired information event, which results in a structure event from every ProtocolComponent of the Simulation Model. Since the learner chose to view just the topmost level, only events of ProtocolComponents of level 1 of the Simulation Model are forwarded through the Adaptor. This leads exactly to the visualizations as shown in Fig. 2.

In the same way only actions events regarding changes on this level are forwarded to V/A-Component, resulting in the animation of moving messages between sender and receiver.

When the user interacts with one of the displayed elements, as for instance clicking on a message (as shown in Fig. 3), an information event is generated, which is interpreted by the Adaptor and then forwarded to the Simulation Model. The then generated structure events of level 2 regarding the message are now forwarded by the Adaptor to the V/A-Component thus showing a more detailed view of the message contents.

3.5 The User Interface

The User Interface is of course responsible for presenting all visual information to the user and to provide him with an area to interact with. The data presented to the user are of graphical nature and will be extended around audio for special effects (e.g. timers of protocols). Interaction happens mainly using the mouse and the keyboard.

3.6 The Script Component

A Simulation Model of a certain protocol, which is derived by processing the specification of this model, results in putting all protocol entities in their initial state. To start an actual simulation, there have to be impulses to produce reactions which establish a simulation and which can be visualized. These impulses can either be given by the user or come from some previously stored file.

These files are needed, because a learner with no or very low knowledge of the current protocol is not able to provide the protocol machine(s) with appropriate input. Therefore, some prescribed behaviour in the form of some previously defined sequence of actions must be available to the learner.

In this way the learner can first view, as in a simple animation, the protocol work. After getting a first impression, she can change the level of detail of this animation to get information about the messages, the partners etc. Only after this she is able to interpret self executed inputs in an appropriate manner. The level of simulation, where the Simulation completely is driven by user inputs should be one of the last stages of education.

As a whole, this component is responsible for keeping one or more prescribed sequences of events for controlling the simulation. These prescriptions are called scripts, since they care for producing an animation like a script does for a movie picture. In addition these scripts will be created using a script-like language, which says,which events are to be fired, which placement method to choose etc.

By creating scripts, a tutor creating an applet for a protocol, can first show important aspects of the protocol to the learner before transferring the control to the learner.

4 The HiSAP System and Its Usage in Distance Education

The HiSAP project aims at providing support for teachers to get interactive and animated simulations of learning material in a comfortable way. Teachers shall not be disturbed with learning any internals of simulation applets to prepare their presentations. Especially they should not worry about the simulation model but use their own model of learning material instead.

The state of the HiSAP project is the following: Protocol specification is done by formal specifying the protocol using the fomal description technique SDL (Specification and Description Language, [Tur93]). SDL is based on a hi- erachical structure of systems, blocks, channels and processes, where the latter are modelled with extended finite state machines.

At the moment we establish the simulation model of a certain protocol by transforming its SDL based specification together with additional configuration information into a Java based representation of the SDL structure hierarchy. This is done by using an interpreter, which creates for each SDL element a correponding Java class, which contains the same information as the SDL element. On the lowest level of this simulation model hierarchy reside the FSA's which establish the behaviour of the single protocol entities.

We realized the V/A-Component by creating a Visualization Toolkit, which is built of visualization elements for every kind of information of the Simulation Model. The toolkit is implemented in Java following the Java Beans concepts. So you can find visualization elements as well for a process, as modelled in the time-sequence diagram, as for messages and the movement of messages, as shown in Fig. 2. Communication between the Simulation Model and the V/A-Component happens just as explained in Sec. 3.4.

To this moment we have established control of animation and visualization. Regarding the control of the simulation the manipulative control still has to be implemented. It is also not possible to automatically generate interactive simulation applets with HiSAP, but they can be generated manually with the existing components.

Information regarding the HiSAP Project are available at the following webadress:

http:\\www.informatik.uni-stuttgart.de\ipvr\vs\projekte
\ProtoVis\protovis.html

Due to running developments, it may be, that the page is sometimes only available to authorised users. In this case contact the authors for a short time access.

5 Summary and Outlook

In this paper we introduced the concept of interactive protocol simulation applets as a tool for distance education, but also for traditional education in classroom. These applets base on a complex simulation model of the protocol to teach and provide a sophisticated interface for a interaction with the simulation on three different levels. This high degree of interaction aims at creating a deep understanding for the simulated protocol. We then showed how the HiSAP system for generation of such interactive simulation applets can be used as an instructional tool.

Future activities of the HiSAP project will include the following:

– Implementing all levels of interaction.
– Creating a scripting language and script recording component.
– Realizing automatic generation of applets.
– Protocol specification with Petri Nets.
– Creation of courses using HiSAP.
– Validation of educational value of interactive simulation applets by testing in real educational environments.

The "final" goal is to have a system, which enables users to create highly interactive educational units in the area of protocols. This system is to be accompanied by a repository of interactive protocol simulation applets for most of the known protocols, similar to such systems as OPNET ([MIL3]) of MIL3 or the ns/nam system of the University of Berkeley ([FV98]), which also come with a set of already implemented protocols.

References

[BN96]   Marc H. Brown and Marc A. Najork. Collaborative active textbooks: A webbased algorithm animation system for an electronic classroom. Technical report, digital Equipment Corporation - Research and Development, 1996.

[EHS97] Geralf Einert, Franz Huber, and Bernhard Schatz. Consistent graphical specification of distributed systems. In John Fitzgerald, Cliff B. Jones, and Peter Lucas, editors, FME' 97 - 4th International Symposium of Formal Methods Europe, volume 1313 of Lecture Notes in Computer Science, pages 122 – 141. Springer Verlag, 1997.

[Hal92] Fred Halsall. Data Communications, Computer Networks and Open Systems. Addison-Wesley Publishing Company, 1992.

[MH94]   Arnulf Mester and Peter Herrmann. Audiovisuelle Animation von verteilten Algorithmen und Kommunikationsprotokollen. Technical report, Arbeitsgruppe Rechnernetze und Verteilte Systeme, Universitat Dortmund, 1994.

[Tur93] Kenneth Turner, editor. Using Formal Description Techniques - An Introduction to ESTELLE, LOTOS and SDL. John Wiley & Sons Ltd., 1993.

[YSY84] Y. Yemini, R. Strom, and S. Yemini, editors. Protocol Specification, Testing and Validation. Proceedings of the IPFP Workshop. North-Holland Publishing Company, 1984.

[MIL3]   http:www.mil3.comhome.html.

[FV98]   Kevin Fall, Kannan Varadhan, editors. ns Notes and Documentation - The VINT Project. Technical Report, University of Berkely, 1998.

Visual Techniques to Accommodate Varying Network Performance in Virtual Environments

J. Robert Ensor, Gianpaolo U. Carraro, John T. Edmark

Bell Laboratories
101 Crawfords Corner Road, Holmdel, New Jersey USA
jre@bell-labs.com, paolo@bell-labs.com, edmark@bell-labs.com

Abstract. This position paper briefly reviews how we created virtual worlds for a real-time, multiparty simulator. These worlds are partitioned into regions. Some regions are displayed as three-dimensional objects, and other regions are displayed as still images or video streams. We hypothesize that the size and placement of these regions can be configured to accommodate various user requirements. Such configurations can be based on static descriptions of the computing and communication resources that are available to users. We also hypothesize that dynamic region configurations can be used, in distributed systems, to accommodate run-time variations in computer and network performance. These configuration changes can be based on real-time measurements of system elements.

1 Introduction

We are building virtual environments that combine two types of sub-spaces or regions. Some regions are displayed as three-dimensional objects, and other regions are displayed as still images or video streams. We have built such worlds as part of a simulator called Peloton[1, 2]. This program creates virtual environments for bicycling, running, and walking. Users participate in simulations by walking or running on treadmills or by pedaling stationary bicycles. The simulator's virtual environment is illustrated by a synthetic, three-dimensional landscape, modeled in the Virtual Reality Modeling Language (VRML)[3]. Fig. 1 is a view from a Peloton virtual world, which models New York City's Central Park. The central portion of this view is a video stream, which is displayed as a texture on a large rectangle—a video "screen." In the surrounding region, graphical elements represent the road and some roadside objects. The bicyclist avatars represent multiple users who are exploring this world concurrently.

As simulation participants move along a virtual roadway, their avatars can move from one region to another. Collections of avatars often spread over different regions of a virtual world, and each participant is likely to see competitors' avatars move to and from image/video regions. In Fig. 1, for example, the right avatar is on a section of road displayed as three-dimensional objects, while the middle and left avatars have moved ahead to a road segment displayed as a video region. User viewpoints also move within Peloton's virtual worlds. As participants move around the virtual environment, they see image/video displays from changing positions. These still images and video clips represent sub-spaces within an encompassing, coherent three-dimensional space. To maintain visual continuity with their surrounding regions, these two-dimensional displays must dynamically respond to the moving user viewpoints.

Fig. 1. View of a Peloton Virtual World

While creating these worlds, we have developed techniques to deal with the movement of objects into and out of video regions and also to support the integration of images into their three-dimensional contexts. Two techniques deal with object movement. In one—*media melding*—when an object moves from one region to another, the media used to represent that object correspondingly change. The middle avatar of Fig. 1 demonstrates media melding. Upon entering a video region, it became a video object. In the second technique—*object tracing*—when an object moves from one region to another, its actions in the second region are represented by a *trace object* in the first region. The left avatar of Fig. 1 is a three-dimensional trace object representing a cyclist in the video region. Visual integration of two-dimensional panels with surrounding three-dimensional regions is aided by the third technique. *Pyramidic panels* and their associated transforms provide means for dealing with viewpoint changes, so that two-dimensional images and video clips can successfully represent three-dimensional spaces. These three techniques are described more fully in [4].

Through Peloton, we have demonstrated that some portions of a virtual world can be displayed as three-dimensional objects and others can be displayed as images or video. We have also shown that the size and placement of these regions can vary. We hypothesize that regions can be configured to match the computing and communication resources of system users. People with powerful machines but poor network connections can specify that a world be displayed primarily (or exclusively) as locally rendered three-dimensional objects. On the other hand, users with network computers—offering high-end network connections but less processing power—can specify that a world be displayed primarily as streamed video. Of course, dynamic variations can occur within users' computing and communication infrastructure. Since image and video textures are shared among multiple remote users, image and video transmission delays can create performance variations. Similarly, available computing power can limit three-dimensional object rendering, causing users to experience performance degradations. We hypothesize that these dynamic changes in system performance can be accommodated by changes in region configurations.

2 Background

Other simulators, *e.g.*, [5], [6], [7], and [8], create virtual environments for shared simulations among multiple people. *Cycling World: The Virtual Tour*[9] is a VRML based, single-user bicycling game on the World Wide Web. The virtual worlds of these games and simulators do not contain video regions.

Photographs are commonly used as textures and background elements in three-dimensional models. Image based modeling techniques, *e.g.*, [10] and [11], permit creation of three-dimensional models from two-dimensional photographs. However, these systems do not treat the image textures themselves as three-dimensional spaces. Hence they do not vary what space is represented in each medium, and they do not accommodate object movement to and from the textures.

Computer-generated graphics and recordings of live action are often combined in special effects for movies, *e.g.*, *Who Framed Roger Rabbit?* These movies are fixed compositions; their effects cannot vary. On the other hand, Peloton's effects are generated as real-time responses to user actions and viewpoint changes.

Virtual sets, *e.g.*, [12], [13], and [14], are studios that permit live actors to move within computer-generated settings. Augmented reality systems, *e.g.*, [15], compose computer-generated graphics over video inputs. The Interspace system[16] creates virtual spaces on the Internet in which avatars have live video streams as "heads." The graphical objects in these systems can be manipulated in response to real-time events, *e.g.*, changes of camera position. However, none support movement of objects between their graphical and video elements.

[17] and [18] discuss virtual reality systems, containing video displays, in which graphical objects are assigned priorities, and these priorities help control video transmission streams. These priority schemes deal with performance limitations by changing the update frequency and size or resolution of images. Surrounding

graphical displays are not adjusted to compensate for the changes in the video displays.

The MPEG-4 proposal[19], currently under development, is expected to permit specification of data displays as compositions of video and graphical objects. Hence, this standard might provide a means of specifying hardware and software infrastructure to support our techniques straightforwardly and efficiently.

3 Region Configurations

Major elements of a Peloton virtual world can be represented in multiple ways—as graphical objects, as still images, and as video clips—hence, they can be part of both graphical and video regions. These multiple object representations allow Peloton to create multiple region configurations for a world. Figures 2 and 3 show two region configurations of the same world. The configuration shown in Fig. 2 creates a large video region, which contains a user's avatar, much of the roadway, and many roadside objects. The configuration of Fig. 3 replaces part of the video region with additional graphical regions. Hence, the avatar, roadway, and distant trees are now displayed as graphical objects.

Fig. 2. Virtual World View with Large Video Region

When the configuration of a world's regions changes, the computing and communication resources needed to display that world typically change also. We believe that static descriptions of system resources and/or measurements of their performance can control the configuration process, thus allowing an application to match its displays to user resources and to accommodate variations in resource loads.

Control parameters for region configuration could include a classification of each user's local rendering engine and network connections. In addition, explicit user controls could specify world complexity metrics for regions, region subsection methods, *etc.* Performance measures could include message delivery rate and delay, video display rates and graphical rendering rates. Also, an application could affect region configurations directly. For example, a simulator could control configurations based on an avatar's speed, replacing video regions with graphical regions (or *vice versa*) as the avatar moved faster.

Fig. 3. Virtual World View with Reduced Video Region

4 Other Opportunities

This paper has briefly discussed virtual worlds that contain both graphics and still images or video streams. It has suggested new techniques for matching the configurations of the graphical and video sub-spaces of these worlds to their user resources and to the performance characteristics of underlying computing and communication systems.

The multiple regions and variable configurations of these worlds could also be used for other purposes. For example, an education application could present course material to students through such displays. More specifically, a student could watch a documentary and, when seeing something of special interest, he or she could pick that object from the video, move it into a region of three-dimensional objects, and study it there by viewing and animating its three-dimensional representations. Similarly, shopping applications could allow shoppers to pick objects from a catalog and see them displayed in a movie. Furthermore, a region can serve as a level of detail specification for groups of objects. For example, a surveillance application could display a region near the viewer (camera) in one medium, while displaying more distant parts of a virtual world through other media.

References

[1] Ensor, J. R. and Carraro, G. U.: Peloton: A Distributed Simulation for the World Wide Web. In: Fishwick, P. A., Hill, D. R. C., Smith, R. (eds.): 1998 International Conference On Web-Based Modeling and Simulation. Simulation Series, Vol. 30, No. 1. Society for Computer Simulation International, San Diego (1998) 159-164.

[2] Carraro, G. U., Cortes, M., Edmark, J. T., Ensor, J. R.: The Peloton Bicycling Simulator. Proceedings VRML 98. ACM, New York (1998) 63-70.

[3] Virtual Reality Modeling Language (VRML) Version 2.0. In VRML Consortium Web Site: http://www.vrml.org/Specifications/VRML2.0/

[4] Carraro, G. U., Edmark, J. T., Ensor, J. R.: Techniques for Handling Video in Virtual Environments. SIGGRAPH 98. ACM, New York (1998).

[5] CompuTrainer. In: Computrainer Web site: http://www.computrainer.com

[6] Virtual Reality Bike. In: Tectrix Web Site: http://www.tectrix.com/products/VRBike /VR_Bike.html

[7] UltraCoach VR. In Ultracoach Web Site: http://www.ultracch.com

[8] Waters, R. et al.: Diamond Park and Spline: Social Virtual Reality with 3D Animation, Spoken Interaction, and Runtime Extendability. Presence. Vol. 6, No. 4. MIT Press. 461-481.

[9] Cuesta J.: Cycling World. In El Faro Web Site: http://www.elfaro.com/vrml20/cycling/ thegame

[10] Debevec, P., Taylor, C., Malik, J.: Modeling and Rendering Architecture from Photographs: A hybrid geometry- and image-based approach. SIGGRAPH 96. ACM, New York (1996) 11-20.

[11] McMillan, L., Bishop, G.: Plenoptic Modeling: An Image-Based Rendering System. SIGGRAPH 95. ACM, New York (1995) 39-46.

[12] 3DK: The Virtual Studio. In GMD Web Site: http://viswiz.gmd.de/DML/vst/vst.html

[13] Katkere, A., Moessi, S., Kuramura, D., Kelly, P., Jain, R.: Towards Video-based Immersive Environments. Multimedia Systems. May (1997) 69-85.

[14] Thalmann, N., Thalmann, D.: Animating Virtual Actors in Real Environments. Multimedia Systems. May (1997) 113-125.

[15] Feiner, S., Macintyre, B., Seligmann, D.: Knowledge-Based Augmented Reality. Communications of the ACM, Vol. 36, No. 7. June (1993) 53-62.

[16] Interspace VR Browser. In NTT Software Corp. Web Site: http://www.ntts.com Interspace

[17] Oh, S., Sugano, H., Fujikawa, K., Matsuura, T., Shimojo, S., Arikawa, M., Miyahara, H.: A Dynamic QoS Adaptation Mechanism for Networked Virtual Reality. Proceeding Fifth IFIP International Workshop on Quality of Service. New York, May (1997) 397-400.

[18] Yamaashi, K., Kawanata, Y., Tani, M., Matsumoto, H.: User-Centered Video: Transmitting Video Images Based on the User's Interest. Proceeding Chi '95.

[19] MPEG Home Page. In http://drogo.cselt.stet.it/mpeg

An Address Resolution and Key Exchange Protocol for Conferencing Applications on the Internet

Michael Fromme, Lutz Grüneberg, and Helmut Pralle*

Lehrgebiet Rechnernetze und Verteilte Systeme
Universität Hannover
Schloßwender Straße 5
D-30159 Hannover
{fromme,gruen,pralle}@rvs.uni-hannover.de

Abstract. Many multimedia conference initiation and control protocols like the Session Invitation Protocol or ITU-T H.323 are likely to co-exist on the Internet. Although these protocols have different invitation schemes and different addressing mechanisms, they all need transport addresses to send conference calls. Considering users mobility, address redirection mechanisms were built into invitation protocols, but in a way specific to that particular protocol. The Confman Address Resolution Protocol (ConfARP) is a simple protocol designed to allow address translations from logical addresses to transport addresses independent of the applied conference initiation protocol. Further ConfARP can deliver encryption keys for the conference setup along with the transport addresses to support encrypted conference calls.

1 Introduction

Internet multimedia conferencing is one of the hottest networking applications today. In the near future the desktop computer will become more and more important as a communication terminal which allows people to communicate by audio, video, and network enhanced applications.

As long as IPv4 is used, the Internet suffers from its small 32-bit address space. The intentionally one-to-one association of addresses to network equipment - one address specifies one host - is circumvented by dynamic address assignment procedures like DHCP [6] in LANs or IPCP [15] of PPP [21]. So mobile users as well as PPP-using home users have to undergo changing IP addresses. For their current Internet use like exchanging E-Mail, reading News or surfing the WWW, this has few significance, because in these cases their computers act as clients. But conferencing is different. To be reachable for conference calls implies that the callee address is known to the caller or can at least be looked up.

* This work is supported by the German Academic Network Organisation (DFN-Verein) with funds from the Federal Ministry of Education, Science, Research and Technology (BMBF).

2   Address resolution for conference calls

Setting up a typical multimedia conference is done by a sequence of procedures:

1. The participant list has to be built.
2. The actual Internet addresses of the participants have to be looked up.
3. The participants have to be called by a conference initiation protocol.
4. When the participants agree to take part in the conference the media tools and their properties have to be negotiated.

This paper is focusing on the second procedure. Various methods for translating a callee identification to an Internet conference address are in use today, such as direct addressing without the need to find addresses, address translation done by session initiation protocols or lookups in directory services. Another issue regarding conference calls is security. Privacy on the Internet demands encrypted communication. Besides political issues, that directly raises the problem of managing keys needed for ciphered data transmissions.

In this paper we are going to propose a protocol that allows conference address resolution and key negotiation. This protocol allows queries to be sent to a conference address server or to be multicasted. They will be answered by either a server or a terminal providing the wanted host address. This protocol has been developed for *Confman*, a conference control system built at RVS.[1] At the time of writing, Confman Version 2.0 is under development, a functional prototype has been released.

3   Address resolution in related protocols

There are a number of protocols that can be used for address resolution in conferencing systems. First of all the directory service approach should be mentioned taking the *Lightweight Directory Access Protocol* [23] (LDAP) as an example. The current MBone [7] conference initiation protocols *Session Initiation Protocol* [11] (SIP) and *Session Announcement Protocol* [9] (SAP) define their own way of address resolution. Further the ITU H.323 Protocol [12] allows address translation to be done by its *gatekeeper*.

3.1   The LDAP solution

LDAP implements a very general directory service approach and is used today by conferencing solution vendors like Microsoft or Netscape to store address information. Much of the data that is stored in a directory service is static. Attributes like names, E-Mail addresses and further personal data require no updates except for the odd occasion. So the main task of a directory service is to look up and answer queries. Data updates can be regarded as seldom administrative tasks. This allows easy implementation of efficient distributed caching structures. For conference addresses, the situation is different since changes of address properties might occur often while these changes lead to updates.

---

[1] See http://www.rvs.uni-hannover.de.

3.2   The SIP solution

The *Session Initiation Protocol* (SIP) is intended to be a simple protocol that enables users to invite people to participate in a multimedia conference. It contains an address resolution mechanism that uses the Internet *Domain Name Service* (DNS) [5] and aims user mobility by supporting proxy operation and redirections. In SIP every user is identified by a unique address, which is similar to an E-Mail address and contains a user name and a host or domain name, for example "somebody@foo.com". If the host part of the address points to an existing host - that means "foo.com" can be translated by DNS to an IP address, SIP assumes the user to be found on that host. If the user is absent, there might be a SIP server running on that host. If the SIP address contains a domain part instead of a host part, there is no host with that name to be contacted directly. In this case SIP tries to find a DNS mail exchange record for that domain. SIP assumes a server running on the mail host, which enables the user to use her E-Mail address as SIP address. A SIP server can operate in two modes. First of all it can return another address for a query. This mode is called the redirection mode. Another mode is proxy mode. In proxy mode the server itself forwards the invitation to the host where the user is currently logged on.

3.3   The SAP solution

The *Session Announcement Protocol* (SAP) offers a different approach for starting online conferences. SAP can be considered as a rendezvous-mechanism for conference participants. It is used to transmit MBone conference announcements to an unspecified group of users via multicast. Due to its nature this protocol offers neither negotiation of media tools and their parameters nor does it offer the specification of address redirections. The SAP announcements simply contain a description of the conference and the media tools.

3.4   Address resolution in H.323

H.323 systems deployed in a LAN might contain a central instance called "*gatekeeper*" which performs various tasks like address translation, admission control, bandwidth control and zone management. Referring to the address translation mechanism, the gatekeeper has to translate alias addresses into transport addresses for the current LANs. These alias addresses might be logical names or E.164 addresses for H.320 or POTS gateways.

4   Confman address resolution protocol

The *Confman Address Resolution Protocol* (ConfARP) has two purposes: to translate the conference identification to an IP number where the to-be-called person can be reached and to negotiate the encryption keys that are necessary to contact the conferencing system. The address translation itself can be done in an encrypted and authenticated way to provide as much privacy as possible. ConfARP can be used by three kinds of programs: by a conference control program, by a proxy server or by an address translation server. A technical protocol description can be found in [8].

4.1 ConfARP implementation in a conference control program

A ConfARP implementation in a conference control program handles the addresses of the current user. If a control program receives a ConfARP request querying one of the configured addresses at which the user can be reached, it will respond with the actual address and protocol parameters of the running program. This can be for example a SIP address. The answer can also contain an encryption key identifier that has to be used for the conference call.

A ConfARP reply can return more than one address. In this case a ConfARP reply contains all addresses that can be used to call the user of the particular conference control program. If the program implements more than one conference initiation protocol (for example SIP and H.323), ConfARP replies with both addresses and let the caller choose the protocol to be used.

4.2 ConfARP address translation servers

ConfARP address translation servers do not have direct access to the properties of a conference control program as they run without direct user interaction. These servers store address information of a group of users and reply to requests according to their configured address translation table as illustrated in fig. 1. There are various scenarios where ConfARP address translation servers might be used:

- Redirection when a user moved to a new address.
- Using a centralized well known server for an institution that redirects calls to the real addresses of their personnel.
- Using a ConfARP server to allow ConfARP address translations to be done on behalf of conferencing programs that do not incorporate ConfARP.
- Redirection for logical group addresses like "hotline@foo.com". This allows to implement a group calling feature within ConfARP.

A ConfARP address translation server has three types of replies for a ConfARP query:

- *Refusal:* If the requested address is not known to the server or the caller is not trusted due to authentication, the server refuses to answer.
- *Address translation:* The server knows the queried address and returns it to the caller. The caller should be able to call the callee by using the delivered protocol and address parameters.
- *Redirection:* The server redirects the query to another ConfARP server. In this case the reply contains the address parameters for the other ConfARP server to be queried. It lies in the responsibility of the caller to do a further ConfARP request.

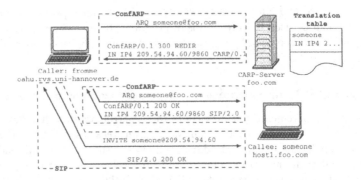

Fig. 1. ConfARP address translation server operation

ConfARP servers can reply with multiple addresses, if a user has configured more than one address. This holds for address translations as well as for redirections.

4.3 ConfARP proxy servers

Proxy servers act like address translation servers but do not return ConfARP redirections. The proxy server itself does further needed ConfARP lookups before sending the reply message. Since the proxy lookup might be done by multicast, the proxy can return several different reply messages for one request. Proxy servers are used in the following scenarios:

- Bridging a firewall between two networks. A ConfARP proxy is used on either side of the firewall which is configured to allow communication between these two proxies.
- Allowing hidden address resolutions. For example, the proxy might use a ConfARP multicast resolution in a corporate network to resolve the conference addresses of the callee.
- Checking if a callee can be reached before returning its address.

In fig. 2 the client sends a query to a proxy server that checks the reachability of the callee before replying. The request by the proxy can be send by unicast or multicasted with a small scope.

From the client's point of view, there is no clear distinction between an address translation server and a proxy. ConfARP servers might act the one or the other way. Since proxy operation is transparent to the caller, there is no way to differentiate between these two operation modes.

4.4 Protocol operation

The protocol is a simple request and reply protocol that uses UDP as transport protocol. Request messages are sent to a defined ConfARP server transport

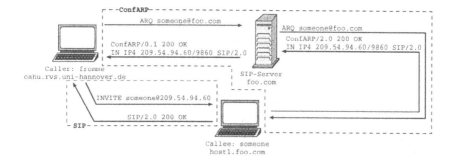

Fig. 2. ConfARP proxy server operation

address or are multicasted to an unspecified number of receivers. The request
and reply messages have a layout similar to the popular HTTP protocol [16, 20].
They have three sections: the request line or the reply code; header information
and a payload that carries the resolved addresses or redirection information
for replies. Encrypted packets have an encryption header and carry a ciphered
ConfARP packet as payload. All information - besides encrypted payload - is
encoded in ASCII. This allows debugging and tracing the protocol operation
with network packet printing tools like **snoop** [22]. The HTTP-like layout makes
it possible for ConfARP to co-exist with similar protocols like SIP within one
centralized network handler and message parser of a conferencing system.

ConfARP has only one request message type, which contains sender, recipient
and address information for the reply packet. A request can be answered by one
of three reply messages:

- A *positive reply* is sent if the ConfARP server was able to translate the
  requested address. The payload carries the resolved conference call addresses.
- A *negative reply* is sent whenever the ConfARP server was not able or refused
  to resolve the queried address.
- If the ConfARP server is uncertain about the addresses, it will send a *redirect
  reply*. This reply contains ConfARP addresses, where the caller should be
  able to get the desired addresses resolved.

5 Multicast address lookup

Multicasted ConfARP requests are sent to an unspecified number of ConfARP
servers. The ConfARP servers which are able to resolve the address will answer
the request while others keep silent. This way allows clients to request address
translation without any knowledge of host addresses belonging to ConfARP
terminals or servers. So multicast ConfARP seems to be a good choice for plug-
and-play installations of conferencing systems. To become reachable a user just

has to start the conference control program. There is no need for centralized servers and the user does not have to maintain address books, either.

In multicast mode only positive or redirect replies are sent. The absence of replies must be regarded as a negative response. Since UDP is unreliable, multicast requests are repeated several times like unicast requests before the caller has to give up. Unfortunately this solution cannot be used on the MBone without restrictions. If such multicasted ConfARP requests were ubiquitously used and distributed worldwide, it would put a high load on the net and on the running ConfARP servers as well. But if it is restricted to a smaller scope like a campus network, these scaling issues are less harmful and do not outweigh the benefits.

It is possible to extend multicast lookups on campus networks with proxy servers, which build a server mesh. The topics on building and maintaining server meshes are not addressed in this paper. Nevertheless the ConfARP protocol should be suitable to interconnect proxies.

There are two cases where multicast lookups occur: the client initiates a multicast lookup itself or the client sends a request to a proxy server that uses multicast for further lookups. This makes an interesting point: even in unicast mode a client has to expect multiple replies and has to wait as long as in the multicast mode until a transaction is finalized. Further the client should not expect to receive INVALID responses in this case since they are omitted by the multicast operation. If on the other hand the unicast request was sent to a simple server, a proxy without multicast operation or an address translation server the client can expect one single reply. A ConfARP implementation should not make an application wait for a multicast lookup if no further addresses are expected. To allow clients to separate the true unicast and the multicast cases, true unicast replies carry status codes different from replies that are part of a multicast mode answer.

6 Encrypted messages

Within ConfARP, all communication can be done encrypted. ConfARP offers an open encryption mechanism similar to SHTTP [18] that allows several encryption mechanisms to be used: public key procedures like RSA [17] or PGP [24] encryption and DES [1] encryption with single keys or key domains. Using encrypted communication enforces privacy and allows simple authentication. If encryption is required to send both requests and replies, DES key domains allow client and server to prove that they belong to a group which members have knowledge of the domain keys.

Encrypted ConfARP messages are enclosed in encryption messages. These messages have a layout similar to a request message, they have a request line, header fields and carry the encrypted message as a payload. The request line contains the special request code SECURE to indicate encrypted operation while the header fields contain key parameters and necessary address information. To defend against known-text attacks, the original message is preceded by a variable length random padding field.

6.1 Encrypted conference calls

ConfARP servers can respond with an encryption method and an encryption key in addition to address properties. Exchanging keys with address information allows conference calls to be done encrypted even if the used conference call protocol has no key management facilities.

The caller can request a specific encryption mechanism for the ongoing conference call like DES. The callee might agree to that method and provide a key or might choose another encryption method and key in his reply. In general the request of a conference key by the caller should be honored by the callee, since the caller explicitly expressed his wish for encrypted communication. Further the server replies with a conference key, if the called party insists on encrypted calls.

6.2 PGP encryption

Pretty good privacy is a widely used encryption program for E-Mail. It uses key pairs like RSA and has built-in facilities to handle keys. ConfARP can use PGP encryption in two ways:

- the request message can be encrypted with the public key of the server. This allows the client to be sure that only one specific server is able to send a reply since this is the only one to decipher the request packet.
- the client can request that a server should encrypt the reply. The public key identification like the E-Mail address of the caller or the PGP key itself is sent in the request packet.

If authentication is desired, the sender must encrypt the message with the PGP public key of the sender and transmit only the key id as illustrated in fig. 3. The server might check the given key against the *From*-header and against a trusted user database. The management of the PGP keys is outside the scope of ConfARP. If a PGP encrypted request is sent via multicast, it can be answered only by those servers that possess the necessary secret key. In this way the address-less multicast lookup can be combined with enforcement of strong authentication between the two partners.

6.3 RSA encryption

RSA encryption can be used if public key encryption is desired but PGP operation and key management are too tedious. The caller provides a public key in the query that is used for the encryption of the reply. This encryption mode allows unencrypted queries to be sent to yet unknown callees but requesting the answer to be encrypted in a way that only the caller is able to decipher it. Encrypting

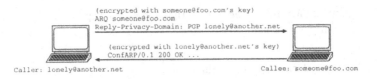

```
                        (encrypted with someone@foo.com's key)
                        ARQ someone@foo.com
                        Reply-Privacy-Domain: PGP lonely@another.net

                        (encrypted with lonely@another.net's key)
                        ConfARP/0.1 200 OK ...
Caller: lonely@another.net                      Callee: someone@foo.com
```

Fig. 3. PGP encrypted communication

the reply is necessary if the reply contains keys that are used for the ongoing conference call. Authentication is not supported by this encryption type since no key management facilities are used.

6.4 DES key domains

A work group that is closely related can agree on using some DES keys. Such agreements define key domains. The keys of a domain are distributed by other means than ConfARP, for example by phone, fax or E-Mail. Each key domain is given a specific name that allows the domain to be uniquely identified by all members, every key within the key domain has another domain-wide unique identifier. Keys in a key domain can be restricted to a limited lifetime for active use or acceptance.

7 Protocol overview

ConfARP is a stateless request-reply protocol. A request causes a reply to be sent to the originator of the request. A proxy server maintains state information for the relayed transaction, but servers do not maintain states between transactions. An address resolution done with ConfARP includes one or more ConfARP request-reply transactions. If the client gets a reply with redirections it should start another ConfARP request to resolve the redirection.

7.1 ConfARP transport protocol needs

ConfARP needs a multicast capable datagram service. In the Internet, UDP is the protocol of choice. However, any datagram oriented transport service, for example AAL 5 [13] of ATM, should fit for ConfARP as well. Reliable transport services like TCP can be used for ConfARP, too. But as ConfARP is designed to run on unreliable transport systems, their reliability will add unneeded redundancy.

7.2 ConfARP request message

Like the HTTP request message, a ConfARP request contains a request line, a header and a payload. Header and payload are separated by an empty line, while the payload length is coded as value of the "Content-Length" header field. The only valid request is an ARP request that is used to initiate an ConfARP address translation. The header contains the field that carry the destination address where replies should be sent to, the address to be looked up, a transaction ID and further fields for encrypted operation.

7.3 ConfARP reply messages

A reply message contains a reply code, a header and a payload. Like for the request message, header and payload are separated by an empty line and the payload length is transmitted in the "Content-Length" header field. The payload contains the resolved addresses.

7.4 ConfARP reply codes

The following table lists the currently defined reply codes of ConfARP:

Code	Text	Description
200, 221	OK	Success. The desired address could be resolved.
500	INVALID *Reason*	Invalid. The address could not be resolved.
300, 321	REDIRECT	The reply contains redirections.

The $x21$ reply codes are equal to their $x00$ counterparts, but express explicitly that this reply is the final and only response to the current transaction.

7.5 Unicast protocol procedures

A ConfARP lookup is initiated by sending a request (ARQ) message to a Conf-ARP server. The server will respond by sending the appropriate reply which is either an OK, a REDIRECT or an INVALID. Since messages are transmitted by UDP, a datagram service that does not provide reliable message delivery, the request or the reply message might be dropped by the network. So request messages are repeated if a reply has not been received within a timeout period. After several unsuccessful retransmissions the request has to be canceled and the server is regarded as unreachable or down.

Due to proxy operation, even a unicast request might result in multiple replies to be sent. So a client has to finalize a ConfARP transaction only if it receives a *221 OK FINAL, 321 REDIRECT FINAL* or a *400 INVALID* response. In any other case it has to wait until the timeout of a multicast transaction has passed. The values for the timeout and the number of retransmissions are not easy to choose, as they have impact on the reliability, the responsiveness and the efficiency of the protocol. The chosen values are under further study, for the time being we use a series of exponential timeout values given by $T_n = 1\mathrm{s}\,1.15^n$ with $n = 0 \ldots 15$. This gives a total transaction time of about 55 s.

7.6 Multicast protocol procedures

The multicast mode uses the same request-reply procedure as defined for unicast with two exceptions: servers do not respond with an INVALID message and clients retransmit their request until the maximal retransmission count is reached. The client has to regard a request as unresolvable if it does not receive a valid answer after several retransmissions.

7.7 Loop detection

Address translation and proxy operation can result in loops. In the address translation case the client is responsible for loop detection, it should never try to resolve an already translated address within one transaction.

Loop detection in proxy servers can be done by checking the transaction ID. If the ID of an incoming request is equal to a request which is already in-process, the request should be denied by returning a 500 message. If a proxy server receives a *REDIRECT* message, the message should be forwarded to the client. The proxy should not try to resolve redirections by itself.

8 Conclusion

ConfARP implements an easy way to translate logical addresses into transport addresses for conference calls and allows a simple key negotiation of keys for encrypted calls. ConfARP can be implemented in various ways including server, proxy server and multicast scenarios. Since ConfARP is independent of the conference initiation and control protocol, it can be used to enhance conferencing systems using SIP, H.323 etc.

At the time of writing ConfARP is implemented in a conference control system called Confman [4]. Implementations for address translation and proxy servers should be developed in the future. The retransmit count and retransmit timeout parameter values should undergo further study in LAN and WAN environments and on low data-rate transmission systems like ISDN.

9 Acknowledgments

The ConfARP implementation in *Confman 2.0* was done by Lars Friebe, RVS. The development of *Confman 2.0* is supported by by the German Academic Network Organisation (DFN-Verein) with funds from the Federal Ministry of Education, Science, Research and Technology (BMBF).

References

1. ANSI X3.92. American standard for data encryption algorithm (DEA), 1981.

2. Audio-Video Transport Working Group, H. Schulzrinne, S. Casner, R. Frederick, and V. Jacobson. RFC 1889: RTP: A transport protocol for real-time applications, Jan. 1996.
3. T. Berners-Lee, L. Masinter, and M. McCahill. RFC 1738: Uniform resource locators (URL), Dec. 1994.
4. B. Böker, C. Fricke, L. Grüneberg, and H. Pralle. Entwicklung eines Management-Systems fr multimediale Online-Konferenzen. In *Proceedings der Fachtagung SI-WORK 96*, Mai 1996. http://www.rvs.uni-hannover.de/reports/siwork.html.
5. R. T. Braden. RFC 1123: Requirements for Internet hosts — application and support, Oct. 1989.
6. R. Droms. RFC 2131: Dynamic host configuration protocol, Mar. 1997.
7. H. Eriksson. MBONE: The multicast backbone. *Communications of the ACM*, 37(8):54–60, 1994.
8. M. Fromme. The Confman Address Resolution Protocol. Protocol description. http://www.rvs.uni-hannover.de/projekte/mbwz/confarp.txt, *Work in progress.*, May 1998.
9. M. Handley. SAP: Session announcement protocol. Internet Draft draft-ietf-mmusic-sap-00.txt, *Work in progress*, November 1996.
10. M. Handley, J. Crowcroft, C. Bormann, and J. Ott. The internet multimedia conferencing architecture. Internet Draft draft-ietf-mmusic-confarch-00.txt, *Work in progress*, July 1997.
11. M. Handley, H. Schulzrinne, and E. Schooler. SIP: Session initiation protocol, November 1997. Internet Draft draft-ietf-mmusic-sip-04.ps, *Work in Progress*.
12. International Telecommunication Union. Draft ITU-T recommendation H.323: Visual telephone sytems and equipment for local area networks which provide a non-guaranteed quality of service, November 1995.
13. International Telecommunication Union. Recommendation I.362: B-ISDN ATM Adaption Layer (ATMAL) Functional Description, March 1993.
14. ISO/IEC JTC 1/SC21. Information Processing Systems – Open Systems Interconnection – the directory: Overview of concepts, models and service. International Standard 9594-1, 1988.
15. G. McGregor. RFC 1332: The PPP Internet Protocol Control Protocol (IPCP), May 1992.
16. C. Newman. Application protocol design principles, July 1997. Internet Draft draft-newman-protocol-design-01.txt, *Work in Progress.*
17. R. L. Rivest, A. Shamir, and L. M. Adleman. A method for obtaining digital signatures and public-key cryptosystems. *Communications of the ACM*, 21(2):120–126, February 1978.
18. A. Schiffman and E. Rescorla. The secure hypertext transfer protocol. Internet Draft draft-ietf-wts-shttp-05.txt, *Work in progress*, November 1997.
19. H. Schulzrinne. Personal mobility for multimedia services in the internet. In B. Butscher, E. Moeller, and H. Pusch, editors, *Interactive Distributed Multimedia Systems and Services*, 1996. European Workshop IDMS'96.
20. H. Schulzrinne. Assignment of status codes for HTTP-derived protocols, July 1997. Internet Draft draft-schulzrinne-http-status-01.ps, *Work in Progress.*
21. W. Simpson. RFC 1661: The point-to-point protocol (PPP), July 1994.
22. Sun Microsystems. snoop - capture and inspect network packets, January 1995. SunOS 5.5 manual page.
23. W. Yeong, T. Howes, and S. Kille. RFC 1777: Lightweight directory access protocol, Mar. 1995.
24. P. Zimmermann. *The Official PGP Users's Guide*. MIT Press, 1995.

An Integrated Platform for Cooperative Teleteaching

Thierry Villemur, Véronique Baudin, Stéphane Owezarski, Michel Diaz

LAAS du CNRS
7, Avenue du Colonel Roche
31077 TOULOUSE CEDEX 4. FRANCE
e-mail: {villemur, vero, sowe, diaz}@laas.fr

Abstract. This paper presents the architecture and the design of a distributed teleteaching platform adapted to the professional education of Airbus air-plane pilots and maintenance agents. Starting from the studies of the current teaching given in classical classrooms, an analysis of the different interactions between trainer and trainees has been conducted. These interactions are supported in a distributed way by the developed tools, which consist of a videoconference, an electronic board and a shared whiteboard running on top of an ATM network.

1. Introduction

Airbus Training is a branch of Airbus specialized in the education of air-line pilots and maintenance agents. It manages several hundreds of hours of multimedia courses to train pilots and maintenance agents to the new versions of AIRBUS planes. For the moment, courses are given using Personal Computers locally grouped together inside a same classroom. The current TOPASE[1] project aims at extending these courses to a whole geographically distributed classroom. The trainers will be inside the AIRBUS training center and the trainees of the flying companies will learn from other places such as companies' main centers or the most important airports.

This paper presents the definition, design and realization of a new generation of distributed architecture for the professional teletraining domain, adapted to virtual classrooms. Starting from formal analysis of cooperation relationships between the members of the group, studies of the distributed cooperation system have been conducted to define the notion of "virtual classroom". News tools, presented in the sequel, supporting the interactions of the geographically distributed members of the classroom have been proposed and developed on top of an ATM network. This article focuses on the architecture and the design of this advanced multipoint teleteaching platform.

This paper is composed of the following sections: section 2 reports some related work. Section 3 describes the model used to represent cooperative groups and section

---

[1] TOPASE project on the design of tools for teleteaching for AIRBUS TRAINING, under grant 96 2 93 0291 from the French Ministry of Industry

4 presents its application to the specific Airbus Training teleteaching situation. Section 5 gives the functionalities of the teleteaching tools developed and section 6 describes the architecture of the whole platform.

2. Related work

Distributed synchronous teleteaching environments are now technologically possible thanks to the use of multimedia information. The major challenge is the building of teleteaching systems that can support current interactions between trainer and trainees in a distributed way: some projects as "Virtual clasroom" [11] present the use of integrated video communications with videoconference systems, communication boards and shared spaces, build on top of multipoint communication services. Inside the "CHeaP" project [7], vote mechanisms and global pointer have been proposed as general supports for distributed interactions between trainers and trainees.

"TeamWorkStation" [4] is a live video environment composed of two tools: a videoconference and a video shared space. The video shared space is composed of the superposition of two or several video pictures coming from different sources, merged and mixed as if they were slides. This general environment is used inside a trainer/trainee relationship: a trainee performs sketchings and the trainer corrects the mistakes through the transparent images.

"BETEL" and "BETEUS" projects [8] are an experimental platform on top of an ATM network. A set of trainees, grouped in a same room, have access to the trainer's environment located in a distant place through a 34 Mb/s ATM link. This platform handles live video data but is limited to point to point communications.

The "MultiTeam" project, is a Norvegian project to link distributed classrooms over an ATM network [5]. An electronic whiteboard the size of an ordinary blackboard, has been developed to transmit all the trainer's documents to the distant classroom. The view of the trainer is transmitted using a videoconference. The first evaluations were limited to two distributed classrooms, but will be extended to several sites. The hardware equipment to support the electronic whiteboard is therefore dedicated to classrooms, trainees being regrouped in specially equipped classrooms and not fully distributed and communicating with private workstations, as in our proposed environment.

3. Model for cooperation

To represent the cooperation structure used to define the distributed behaviour of a set of group members and the way cooperation information are shared and exchanged between them, a formal model, based on graphs, has been introduced [1], [9]. This model appeared to us simple enough to be handled in a natural way by the application layer, and general enough to be adapted to numerous and various cooperative situations. Moreover, it can be used with any kind of data, classical or multimedia.

3.1. Data knowledge relations between group members

A cooperative group is formed of users which are organized to define the relationships between the members of the group (Figure 1). The cooperative work is the common task associated to the group. The structure of the cooperation is represented by a directed graph, the cooperation graph, as shown in Figure 2. The vertices represent the members, the edges represent the relations between them. Each member has a set of data of which he is the owner. A participant can only modify his own data. An edge from participant "A1" to "A2" means that "A1" owns data transmitted to "A2" when their values change, as shown in Figure 2. It is important to note that an edge does not represent data ownership, given by the vertices, but represents the relation **Rd** of data exchange between two members. The approach retained for cooperation is that of information sharing between group members. Participant "A2" cooperates with participant "A1" if he sends some of his information to "A1".

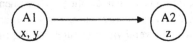

Fig. 1. Group member A1 sends "x" and "y" values to member A2: A2 knows data values of A1, but A1 does not know those of A2

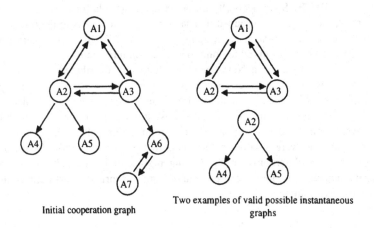

Initial cooperation graph

Two examples of valid possible instantaneous graphs

Fig. 2. A cooperative group

3.2. Dynamic groups

Let us now consider how the activity or the cooperative work associated to the group is initiated. The trivial solution corresponds to the case in which cooperation is considered to begin when all the members are ready to start. Of course, this view is too restrictive as a cooperative work can be performed as soon as an adequate and sound set of participants comes into existence. This means that at a given instant it is not necessary for all members to be present to start or conduct the cooperative work. As a consequence, the conceptual model is extended to define which participants must cooperate at the same time to perform the cooperative work. At any time the way the members interact between them and the number of cooperating members can be different.

The application associated with the cooperative group has to define the subsets of participants which have a meaning for the implementation and the performing of the cooperative work. In fact, if a pictorial representation is considered, these allowed subsets of participants form subgraphs of the cooperation graphs. Among all the subgraphs of the cooperation graph, the application chooses those semantically possible. The subgraphs retained by the application are called valid instantaneous graphs. Figure 2 shows two valid instantaneous graphs that could come from the initial cooperation graph.

3.3. Group decision for dynamic evolution

The current group configuration evolves in time, considering the potential arrivals and departures of the cooperative members inside the group. At any time, the current configuration corresponds to a valid instantaneous graphs, but several valid instantaneous graphs can be obtained at different moments.

Several cases are possible to change the cooperation configuration. The first one is to modify it as soon as possible. The service that manages the cooperation enforces the modification for each new configuration. The second one, selected here, considers the modification decision as a cooperative decision. As a consequence, the opportunity of changing is proposed to the actual set of cooperating members. The cooperating members vote [3] to accept or to deny the configuration change. The vote policy is specified by the cooperative application. According to the vote result, the valid configuration is changed or not. The current cooperation structure remains unchanged if the modification is refused.

Vote has been retained as a generic mechanism to implement a group decision technique. Moreover, combined with weights [3], votes offer very rich policies according to the different positions and importance of the cooperative group members. Some classical examples of votes policies are unanimity, majority vote, but more complex policies can be obtained such as giving the whole decision to a subset of participants or to a single participant.

4. Application to the Airbus Training teleteaching context

The model for cooperation has been used to characterize the data relations and exchanges between the members of a specific classroom. Studies have been conducted in the special case in which trainees are air-line pilots, but have been kept as generic as possible to be applied to various teleteaching and distributed cooperative situations.

4.1. Course presentation

The Airbus Training education class is composed of a trainer and twenty trainees at the utmost. The air-line pilots courses have a duration of 54 hours, on a two week period.

Each trainee owns an autonomous multimedia PC with two screens to visualize information for more convenience. The courses are carried out using the Video and Audio Computer Based Instruction (VACBI) environment, an hypermedia computer aided learning support, and are composed of hypermedia modules containing graphic, text, audio and video sequences presented in a sequential way. Each trainee owns a paper copy of the trainer course in which he can take notes. He studies his specific VACBI sequences in an autonomous way.

During his lesson, the trainer uses a multimedia PC running VABCI to show the important sequences or the specific parts of the VACBI modules to the whole classroom. His presentation is made with a retroprojector either to show his slides or some VACBI sequences. He uses a classical white board for writing or drawing, and a giant cockpit poster to point out the important parts of the studied plane.

A classical lesson is composed of three separated phases during a day:

The briefing session is a twenty minute presentation of the lesson contents. The trainer gives an introduction of the lesson, presents the global content of the VACBI modules to be studied by the trainees, and insists on some important points or on some important sequences discovered by the trainees. All the data of the session (slides, text notes, VACBI modules) belong to the trainer, and are shown by him to the whole classroom. During this session, trainees can ask questions to the trainer about the information he displays , creating a question/response dialogue between trainer and trainees. The briefing session is very close to a classical lesson.

The self-learning session looks like practical work. The trainees are independent to carry out, inside the VACBI application, all the exercises presented during the briefing session. Each trainee studies the content of the VACBI modules at his own rate. The progression of the trainees can be different and a personal context describing their progression is maintained by the local system. The trainer supervises the trainees and controls their progress. During this session, he helps the trainees that encounter difficulties and answers to the questions asked. The answers are only made to the requesting student in the case of personal help. The trainer can assist a trainee in his personal VACBI modules handling. He can speak to a subgroup or to the whole classroom if the information interests several trainees: it is a kind of general help.

The debriefing session is a general discussion between trainer and trainees once self-learning is over. The members can discuss on the difficulties encountered, insist on some unclear points, or have an evaluation of the previous sessions studied. It is an informal session, conducted as a global meeting.

4.2. Situation analysis

The different situations required for the running of an Airbus Training education have been first analyzed by Human Computer Interface researchers and ergonomists, to isolate the different dialogues and information exchanges used for each session. The classical Airbus Training education has been observed and studied for several days, using different trainers and trainees. All these studies form the bases used for the definition of the different phases, the different functionalities and the various data exchanges to support interactions between trainer and trainees.

The graphs of cooperation are a general model to define the relations between the members of a cooperative group. From the previous studies, inside each situation, the different flows of information have been identified and modeled to correspond to those supported by the cooperative teleteaching platform. A set of functionalities (classroom vizualization, information multicast...) required by each member of the group has been defined for each main teaching phase (briefing, question inside briefing, self-learning, question inside self-learning, debriefing...). The data flows are described as precisely as possible for each functionality. Their different quality of service have been given in [10], and their values have been evaluated inside the cooperative teleteaching platform realized.

The initial graph of cooperation is decomposed into a set of graphs, one for each data type. The meaning of these data graphs is given by Figure 3. The use of a functionality inside a new teaching phase requires the creation of new information flows: in some case, this creation needs the agreement of some cooperative members. For instance, when a trainee asks a question, the trainer has to take into account the request, and to accept it before the trainee's intervention is broadcasted to the whole classroom. The information flow control graphs that supervise the data exchanges are then introduced and presented in Figure 3. Member A1 can send video data to member A2 only when A3 agrees.

Fig. 3. Agent A1 sends video data to A2, once A3 has accepted this sending

The rest of this section presents the phases and the functionalities required to support the interactions between cooperative members. A detailed description of the structure of the data and control flows graphs is given in [10].

a) Normal briefing
The trainer has access to the image of each trainee's face and sends the image of his face and speech to each trainee. The trainees can not communicate between them (view of the whole class). The trainer multicasts the running of a multimedia application with an audio and a video channel. A channel is equivalent to an information flow. His slides and notes are multicasted with his pointer image to the trainees (multicast of multimedia and graphical documents).

b) Briefing with a question

A trainee asks a question. His request is signaled to the trainer who takes into account the trainee's intervention. The question has to be acknowledged by the trainer and can be delayed or refused by him: the trainer has a moderator role with respect to the set of trainees. He controls the start and the end of this specific phase. The dialogue between the trainer and the requesting trainee is communicated to the set of other trainees. The trainer owns several applications that are broadcasted to the set of trainees. At the beginning, he has the control of his applications. But, after his agreement, he can hand out control to the trainee that has asked a question: the authorized trainee pilots the trainer's environment (remote control). It is a useful functionality as a support for questions.

c) Self-learning: supervising the trainees

The trainer has access to the image of each trainee's face and sends his face image to each trainee, as in the normal briefing phase. At some time, the trainer wants to have a look at the trainee work progression, and know his current state. This functionality, similar to the glance function of [2] to know if somebody is present inside a distant room, corresponds to the remote access to the trainee's environment.

d) Self-learning: individual help

Sometimes, inside the self-learning session, a trainee needs help from the trainer: this individual help can start either on a trainee's request or on a trainer's observing the trainee's work performed so far. The dialogue remains private between the two members because it is an individual help. The trainer needs remote access to the trainee's environment to help him and to remotely pilot, if necessary, all the trainee's applications and more precisely the local VACBI application.

e) Self-learning: general help

The previous dialogue between the trainer and a helped trainee is multicasted to the whole set of trainees, together with the helped trainee's environment. This phase is used by the trainer when a particular question or remark can interest the whole class, to save the other trainees the bother of the same problem.

f) Debriefing

The informal discussion between all the members is supported by the same functionalities as those of the briefing phase. Moreover, the trainer can hand out the control of his applications to a remote trainee.

5. The teleteaching platform

Starting from the analysis of the data flows required to support all the remote interactions, a set of tools has been developed. They are presented in this section.

5.1. N-TSVS

The visualization of all the classroom members is carried out by using a synchronized videoconferencing system called N-TSVS (N-Timestamp Synchronized Videoconference System). It manages all the video and audio data required to view the different distributed class members, and more precisely, it is concerned with the capture, compression, transmission, decompression and presentation of the multimedia data through multipoint communications. N-TSVS defines and manages the group quality of service for the images of the videoconference participants. It synchronizes the different media, guarantees the temporal validity of the video and audio data presented (intra-flow synchronization) and controls the temporal shift that can appear between audio and video flows (inter-flow synchronization, for instance lip synchronization).

The N-TSVS visual interface is composed of two types of video windows: a local video, captured by the local video camera, monitors the images sent to the other members. The other video windows displays the images of the distant members.

Each member present inside the distributed classroom owns his local video window. The trainer always owns an image of the trainees present. But, following the previous defined phases, the trainees have access to a single distant video (in the briefing and in the self learning phase), to two distant videos (when another trainee asks an accepted question displayed to the whole classroom), or to all the other distant videos in the debriefing phase. During each phase changing, the videos windows are dynamically modified.

When a member talks inside an authorized phase, his corresponding video window is surrounded by a blinking red border. The local video border becomes red on the sender machine, and one of the distant video becomes red on the receiving machines. This visual signal is useful to indicate who is currently speaking, and it strongly helps users to follow discourses when the group size increases. Moreover, when two users are speaking at the same time, the concurrent red signals easily identifies the audio collision, and the speakers can solve the problem.

Data synchronization is provided using a temporal timestamp technique: a timestamp is associated to each captured and sent object, and is used to define the presentation date on each receiving machine. This synchronization principle respects the temporal line paradigm, and guarantees both intra and inter-flow synchronizations.

The audio flows coming from the other N-1 cooperative members must be multiplexed inside the single audio output of a local workstation. To avoid a flow congestion inside the audio output, a silent detection is realized before any audio sending, and the audio data that correspond to real sounds are sent. Several persons speaking at the same time generate voice hubbub. Inside a receiving machine, the different audio flows are randomly interleft and the audio flow obtained is inaudible. The created cacophony is gracefully avoided by using the red window surrounding signals.

The N-TSVS user modules, at application level, are based on a "multithreaded" architecture, that gives a high degree of parallelism, guaranteeing a fine-grain synchronization of the multimedia data flows. Each thread is in charge of an elementary operation on a single identified data flow (for instance, a video flow display).

Data exchanges are made using a multipoint communication library build on top of IP multicast. This library gives each N-TSVS user module general primitives for unreliable multicast data exchanges and for multicast group management.

5.2. Shared electronic board

The shared electronic board is a general tool for sharing any application put inside its window. It gives remote views of applications under its control and supports the remote control of these applications. Each member's interface is composed of a video window area that catches the images of the shared applications of a chosen member and displays their video images to the screens of some or all the other members. Applications are shared by a single member, that owns them, and can allow any other group members to control them from a distance. But, following the teletraining phases, the people that share applications are different.

During the normal briefing phase, the trainer puts his local VACBI application shown by all the trainees inside his shared space. When a trainee is authorized to ask a question by the trainer, all the remote commands coming from the trainee are sent to the trainer's VACBI application, and act on it. The most surprising effect is that the authorized trainee remotely pilots an application, having only access to a video picture of it: the main advantage of this system is that any application (multimedia or not) can be shared through the shared electronic board, because only video copies of the application windows and remote commands are exchanged. This choice guarantees that the shared electronic board is a true generic tool that can be used in very different platforms to share varied applications.

The notes transmitted to all the members are also possible through the shared electronic board. They can either come from the owner of the shared applications or from a remote authorized member.

During self-learning session, the roles are reversed: during the supervising phase, the selected trainee shares his local applications, the trainer has access to a video picture of them. For individual help, the trainer remotely pilots the trainee's applications and for general help, the video picture of the environment of the helped trainee is multicasted to the whole class.

The design of the shared electronic board has been made using the same mechanisms as those described for N-TSVS. Data exchanges use IP multicast, tool architecture is based on multithreading and synchronization is based on timestamps.

5.3. Shared whiteboard

The shared whiteboard is only used at the present time inside the briefing session. With it, the trainer displays slides written in GIF or JPEG format and writes notes during the briefing session. This tool aims at reproducing the behaviour of a retroprojector and of a classical whiteboard, supports of lectures. The slides and trainer's notes are sent to the trainees, who can add personal notes unknown by the other members and save them in association with the information transmitted by the trainer. The trainer is always the sender of graphical data, the trainees are the receivers. The interface of the shared whiteboard is composed of a graphical window for each member.

Graphical data are multicasted to the trainees using a multicast library developed of top of IP multicast. All information are sent with a temporal timestamp to be synchronized and presented at the right time.

6. Architecture and implementation

The architecture of the platform, given by Figure 4, is based on the layering principle of the Open System Interconnection reference model (OSI).

- The application tools of the teleteaching platform, the tool application manager and the set of cooperation rules that gives group valid configurations have been put inside the application layer. Each application entity is connected to the dynamic membership cooperation service through Service Access Points (SAPs) and uses a set of service primitives defined in [9].
- The group membership service has been built on top of a connected reliable multicast transport service, based on TCP connections for convenience. As a consequence, it can be considered as a session membership service.
- The application tools directly use different transport multicast services for their specific data transmissions.

The group membership service [9], composed of the cooperation protocol modules and of the cooperation manager, manages the entries and exits of the members to keep the group in a coherent state, and controls data relations between members. It aims, when possible, at passing from a valid configuration (where members are cooperating) to another one, by considering the requests of entry in cooperation and the requests to leave cooperation coming from the members. It manages the vote process and, following the vote rules also given at application level, gives the vote result to the cooperative members. It synchronizes the change of cooperation structure with the application data exchanges when cooperation is modified. It is a generic service because it can support any cooperative configuration.

The "cooperation rules" module shares data with the manager and contains the conditions of validity to build the possible valid instantaneous graphs. Using these conditions, which are application dependent, the manager knows whether any cooperation change is possible. Very generic rules can be programmed with any kind of vote with weights. In the specific case of teleteaching environment, the rules coming from the observation of the current Airbus Training educations, that have been retained, are:

- in the briefing session, the trainer and all the trainees need to be present. The only valid possible configuration contains all the members. With such a choice, vote is not required. A weaker hypothesis could start the briefing session with the trainer and a subgroup of trainees. In this case, the vote decision will be given to the trainer;

- in the self-learning session, the trainer and at least one student must be present, the trainees studying the VACBI application at their own rate. The whole vote decision is given by the trainer that can control the arrivals and departures of the trainees;
- the debriefing session is a very informal session. At least one student must be present and all vote decision is given to the trainer.

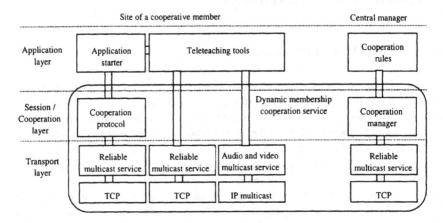

Fig. 4. Software architecture of the platform

The application starter, at application level, has two roles: first, it manages the different tools, giving them all the information required for their personal configuration (current phase, trainee who has been authorized to ask a question...) and second it displays all the information of the current context of the cooperative group (number and name of the people, phase and session, state of the different tools...).

The teleteaching platform has been implanted on top of a SUN workstation platform using SOLARIS 2.5 Operating System, equipped with Parallax video cards and connected through private Ethernet and ATM networks. Tests have been made using Internet Protocol over Ethernet and over ATM. Of course, the maximum bandwidth of the 10 Mbits/s Ethernet cable is rapidly reached with only three members: ATM supports more users.

7. Conclusion

This paper has presented the design of a teleteaching platform adapted to the education of air-plane pilots and maintenance staffs. Tools developed aim at supporting the interactions that take place in a classical classroom (questions, share of documents, help of the trainer..) through the distributed teleteaching environment.

Starting from studies of current traditional education, the different interactions and exchanges have been modeled to be supported by the distributed tools proposed.

The next step is to evaluate the proposed platform, with some air-plane students and with a trainer. Evaluations are under progress, but the first results seem encouraging. Air-plane education has given us a true framework for the design of our teleteaching tools. Although remote interaction tools have been adopted to the specific requirements of this education, their design has been kept as generic as possible to be easily adapted to other teleteaching domains. Another direction of research will be to improve and to test them for other teleworking domains as telecodesign.

Finally, more fundamental researches have to be conducted for the definition and the use of other synchronization algorithms. Indeed, synchronization algorithm based on global timestamps, does not ensure perfect synchronization or require to globally synchronize the clocks of the different distributed machines. Other work, based on Petri Nets [6], more complete than timestamp models, have richer synchronization semantics and are more adapted to the asynchronism of current communication systems.

References

1. M. Diaz and T. Villemur. Membership Services and Protocols for Cooperative Frameworks of Processes. Computer Communications, 16(9):548-556. September 1993.
2. R. S. Fish, R. E. Kraut, R. W. Root et R. E. Rice. Video Informal Communication. Communications of the ACM, 36(1):48-61, January 1993.
3. H. Garcia-Molina and D. Barbara. How to assign votes in a distributed system. Journal of the ACM, 32(4):841-860. October 1985.
4. H. Ishii and N. Miyake. Toward an Open Shared Workspace: Computer and Video Fusion Approach of Teamworkstation. Communications of the ACM, 34(12):37-50, December 1991.
5. MultiTeam project. Web site: http://www.unik.no/ENGELSK/ multiteam.html
6. P. Owezarski and M. Diaz Models for enforcing multimedia synchronization in visioconference applications. Proceedings of the 3rd International Conference on Multimedia Modeling (MMM'96), pages 85-100, Toulouse, France, 12-15 November 1996.
7. J. Sousa Pinto and J.Arnaldo Martins. CHEaP: a cooperative Hypermedia Editor and Player. Special issue of IEEE Transaction on education, august 1996.
8. Y. H. Pusztaszcri 94, M. Alou, E. W. Biersack, P. Dubois, J.-P. Gaspoz, P. Gros and J.-P. Hubaux. Multimedia Teletutoring over a Trans-European ATM Network. Proceedings of the 2nd IWACA Workshop, Heidelberg, 1994.
9. T. Villemur. Conception de services et de protocoles pour la gestion de groupes coopératifs. PhD dissertation, University of Toulouse III, January 1995.
10. T. Villemur. Rapport Coopération. project report TOPASE 3464. Internal LAAS report no 97228, 30 pages, 1997.
11. J.M. Wilson and D.N. Mosher. Interactive MultiMedia Distance Learning (IMDL): The prototype of the Virtual Classroom. Proceedings of the Word Conference on Educational Multimedia and Hypermedia, pages 563-570, june 1994.

CCS: CORBA-based Conferencing Service[1]

Dirk Trossen, Karl-Heinz Scharer
Technical University of Aachen
Dept. of Computer Science IV
Ahornstr. 55
D-52074 Aachen, Germany
trossen@i4.informatik.rwth-aachen.de

Abstract: An efficient conferencing service facilitates the implementation and the run-time control of conference applications. Key features of a conferencing service are conference management, multicast communication support, application state synchronization and user data marshalling. The paper defines a conferencing service to fulfil the requirements of conferencing applications. An object model of the service is defined and implemented using the CORBA distributed platform. The conference control protocol, which is used for our conferencing service, is introduced together with architecture of our implementation.

1 Introduction

Conference applications enable the communication and cooperation of widely distributed end-systems. The key function in these applications is the *multi-point communication* among several users. In heterogeneous environments this involves *marshalling* and *demarshalling* of user data. These features are crucial for applications such as cooperative working on documents and multi-user games. However, additional functions are needed in most conference applications. Due to concurrent activities, the need arises for *coordination* and *synchronization* of distributed program entities and users. Furthermore, functionality to inquire for information about the state and structure of existing conferences may be needed, e.g. to join a conference or to invite other users. All these features of conference applications are mostly independent of specific scenarios. Therefore it is useful to provide them by a generic system layer. Usage of the generic functionality accelerates and simplifies the implementation of conference applications.

In our paper we aim at developing a CORBA-based conferencing service by introducing the main features of the conference control protocol as the basis of our conferencing service. An object model and architecture for a CORBA-based service is proposed. Multipoint communication is one of the key features of a conferencing service. CORBA [5] provides a service to support multipoint in heterogeneous environments. We shortly introduce one implementation for its usage in a conference environment.

The paper is organized as follows. In section 2, we present some related work. In section 3, the conference control protocol is described, before introducing the realization in a CORBA environment in section 4. In section 5 conclusions are presented.

2 Related Work

Most of the requirements of a conferencing service are common to some applications. To standardize protocols for data communication the ITU designed the T.120 protocol stack [4]. This protocol family includes multipoint communication and generic conference support over different networks using profiles. A tree topology of providers is used with a dedicated top provider. Due to the lack of delta refreshes of database contents and the missing support of multicast in the control and data stream, the T.120 protocol stack

---

1. The work presented in the paper results from a joint project between Philips Research and Technical University of Aachen. The project was funded by Philips

is not well scalable as shown in [2]. Approaches [3] exist to combine the T.120 and CORBA [5] platforms to fulfil the requirements of a conferencing application.

The IETF (*Internet Engineering Task Force*) defines conference and multicasting services that can be compared with the features of the T.120. They, for example, define a *simple conference control protocol* [1], a *simple conference invitation protocol* [7] and multicast transport protocols such as RTP (*real-time protocol*) to transport real-time streams over IP multicast. The services and features of the conference control protocol of this approach are comparable with the T.120, but unfortunately this protocol is not described in more details.

Another approach for a distributed conferencing service was developed in the *HORUS* project [8]. There, a description is given how to realize a framework for distributed conference applications. User data marshalling is realized by using CORBA. Multipoint conferences are supported but there is no standardized communication platform.

3 Conference Control Protocol

A number of features are inherent to different conference applications. These features can be offered in a generic way by a conferencing service infrastructure. In [3] a detailed definition of application requirements and features of a conferencing service can be found. Since the wide variety of features can not be adequately treated in a single paper, we restrict ourselves in the following to only four essential features, namely *conference management, multicast support, state synchronization* and *user data marshalling*. Aspects like security, streaming, application functionality are not stated in this paper. In this section we propose a conference control protocol to fulfil these requirements of a conferencing service together with a high scalability in large scenarios.

The core of our conferencing service is the control protocol, which is used to provide the functionalities of our service. The aspect of user-data marshalling in heterogenous environments is provided by a layer on top of our service, which is not described in this paper. Figure 1 shows the architecture of the proposed protocol stack. The conference

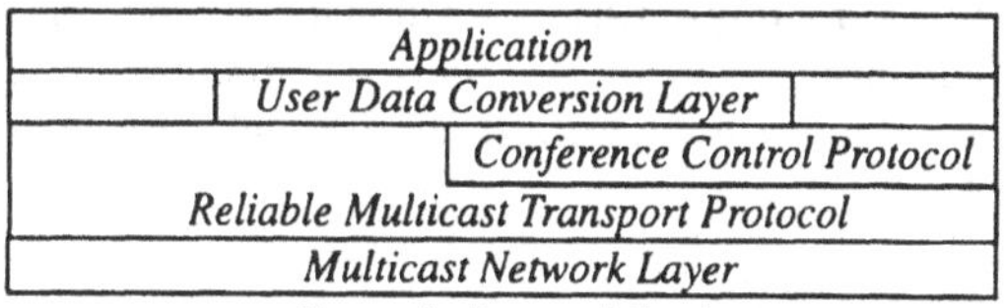

Application		
User Data Conversion Layer		
	Conference Control Protocol	
Reliable Multicast Transport Protocol		
Multicast Network Layer		

Figure 1: Protocol Stack

control protocol uses a reliable multicast transport protocol. It maps multipoint connections of the conference to multicast connections of the underlying multicast transport protocol, but user data may be sent directly using the multicast protocol.

The protocol is provided by *conference servers*, which are organized in a hierarchical tree topology. Conference clients are connected to one of these servers. Each control request is sent upward in this topology, some indications like database refreshes are sent back via a *multicast indication cloud*, which is established during setting up the conference. This cloud is a dedicated multicast channel, each provider is connected to when joining the conference. The database of conference members and applications is replicated at each provider in the tree. Thus, read requests are minimized. If a database entry changed, the database is only partially refreshed. This is called *delta refresh*, which is sent using the multicast indication cloud. Therefore scalability is improved.

3.1 Reconfiguration of a Conference

As a major part our conference control protocol allows the reconfiguration of conferences, e.g. *merging* or *splitting* conferences, changing the top provider, without a complete re-setup of the conference. The resource administration is changed at reconfiguration and new provider-provider connections are established. Resource conflicts are resolved without releasing resources. This is done by remapping identifiers if possible. During the merging of two conferences the merge request including the database of the lower conference is sent upward to the new top provider. The new merged database is generated and indicated with delta refreshes using the multicast channel. The conflicting resources are sent downward to the old top provider of the lower conference receiving also the complete new database. The new database and the conflict resources are indicated by the old top provider using the old multicast channel. The remapping of conflict resources is done in the appropriate providers of the lower conference. If a conflict resolving is not possible, the resource is released. Otherwise the resource is remapped to another identifier. At last, the old multicast channel is deleted and the lower providers join the multicast channel of the merged conference. The extended resource resolving mechanism differs e.g. from the T.120 [4] approach. This protocol solves the resource conflicts by releasing the conflict resources.

3.2 Multipoint Transfer

Our conference control protocol provides multicast communication by using a flexible *channel* concept. The channels are mapped to dedicated multicast connections of the underlying transport layer. The protocol supports *public* and *private* channels. Private channels are convened by a dedicated member of the conference, who may invite other members to join the channel. Members can also ask for invitation. The convener may eject members or release the channel. Public channels can be joined by all members in the conference. The channel is released if all members left this channel, which results in closing the multicast connection.

In the protocol there is no routing of user data within the tree topology of providers. The channels are only administrated by the providers. The routing of user data is done by the underlying multicast transport protocol. Therefore multicast communication is used directly for user data.

3.3 State Synchronization

The protocol provides state synchronization by a *token* concept. These tokens are an abstraction for states and application resources in a group communication scenario. Tokens may be grabbed exclusively by one conference member or inhibited non-exclusively by several members. The status of a token may be asked and the ownership may be given to another member. It is also possible to ask the owner for a token. This functionality is very similar to the concept of the T.120 protocol. Additionally, the owner(s) of a token may be inquired by any member, which is not provided by the T.120.

3.4 Resource Allocation

One of the main scalability factors is the response time of *resource requests*, which are requests for tokens and channels. For instance, in the T.120 standard a central database is used, which is stored at the top provider. This results in high response time of resource requests, like grabbing or giving tokens or joining channels.

In [9] an improved resource management scheme is proposed, which is used in our protocol for the resource management. This scheme results in higher performance of resource requests. The main idea of this scheme is, that the requests are sent upward in the tree until a provider is reached, who is able to generate a confirm or indication. For further details about the complete scheme and the overall performance see [9].

This allocation method provides higher scalability of our tree-based administration.

4   Realization of a CORBA-based Conferencing Service

After the introduction of our conference control protocol, we want to show the realization based on a CORBA approach. For that, our object model to realize the conferencing service is described followed by the architecture, we used to implement the service.

4.1   Object Model of our Conferencing Service

Figure 2 shows the object model of the conferencing service and its correlation in *Uni-*

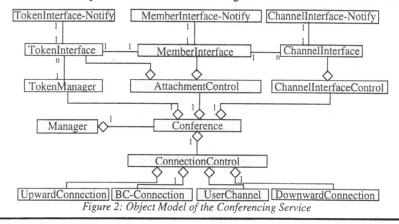

Figure 2: Object Model of the Conferencing Service

fied Modeling Language (UML) notation.

The core of the model is the *Manager* object. It provides methods to create local conferences, to append and join remote conferences. The *Conference* object is created by the Manager object and it is the core of one conference which provides methods for the conference database. There are three *factory objects* which create different interfaces at runtime. The *AttachmentControl* factory is responsible for the creation of the *Member-Interface* and the *TokenInterface*. The *MemberInterface* object is created when a new participant enters the conference. This object provides methods to get database entries like name and address of the endsystem, represented by the member object. Additionally a *TokenInterface* is created by the AttachmentControl factory for the token mechanism. When a local member in the conference joins a channel the *ChannelInterface-Control* factory creates a *ChannelInterface* which provides methods for the data transfer. This object is associated to a dedicated multicast address of the underlying multicast transport protocol.

The *ConnectionControl* factory is responsible for creating different objects to realize the provider-to-provider communication. There may be upward and downward connections and there is a broadcast channel for some indications of the control protocol. The *UserChannel* object is created as an abstraction of a dedicated multicast address when a local conference member has joined a channel. Different objects in our model correspond with notification objects to signal information changes like altering the state or adding new members to the conference.

4.2 Architecture of a CORBA-based Conferencing Service

As stated in section 3 our conference control protocol is offered by *providers* organized in a tree topology. Each provider consists of different client and server parts running in a multi-threaded environment. Figure 3 shows the resulting architecture. The applica-

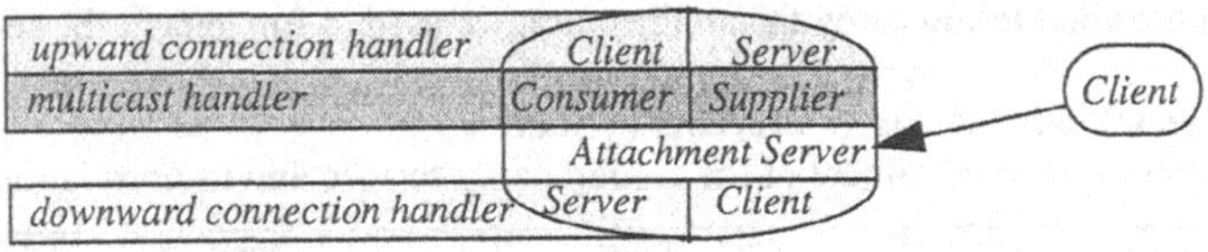

Figure 3: Architecture of Conference Service Providers

tion is a CORBA client connected to a *attachment server* part of the provider. The upward and downward provider-to-provider connections are realized by *upward* and *downward connection handlers*, which are crossed client-server threads. Each direction of a provider-to-provider connection is realized by an own client-server thread. The uppermost top provider has no upward connection. The different threads in each provider communicate via inter-thread communication (e.g. semaphores) with each other. Instead of exchanging *protocol data units* (PDUs) the control requests and indications are realized by method invocations in the appropriate servers by the appropriate client. Thus the requests are marshalled by the CORBA environment. For the *multicast indication cloud*, which is used in our conference control protocol, our architecture uses the multipoint communication concepts of CORBA. The *multicast handler* is registered as a consumer and supplier to an event channel to receive and send messages to the indication cloud.

4.3 Multicast Communication Using CORBA

Our conference control protocol uses multicast to transport indications like database refreshes. Therefore we require a multicast mechanism to build our conferencing service. The OMG standardized the *Event Service* [6] to provide asynchronous, multipoint communication. Different implementations of this service exist. We use one of these products, called *OrbixTalk* from Iona, Inc. The OrbixTalk model defines *talkers* and *listeners*, which have to be registered using to a specific *topic name*. These topics are mapped to multicast addresses. In an OrbixTalk scenario there may be M talkers and N listeners, who are communicating using the *OrbixTalk Reliable Multicast Protocol* (OTRMP) built on top of IP multicast on the network layer.OTRMP is responsible for the reliable transfer from the talkers to the listeners including fragmenting and reassembling of large messages. It is not specified how the multicast protocol works exactly, i.e. to provide reliability or ordering of messages. OTRMP is used by the event service implementation from Iona or it can be used by applications directly via an object oriented interface. To get maximum performance in our implementation we use the object oriented interface of the reliable multicast protocol directly.

Unfortunately, measurements in our department showed that the OrbixTalk protocol is not very stable and predictable. Message bulks are sent with low throughput and sending on different channels results in degraded performance. The reason for this may be the implementation and the internal design of the OrbixTalk protocol. For that, we are currently developing an object-oriented interface to other multicast transport protocols to get higher performance.

5   Conclusions

The paper discussed early results of a *CORBA-based conferencing service* (CCS) with a new developed conference control protocol. For that we focussed on four main requirements of conferencing applications, *conference management, multicast support, state synchronization* and *user data marshalling,* which are common to most scenarios. We introduced our conference control protocol, which supports conferencing using a tree-based approach. To improve scalability, delta refreshes and real multicast is used. Multipoint connections are directly mapped to corresponding multicast connections of the underlying multicast transport protocol. Synchronization is provided by tokens very similar to the T.120 standard. To improve resource response times, an enhanced resource management scheme is used to reduce the response time and the provider and link load in some scenarios. The protocol may be used in any multicast environment.

The object model and architecture was described to provide the conferencing functionalities of our protocol when using CORBA. Additionally a short introduction of a multipoint mechanism in CORBA was given.

To sum it up it can be said, that we defined a conferencing service, which was developed on a multipoint CORBA environment. For that we defined a control protocol, which can be easily adapted to other multicast platforms, especially it can be used to develop a standard C++ environment with any multicast protocol.

Our next steps will be to evaluate our system and to specify our conferencing service formally e.g. in SDL. Implementing the service in C++ using a multicast transport protocol will be a next step in our development to compare it with our CORBA implementation to get perhaps higher performance especially when using multicast.

References

[1]   C. Borman, J. Ott, C. Reichert (1996): Simple Conference Control Protocol, ftp://ftp.ietf.org/internet-drafts/draft-ietf-mmusic-sccp-00.txt

[2]   T. Helbig, D. Trossen (1997): The ITU T.120 Standard Family as Basis for Conferencing Applications, Proceedings of SPIE International Symposium Voice, Video, & Data Communications, November 1997, Dallas, USA

[3]   T. Helbig, S. Tretter, D. Trossen (1997): Combining CORBA and ITU-T.120 to an Efficient Conferencing Service, Proceedings of the International Workshop on Interactive Multimedia Systems and Telecommunication Services, September 1997, Darmstadt, Germany

[4]   ITU-T T.120 (1996): Data Protocols for Multimedia Conferencing

[5]   OMG (1993): Common Object Request Broker: Architecture and Specification

[6]   OMG (1995): Common Object Services Specification

[7]   H. Schulzrinne (1996): Simple Conference Invitation Protocol, ftp://ftp.ietf.org/internet-drafts/draft-ietf-mmusic-scip-00.txt

[8]   R. Renesse, K. Birman, S. Maffeis (1996): Horus: A flexible Group Communication System, Communication of the ACM, April 1996

[9]   D. Trossen, P. Papathemelis, T. Helbig (1998): Improved Resource Management for the ITU T.122 Standard, Proceedings of the IEEE Workshop on Systems Management, April 1998, New Port, USA

The Application of TINA in the MESH Project

Marten van Sinderen and Luís Ferreira Pires

Centre for Telematics and Information Technology, University of Twente, PO Box 217
7500 AE Enschede, the Netherlands
{sinderen,pires}@cs.utwente.nl

Abstract. This paper discusses the application of TINA concepts, architectures and related design paradigms in the MESH project. MESH adopted TINA as a means to facilitate the design and implementation of a flexible platform for developing and providing interactive multimedia services. This paper reports on the activity in which the TINA specifications have been studied and implementation options for the TINA components have been selected. This paper also discusses the role and position of protocols and objects in this context.

1 Introduction

User demands with respect to telecommunication services are becoming increasingly stringent. These demands are not only related to functionality, performance and capacity, but also to reuse, adaptability and composability. That is, telecommunication systems should not only satisfy current requirements, but they should be designed in such a way that they can be easily maintained and modified to satisfy future requirements as well.

This challenge was taken up by the MESH[1] (Multimedia-services for the Electronic Super Highway) project. MESH aims at the development of a flexible distributed services platform to support some specific business domains, including education and health care. MESH is the continuation of the PLATINUM (Platform providing Integrated-services to New Users of Multimedia) project [3]. In PLATINUM a platform consisting of an ATM-based transport system with multiparty connection support, a middleware layer providing multiparty/multimedia sessions, and a set of application components has been developed. While re-using these results as much as possible, MESH should achieve higher adaptability and flexibility than the PLATINUM system, and should link up with current standards developments.

After surveying current developments in standards for multimedia telecommunication services, we have concluded that the requirements above can be properly addressed by following an approach such as the one taken in TINA (Telecommunica-

---

[1] MESH is carried out by a Dutch consortium of research institutes, industry and end-users and is partially sponsored by the Dutch Ministry of Economic Affairs. The project started in December 1996 and will end in December 1998.

tions Information Networking Architecture) [4, 9]. The TINA approach assumes the availability of a Distributed Processing Environment (DPE), which supports the development, deployment and operation of interacting objects, independent of the operating system, software and hardware of the different computing nodes. In line with the TINA approach, we decided to use CORBA (Common Object Request Broker Architecture) [7, 8] as the DPE for the MESH platform.

The particular combination of ingredients (ATM, TINA and CORBA) makes it necessary to consider two different paradigms for distributed system design, viz. a protocol-centred and an object-centred paradigm. The protocol-centred paradigm has traditionally been used by the telecommunications community. It focuses on the rules for message exchange between (protocol) entities that allow the support of some defined cooperative behaviour or service. The object-centred paradigm originated in the computing community. This paradigm is primarily concerned with the operations that can be invoked on (remote) objects and their possible returns. Since the two paradigms represent different cultures and comprise different, but partially overlapping concepts, their combined use in a single project may lead to confusion and inconsistent (intermediate) designs, unless the paradigms are precisely characterized and mutually related [2].

This paper discusses the application of TINA in the design of the MESH platform. It also discusses the role and position of protocols and objects in a TINA-based platform.

The remaining of this paper is organized as follows: Section 2 discusses the high-level decisions taken in the design of the MESH platform and their implications; Section 3 presents the MESH platform architecture; Section 4 discusses the role of objects and protocols in this architecture; and Section 5 draws some final conclusions.

2 Design Decisions and Implications

The Platinum system was limited in the sense that it was based on a single network technology, did not conform to open standards, did not provide a clean separation of network and middleware/application concerns, and was not easy to extend or modify. The main architectural challenge for the designers of the MESH platform was to provide an open and more flexible architecture through the adoption of TINA concepts, principles and components, and to re-use as much as possible of the Platinum results.

TINA is an open architecture consisting of a set of concepts, principles and components for the development, deployment and operation of telecommunication systems. Re-use of specifications and software, high availability, interoperability and flexibility are crucial requirements for advanced telecommunication systems. For this reason, TINA is based on object-orientation, distributed computing and other standards from the telecommunications and computing industries.

TINA-compliant systems are distributed computer systems, consisting of interconnected *computing nodes*. Different computing nodes in a TINA system may be produced by different manufacturers, which implies that they may use different hardware and software technology. *Telecommunication applications* therefore can assume the availability of a *Distributed Processing Environment* (DPE), which allows one to develop and deploy a collection of interacting objects that implement the applications, independent of the operating system, software and hardware of the computing nodes, and the network technology used to interconnect these nodes.

TINA identifies different sub-architectures for different aspects of telecommunication systems, and uses different models to completely define these sub-architectures. For the development of the MESH platform, the crucial sub-architectures were the service architecture (covering telecommunication applications) [5] and the network architecture (covering data transport) [6]. The most important models were the information model and the computational model. These architectures and models were also used in the evolutionary path from the PLATINUM system to the MESH platform. In this path we had to find a proper mapping from the PLATINUM components and models (e.g., multiparty/multimedia sessions) onto TINA architectures and models.

The MESH platform uses CORBA as DPE. When this choice was made, the available commercial CORBA implementations were not capable of supporting interactive multimedia services[2]. Therefore, multimedia support in the MESH platform had to be realized outside CORBA, using PLATINUM components.

3 Platform Architecture

The MESH platform architecture basically consists of the TINA service and network architecture, limited by some specific choices. This section illustrates the application of TINA, the use of CORBA and the encapsulation of PLATINUM components.

Fig. 1 illustrates a multipoint-to-multipoint relationship (service session) between service users (parties) that can be supported by the MESH platform, according to the TINA service architecture and using the information model concepts. Components are able to establish, change and dissolve relationships through the manipulation of information model concepts.

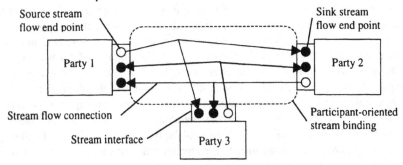

Fig. 1. Example of mp-mp service session

---

[2] IONA Technologies recently announced an extension of Orbix, called OrbixMX, which supports multimedia and is ATM-aware. OrbixMX is expected to be available in Q3 98.

Fig. 2 illustrates the distribution of service components supported by the MESH platform, according to the TINA service architecture and using the computational model concepts. The distribution is based on the distinction between access to services and usage of services, and the existence of domain boundaries. Component interactions that cross domain boundaries require conformance to the external interfaces specified in the TINA service architecture. Although TINA also specifies component interfaces that are used by other components in the same domain (internal interfaces), conformance to these interfaces is not mandatory.

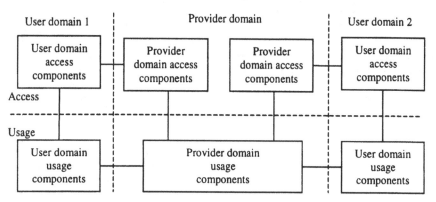

Fig. 2. Distribution of service components

One of the user domain usage components is the *service session User Application* (ss-UAP). The ss-UAP of the MESH platform consists of three sub-components (see Fig. 3): a generic component for interfacing with the provider domain usage components, a service specific component that contains the user applications and also interacts with the user domain access components, and a medium realization component that provides stream interfaces for the exchange of continuous data (audio and video).

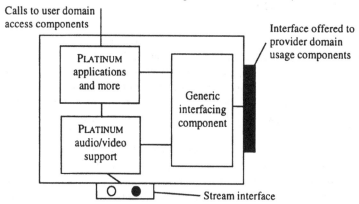

Fig. 3. Decomposition of the service session User Application component

The medium realization component is necessary since the CORBA implementation that we use does not support stream interfaces. This component re-uses the PLATINUM middleware layer functionality for linking network devices and multimedia user interface devices within a terminal. An alternative medium realization component, based on the H.323 series of standards [1], is under consideration. The service specific component also re-uses part of the PLATINUM system, viz. the application components (e.g., a conference management application with shared whiteboard). These applications need the stream support provided by the medium realization component.

The MESH platform uses CORBA to support the interactions between its service components, provided these interactions are based on operational interfaces. CORBA, in turn, uses the Internet transport system (TCP/IP) to exchange messages between different ORBs (see Fig. 4). The PLATINUM transport system is used for the exchange of continuous data through stream interfaces.

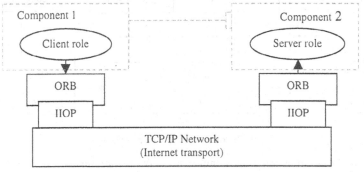

Fig. 4. Component interaction using CORBA

4 Protocols and Objects

The TINA architecture isolates service issues from network issues, such that telecommunication applications can be designed and deployed independently of the network technology used to support these applications. The interactions between the application (service) components, and their constituting objects, are supported by the DPE. The DPE, or actually its ORB part, hides the protocols that provide the interaction support. This allows interactions to be specified at the application level in terms of (patterns of) invocations of methods on interfaces of components.

The DPE boundary reflects the state-of-the-art with respect to middleware technology: below this boundary, functionality is provided out-of-the-box, while above the DPE boundary, functionality is user-defined, although application frameworks may facilitate the development of user-defined functionality. We expect the DPE boundary to shift in time. For example, next generation DPEs will probably support stream interfaces and multipoint communication. In general, recurring patterns of interaction are potential candidates for future DPE (ORB) extensions, and complex coordination of components may be replaced by simpler interactions if protocols that provide richer interaction support are incorporated in the DPE.

5 Final Remarks

The MESH platform architecture presented in this paper is an intermediate result of the MESH project. The platform is currently being implemented. This implies that the architecture may still be modified, extended or simplified, depending on the problems and opportunities encountered in the implementation process. For example, tools and technologies for WWW programming will be used to create a wide range of additional applications, without losing the benefits of TINA and TINA compliance.

TINA turned out to be useful in the achievement of the project goals. However, the interpretation and application of TINA specifications is not straightforward: the TINA specifications are quite complex and general, forcing designers to make choices and interpretations, such that the resulting system complies with the intended requirements in a reasonable time scale. Furthermore, TINA was still under development during the design of the MESH platform, and consequently the specifications were not always complete and consistent. In retrospect, however, we feel that it is important to exercise the TINA concepts in order to get a better understanding and control of complex telecommunication systems and services.

References

1. International Telecommunication Union. Audio/video communication. Recommendation H.323v2 (forthcoming), ITU-T, 1998.
2. M. van Sinderen, L. Ferreira Pires. Protocols versus objects: can models for telecommunications and distributed processing coexist? Sixth IEEE Workshop on Future Trends of Distributed Computing Systems (FTDCS'97), IEEE Computer Society Press, 1997, pp. 8-13.
3. M. van Sinderen, P. Chimento, L. Ferreira Pires. Design of a shared whiteboard component for multimedia conferencing. Third International Workshop on Protocols for Multimedia Systems (PROMS'96), Dpto. de Publicaciones de la ETSIT, Ciudad Universitaria, Madrid, Spain, 1997, pp. 1-16.
4. Telecommunications Information Networking Consortium. Overall concepts and principles of TINA. Version 1.0. February 1995.
5. Telecommunications Information Networking Consortium. Service architecture. Version 5.0. June 1997.
6. Telecommunications Information Networking Consortium. Network resource Architecture. Version 3.0. February 1997.
7. S. Vinoski. CORBA: integrating diverse applications within distributed heterogeneous environments. IEEE Communications Magazine, 35(2):46-55, Feb. 1997.
8. http://www.omg.org/
9. http://www.tinac.com/

Flexible Multiplexing in MPEG-4 Systems

J. Deicke[1], U. Mayer[1], A. Knoll[2], and M. Glesner[1]

[1] Darmstadt University of Technology
Institute of Microelectronic Systems
E-Mail: {deicke|mayer|glesner}@mes.tu-darmstadt.de

[2] Deutsche Telekom Berkom GmbH
E-Mail: knoll@berkom.de

Abstract. System design for terminals communicating audiovisual information becomes more and more complex. MPEG-4 Systems is the part of the upcoming standard that cares exactly about this issue. Because MPEG-4 addresses many applications at once, it has to be understood as a tool box, where application developers can choose appropriate tools to support their development efforts. In particular, the multiplexing tool of MPEG-4 Systems has the difficult task, to apply scheduling and dropping algorithms to multimedia data streams in order to optimize the end-to-end quality of the whole application. Therefore, it has to take into account bitstream characteristics and parameters set by the author of the multimedia content as well as information from the underlying network. To ensure the interoperability of MPEG-4 terminals and to hide network specific details from the MPEG-4 application developer, MPEG has defined the Delivery Multimedia Integration Framework (DMIF). This paper gives a short introduction into MPEG-4 Systems and DMIF. Moreover, we present our prototype realization of a DMIF layer, including FlexMux control, by means of OMT diagrams and block diagrams.

1 Introduction

In May 1998, MPEG-4[1] (version 1) reached the status of a Final Committee Draft (FCD) in the progress of becoming an International Standard (IS). The main innovation of MPEG-4 compared to existing audiovisual communication standards (e. g. [6] or [13]) is that it introduces objects instead of frames as smallest accessible units [17]. In MPEG-4 the well-known news speaker can be encoded with a higher quality (e. g., resolution) than the less interesting background object. Among other new features like extendibility and flexibility[18], this scalability leads to much more complex problems in designing MPEG-4 systems. An excellent introduction to the MPEG-4 standard is given in the official MPEG-4 Overview paper[2] [16].

One of the central points in the MPEG philosophy is the idea not to invent something twice (*one functionality – one tool*). And this is the way MPEG-4 has to be understood: as a tool box. Any of the six parts (Systems, Visual, Audio, Conformance, Reference Software and DMIF) tries to identify tools to offer to the application developer. MPEG-4 Systems consists of the following tools [15]:

---

[1] MPEG = Moving Picture Experts Group: The ISO number of the MPEG-4 standard is 14496.

[2] http://drogo.cselt.stet.it/mpeg/standards/mpeg-4.htm.

- a terminal model for time and buffer management
- a coded representation of interactive audiovisual scene information
- a coded representation of identification of audiovisual streams and logical dependencies between stream information
- a coded representation of synchronization information
- multiplexing of individual components in one stream
- a coded representation of audiovisual content related information

In this paper, we want to describe the multiplexing tool of MPEG-4 Systems, the FlexMux and as much from the surrounding parts of an MPEG-4 system as necessary to understand the task of the FlexMux. Furthermore we will present our prototype realization of DMIF and the FlexMux which were used in order to realize a prototype of a QCIF[3] video server [10]. In general, MPEG-4 does define the terminal and stays silent about the server; the server is considered as an implementation issue. This paper will focus on the server.

To achieve a sufficient understanding it is necessary to present many of the central concepts of MPEG-4 Systems; this led to the structure of this paper: In section 2 we will give a short overview of the Systems part, present it's architecture and introduce some of the most important terms and concepts. Section 3 gives insight in the main DMIF concepts and the FlexMux will be introduced. Besides that, it considers especially the collaboration between DMIF and the FlexMux. Then section 4 describes the software architecture of our prototype realization of the DMIF layer, finally section 5 ends the paper with some concluding remarks and an outlook on future work.

2 MPEG-4 Systems

2.1 Terminology and Layers

The variety of functionality provided by MPEG-4 Systems highly recommends a layered design. Referring to the end-to-end argument [11], that states that a lower layer protocol should not provide a service that a higher layer protocol or application must also provide, and to the *one functionality – one tool* philosophy, four functional layers of MPEG-4 Systems have been identified (figure 1: Compression Layer, Access Unit Layer, FlexMux Layer, TransMux Layer). In a fast walk down the protocol stack, we will introduce some important MPEG-4 Systems terms. The content producer (author) creates digital data that will be individually compressed in the Compression Layer, depending on the media type of the data. The resulting compressed data streams are called *ElementaryStreams*. ElementaryStreams are sequences of *AccessUnits* and are passed to the so called AccessUnit Layer. An AccessUnit is the smallest semantic unit, MPEG-4 knows. E. g., one frame from an MPEG-1 video sequence is one AccessUnit (could be an I-, a P- or a B-frame[4]). In that layer, the AccessUnits will experience fragmentation and header addition. The resulting streams are called

---

[3] QCIF = Quarter Common Intermediate Format.

[4] I: Intra, P: Predicted, B: Bidirectionally predicted.

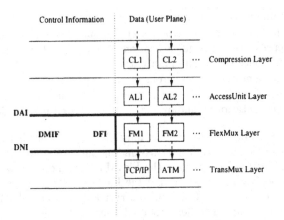

Fig. 1. The Layer Model of an MPEG-4 Server

AL-Packetized Streams (a sequence of AL-PDUs[5]). These streams are multiplexed by the FlexMux layer (see section 3.2). Leaving the FlexMux Layer, the multiplexed streams change their name to *FlexMux Streams* and are passed to the TransMux Layer.

2.2 Audiovisual Objects and SceneDescription

The essential innovation in MPEG-4 is the object concept. An object is called AVO or Audiovisual Object and can be synthetic or natural, auditive or visual, static or dynamic. It can be possible to have user interaction with an object to change some of its parameters or objects can have dynamic behaviour on their own (e. g., rotating images). To enable this broad range of functionalities, MPEG-4 introduced a scene description language and its binary representation BIFS[6]. Most of the concepts are borrowed from the VRML[7] community [1]. This is because MPEG was aware of the great success of VRML 2.0 as the de-facto standard for describing *synthetic worlds* on the World Wide Web and recognized how fruitful a cooperation between the two communities would be for both.

Like VRML, the MPEG-4 scene description also uses *nodes* to create hierarchical structures in scenes. E. g., you can think of a very simple scene consisting of a natural video sequence displayed in front of a static background. The natural video can be represented in the scene graph as a `VideoObject2D` Node, the static background e. g. as a JPEG[8] picture through the `Background Node`, a `Group2D` Node would group all visual nodes together and serve as the top of the visual nodes. A `World Info Node` for additional textual explanation of the scene and the top `Scene Node` that is the root of the scene tree (figure 2) complete the

---

[5] AL-PDU = AccessUnit Layer - Protocol Data Unit.

[6] BIFS = Binary Format for Scenes.

[7] VRML = Virtual Reality Modeling Language. VRML is also a ISO/IEC standard. Number: 14772.

[8] JPEG = Joint Photographic Experts Group.

scene. By definition, the `Scene Node` has to contain exactly the topmost real grouping node and the `World Info Node`. A very important difference, com-

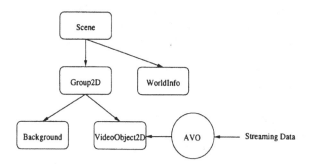

Fig. 2. The scene tree for a very simple example scene

pared the MPEG approach with the VRML way, is the idea of streaming data to support distributed applications. So it is not necessary to download the whole video that should be displayed through the `VideoObject2D Node` in the scene, but it is sufficient to connect an AVO with associated data streams consisting of video data to that node. It is important to note that there are *nodes* that make up a scene and *objects* that are the link between scenes and streaming data. The syntax and semantics of those objects are described in the next subsection. At the beginning of a session, the scene description is sent to the receiving termi- nal in its own stream (`SceneDescriptionStream`). Also the object definitions are transmitted downstream in the so called `ObjectDescriptorStream`. When in the following the syntax of ObjectDescriptors will be discussed, it will be- come clear, that only if the ObjectDescriptors are known, a useful access to the streaming data will become possible.

2.3 Objects and Object Descriptors

ObjectDescriptors are the link between streaming data and the scene description. The syntax of the `ObjectDescriptor` can best be defined by using the Syntactic Description Language (SDL), that is also described in [15]:

```
class ObjectDescriptor () {
      uint(10) ObjectDescriptorID;
      uint(5) streamCount;
      for(j=0; j<streamCount; j++) {
            ES_Descriptor ();
            ...
      }
}
```

An Object has a 10 bit long identification number and up to 32 $(= 2^5)$ streams can be plugged into it. Those streams are called *ElementaryStreams* (ES) and are one of the central abstractions in MPEG-4. For instance, an MPEG-1 video stream could be such an ElementaryStream. The reason for the freedom to have more than one ES at an object is the realization of one aspect of scalability. One can have different additional video streams (EnhancementLayer) to an independent video ES (BaseLayer), each enhancing the quality of the video. The quality can be scaled down, when resources become tight by transmitting fewer or none enhancing streams.

The remaining definition of the syntax consists mainly of the ES_Descriptors that describe the single ElementaryStreams assigned to it. The Descriptor of an ElementaryStream looks like the following:

```
class ES_Descriptor () {
      uint(5) ES_Number;
      uint(1) streamDependence;
      ...
      if (streamDependence) {
            uint(5) dependsOn_ES_Number;
      }
      aligned(8) DecoderConfigDescriptor decConfigDescr;
      if (decConfigDescr.streamType!=initialObjectDescriptor) {
            ALConfigDescriptor alConfigDescr;
            QoS_Descriptor qosDescr;
            ...
      }
}
}
```

The **ES_Number** field leads to the possibility to identify ElementaryStreams. This is done by the ES_Number field together with the ObjectDescriptorID of the associated ObjectDescriptor. To know about the dependencies between BaseLayer (independent) streams and EnhancementLayer (dependent) streams, each ES has the **streamDependence** flag and maybe the five bit **dependsOn_ES_Number** field to point to the stream it depends on. The **DecoderConfigDescriptor** provides information for each single ES to the decoder.

Because the lengths of AccessUnits vary in a broad range, it is necessary to fragment them to appropriate sizes for the underlying network. The AccessUnit Layer gets AccessUnits and fragments them to AL-PDUs. AL-PDUs consist of an AL-PDU-Header and AL-PDU-Payload (one whole or a fragment of an AccessUnit). To tell the receiver how it's AccessUnit Layer has to parse the AL-PDU-Header, it is necessary to assign an **ALConfigDescriptor** to any ElementaryStream that configures the parser for the AL-PDUs. Inside the AL-PDU-Header is not only all the timing information, but also some flags that are very relevant for the receiving AccessUnit Layer as well as for the sending Flex-Mux Layer [15]. The last descriptor within the ES_Descriptor is very important for the FlexMux. The most significant parameter for the multiplexer inside the QoS_Descriptor is the **streamPriority**. Any ES has a **streamPriority** value between 0 and 31; this is the relative importance of an ES that is considered by the FlexMux when resources become tight and decisions have to be made which ES must be dropped.

3 DMIF and FlexMux

3.1 DMIF

A key part of the MPEG-4 standard is the Delivery Multimedia Integration Framework. DMIF goals are twofold [14]:

- hide the delivery technology details from the DMIF user, i. e., from the MPEG-4 application
- ensure interoperability in the control plane between end systems

The DMIF architecture is such that applications which rely on DMIF for communication do not have to care about the underlying communication method. The implementation of DMIF takes care of the technology details presenting a simple interface to the application.

Like depicted in figure 1, DMIF can be seen as a control layer that interacts with the outside world (other layers) through interfaces. To the application, DMIF communicates via the DMIF Application Interface (DAI). The DAI is the only normative DMIF interface. The DMIF network interface (DNI) is the interface between DMIF and the underlying network. That means, that there has to be one DNI implementation per supported network technology (e. g., ATM). The third interface is the DMIF FlexMux interface (DFI), an internal reference point that defines the collaboration of DMIF and the FlexMux(es) (figure 3).

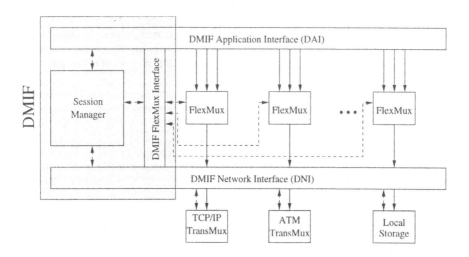

Fig. 3. Modules in the DMIF Layer

DMIF is a multimedia middleware between a local application (e. g., an MPEG-4 terminal that is able to present MPEG-4 content), the remote application (e. g., an MPEG-4 video server) and the network. Conceptually, the local application can not tell the difference between content coming from local storage or content coming via the net (broadcast or remote interactive). The visible communication primitives at the DAI are internally mapped to the adequate communication protocol. It is also possible to emulate remote applications on the local consuming host.

3.2   FlexMux

One of the tools in the MPEG-4 Systems tool box is the FlexMux tool. Semantically, the FlexMux belongs to DMIF, but because MPEG-4 Systems defines the data plane and DMIF defines the control plane, the FlexMux is defined in Systems. It is classified as optional, that means any receiver that wants to be MPEG-4 compliant has to implement a simple FlexDemux. Opposite to the demultiplexing part, the FlexMux at the producing peer can become quite complex. It it important to note that it is common in the telecommunications world to specify multiplexers for specific terminals. Among others, there exist ITU-T[9] specifications for terminal-multiplexer pairs in the fields ISDN[10] [7], [3], PSTN[11] [9], [4], and LAN/Internet [8], [5]. So it is not surprising that MPEG defines a multiplexer, too. But the MPEG-4 FlexMux is *not* only *yet another multiplexing tool* because of the large amount of parameters that are available for statistical multiplexing in the FlexMux Layer.

The main task is to multiplex those ElementaryStreams, that require a similar QoS and pass them to the TransMux Layer. It is useful to learn some terms that describe the FlexMux (compare figure 4): The FlexMux is a n:1 multiplexer that connects n inputs (called FlexMux channels) to one output (called FlexMux stream, consisting of FM-PDUs[12]). Each AL_Packetized stream is delivered to one FlexMux channel. There can be more than one FlexMux entity, one for each TransMux channel which picks up the FlexMux streams. How channel establishing and releasing is organized will be covered in section 3.3.

The FlexMux is a statistical multiplexer. That means it has the task to forward the incoming data as good as possible to the output by considering the dynamic behaviour of both sides. To keep things simple, think of just one FlexMux that is connected to one CBR[13] channel; this could be an ATM[14] CBR channel, an N-ISDN channel or simply a modem on a telephone line (PSTN). From the MPEG point of view, these network technologies are all simply TransMuxes. A TransMux could also be a very sophisticated ATM VBR[15] channel or a best-effort TCP/IP network (but in the latter case a statistical multiplexing would not be very useful).

The FlexMux is aware of the channel capabilities and has all the necessary information of the incoming data streams that it needs to apply *scheduling and dropping algorithms* and decide which data should be discarded and which data

---

[9] ITU-T = International Telecommunication Union – Telecommunication Section.

[10] ISDN = Integrated Services Digital Network.

[11] PSTN = Public Switched Telephone Network.

[12] FM-PDU = FlexMux - Protocol Data Unit.

[13] CBR = Constant Bitrate.

[14] ATM = Asynchronous Transfer Mode.

[15] VBR = Variable Bitrate.

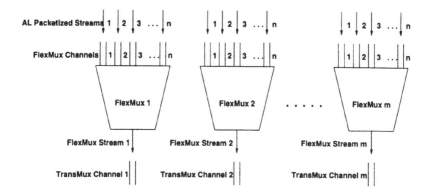

Fig. 4. FlexMux Entities

should get which amount of available bandwidth (datarate). The FlexMux considers the following kinds of information:

- timing information
- streamPriority
- information about the channel capabilities
- stream dependencies

These parameters and the freedom to delay or drop data and preserve AccessUnit borders at the same time, let the FlexMux become an interesting tool in improving QoS in low-bandwidth environments. The FlexMux has to deliver AccessUnits (or their fragments, respectively) in time, i. e., it has to consider the DecodingTimeStamp (DTS) of AccessUnits (the time, when an AccessUnit has to be at the decoder to be displayed in time) as a delivery deadline. A constant end-to-end delay of the network can be assumed for many cases.

Any ElementaryStream has a `streamPriority`. In the case of insufficient bandwidth, the ElementaryStream with the lowest priority has to be delayed, maybe some of its AccessUnits have to be skipped. The multiplexer shall be aware of the skipping consequences because it is not possible to continue with the transmission at any AccessUnit. There are flags that label `RandomAccessPoints` for continuing with transmission (e. g., in an MPEG-1 videostream, the beginning of an I-frame would be such a `RandomAccessPoint`).

To know about the bandwidth resources of the underlying TransMux channel, the FlexMux has to be aware of its delivery capabilities. This information is given to the FlexMux through the DNI (refer to subsection 3.1).

There are two multiplexing modes: Simple Mode and MuxCode Mode. These are the two ways how the FM-PDUs can be structured (see figure 5 and 6). In

Fig. 5. FlexMux-Protocol Data Unit (FM-PDU) in Simple Mode

Fig. 6. FlexMux-Protocol Data Unit (FM-PDU) in MuxCode Mode

the Simple Mode case, one AL-PDU goes into one FM-PDU. This is obviously the best choice for large AL-PDUs because due to the eight bit length field that follows the eight bit index field of the FM-PDU-Header, the FM-PDU payload can not be bigger than 255 bytes (for the exact syntax of FM-PDUs refer to [15]). The larger amount of overhead in the MuxCode Mode would be appropriate only in the case of small AL-PDUs.

Finally, the dependencies between ElementaryStreams have to be taken into account by the FlexMux. It is certainly not useful to transmit enhancing streams when the base stream that they depend on has been skipped. This is also information that has to be considered in the dropping strategy of the FlexMux.

3.3 Collaboration between DMIF and the FlexMux(es)

After the explanation of the functionality of the FlexMux and DMIF during the last two subsections, we can now describe their collaboration.

The easiest way to understand the collaboration is to look at a setup scenario and the following transmission phase step by step. The DAI has four types of communication primitives, each representing a period during a transmission:

- service primitives
- session primitives
- channel primitives
- data primitives

First of all, the client initiates a session by asking the server for a service. It is very important to distinguish the terms service and session. A service is something that the provider offers to the consumer. Imagine an http link to a JPEG picture on the Web. This is the offer from the provider. After you click on the link and when you see the picture on your screen you have received this service. A session is the sum of the necessary ressources (e. g. connections) between the producing and the consuming peer required for the delivery of one or more service(s).

After the consumer (client) has asked for a first service, a session is established between the two peers. The client receives the `InitialObjectDescriptor` with the scene description in a so called *first stream*. Now the client knows which ElementaryStreams it will receive during the session to deliver the demanded service. Also a `StreamMapTable` that assigns ElementaryStreams to channels will be passed to the client. Now, the actual transmission begins.

At the server side, the application passes `channelAdd` primitives to the DAI and asks DMIF for channels with an ElementaryStream specific QoS. DMIF then passes channel handles to both peers and the real data transmission can begin. Besides this, DMIF instantiates one FlexMux per requested QoS; channels requesting a similar QoS are put together on the same FlexMux. Furthermore, at the client and the server side the DMIF layer connects TransMuxes with FlexMux streams.

The observation of the TransMux channel during the transmission is the task of the FlexMux. The FlexMux passes the FlexMux streams to the TransMuxes via a channel estimation buffer. The TransMux *pulls* the data from that buffer and the FlexMux can monitor the TransMux datarate by checking the amount of data in the buffer. These datarate measures are passed through the DFI and are held in the SessionManager, so any FlexMux can ask for the bandwidth situation of other FlexMuxes, if any. This opens the optimization potential to initiate a `channelMove` through the DFI and pass a FlexMux channel from an high-loaded FlexMux to an idle or low-loaded FlexMux with a similar QoS.

The task of the so called session manager in DMIF is to negotiate with the network and to establish new TransMux channels and FlexMuxes when they are needed. The borderline between the responsibilities of DMIF and FlexMux is the exchange of channel administration information from DMIF to the FlexMux(es) and in-band datarate control from the FlexMux(es) to DMIF and the other FlexMux(es). Exactly that collaboration is provided by the DFI.

The release of a session can be instantiated by the producing as well as by the consuming peer. DMIF will react by releasing channels and finalizing FlexMuxes in an appropriate way.

4 Objects in the DMIF Layer

In this section, our prototype realization of the DMIF layer including the Flex-Mux is described by means of the widely accepted OMT[16] notation [12], [2]. The diamond symbol represents an aggregation, the triangle symbol stands for inheritance, the filled dot for zero or more relations and the non-filled dot for a one or zero relation. The class names in italics refer to abstract classes or interfaces in our Java implementation, respectively.

In figure 7, all classes of the DMIF layer are shown (for the purpose of better readability, no association relations are taken into account). The main class is the DMIF class that implements all DMIF interfaces (DAI, DNI and DFI). The implementations of the (Java) interfaces define the syntax according to the DAI semantics of all communication primitives used in any of the interfaces. The actual implementation work is done in the DMIF class. Moreover, the DMIF class instantiates most other classes in the DMIF layer. There is one SessionManager for each DMIF session (optional with a graphical management tool, the DMIF-ManagementInterface); DMIF instantiates and finalizes also all FlexMux entities. Finally, the DMIF class also instantiates and controls the different TransMux entities that are subclasses from a common SuperTransMux class which implements dummy functions as substitutes when a TransMux does not implement the whole DNI function set. The actual implementation of the functions is done in the real TransMuxes. At the server side, the MPEG-4 Application (e. g., the QCIF MPEG-4 video server described in [10]) consists of the following main components (figure 8): The MPEG-4 Service and DMIF should be two commu-

---

[16] OMT = Object Modeling Technique.

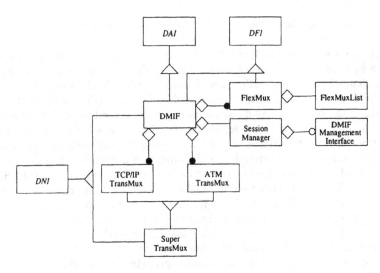

Fig. 7. OMT Diagram of the DMIF Layer

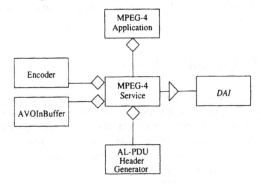

Fig. 8. OMT Diagram of the Application Layer

nicating processes. In our prototype realization, we have implemented them as two separate threads.

5   Conclusions and Future Work

During this paper, a brief introduction into MPEG-4 has been given. In particular MPEG-4 Systems and DMIF have been considered. Important concepts in the MPEG-4 Systems context have been identified and explained. The tool box character of MPEG-4 lead to the identification of the different tools in MPEG-4 Systems. We concentrated on the description of the FlexMux, the multiplexing tool of MPEG-4 Systems. To understand the FlexMux, it is necessary to know about the MPEG-4 layers and DMIF. Therefore a very brief introduction into DMIF has also been given. The cooperation between DMIF and the FlexMux and the task for the FlexMux have been described. MPEG-4 stays silent about implementation issues on the server side, therefore we have presented a possible object-oriented design of the DMIF layer, including FlexMux control for the server. Up to now, our prototype realization can communicate with two of the possible TransMuxes (i. e., underlying network technologies): TCP/IP and ATM CBR.

Future work will consist of implementing more network technologies under the hood of the DMIF layer, especially advanced Internet protocols like the Real-Time Transmission Protocol and the Resource Reservation Protocol. But the focus of our future work will be the development of scheduling and dropping algorithms for the FlexMux. The high dynamic of the presented MPEG-4 multiplexing problem defines a new challenge in packet scheduling strategies.

References

1. A. L. Ames, D. R. Nadeau, and J. L. Moreland. *VRML 2.0 Sourcebook.* Wiley Computer Publishing, New York, second edition, 1997.
2. Erich Gamma, Richard Helm, Ralph Johnson and John Vlissides. *Entwurfsmuster: Elemente wiederverwendbarer objektorientierter Software.* Addison-Wesley, Bonn, 1996.
3. ITU-T Recommendation H.221. Frame structure for a 64 to 1920 kbit/s channel in audiovisual teleservices, July 1997.
4. ITU-T Recommendation H.223. Multiplexing protocol for low bitrate multimedia applications, March 1996.
5. ITU-T Recommendation H.225.0. Media stream packetization and synchronization on non-guaranteed quality of service LANs, November 1996.
6. ITU-T Recommendation H.263. Video coding for low bitrate communication, July 1995.
7. ITU-T Recommendation H.320. Narrow-band visual telephone systems and terminal equipment, July 1997.
8. ITU-T Recommendation H.323. Visual telephone systems and equipment for local area networks which provide a non-guaranteed quality of service, November 1996.
9. ITU-T Recommendation H.324. Terminal for low bit rate multimedia communication, March 1996.
10. J. Deicke, U. Mayer, and M. Glesner. An object-oriented client/server architecture for video-on-demand applications. In *Interactive Distributed Multimedia Systems and Telecommuncation Services (Fourth International Workshop, IDMS'97)*, Lecture notes in computer science, pages 440–449, Berlin, September 1997. Springer.
11. J. H. Saltzer, D. P. Reed, and D. D. Clark. End-to-end arguments in system design. *ACM Transactions on Computer Systems*, 2(4), November 1994.
12. James Rumbaugh, Michael Blaha et al. *Object-oriented modeling and design.* Prentice-Hall Inc., Englewood Cliffs, 1991.
13. ISO/IEC JTC1/SC29/WG11. IS 13818: Generic coding of moving pictures and associated audio, November 1994.
14. ISO/IEC JTC1/SC29/WG11. MPEG-4 DMIF committee draft, November 1997.
15. ISO/IEC JTC1/SC29/WG11. MPEG-4 Systems committee draft, November 1997.
16. ISO/IEC JTC1/SC29/WG11. Overview of the MPEG-4 version 1 standard, November 1997.
17. A. Knoll. MSDL: MPEG-4 Systems and Description Languages (in German). *Fernseh- und Kinotechnik*, 50. Jahrgang:459–465, August/September 1996.
18. F. Pereira. MPEG-4: A New Challenge for the Representation of Audio-Visual Information. In *Picture Coding Symposium*, Melbourne, Australia, 1996.

Video Encryption Based on Data Partitioning and Scalable Coding - A Comparison

Thomas Kunkelmann[1] and Uwe Horn[2]

[1] Darmstadt University of Technology, Department of Computer Science
Information Technology Transfer Office, D-64283 Darmstadt, Germany
kunkel@ito.tu-darmstadt.de

[2] GMD - German National Research Center for Information Technology
Institute for Media Communication, D-53754 Sankt Augustin, Germany
Uwe.Horn@gmd.de

Abstract. Many of today's multimedia applications require confidential video transmission over the Internet. Appropriate encryption methods require a high computational complexity and are likely to become a performance bottleneck within software-only applications. To reduce the computational encryption effort, partial video encryption methods have been proposed in the past. Promising approaches are based on data partitioning where the encoded video stream is partitioned into two streams, one containing the most important data, the other one containing the least important data. Encrypting the most important data only can reduce the required computational complexity to 10 - 50 % compared to encryption of the whole data stream. Besides the known standardized DCT based video codecs, scalable codecs become more and more popular. Scalable codecs have the advantage that no additional effort is needed to obtain the required data partitioning. In this paper, a novel approach to partial video encryption based on data partitioning applicable to every DCT-based video codec is presented. It is compared to base layer encryption of a video stream encoded with a scalable codec based on a spatio-temporal resolution pyramid. Besides partial encryption, transparent encryption is discussed as well.

1 Introduction

A striking feature of today's communication systems is the incorporation of live video. In computers, this kind of communication is handled by multimedia conferencing applications, supporting synchronous communication and cooperation between different individuals or groups. Unique to these systems is the combination of live media like real-time audio and video and the possibility of sharing documents and applications. Currently, security plays only a minor role in multimedia conferencing systems, but the need for confidentiality and privacy becomes more and more important, especially for multimedia applications that operate on open networks like the Internet.

Besides other security requirements like access control, authentication, data integrity and non-repudiation, data confidentiality plays a major role for video transmissions. Data confidentiality means that the content of a video transmission cannot be revealed by any unauthorized eavesdropper. Suitable encryption methods which can guarantee an appropriate level of video data confidentiality [1] require a high computational complexity and are likely to become a performance bottleneck in software-only multimedia applications. Therefore, partial video encryption schemes have been proposed in the past [2–4]. The idea behind partial encryption is to encrypt only the most important parts of an encoded video stream. Partial encryption methods for standardized DCT-based video codecs like MPEG-1 or MPEG-2 include the protection of Intra-coded information only [2], the permutation of DCT coefficients [3], or they are based on data partitioning. Data partitioning means that DCT coefficients are partitioned into two classes where one class contains the most important low-frequency coefficients and where the other class contains the less important high-frequency coefficients [4]. By encrypting only the low-frequency DCT coefficients, the encryption effort can be reduced to 10 - 50 % compared to encrypting the whole data stream [5]. Nevertheless, attacking such an encrypted video can still reveal details of the original video. Therefore we are especially interested in methods achieving the highest video data confidentiality at the lowest encryption effort.

Apart from protecting confidential video data, there is often a need for transparent encryption [6]. Transparent encryption tries to restrict the access to the best video quality. Receivers not possessing the correct decryption key can decode only a lower quality. This scenario makes perfectly sense for Pay-TV applications, where the content provider offers free previews at a lower image quality.

Besides video standards like MPEG-1 [7], H.261 [8] and H.263 [9], scalable video codecs are becoming more and more popular [10,11]. A scalable codec transmits a video signal in different layers, each encoded at its own bitrate. As explained later, both partial and transparent encryption are easy to achieve with a scalable video codec.

This paper compares partial and transparent video encryption based on DCT data partitioning as a suitable approach applicable to all standardized video codecs, with base layer encryption of scalable video streams obtained from a video codec presented in [11]. Scalable coding has the advantage that neither partial nor transparent encryption requires bit stream parsing of an already encoded video, as it is otherwise the case if a non-scalable codec like MPEG-1 is used.

In the following, we first give an introduction into DCT based hybrid coding. We describe partial encryption schemes known from literature which are suitable for standardized video codecs and present our approach to partial encryption which allows bitrate scaling of the data to encrypt. After that we describe our scalable codec based on a spatio-temporal resolution pyramid combined with lattice vector quantization. Finally, we present simulations results for the partial encryption method we propose for standardized video codecs and compare them with results obtained with our scalable codec. DCT-based video coding is carried out by an MPEG-1 codec. In our comparisons we take into account the complexity of each method and its ability to perform the desired task, which is for partial encryption to hide most of the scene content at the lowest computational effort, and for transparent encryption to give a lower quality video, which is nevertheless still viewable.

The domain of application for encryption support in scalable video codecs can be subdivided in *Pay-TV*, *video conference* support and *archives*.

Pay-TV and video-on-demand services. For broadcast TV applications, there is no need to protect the video content with highly secure mechanisms, since it contains no confidential information. The purpose of encryption is here to prevent anyone who has not legally joined the service accessing the video content. Therefore, the encryption methods used here are still suitable if they only restrict the pleasure of watching the video in full quality. However, this behaviour can be a useful feature of the encryption method, as the transparent encryption example shows. Here the encryption method offers the possibility of a preview of the broadcast material at no cost, while the full quality access requires the purchase of the correct decryption key.

Video conference support. In these applications the need for strong encryption is obvious, since video conferences may often contain highly confidential content. The need for a fairly good protection is furthermore increased if the video data passes open networks like the Internet. If partial encryption methods are used here, their effectiveness for protecting the video content has to be evaluated first.

Video archives. For already digitized and stored video material, the usage of a scalable video codec and the encryption with different keys for the video coding layers gives some advantages. With transparent encryption a search and retrieval in video databases is still possible on the lower-quality material. Also, for content-based retrieval there is no need to decrypt the whole material prior to the search, since most similarity-based algorithms operate mainly on the base layer information of a scalable video stream. So the decryption effort can be drastically reduced for each retrieval.

2 Partial Encryption Methods for DCT-based Video Codecs

All standardized video codecs are based on motion-compensated hybrid coding as shown in Fig. 1 [7, 12]. A frame can be encoded as Intra- or as Inter-Frame. An Intra-Frame is decomposed into 8×8 blocks and a DCT (Discrete Cosine Transform) is applied to each block. The resulting DCT coefficients are quantized, reordered by a zig-zag scan, run-length entropy-encoded, and transmitted to the receiver. An Inter-Frame is encoded with reference to an already transmitted frame. Frames referring only to a past image are called P-Frames. A motion estimator tries to find for each block of the P-Frame a good match in the reference

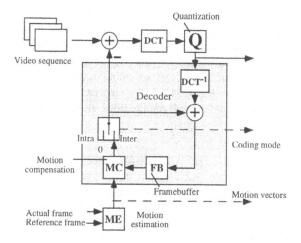

Fig. 1. Motion-compensated hybrid DCT coder as used by MPEG

frame. Typical block sizes used for motion-compensation are 8×8 or 16×16. From estimated motion vectors, a motion-compensated prediction for each block in the actual frame is computed. It is decided adaptively whether a block should be encoded in Intra- or in Inter-mode. In Intra-mode, the block is encoded like in still image compression schemes. In Inter-mode, only the difference between the original block and its motion-compensated prediction is encoded together with the corresponding motion vector. Intra-coding of a block in an Inter-Frame is selected if motion estimation fails. This is often the case if a scene contains a high amount of motion. However, the highest compression gain is obtained from Inter-Frame coding [13].

Several methods for partial encryption of DCT-based video codecs have been proposed in the past and are summarized in the following. A more detailed comparison of DCT-based partial encryption schemes can be found in [5].

Padding. Statistical analysis of MPEG streams justifies the application of encryption to only one half of the video stream and use of these data as a secure one-time pad for the other half of the stream [14]. The encryption effort for this method is only 53% of the effort required for encrypting the whole data stream, but cannot be reduced furthermore.

Encryption of intracoded frames. In [2] it is proposed to encrypt only the Intra-Frames of an MPEG stream. As shown in [15], this approach can lead to a fairly good protection of the video content, although video sequences with a high degree of motion still show a lot of details from the original scene.

Better results can be achieved by encrypting the Intra-coded macroblocks within Inter-Frames as well. Note that this requires a content parsing of the video stream down to the macroblock level. However, the remaining Inter-coded macroblocks can still reveal details of the original sequence. By increasing the amount of Intra-coded information at encoding time, a better level of confidentiality can be achieved, but this will also increase the bit rate of the video stream, which is impractical for most applications, since transmission bandwidth is a limited resource.

SEC-MPEG. SEC-MPEG [16] is an implementation for partially encrypting MPEG-1 data, based on the Intra-coded data encryption method mentioned above. The aim of this toolkit is to achieve confidentiality and integrity checks. Confidentiality is achieved using the DES algorithm, integrity checks are carried out by a cyclic-redundancy check (CRC) due to performance issues, at the expense of a weak integrity certification. The toolkit supports four levels of confidentiality and three levels of integrity, beginning with encrypting the header information, up to an encoding of the whole MPEG stream. In confidentiality level 2 a subset of Intra-coded macroblocks is selected, which will be encrypted, while level 3 encrypts all Intra-coded image information.

3   Rate-Scalable Encryption of DCT Coefficients

In [4] we describe a rate-scalable partial encryption method, which allows a security level of nearly every granularity and which is applicable to all DCT-based video compression schemes. In contrast to the approaches described above our method also protects Inter-coded information. The encryption scheme is based on the observation that the first few low-frequency DCT coefficients are the most important ones with respect to the quality of the reconstructed image. Our algorithm starts with encrypting a data block at the beginning of a DCT block and guarantees protection of the first n DCT coefficients. By varying n, the bitrate of data selected for encryption and therefore the encryption effort can be adjusted. Note that for a given n the resulting amount of data selected for encryption depends on the scene content. Typically, the lowest obtainable encryption rate lies between 20 % and 45 % of the overall bitrate and can be as high as almost 100 % for $n \rightarrow 64$.

Fig. 2 shows the idea of rate-scalable DCT coefficient encryption applied to an MPEG-1 coded video stream. Also shown is an extension where motion vectors are encrypted as well. Although in the latter case the amount of encrypted data increases, no significantly better protection of the scene content is observed. Encryption of header data has not been considered since these data contain a lot of redundant information which can easily be computed by implicit knowledge about the video stream, e.g. by the image size and the encoder type that was used to produce the video stream.

An advantage of this method is the scalability of the encryption effort even for already encoded video material, as needed for applications dealing with videos

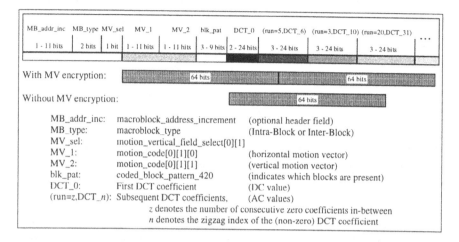

Fig. 2. Rate-scalable encryption of an MPEG-1 bit stream with the method described in [4]. The top row shows the macroblock syntax of an MPEG-1 video stream [17]. The second row shows the number of bits occupied by each symbol. The brightness of the third row indicates the importance of the specific field for scene reconstruction (black: essential, white: unimportant). The two rows at the bottom specify which symbols are encrypted with and without motion vector encryption. We assume a block cipher with a block size of 64 bits. Motion vector encryption often results in one more 64-bit block, increasing the total amount of encrypted data by approx. 5 − 7%.

on CD-ROM or video archive material. Encryption rate scalability can also be achieved in level 2 of the SEC-MPEG package. The method proposed there has the disadvantage that the reduction of the encryption effort leads to more and more unprotected Intra-coded macroblocks, resulting in a weaker confidentiality level.

4 Scalable Video Coding with a Spatio-Temporal Pyramid

Scalable video codecs have been proposed in the past to address the problem of video integration into heterogeneous multimedia environments, especially in the context of Internet video transmission [18–20,11]. A scalable video coder produces a data stream which can be decoded at different bitrates. It allows computation time and memory limited decoding on less powerful hardware platforms [10], and it can substantially improve the quality and acceptance of video services on the Internet. For video servers, sequences need to be encoded only once. Depending on the available bitrate, the server selects more or fewer bits from the data stream to be sent to the receiver. For broadcast applications a layered multicast scheme can be used. The different bitrates can be distributed into several layered multicast groups. Picture quality increases with the number of received multicast groups.

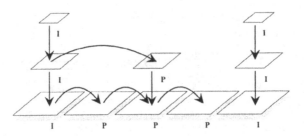

Fig. 3. An example for a spatio-temporal resolution pyramid with three layers. Note that we use a two-layered pyramid with no temporal subsampling for our experiments.

Our approach to scalable video coding is based on a spatio-temporal resolution pyramid. This kind of a multiresolution decomposition was first proposed by Uz and Vetterli in 1991 [21, 22]. The idea is shown in Fig. 3 for a regular spatio-temporal pyramid with three layers. The original video signal is first decomposed into three spatial resolution layers where each layer is at the same time transmitted at a lower temporal resolution. Compared to the original video signal, the overall amount of samples to encode is increased by approximately 13 % in this example. Advantages of this overcomplete representation are that downsampling and interpolation filters can be chosen freely and that multiscale motion-compensation can be easily included.

Besides I-Frames we are also using P-Frames in our coding scheme. Motion-compensated prediction is based on 16 × 16 blocks and works within each layer similar to motion-compensated hybrid coders [23, 24]. Motion vectors are estimated and coded in a hierarchical way. Motion vectors found for a lower resolution layer are used to predict motion vectors in the next higher layer. Within P-Frames, we distinguish between Inter- and Intra-layers. An Inter-layer can include temporal references to the previously transmitted layer of the same resolution. Therefore, each block can be predicted either spatially or temporally. Within Intra-layers, blocks can only be predicted spatially.

More details about the scalable video codec can be found in [11]. Within the context of this paper it is only important to understand that this codec produces video data streams at different rates, where data streams corresponding to lower spatial resolution layers contain the most important data. Applying partial or transparent encryption to a scalable video stream is straightforward. For partial encryption, only the first lower resolution layers starting with the base layer are encrypted. For transparent encryption, an appropriate number of layers starting with the least important layer are encrypted.

5 Simulation Results

In this section, we present simulation results for a comparison between partial and transparent encryption schemes applied to MPEG-1 and our scalable video codec. We assume that an eavesdropper can identify, separate and reconstruct any unprotected video data, but cannot reconstruct any protected video data. Any information contained in protected parts of the video stream is set to some reasonable default value. As test sequences we use *Coastguard* and *Akiyo*, both in CIF resolution (352 × 288 pixels) at 25 Hz. Coastguard is a video clip with a high degree of motion (camera movement), Akiyo is an example for a scene with no camera movement and a low amount of motion (head-and-shoulder scene). For our experiments we use a two-layered pyramid with no temporal subsampling. The base layer contains the input signal at the full temporal resolution but at a quarter of the original spatial resolution. Both the scalable codec and the MPEG-1 codec encode every 15th frame as an Intra-Frame, the frames in between are encoded as P-Frames. The overall bitrate needed by the scalable codec is comparable to the bitrate obtained from the MPEG-1 codec.

5.1 Confidentiality Level

Tab. 1 shows simulation results concerning the confidentiality level. For partial MPEG-1 encryption we use the method described in Section 3. As can be seen, MPEG-1 needs 1071 kbps to encode Coastguard at a PSNR of 28.7 dB and 128 kbps to encode Akiyo at a PSNR of 33.7 dB. The corresponding rates needed by the scalable codec depend on the rate spent within the base layer. The values show that at low and medium base layer rates the scalable codec outperforms MPEG-1 (without using B-Frame compression) in terms of coding efficiency.

The energy values E of both methods indicate that the protection obtained from base layer encryption with our scalable codec is comparable to the best known partial MPEG encryption method. For Akiyo, the scalable codec achieves an even better protection with the same encryption effort. Since base layer encryption needs no content parsing, the computational complexity is much lower than partial DCT encryption. Note that E is only a first approach for measuring the amount of original information decodable from a crypted video stream. A more accurate comparison would require subjective tests which are beyond the scope of this paper. An impression of the viewable scene content after partial encryption is given in Fig. 4.

5.2 Transparent Encryption

The idea of encrypting a scalable video stream transparently can be applied straightforward by protecting the whole enhancement data stream. Receivers who want a low-quality preview of the video can then still decode the base layer and scale it to the video's full size (and possibly to the full temporal resolution). This scaling step, of course, cannot reconstruct the video information contained in the enhancement layer, so the quality will be less than the quality obtained by decryption and decoding of the complete video stream.

With the partial encryption method of [4] we also can achieve transparent encryption for DCT-based video codecs. Here we do not protect the DCT coefficients with a frequency lower than the threshold value, but only those with

Table 1. Simulation results for partial encryption with MPEG-1 compared to our scalable codec. Encryption rate percentage is the percentage of the encrypted bitrate with respect to the overall bitrate. For the scalable codec this percentage is identical to the percentage of the base layer bitrate with respect to the overall bitrate. The overall bitrate is the bitrate needed for transmitting a test sequence at the given PSNR. E denotes the energy contained in the decodable frames after the given rate percentage has been encrypted. It is a first approach to an objective measurement, reflecting the amount of original information decodable from a crypted video stream. All values are computed as averaged values over the first 100 frames of each test sequence. The value E_{MV} denotes the energy for an additional MPEG motion vector encryption, leaving the overall amount of encrypted data constant.

Test sequence	Encryption rate percentage	MPEG-1				Scalable codec		
		Overall bit rate [kbps]	PSNR [dB]	E	E_{MV}	Overall bit rate [kbps]	PSNR [dB]	E
Coastguard	≈ 25%			344	620	948	29.4	212
	≈ 50%	1071	28.7	162	334	984	28.9	130
	≈ 75%			49	115	1044	28.4	91
Akiyo	≈ 50%			103	119	122	33.7	32
	≈ 66%	128	33.9	61	95	132	33.6	22
	≈ 75%			43	62	136	34.9	13

a larger index. These coefficients contain the minor details of the video scene content and can be compared with the enhancement layer information of the scalable video codec.

An important issue for this kind of transparent encryption is the usage of a stream cipher method [25] operating on single bits, since we do not want to overwrite any header information of the video stream, which would occur if we apply a 64-bit block cipher method on the video stream with no splitting of the stream. To explain this fact, take a look at Fig. 2 where all encryption on the video stream takes place in consecutive blocks of 64 bits. If we would use this technique here, some of the header data of the following block would fall into the 64-bit boundary and therefore they would also be encrypted, rendering the video stream useless for normal decoding. With a stream cipher, we can protect any single bits in the video stream, restricting encryption to the particular bits defining the high frequency DCT coefficients. The drawback of this single-bit encryption is the loss in performance, depending on the stream cipher algorithm used.

For transparent encryption in DCT-based coding, data partitioning could lead to a drift problem caused by motion-compensated predictive coding [26]. If the encoded data stream is split into two bit streams and only the lower rate bit stream can be decoded, different reference frames for motion compensated prediction are used at encoder and decoder. The error in the decoded image introduced by this mismatch is difficult to control and remains visible as long

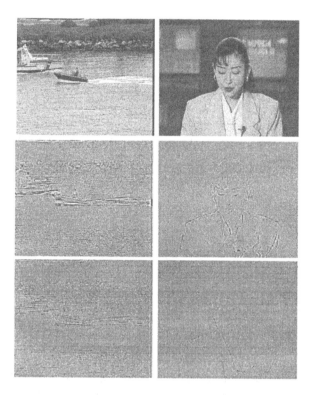

Fig. 4. Reconstruction of partial encrypted video frames: Original (top), MPEG-1 (middle), scalable codec (bottom). Left column: Coastguard, frame 30, ≈ 25% encrypted data. Right column: Akiyo, frame 45, ≈ 66% encrypted data.

as only Inter-coded frames are received. Fig. 5 presents an example obtained by encrypting a scalable video and an MPEG stream transparently. The images show that this drift problem is not visible in the MPEG example, since the transparent encryption obscures other artifacts in the video image. Also, since only high-frequent coefficients are encrypted, the drift is attenuated by the filter-in-the-loop of motion compensated prediction.

6 Conclusion

There are several sophisticated approaches for applying partial encryption methods to non-scalable standard-based hybrid video coding schemes like MPEG-1. We propose to use a rate-scalable partial encryption method, which allows a security level of nearly every granularity and which is applicable to all DCT-based video compression methods. Although this approach is superior to other approaches known from literature, a scalable codec offers several advantages for

Fig. 5. Transparent encryption with ≈ 75% protected data. Top left: fully decoded Coastguard frame 60 (I-Frame), top right: scalable codec, bottom left: MPEG encryption, bottom right: MPEG encryption for frame 59 (last P-Frame of GOP).

both partial and transparent video encryption. Simulation results show that the protection obtained from simple base layer encryption is comparable to rate-scalable partial DCT encryption, and can even outperform these method at low encryption rates. Note that base layer encryption does not require content parsing and therefore has a much lower overall computational complexity than partial DCT encryption. By using more than two layers, different confidentiality levels can be obtained from a scalable codec without additional effort, even if a video has already been encoded. Furthermore, the scalable codec has the advantage that transparent encryption does not suffer from the drift problem which can otherwise occur with standardized codecs.

References

1. B. Schneier. *Applied Cryptography*. John Wiley, New York, 2nd edition, 1996.
2. T.B. Maples and G.A. Spanos. Performance study of a selective encryption scheme for the security of networked real-time video. In *Proc. 4th Int'l Conference on Computer and Communications*, Las Vegas, NV, 1995.
3. L. Tang. Methods for encrypting and decrypting MPEG video data efficiently. In *Proc. 4th ACM Int'l Multimedia Conference*, Boston, MA, 1996.
4. T. Kunkelmann and R. Reinema. A scalable security architecture for multimedia communication standards. In *Proc. 4th IEEE Int'l Conference on Multimedia Computing and Systems*, Ottawa, Canada, Jun. 1997.

5. T. Kunkelmann, R. Reinema, R. Steinmetz, and T. Blecher. Evaluation of different video encryption methods for a secure multimedia conferencing gateway. In *Proc. 4th COST 237 Workshop*, Lisboa, Portugal, Dec. 1997.

6. B.M. Macq and J.J. Quisquater. Cryptology for digital TV broadcasting. *Proc. of the IEEE*, 83(6):944–957, Jun. 1995.

7. D. J. LeGall. MPEG: A video compression standard for multimedia applications. *Comm. ACM*, 34(4):46–58, Apr. 1991.

8. ITU-T. Recommendation H.261: Video codec for audiovisual services at $p \times 64$ kbit/s, 1993.

9. ITU-T. Recommendation H.263: Video coding for low bit rate communication, 1996.

10. B. Girod. Scalable video for multimedia systems. *Computers & Graphics*, 17(3):269–276, 1993.

11. U. Horn and B. Girod. Scalable video coding for the Internet. *Computer Networks and ISDN Systems*, 29(15):1833–1842, Nov. 1997.

12. D. J. LeGall. The MPEG video compression algorithm. *Signal Processing: Image Communication*, 4(2):129–140, Apr. 1992.

13. B. Girod. Motion-compensating prediction with fractional-pel accuracy. *IEEE Trans. on Communications*, 41(4):604–612, Apr. 1993.

14. L. Qiao and K. Nahrstedt. A new algorithm for MPEG video encryption. In *Proc. 1st Int'l Conf. on Imaging Science, Systems and Technology*, Las Vegas, NV, 1997.

15. I. Agi and L. Gong. An empirical study of secure MPEG video transmissions. In *ISOC Symposium on Network and Distributed System Security*, San Diego, CA, 1996.

16. J. Meyer and F. Gadegast. Security mechanisms for multimedia data with the example MPEG-1 video. http://www.mpeg1.de/doc/secmeng.ps.gz, 1995.

17. ISO/ IEC. International Standard 13818-2: Generic coding of moving pictures and associated audio information: Video, 1996.

18. N. Chadda, G. Wall, and B. Schmidt. An end-to-end software-only scalable video delivery system. In *Proc. NOSSDAV'95*, Apr. 1995.

19. D. Hoffman and M. Speer. Hierarchical video distribution over Internet-style networks. In *Proc. ICIP'96*, volume I, pages 5–8, Lausanne, Sep. 1996.

20. W. Tan, E. Chang, and A. Zakhor. Real time software implementation of scalable video codec. In *Proc. ICIP'96*, volume I, pages 17–20, Lausanne, Sep. 1996.

21. M.K. Uz, M. Vetterli, and D.J. LeGall. Interpolative multiresolution coding of advanced television with compatible subchannels. *IEEE Trans. on Circuits and Systems for Video Technology*, 1(1):86–99, Mar. 1991.

22. M. Vetterli and K.M. Uz. Multiresolution coding techniques for digital television: A review. *Multidimensional Systems and Signal Processing*, 3:161–187, 1992.

23. B. Girod, U. Horn, and B. Belzer. Scalable video coding with multiscale motion compensation and unequal error protection. In Y. Wang, S. Panwar, S.-P. Kim, and H. L. Bertoni, editors, *Multimedia Communications and Video Coding*, pages 475–482. Plenum Press, New York, Oct. 1996.

24. U. Horn and B. Girod. Performance analysis of multiscale motion compensation techniques in pyramid coders. In *Proc. ICIP'96*, volume III, pages 255–258, Lausanne, Sep. 1996.

25. M.J.B. Robshaw. Stream ciphers. Technical Report TR-701, RSA Laboratories, Jun. 1995.

26. R. Mathew and J.F. Arnold. Layered coding using bitstream decomposition with drift correction. *IEEE Transactions on Circuits and Systems for Video Technology*, 7(6):882–891, Dec. 1997.

An Architecture for an Interactive Multimedia System Based on MPEG-2

Naceur Lagha[1], Hossam Afifi[1]

[1]ENST Bretagne, Networks & Multimedia Services Department
2, rue de la chataigneraie, 35510 Cesson sévigné, France
{lagha,Afifi@rennes.enst-bretagne.fr}

Abstract: The standardization of video coding techniques as well as data networks has attained a maturity that enables to consider wide and successful deployment of public video services. Today, numerous implementations of Video-On-Demand and Tele-medical applications are operational and are based on MPEG and ATM standards. Based on these standards, many other applications can rapidly be deployed. In this paper we present a new simple MPEG-2 based architecture to fulfill a subset of the MPEG-4 specified functionalities especially content based coding and interactivity. A prototype is also presented and evaluated.

1 Introduction

The need to optimize bandwidth utilization for statistical multiplexing and cost reduction has raised new data compression requirements [5]. In this context, several standards have been developed. The JPEG Standard (Joined Expert Photographic Group) defines a compression algorithm of the fixed image based on DCT transformation and on quantization[4]. It also supports the choice of user compression parameters. This principle was adopted by the MPEG standard (Moving Picture Expert Group). It adds a coding technique for movement and takes in account the correlation between the successive images (temporal redundancy). The MPEG working group produced MPEG-1 and MPEG-2 standards [3].

MPEG-1 was conceived to produce near VHS video quality and MPEG-2 was designed to cover a broader spectrum. For this reason it introduced the concept of levels and profiles (that correspond to several compression alternatives). Applications are defined by the couple {level, profile} correspondence. MPEG-2 does not exceed high definition television HDTV [6] quality.

MPEG-4 [10] that is still in the standardization process should provide a video representation environment allowing content-based functionalities. These functionalities include audio-visual object manipulation, low bit rate coding and scalability.

We present in this paper an MPEG-2 based architecture to fulfill partial MPEG-4 improved functionalities. Our motivation is to enrich a very large number of MPEG-2 legacy terminal equipments with these functionalities. We also analyze the ability of MPEG-2 algorithm to support such functionalities and suggest a necessary but minimal set of modifications in MPEG-2 encoders. An architecture using MPEG-2 is detailed in section 2. The third and the fourth sections give details of the new functionalities offered by our new approach and the associated results.

2 MPEG-2 Based Architecture

Although a full coding-decoding MPEG-4 process would represent an ideal and powerful facility, a quick realistic view can judge on problems facing the availability of such a product. First, the standardization process is slow and details have yet to be discussed. Second, one can see that a huge number of MPEG-2 coding and decoding products are now available. Finally, current hardware technologies are still less performing than MPEG-4 requirements.

For these reasons, we propose a scheme that would offer an important MPEG-4 functionality with an off-the-shelf MPEG-2 encoding process. In this way, users would have the selective functionalities of MPEG-4 without needs to the standard itself as a first step of testing and profiling. This functionality consists in offering different coding quality within a scene for different objects. We first describe the general architecture of the proposed scheme and give the descriptions of the resulting MPEG-2 encoder.

2.1 The Architecture

The proposed architecture [Fig. 1]consists of an encoder and a decoder connected through a network. We assume that the network offers an end-to-end constant bit rate connection (DP+TP). The scheme offers two ways of feedback: remote and local. We assume that there exists a backward connection (TP_2+DP_2) from the decoder to the encoder offering through a bounded delay stream for feedback (remote) control informations (c.f. User events). These informations consist in boundaries coordinates for a region that the user wishes to enhance in the current stream. The architecture offers also a local access to the encoding process as a way to control coded regions using segmentation methods. In this case the feedback information is local to the encoder (segmentation module). A special process is responsible for determining image boundaries by a novel real time stereoscopic algorithm (not presented in this work) and the boundaries are given to the coder.

We now describe an additional layer that will upgrade the coding process. This layer is capable of object manipulation and leads to a more flexible and scalable coding MPEG-2 architecture. It will control the image quality by using external events and specifications from the user (remote) or from the segmentation module (local).

In the MPEG-2 Test Model 5 [13] the quantization parameter is updated according to the output buffer fullness to maintain a specific bit rate [Fig. 2]. In our case the coding control layer performs also additional degradation/enhancement according to priorities between video object planes (VOP) already specified by user events and according to the required rate control. The user or the segmentation module provides hence VOP specifications (shape and spatio-temporal resolutions) and associated priorities.

2.2 Modifications in the MPEG-2 Encoder

An encoder deals with images at a macro-block level constituting a unit element.

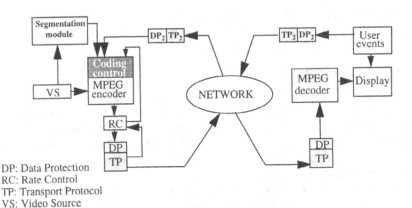

DP: Data Protection
RC: Rate Control
TP: Transport Protocol
VS: Video Source

Fig. 1. General Design Architecture

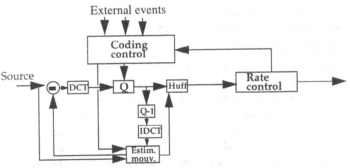

Fig. 2. Modified MPEG encoder

This means that each element is coded independently of other elements in the same slice. We take profit of this property in order to introduce a new *Region Concept* (VOP) that is simply a set of macro-blocks.

The quantization coefficient Q is responsible for the visual quality within a frame. We use it to deliver the required spatial quality in a region. In what concerns the temporal visual quality we reflect this coefficient on the motion estimation process. Depending on the required quality we will choose between various coding decisions like: motion vector, error value and/or complete macro-block coding. As an example, if the user decides to code a region at a very low coding bit rate (ex: 2 images/s) the encoder will apply a null motion, a null estimation error for all macro-blocks of this region in P and B frames.

We restrict the study to an encoder process at constant bit rate. When we want to apply a different quantization coefficient on different objects within a scene, we have two possible solutions; one could apply a constant Q on the selected region and vary the second coefficient for the rest of the scene. Another solution consists in fixing a maximum Q (meaning a very low visual quality) outside the region of interest and varying it within the region. This latter solution would lead to an optimal quality of the selected region within the available bandwidth.

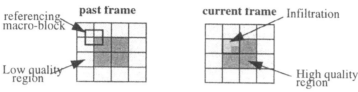

Fig. 3. Data infiltration

The first scheme may cause a problem due to buffer overflow. In fact, when we decide to use a constant Q for coding some heterogeneous regions we may exceed the available channel bandwidth leading to a buffer overflow in some situations. We use the second scheme in the remaining part of the study.

When the network flow control requires additional compression, the controller acts gradually on macro-blocks having the lowest priority, by changing both the motion estimation quality and the Q coefficient.

3 A Prototype Implementation

The goal of our prototype is to evaluate the gain obtained by using MPEG-4 content based coding in comparison with a plain MPEG-2 coder.

We have used the Berkeley MPEG-2 software and have limited our model to one region per frame (specified by the user). We implemented the second method where the outer macro-blocks are coded with a fixed Q and inner macro-blocks are coded according the remaining network bandwidth. The controller feeds the encoder with sequences of instructions corresponding to the region dimensions for each group of pictures (GoP). This prevents from introducing low quality data in the high quality region. Interference may take place if the concerned region moves within a GoP. In this case, high quality macro-blocks would have used low quality ones as referencing macro-blocs. This may reduce the quality and is hence forbidden. Even while acting at the GoP scale, motion estimation may in certain situations lead, as in [Fig. 3], to code some macro-blocks in the high quality region with macro-blocks by including data from the other region. In this situation some interference from the low quality region and hence some degradation will be induced in the high quality region. We must hence proceed with a different mechanism for contours in order to prevent any infiltration between the two zones. We propose a simple solution where contour macro-blocks are coded as intra information, i.e. no motion estimation is applied on them.

In this prototype user events correspond to a set of commands. A command specifies coordinates, size and quality of the rectangular region. The coding process is performed with respect to these commands at the beginning of every GoP. Through commands the user may change quality, size and position of his desired region.

4 System Performance

We have performed series of tests on a video sequence of 500 frames (20 s.) for a scene of 24x18 macro-blocks. We measured in all cases a throughput bounded by 500 Kb/s.

In [Fig. 4]we evaluate the required Q coefficient for the high quality region when we increase its size (number of macro-blocks). We notice that with 25 macro-blocks we

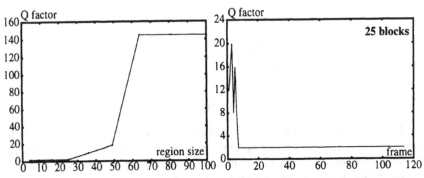

Fig. 4. Average Q factor in the high quality macro-blocks versus region size

Fig. 5. Q factor in the high quality macro-blocks versus frame number

still have a very reasonable Q (usually with throughput <500 Kb/s). Note also that 64 blocks is a limit beyond which the quality factor is so high that the visual quality in the important area becomes very deteriorated. Undesirable effects start showing beyond this limit (Q=140).

In [Fig. 5]we plot the Q factor for the previous sequence (for high quality region of 25 blocks) and we can see that it is quite constant except a short transient period at the beginning of the coding process. The constant Q factor measured is the best value that MPEG-2 can deliver (Q=2)

In [Fig. 6]we notice a large transient period before Q factor becomes constant. Bad quality affects B frames due to the small target rate reserved for this kind of frames [13].

When we compare our results in terms of quality factor and throughput with the conventional TM5 model [13] we find that a considerable gain is obtained. We are able to send a video sequence with a 500 kb/s throughput and an average Q of 2 (in the high quality region) while MPEG-2 requires to reduce the quality down to Q=45.5 to obtain the same throughput.

We must finally point out some problems that appear when the selected region exceeds 36 blocks [Fig. 7]e.i available bandwidth is not enough to deliver best quality in the selected region. The Q factor is very low for I and P frames (high quality) and very high for B frames (low quality). This undesirable result is due to the choice of virtual buffer sizes given by the TM5 model [13] which does not take in account the selective coding. The ideal scheme is the one that increases Q factor uniformly in the I,P and B frames. We treat this problem in ongoing work.

5 Conclusion

In this paper we have presented a new method for mapping MPEG-4 functionalities on top of MPEG-2 standard. This facility opens the way for immediate implementations and tests before standardization in a very simple way. We have described a prototype implementation that offers a selective coding of objects within GoPs. The advantages and critical design issues were also outlined. We have finally presented the system performance compared to a simple MPEG-2 coding mechanism and show the gain that can be obtained by such an algorithm.

112

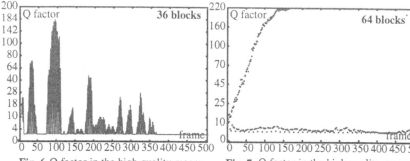

Fig. 6. Q factor in the high quality macro-blocks versus frame number

Fig. 7. Q factor in the high quality macro-blocks versus frame number

6 References

1. J. Choi and D. Park. A Stable Feedback Control of the Buffer State Using the Controlled Lagrange Multiplier Method. IEEE Transactions On Image Processing, 3(5):546-558, September 1994.
2. R.F. Coelho. traffic control for VBR video in ATM networks. ENST Paris. 1995.
3. D. Le Gall. MPEG: A Video Compression Standard for Multimedia Applications. Communications of the ACM, 4(34):305-313, April 1991.
4. ISO-IEC/JTC1/SC29/WG11. Generic Coding of Moving Pictures and Associated Audio: Video. In Recommendation ITU-T H.262, ISO/IEC 13818- 2, November 1994.
5. M. Kunt, A. Ikonomopoulos, and M. Kocher. Second-Generation Image- Coding Techniques. Proceedings of the IEEE, 73(4):549-574, April 1985.
6. A. Puri. Video Coding Using the MPEG-2 Compression Standard. In Proceedings of SPIE Visual Communications and Image Processing, Boston, November 1993.
7. M. Hamdi, J.W. ROBERTS and P. ROLIN. Rate Control for VBR Video Coders in Broadband Networks. IEEE Journal on Selected Areas in Communications, Special Issue. 1997.
8. K. Ramchandran, A. Ortega, and M. Vetterli. Bit Allocation for Dependent Quantization with Applications to Multiresolution and MPEG Video Coders. IEEE Transactions On Image Processing, 3(5):533-545, September 1994.
9. Traffic Characteristics of 3D-DCT Video Compression Algorithm. P. Rolin, H. Afifi, M. Hamdi. Cost-237 Multimedia Workshop. Lancaster. June 1996.
10. N.Lagha. The MPEG4 standard, a state of the art. Technical report. RSM department ENST de Bretagne.
11. MPEG AOE Group, "Proposal Package Description (PPD) - Revision 3", Doc. ISO/IEC ITC1/SC29/WG11 N998, Tokyo meeting, July 1995
12. IM1 MPEG-4 player http://televr.fou.telenor.no/~karlo/compositor/October 97
13. ISO-IEC/JTC1/SC29/WG11. Coded representation Pictures and Audio Information. In MPEG Test Model 5

Classifying Objectionable Websites
Based on Image Content *

James Ze Wang   Jia Li   Gio Wiederhold   Oscar Firschein

Stanford University, Stanford, CA 94305, USA

Abstract. This paper describes IBCOW (Image-based Classification of Objectionable Websites), a system capable of classifying a website as objectionable or benign based on image content. The system uses WIPE$_{TM}$ (Wavelet Image Pornography Elimination) and statistics to provide robust classification of on-line objectionable World Wide Web sites. Semantically-meaningful feature vector matching is carried out so that comparisons between a given on-line image and images marked as "objectionable" and "benign" in a training set can be performed efficiently and effectively in the WIPE module. If more than a certain number of images sampled from a site is found to be objectionable, then the site is considered to be objectionable. The statistical analysis for determining the size of the image sample and the threshold number of objectionable images is given in this paper. The system is practical for real-world applications, classifying a Web site at a speed of less than 2 minutes each, including the time to compute the feature vector for the images downloaded from the site, on a Pentium Pro PC. Besides its exceptional speed, it has demonstrated 97% sensitivity and 97% specificity in classifying a Web site based solely on images. Both the sensitivity and the specificity in real-world applications is expected to be higher because our performance evaluation is relatively conservative and surrounding text can be used to assist the classification process.

1   Introduction

With the rapid expansion of the Internet, every day large numbers of adults and children use the Internet for searching and browsing through different multimedia documents and databases. Convenience in accessing a wide range of information is making the Internet and the World-Wide Web part of the everyday life of ordinary people. Because there is freedom of speech, people are allowed to publish various types of material or conduct different types of business on the Internet. However, due to this policy, there is currently a large amount of domestic and foreign objectionable images and video sequences available for free download on the World-Wide Web and usenet newsgroups. Access of objectionable graphic images by under-aged "netters" is a problem that many parents are becoming concerned about.

* We thank the Stanford University Libraries and Academic Information Resources for providing computer equipment during the development and testing process. Correspondence to: wangz@cs.stanford.edu

1.1 Related Work in Industry

There are many attempts to solve the problem of objectionable images in the software industry. Pornography-free web sites such as the *Yahoo! Web Guides for Kids* have been set up to protect those children too young to know how to use the web browser to get to other sites. However, it is difficult to control access to other Internet sites.

Software programs such as *NetNanny*, *Cyber Patrol*, or *CyberSitter* are available for parents to prevent their children from accessing objectionable documents. However, the algorithms used in this software do not check the image contents. Some software stores more than 10,000 IP addresses and blocks access to objectionable sites by matching the site addresses, some focus on blocking websites based on text, and some software blocks all unsupervised image access. There are problems with all of the approaches. The Internet is so dynamic that more and more new sites and pages are added to it every day. Maintaining lists of sites manually is not sufficiently responsive. Textual matching has problems as well. Sites that most of us would find benign, such as the sites about breast cancer, are blocked by text-based algorithms, while many objectionable sites with text incorporated in elaborate images are not blocked. Eliminating all images is not a solution since the Internet will not be useful to children if we do not allow them to view images.

1.2 Related Work in Academia

Academic researchers are actively investigating alternative algorithms to screen and block objectionable media. Many recent developments in shape detection, object representation and recognition, people recognition, face recognition, and content-based image and video database retrieval are being considered by researchers for use in this problem.

To make such algorithms practical for our purposes, extremely high sensitivity (or recall of objectionable websites) with reasonably high speed and high specificity is necessary. In this application, *sensitivity* is defined as the ratio of the number of objectionable websites identified to the total number of objectionable websites accessed; *specificity* is defined as the ratio of the number of benign websites passed to the total number of benign websites accessed. A perfect system would identify all objectionable websites and not mislabel any benign websites, and would therefore have a sensitivity and specificity of 1. The "gold standard" definition of objectionable and benign images or websites is a complicated social problem and there is no objective answer. In our experiments, we use human judgment to serve as a gold standard.

For real-world application needs, a high sensitivity is desirable, i.e., the correct identification of almost every objectionable website even though this may result in some benign websites being mislabeled. Parents might be upset if their children are exposed to even a few objectionable websites.

The following properties of objectionable images found on the Internet make the problem extremely difficult:

- mostly contain non-uniform image background;
- foreground may contain textual noise such as phone numbers, URLs, etc;
- content may range from grey-scale to 24-bit color;
- some images may be of very low quality (sharpness);
- views are taken from a variety of camera positions;
- may be an indexing image containing many small icons;
- may contain more than one person;
- persons in the picture may have different skin colors;
- may contain both people and animals;
- may contain only some parts of a person;
- persons in the picture may be partially dressed.

Forsyth's research group [2, 3] has designed and implemented an algorithm to screen images of naked people. Their algorithms involve a skin filter and a human figure grouper. As indicated in [2], 52.2% sensitivity and 96.6% specificity have been obtained for a test set of 138 images with naked people and 1401 assorted benign images. However, it takes about 6 minutes on a workstation for the figure grouper in their algorithm to process a suspect image passed by the skin filter.

1.3 Overview of Our Work

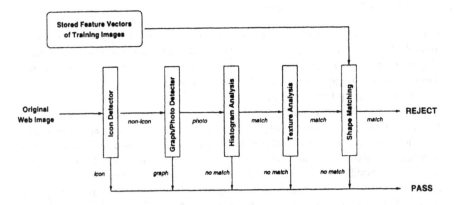

Fig. 1. Basic structure of the algorithm in WIPE.

WIPE Our group has built the WIPE [9, 11] system that is capable of classifying an image as objectionable or benign in a much efficient way, processing an image within 2 seconds on a Pentium Pro PC. Instead of carrying out a detailed analysis of an image, we match it against a small number of feature vectors obtained from a training database of 500 objectionable images and 8,000 benign images, after passing the images through a series of fast filters. If the image is close in content to a threshold number of pornographic images, e.g., matching two or more of the marked objectionable images in the training database within the closest 15 matches, it is considered objectionable. To accomplish this, we attempt to effectively code images based on image content and match the query with statistical information on the feature indexes of the training database. The foundation of this approach is the content-based feature vector indexing and matching developed in our multimedia database research. Image feature vector indexing has been developed and implemented in several multimedia database systems such as the IBM QBIC System [1] developed at the IBM Almaden Research Center. Readers are referred to [5–8, 10] for details on this subject. However, for WIPE we use quite specialized features. Using Daubechies' wavelets, moment analysis, texture analysis, histogram analysis and statistics, the algorithm in the WIPE system is able to produce a 96% sensitivity and a higher than 91% specificity, tested on more than 1,000 objectionable photograph images and more than 10,000 benign photograph images.

IBCOW Based on the WIPE system, we have developed IBCOW, a system that can classify a website as objectionable or benign. The system downloads and classifies the first N images from a new website. If at least a subset of the N images are classified as objectionable by the existing WIPE system, the website is classified as objectionable by the IBCOW system; otherwise, the website is classified as a benign website.

In the real world, IBCOW can be incorporated in a World Wide Web client software program so that a website is first screened by the system before the client starts to download the contents of the website. Once the website is screened, it is memorized on the local storage so that it is considered safe for some period of time. IBCOW can also be used as a tool for screening software companies to generate lists of potentially objectionable World Wide Web sites.

2 Screening Algorithms in IBCOW and Statistical Analysis

In this section, we derive the optimal algorithm for classifying a World Wide Web site as objectionable or benign based on an image classification system like the WIPE system developed by us.

2.1 Screening Algorithms

As discussed in [9, 11], the screening algorithm in the WIPE module uses several major steps, as shown in Figure 1. The layout of these filters is a result of a cost-effectiveness analysis. Faster filters are placed earlier in the pipeline so that benign images can be quickly passed. The algorithm in WIPE has resulted a 96% sensitivity and higher than 91% specificity for classifying a photographic image as objectionable or benign. Figure 2 and 3 show typical images being mistakenly marked by the WIPE system.

Fig. 2. Typical benign images being marked mistakenly as objectionable images by WIPE. (a) areas similar to human body (b) fine-art (c) some dog images are difficult to classify (d) partially undressed (e) hard to tell (bathing) .

Figure 4 shows the basic structure of the IBCOW system. For a given suspect website, the IBCOW system first downloads as many pages as possible from the website by following the links from the front page. The process is terminated after a pre-set timeout period. Once the pages are downloaded, we use a parser to extract image URLs, i.e., URLs with suffixes such as '.jpg' or '.gif'. N randomly selected images from this list are downloaded from this website. Then we apply WIPE to classify the images. If at least a subset, say $r \times N$ images ($r < 1$), of the N images are classified as objectionable by the WIPE system, the website is classified as objectionable by the IBCOW system; otherwise, the website is classified as a benign website. The following subsection will address the ideal combination of N and r given the performance of WIPE using statistical analysis.

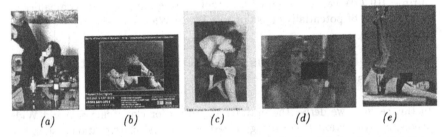

Fig. 3. Typical objectionable images being marked mistakenly as benign images by WIPE. (a) undressed part too small (b) frame (c) hard to tell (d) image too dark and of extremely low contrast (e) dressed but objectionable . Some areas of objectionable images are blackened and blurred.

2.2 Statistical Analysis

In order to proceed with the statistical analysis, we must make some basic assumptions. A World Wide Web site is considered a benign website if none of the images provided by this website is objectionable; otherwise, it is considered an objectionable website. This definition can be refined if we allow a benign website to have a small amount, say, less than 2%, of objectionable images. In our experience, some websites that most of us would find benign, such as some university websites, may still contain some personal homepages with small number of half-naked movie stars' images.

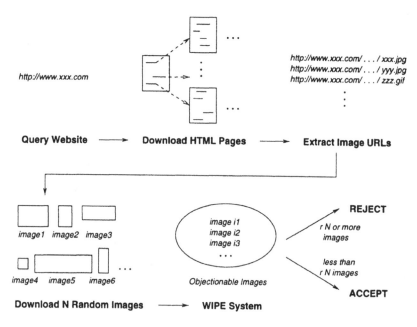

Fig. 4. Basic structure of the algorithm in IBCOW.

For a given objectionable website, we denote p as the chance of an image on the website to be an objectionable image. The probability p varies between 0.02 and 1 for various objectionable websites. Given a website, this probability equals to the percentage of objectionable images over all images provided by the website. The distribution of p over all websites in the world physically exists, although we would not be able to know what the distribution is. Therefore, we assume that p obeys some hypothetical distributions, which are as shown in Figure 5.

The performance of our WIPE system was evaluated by two parameters: sensitivity, denoted as q_1, is the accuracy of detecting an objectionable image as objectionable, and specificity, denoted as q_2, the accuracy of detecting a benign image as benign. The false positive rate, i.e., the failure rate of blocking an objectionable image, is thus $1 - q_1$, and the false negative rate, i.e., the false alarm rate for benign images, is $1 - q_2$.

For IBCOW, we must find out the minimum number of images, denoted as N, from a suspect website to be tested by the WIPE module in order to classify a website as objectionable or benign at a confidence level α, i.e., with a probability $1 - \alpha$ of being correct. The confidence level requirements on objectionable websites and benign websites may differ. For objectionable websites, we denote the desired confidence level to be α_1, while for benign websites, we denote the desired confidence level to be α_2. Furthermore, we must decide the threshold, denoted as r, for the percentage of detected objectionable images at which the IBCOW system will classify the website as objectionable. Therefore, the system tests N images from a website and classifies the website as objectionable if more than $r \times N$ images are detected as objectionable by WIPE. Our objective is that when a website is rated as objectionable with probability higher than $1 - \alpha_1$, it will be classified as objectionable, and when a website is rated benign, with probability higher than $1 - \alpha_2$, it will be classified as benign.

According to the above assumptions, we can calculate the probabilities of misclassifying objectionable websites and benign websites. We start with the simpler case of benign websites.

$$P\{ \; classified \; as \; benign \; | \; a \; website \; is \; benign \; \} = P(I_2 \leq rN) \quad ,$$

where I_2 is the number of images detected as objectionable by WIPE. Since I_2 is a binomial variable [4] with probability mass function

$$p_i = \binom{n}{i}(1 - q_2)^i q_2^{n-i} \; , \; i = 0, \; 1, \; ... \; , \; n \quad ,$$

we have

$$P(I_2 \leq rN) = \sum_{i=1}^{[rN]} \binom{N}{i}(1 - q_2)^i q_2^{n-i} \quad .$$

Similarly, for objectionable websites, we get

$$P\{ \; classified \; as \; objectionable \; | \; a \; website \; is \; objectionable \; \} = P(I_1 > rN)$$

For an objectionable website, suppose that any image in this website has probability p of being objectionable and it is independent of the other images, then the probability for this image to be classified as objectionable image is evaluated as follows:

$$P\{ \; classified \; as \; objectionable \; \}$$
$$= P(A)P(\; classified \; as \; objectionable \; | \; A) +$$
$$P(\tilde{A})P(\; classified \; as \; objectionable \; | \; \tilde{A})$$
$$= pq_1 + (1 - p)(1 - q_2)$$

where

$$A = \{ \; the \; image \; is \; objectionable \; \},$$
$$\tilde{A} = \{ \; the \; image \; is \; benign \; \} \quad .$$

For simplicity, we denote

$$\lambda(p) = pq_1 + (1 - p)(1 - q_2) \quad .$$

Similarly, I_1 follows a binomial distribution with a probability mass function

$$p_i = \binom{n}{i}(\lambda(p))^i (1 - \lambda(p))^{n-i} \, , \, i = 0, \, 1, \, \dots, \, n \quad .$$

For this specific website,

$$P(I_2 > rN) = \sum_{[rN]+1}^{N} \binom{N}{i}(\lambda(p))^i (1 - \lambda(p))^{n-i} \quad .$$

If p follows a truncated Gaussian distribution, i.e., the first hypothetical distribution, we denote the probability density function of p as $f(p)$. Thus,

$$P\{ \text{ classified as objectionable } | \text{ a website is objectionable } \}$$

$$= \int_0^1 \left[\sum_{[rN]+1}^{N} \binom{N}{i}(\lambda(p))^i (1 - \lambda(p))^{n-i} \right] f(p)dp \quad .$$

As N is usually large, the binomial distribution can be approximated by a Gaussian distribution [4]. We thus get the following approximations.

$$P\{ \text{ classified as benign } | \text{ a website is benign } \}$$

$$= \sum_{i=1}^{[rN]} \binom{N}{i}(1 - q_2)^i q_2^{n-i}$$

$$\approx \Phi\left(\frac{(r - (1 - q_2))\sqrt{N}}{\sqrt{q_2(1 - q_2)}} \right) \quad ,$$

where $\Phi(\cdot)$ is the cumulative distribution function of normal distribution [4]. Supposing $r > (1 - q_2)$, the above formula converges to 1 when $N \rightarrow \infty$.

$$P\{ \text{ classified as objectionable } | \text{ a website is objectionable } \}$$

$$\approx \int_0^1 \left(1 - \Phi\left(\frac{(r - \lambda(p))\sqrt{N}}{\sqrt{\lambda(p)(1 - \lambda(p))}} \right) \right) f(p)dp \quad ,$$

where $\lambda(p) = pq_1 + (1 - p)(1 - q_2)$ as defined before.
When $r < \lambda(p)$,

$$\lim_{N \rightarrow \infty} \Phi\left(\frac{(r - \lambda(p))\sqrt{N}}{\sqrt{\lambda(p)(1 - \lambda(p))}} \right) \rightarrow 0 \quad .$$

Obviously, for any reasonable objectionable image screening system, $q_1 > 1 - q_2$, i.e., the truth positive (TP) rate is higher than the false positive (FP) rate. Hence, we can choose r so that $r \in (1 - q_2, \epsilon q_1 + (1 - \epsilon)(1 - q_2))$ for $\epsilon > 0$. The inequality $r > 1 - q_2$ will guarantee that the probability of misclassifying benign websites approaches zero when N becomes large, which we concluded in a previous analysis. On the other hand, the inequality $r < \epsilon q_1 + (1 - \epsilon)(1 - q_2)$ will enable the probability of misclassifying objectionable websites to become arbitrarily small when N becomes large.

To simplify notation, we let

$$\Delta_{r,N}(p) = 1 - \Phi\left(\frac{(r - \lambda(p))\sqrt{N}}{\sqrt{\lambda(p)(1 - \lambda(p))}}\right) \quad .$$

Note that

$$\int_0^1 \Delta_{r,N}(p)f(p)dp \geq \int_\epsilon^1 \Delta_{r,N}(p)f(p)dp \quad .$$

By increasing N, we can choose arbitrarily small ϵ so that $\Delta_{r,N}(p)$ is as close to 1 as we need, for all $p > \epsilon$. Hence, $\int_\epsilon^1 \Delta_{r,N}(p)f(p)dp$ can be arbitrarily close to $\int_\epsilon^1 f(p)dp$. Since we can choose ϵ arbitrarily small, this integration approaches to 1. In conclusion, by choosing r slightly higher than $1 - q_2$ and N large, our system can perform close to 100% correctness for classification of both objectionable websites and benign websites.

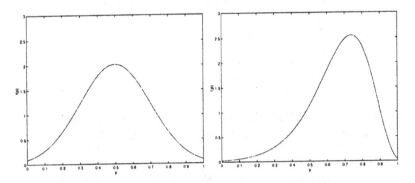

Fig. 5. Distributions assumed for the percentage (p) of objectionable images on objectionable websites.

As we only require a confidence level α, i.e., $1 - \alpha$ correctness, we have much more freedom in choosing r and N. Our WIPE system can provide a performance with $q_1 = 96\%$ and $q_2 = 91\%$. The actual q_1 and q_2 in real world can be higher because icons and graphs on the Web can be easily classified by WIPE with close to 100% sensitivity. When we assume $f(p)$ being a truncated Gaussian with mean

$\bar{p} = 0.5$ and standard deviation $\sigma = 0.2$, which is plotted in Figure 5, we may test $N = 35$ images from each website and mark the website as objectionable once 7 or more images are identified as objectionable by the WIPE system. Under this configuration, we can achieve approximately 97% correctness for classifying both objectionable websites and benign websites.

If we fix the decision rule of our system, i.e., test a maximum of 35 images from each website and mark the website as objectionable once 7 or more images are identified as objectionable, the percentages of correctness for classification of both types of websites depend on the sensitivity parameter q_1 and the specificity parameter q_2. By fixing q_2 to 91% and changing q_1 between 80% to 100%, the percentages of correctness for both types of websites are shown in the left panel of Figure 6. Similarly, the results are shown in the right panel of Figure 6 for the case of fixing q_1 to 96% and changing q_2 between 80% to 100%. As shown in the graph on the left side, when q_2 is fixed, the correct classification rate for benign websites is a constant. On the other hand, the correct classification rate for objectionable websites degrades with the decrease of q_1. However, the decrease of the correct classification rate is not sharp. Even when $q_1 = 0.8$, the correct classification rate is approximately 95%. On the other hand, when $q_1 = 96\%$, no matter what q_2 is, the correct classification rate for objectionable websites is always above 92%. The rate of correctness for benign websites monotonically increases with q_2. Since benign images in an objectionable website are less likely to be classified as objectionable when q_2 increases, the number of objectionable images found in the set of test images is less likely to pass the threshold 7. As a result, the correct classification rate for objectionable websites decreases slightly with the increase of q_2. However, the correct classification rate will not drop below 92%.

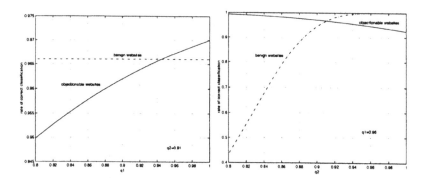

Fig. 6. Dependence of correct classification rates on sensitivity and specificity of WIPE (for the Gaussian-like distribution of p). Left: $q_2 = 91\%$, q_1 varies between 80% to 100%. Right: $q_1 = 96\%$, q_2 varies between 80% to 100%. Solid line: correct classification rate for objectionable websites. Dash dot line: correct classification rate for benign websites.

In the above statistical analysis, we assumed that the probability of an image being objectionable in an objectionable website has distribution $f(p)$ with mean 0.5. In real life, this mean value is usually higher than 0.5. With a less conservative hypothetical distribution of p, as shown in the right panel of Figure 5, we can achieve approximately 97% correctness by testing only 20 images from each website and marking the website as objectionable if 5 or more images are identified as objectionable by the WIPE system.

2.3 Limitations of the Algorithm

The screening algorithm in our IBCOW system assumes a minimum of N images downloadable from a given query website. For the current system set up, N can be as low as 20 for the less conservative assumption. However, it is not always possible to download 20 images from each website. We have noticed that some objectionable websites put only a few images on its front page for non-member netters to view without a password. For these websites, surround text will be more useful than images in the classification process. Also, we are considering to assign probabilities of objectionable to such sites based on accessible images.

In the statistical analysis, we assume each image in a given website is equally likely to be an objectionable image. This assumption may be false for some websites. For example, some objectionable websites put objectionable images in deep links and benign images in front pages.

3 Experimental Results

This algorithm has been implemented on a Pentium Pro 200MHz workstation. We selected 20 objectionable websites and 40 benign websites from various categories. It takes in general less than 2 minutes for the system to process each website. Besides the fast speed, the algorithm has achieved remarkable accuracy. It correctly identified all the 20 objectionable websites and did not mismark any one of the 40 benign websites. We expect the speed to be much faster once image and textual information is combined in the classification process.

4 Conclusions and Future Work

In this paper, we have presented the statistical analysis that provides us with the size of the sampling set and the number of objectionable images in that set needed to classify a website as objectionable. Using the WIPE system we developed, we have obtained a performance which already appears satisfactory for practical applications. Using statistical analysis, we expect the system to perform approximately 97% sensitivity and 97% specificity in classifying websites. Both the sensitivity and the specificity in real-world applications is expected to be much higher because our performance evaluation is relatively conservative and surrounding text can be used to assist the classification process.

We will further test the assumptions used in the statistical analysis part of this paper using real-world data. We are also working on refining both the WIPE and the IBCOW algorithms and the codes so that the system is more useful to real-world applications. Surround text will be used in the screening process. The algorithm can also be modified to execute in parallel on multi-processor systems. Experiments with our algorithm on video websites could be another interesting study.

References

1. C. Faloutsos et al, Efficient and Effective Querying by Image Content, *J. of Intelligent Information Systems*, 3:231-262, 1994.
2. Margaret Fleck, David A. Forsyth, Chris Bregler, Finding Naked People, *Proc. 4'th European Conf on Computer Vision*, UK, Vol 2, pp. 593-602, 1996.
3. David A. Forsyth et al, Finding Pictures of Objects in Large Collections of Images, *Proc. Int'l Workshop on Object Recognition*, Cambridge, 1996.
4. Alberto Leon-Garcia, *Probability and Random Processes for Electrical Engineering*, Addison-Wesley Publishing Company, pp.99-110, 280-287, 1994.
5. Amarnath Gupta and Ramesh Jain, *Visual Information Retrieval*, Comm. of the ACM, vol.40 no.5, pp 69-79, 1997.
6. C. E. Jacobs et al., Fast Multiresolution Image Querying, *Proc. of SIGGAPH 95 Computer Graphics*, pp.277-286, August 1995.
7. J. R. Smith and S.-F. Chang, VisualSEEk: A Fully Automated Content-Based Image Query System, *ACM Multimedia Conference*, Boston, Nov 1996.
8. James Ze Wang et al., Wavelet-Based Image Indexing Techniques with Partial Sketch Retrieval Capability, *Proc. 4th ADL Forum (ADL'97)*, Washington D.C., May 1997.
9. James Ze Wang et al., System for Screening Objectionable Images Using Daubechies' Wavelets and Color Histograms, *Proc. IDMS'97*, Springer-Verlag LNCS 1309, Sept. 1997.
10. James Ze Wang et al., Content-based Image Indexing and Searching Using Daubechies' Wavelets, *International Journal of Digital Libraries(IJODL)*, 1(4):311-328, Springer-Verlag, 1998.
11. James Ze Wang et al., System for Screening Objectionable Images, to appear in *Computer Communications Journal*, Elsevier, Amsterdam, 1998.

Identifying Perceptually Congruent Structures for Audio Retrieval

Kathy Melih and Ruben Gonzalez

School of Information Technology, Griffith University, QLD, Australia.
{K.Melih, R.Gonzalez}@gu.edu.au

Abstract. The relatively low cost access to large amounts of multimedia data, such as over the WWW, has resulted in an increasing demand for multimedia data management. Audio data has received relatively little research attention. The main reason for this is that audio data poses unique problems. Specifically, the unstructured nature of current audio representations considerably complicates the tasks of content-based retrieval and especially browsing. This paper attempts to address this oversight by developing a representation that is based on the inherent, perceptually congruent structure of audio data. A survey of the pertinent issues is presented that includes some of limitations of current unstructured audio representations and the existing retrieval systems based on these. The benefits of a structured representation are discussed as well as the relevant perceptual issues used to identify the underlying structure of an audio data stream. Finally, the structured representation is described and its possible applications to retrieval and browsing are outlined.

1. Introduction

The explosion of distributed multimedia systems has opened the door to storage of vast amounts of multimedia data. Naturally, an increased desire to interact with this data at ever increasing levels of sophistication is also becoming apparent. Many applications would benefit from content-based audio retrieval and browsing methods. The most obvious is the extension of retrieval possibilities for the World Wide Web. Without support for random access and content based retrieval of audio, this will never be a true hypermedia system as intended[1].

Even a very coarse classification based on the audio type (e.g., speech or music) can be useful, especially for browsing. For example, locating a desired section in a concert recording is greatly simplified if it is first segmented into pieces by the location of non-music sections (applause, silence and speech). However, traditional audio coding techniques provide representations that make extracting even this low-level information difficult. Traditional representations are unstructured, aiming only to reproduce the signal (or a perceptual equivalent) while being compact. In contrast, content-based retrieval and browsing benefit from structured representations.

This paper presents a perceptually congruent structured audio representation designed specifically to support content based retrieval and browsing. The next section will review some of the general issues pertinent to audio retrieval as well as examining the benefits of a structured representation. Relevant psychoacoustic principles will then be outlined followed by a description of a new structured audio representation. Methods of content-based retrieval, based on this representation, will be outlined and finally, directions for future work will be discussed.

2.   Audio Retrieval

2.1   Content Based Retrieval

Two things are necessary for content-based retrieval: segmentation and component labeling (indexing). Segmentation involves dividing the data into cognitively significant sections. Using unstructured representations, this is a tedious task in itself. Index key selection is the most significant issue in content-based retrieval since the index keys directly influence the nature and scope of queries supported. Possibilities range from manual annotation to automatically generated statistical feature vectors.

Manual annotation has many drawbacks. Most obviously, it is extremely tedious and not practical for large databases. There is also severe limitation on the scope of possible queries. These limits are imposed by the selection of index attributes which are limited by the fact that some features of audio are difficult, or impossible, to identify using simple textual descriptions (e.g., timbre). For speech, transcriptions derived using automatic speech recognition (ASR) would seem to be ideal, however, manual intervention is required in unconstrained environments[2][3]. Also, a simple transcription cannot describe semantically significant audio features (e.g. prosodics).

Indexing musical data requires a means of accessing melodic information. MELDEX accepts audio queries, transcribes them into musical notation and uses this description to search a database of musical scores[4]. Ghias *et al*[5] propose a melody retrieval system that converts queries into strings of relative pitch transitions. Searches are performed in an index containing similar strings as keys. This index is generated directly from MIDI files. Both systems are akin to searching a speech database using textual transcriptions and suffer similar drawbacks, including the loss of semantically significant information (e.g.timbre). Also, these methods are highly constrained.

Recent general audio retrieval systems use automatically generated statistical feature vectors as index keys[6]. These vectors are generated by performing statistical analyses of the audio signal and describe attributes such as the brightness and bandwidth of signals. Since this technique is automatic, it is of greater practical value. Also, the non-verbal description is unconstrained and thus more flexible. However, the scope of retrieval is still restricted by the feature analytic nature of the attributes: they possess little cognitive significance. For example, bandwidth has little semantic value to an untrained user. Each of these indexing schemes is constrained to non-composite audio data thus the data must undergo an initial segmentation process.

2.2 Browsing

Browsing is required when a user can't specify a query exactly, or to review search results where several possibilities have been retrieved. The first instance requires that broad queries ('find sections of speech/modulation/transitions') be supported while the second requires non-sequential access and a logical, hierarchical structure. This structure may be inherent in the data itself, defined by some grammar, or may result from a classification data attributes. The structure of music may be described in several ways[7][8]. The basic hierarchy divides pieces into phrases composed of notes. Speech is divided by speaker transitions[2][6] then into individual phrases or words by silence detection. Discrete environmental sounds have no grammar upon which a structure can be based. In this case, a hierarchical structure may be developed by performing a categorisation on qualities such as loudness, pitch or harmonicity of the signals[6].

The few existing systems that support use temporal rather than content based structures. Time-line representations[2] or time compressed play-back[9] provide only very low level support. True content based browsing is of much greater value. For example, it is much more likely that a person would prefer to browse a concert recording by piece or movement (identified by occurrence of non-music) rather than by sampling at given time intervals.

Content based browsing, requires the data to have structure. However, perceptually significant attributes also need to be readily accessible at fairly high temporal resolution. For example, a user may wish to recover all sections of a recording that contain a particular rhythm pattern. Statistical analyses of entire contiguous sections of a single type do not have the necessary resolution to support such browsing[2]. This results from reliance on unstructured audio representations and segmentation and classification schemes using attributes with limited cognitive significance.

2.3 Benefits of a Structured Representation

Many problems suffered by existing audio retrieval systems can be attributed to reliance on unstructured representations. Existing audio representations give very little indication of the content of the encoded data. With such representations, processing and storage overheads are an inevitable consequence of the desire to provide support for retrieval and browsing. Also, the underlying structure of the data is not directly apparent in these bit streams which severely limits browsing possibilities.

Several of key attributes appear to be extracted from audio signals during human audio perception[10]. These attributes form an obvious base for a representation that supports content based retrieval and browsing since a mid-level index is 'built in' to the representation. As these attributes are perceptually based, they will most likely support higher level queries. For example, minimal processing is required to determine the type of a sound (e.g. speech) given access to such attributes. Having isolated the key cognitive features of an audio signal, psychoacoustic principles can be applied to identify any inherent organisation in the data.

3. Perceptual Considerations

3.1 Peripheral Processing

The process of audio perception displays several interesting phenomena relevant to the representation presented in this paper. The auditory system subjects short temporal sections of audio signals to a frequency transformation. The result is known as a time-frequency distribution (TFD) and is a representation of the input audio signal in a three dimensional (time, frequency and intensity) space (Fig. 1.).

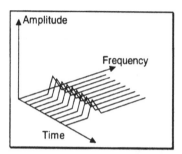

Fig. 1. Simplified TFD of a single frequency tone

The axes are non-uniformly sampled: at high frequencies, frequency resolution is coarse while temporal resolution is fine and vice versa. Also, the amplitude axis displays a frequency dependent non-linearity. Another interesting phenomenon is masking. If two signals in close frequency proximity are presented simultaneously, the less intense sound may be rendered inaudible. The two signals may be tones or noise. Masking can also occur when two signals are presented in close temporal proximity.

3.2 Mental Representation of Audio

The ability of the perceptual system to 'hear out' simultaneous sounds is called stream segregation. During stream segregation the signal is decomposed into its constituent parts (partials) that are then grouped into streams: one for each sound.

There appears to be a set of general principles that are applied to the task of stream segregation. These principles include[10]:

- Similarity: tones similar in frequency tend to be fused.
- Continuation: partials representing smooth transitions tend to fusion. Rapid transitions tend separation.
- Common fate: partials with similar onset times and/or correlated modulation tend to be fused.
- Disjoint allocation: in general, each partial can belong to only one stream.
- Closure: similar partials, separated in time by an obscuring event, tend to be fused by interpolation of the 'missing' section.

At a basic level, one can model audio representation in the human mind as a series of peak amplitude tracks in a time-frequency-intensity space[10]. Three audio classes exist: frequency sweeps, tone bursts and noise bursts. The representation of these classes in the time frequency plane is shown in Fig. 2.

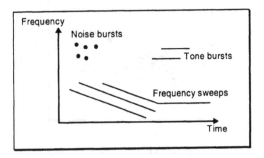

Fig. 2. Mental representation of audio

4. Identifying Audio Structure

The developed representation aims to facilitate direct access to perceptually significant audio structures. Hence, it is essentially a parametric description of the three sound classes identified in section 3.2. The process of generating the representation is summarised in Fig 3.

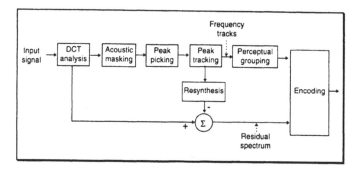

Fig. 3. Coding algorithm

4.1 TFD generation

Sinusoidal transform coding[12] represents audio signals as a sum of sine waves with time varying amplitudes and frequencies as follows:

$$s(n) = a_i(n)\exp(j\phi_i) \tag{1}$$

where $s(n)$ is the sampled audio signal and a_i and ϕ_i are the time varying amplitude and phase respectively of the ith sine wave. Thus, the signal is described as a series of amplitude trajectories through time-frequency space. Conventionally, the parameters are estimated using a short time Fourier transform and the TFD is sampled uniformly in time and frequency. This leads to redundancy, poor noise performance and a poor model of the perceptual process. To overcome these problems, a DCT[13] is used and the axes of the TFD are perceptually tuned, mimicking the time-frequency resolution of the ear. The DCT is used to remove some redundancy and the tuning better models audio perception as well as further eliminating redundancy and providing better noise performance. Fig. 4 shows the resultant tiling in the time-frequency plane.

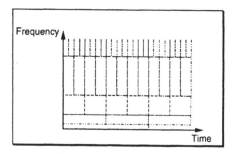

Fig. 4. Time-Frequency resolution of the TFD

Since the resolution of a DCT is proportional to the length of the analysis window, generating a variable resolution TFD requires that the low frequency analyses use longer temporal windows than those used in high frequency analyses. The amount of data generated by this operation is kept to a minimum by a recursive filtering and down sampling operation. The process is described in Fig. 5.

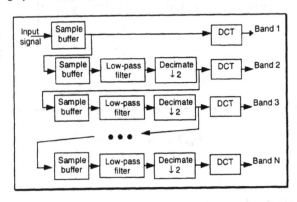

Fig. 5. Perceptually tuned TFD generation

4.2   Masking thresholds

Having generated a variable resolution TFD, acoustic masking and quiet thresholds are applied to eliminate perceptually redundant data. This helps to compact the final representation as well as simplifying the following stages of processing.

The first step in calculating acoustic masking thresholds is to transform the DCT spectrum from the physical frequency domain, f, into the critical band (Bark) domain, z. The transformation is achieved using the expression[14]:

$$z = \frac{26.81f}{(1960+f)} - 0.53 \tag{2}$$

The spectrum is then convolved with the basilar membrane spreading function to generate the masking thresholds. This function models the action of the inner ear that is responsible for masking. The basilar membrane spreading function is obtained from the expression[15]:

$$\Lambda(z)_{dB} = 15.8114 + 7.5(z + 0.474) - 17.5\left(1 + (z + 0.474)^2\right)^{1/2} \tag{3}$$

In addition to acoustic masking thresholds, quiet thresholds are also applied. These thresholds mask out any components that are too low in intensity to be audible. Thresholds are those provided in the MPEG1 audio standard[16]. Linear interpolation is used to derive intermediate values not reported in the standard.

4.3 Peak picking and tracking

The next stage of processing involves peak picking and tracking. Peaks are found by searching for all points in the TFD that satisfy the condition:

$$X_t(f_{i-1}) < X_t(f_i) > X_t(f_{i+1}) \qquad (4)$$

where $X_t(f_i)$ is the amplitude at the ith frequency, f_i, in the current time frame, t.

The result of the peak picking stage is a list of peak amplitudes and frequencies for each time frame. Tracking is performed according to a modified version of the algorithm in [12] which involves matching peaks from adjacent time frames that are closest in frequency within set limits. This algorithm has been modified to overcome some specific problems encountered.

Firstly, the varying resolution of the TFD means that adjacent frames at low frequencies are much further apart in time than those at higher frequencies. This means two frames that are adjacent at low frequencies will not be adjacent in higher bands. Thus, it is possible for the temporal distance between peaks to vary during a sweep. This is resolved by fixing the time index, m, relative to the shortest analysis window and recording the current time index each time a peak is assigned to a track.

Secondly, ambiguous cases often arise where two peaks are equally likely candidate matches for a single track. This is particularly relevant to the case of frequency sweeps in close frequency proximity. To resolve such cases, amplitude matching is performed in addition to frequency matching. However, problems can still arise when two frequency sweeps are close in amplitude as well as frequency. Fig. 9 illustrates this problem. As a more robust solution to this problem, Hough transforms are being considered.

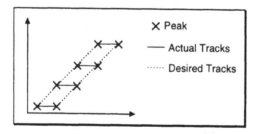

Fig. 6. Problems with existing peak tracking

4.4 Track classification and segregation

Once generated, each track is classified according to type: noise burst, tone burst or frequency sweep. Very short tracks are classified as noise bursts. Examining the frequency contour of the track makes the decision as to whether a long track belongs to the class of tone burst or sweep. Psychoacoustic principles are then applied to segregate them into streams. At this stage, the aim of segregation is simply to remove correlation in the data so only a very basic set of principles is applied. These principles are illustrated in Fig 8. Finally, the tracks are encoded in groups.

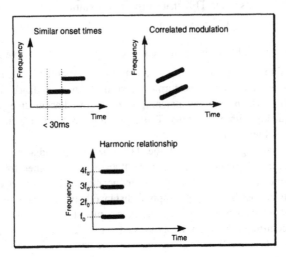

Fig. 7. Psychoacoustic grouping rules

5. Suitability for Retrieval

Determining the nature of a segment of audio follows directly from this representation. The data can be classified into one of four categories: speech, music, silence and noise. Each of these categories exhibits unique characteristics in the time-frequency domain that are directly visible in the track representation. Once a coarse classification has been performed, the track-based structure lends itself to many category-specific analysis tasks.

Given the track-based structure, classification is a relatively straightforward matter. Identifying silence is a trivial matter as it is characterised by the absence of any tracks. Music consists of long harmonically related tracks with few periods of silence. The presence of relatively short noise bursts, tone bursts and frequency sweeps, interspersed with frequent short periods of silence identify speech. Another characteristic of speech directly visible in this representation is its almost unique concave and convex formant structure[17]. Noise consists entirely of noise bursts.

After this coarse classification, individual audio segments can be further analysed based on type. Given that the tracks are parametrically represented, analysis basically involves comparing parameter values of individual tracks. The type of higher level information that can be inferred from the tracks depends on the sound type.

For music data, the melody line can be determined by examining the pitch along tracks. Similarly, rhythm can be extracted by analysing the amplitude contour. The representation should also permit query by example. Queries input via an appropriate audio interface can be analysed into the track representation and then the melody or rhythm information extracted and used as a basis for comparison.

In the case of speech, change of speaker or gender may be determined by examining the pitch. Speaker emphasis is visible in the variation of relative amplitude along tracks. Voicing information is directly visible by the nature of the tracks at an instant (noise or tone). The suitability of this representation for speech recognition is yet to be investigated, however, the work of [18] suggests that query by example should be supported. It is proposed that, although the same utterance spoken at different times will posses slightly different track structures, there will be a simple transformation between the two structures that is constant across tracks.

There are at least two methods by which pitch information can be extracted from this representation: spectral compression and a method involving calculation of two pitch measures (spectral pitch and virtual pitch)[19]. Both methods require that perceptually significant tonal components of the signal first be isolated. The frequency tracks of the representation presented in this paper describe precisely this thus, extraction of pitch information is simplified over existing representations.

Notably, all the indexing attributes currently used in audio retrieval systems can also be derived from this representation. Indeed, the extraction of this information will generally be simplified. Pitch information is one example discussed earlier. Other examples include loudness and harmonicity. Loudness is easily determined from the amplitude contours. Harmonicity follows directly from the track grouping. In addition, the variation of these qualities can be determined over time. Thus, the structured audio presented here is capable of supporting all existing query methods as well as cognitively significant structure based queries.

With index attributes directly accessible, the representation clearly supports content-based retrieval. Support for browsing may be less obvious but is nonetheless accounted for in a number of ways. Firstly, random access is furnished by the track structure since individual semantically congruent passages can be easily recovered and decoded. In the case of signals with inherent structure (ie music and speech) the track representation reveals the perceptually relevant aspects of this structure. Also, broad classification according to type can also be useful for browsing. These access methods are basic extensions of time-based browsing methods. The most significant advantage of structured audio is its ability to support true content based browsing.

Powerful support for content based browsing is provided by the information that is readily accessible in the track description. This is because it is relatively straightforward to recover all sections of a recording that contain some semantically significant attribute. Examples of such attributes include vibrato, specific chord sequences and change of key. This level of information is impossible to extract from holistic statistical descriptions. In some cases, such as vibrato or timbre, even complete transcriptions will fail. Thus by using perceptually congruent structures, an increased level of support for browsing has been achieved.

6. Future Work and Conclusions

A structured audio representation, based on psychoacoustic principles, has been suggested as a solution to the problems posed by content-based audio retrieval and browsing. This representation has been designed to provide direct access to perceptually salient attributes of audio. In addition, the structure has been greatly influenced by cognitive principles. Finally, the suitability of this representation for content based retrieval and browsing has been discussed.

Having developed the audio representation, there are two directions for future work. The first is to resolve encoding issues and the second is to verify the suitability of the representation for its intended purpose of audio retrieval. In addressing the first issue, the desire to provide a compact representation must be carefully approached so as not to compromise access to the salient features of the structure. The second task will receive the most attention and will involve the development of methodologies and algorithms to perform classification, content based retrieval and browsing of audio.

The primary feature of the audio structure presented here is its cognitive congruence. Information that has true semantic significance can be readily extracted from the track description. This is in contrast to the feature sets of existing systems that rely on statistical attributes with only incidental significance.

7. References

1. R. Gonzalez, "Hypermedia Data Modeling, Coding and Semiotics", *Proc of the IEEE*, vol 85, no 7, July 1997, pp 1111-1141.
2. D. Hindus, C. Schmandt and C. Horner, "Capturing, Structuring and Representing Ubiquitous Audio", *ACM Trans. On Information Systems*, v. 11, n. 4, Oct 1993, pp 376-400.
3. G. Hauptmann, M. J. Witbrock, A. I. Rudnicky and S. Reed, "Speech for Multimedia Information Retrieval", UIST '95, pp. 79-80.
4. J. McNab, L. A. Smith, D. Bainbridge and I. H. Witten, "The New Zealand Digital Library MELody inDEX", *D-Lib Magazine, May 1997*, http://www.dlib.org/dlib/may97/meldex/05witten.htm.
5. Ghias, J. Logan, D. Chamberlin and B. C. Smith, "Query By Humming: Musical Information Retrieval in An Audio Database", Proc. ACM Multimedia '95, San Francisco, pp 231-236.
6. E. Wold, T. Blum, D. Keislar and J. Wheaton, "Content-Based Classification, Search and Retrieval of Audio, *IEEE Multimedia*, Fall 1996, pp. 27-36.
7. S. Tanguine, "A Principle of Correlativity of Perception and its Application to Music Recognition", *Music Perception*, Summer 1994, 11 (4), pp. 465-502.
8. P.J.V. Aigrain, P. Longueville, Lepain, "Representation-based user interfaces for the audiovisual library of year 2000", Proc. SPIE Multimedia and Computing and Networks 1995, vol. 2417, Feb 1995, pp. 35-45.
9. B. Arons, "SpeechSkimmer: Interactively Skimming Recorded Speech", Proc. USIT 1993: ACM Symposium on User Interface Software and Technology, Nov 1993.

10. D. P. W. Ellis, B. L. Vercoe, "A Perceptual Representation of Audio for Auditory Signal Separation", presented at the 23rd meeting of the Acoustical Society of America, Salt Lake City, May 1992.

11. B. C. J. Moore, "An Introduction to the Psychology of Hearing", fourth edition, Academic Press, 1997.

12. T. F. Quatieri, R. J. McAulay, "Speech Transformations Based on a Sinusoidal Representation", *IEEE Trans. ASSP*, vol. ASSP-34, no. 6, Dec 1986, pp. 1449-1463.

13. N. Ahmed, T. Natarajan and K.R. Rao, "Discrete Cosine Transform", *IEEE Trans on Computers*, Jan 1974, pp. 90-93.

14. M. Paraskevas, J. Mourjopoulos, "A Differential Perceptual Audio Coding Method with Reduced Bitrate Requirements", *IEEE Trans ASSP*, v. 3, n. 6, Nov 1995.

15. M.R. Schroeder, B. S. Atal, J. L. Hall, "Opimizing digital speech coders by exploiting masking properties of the human ear", *J. Acoust. Soc. Amer.*, **66**(6), Dec 1979, pp 1647-1651.

16 ISO/IEC 11 172-3.

17. J. Hoyt, H. Wechsler, "Detection of Human Speech in Structured Noise", IEEE ICASSP, vol 2. 1994, pp 237-240

18. A. B. Fineberg, R. J. Mammone, "Detection and Classification of Multicomponent Signals", Proc. 25th Asilomar Conference on Computer, Signals and Systems, Nov 4-6, 1991.

19. E. Terhardt, G. Stoll, M. Seewann, "Algorithm for extraction of pitch and pitch salience from complex tonal signals", *J. Acoust*

An Image Coding and Reconstruction Scheme for Mobile Computing

Edward Y. Chang

Department of Electrical Engineering
echang@cs.stanford.edu

Stanford University

Abstract. An asynchronous transfer mode (ATM) wireless network has bursty and high error rates. To combat the contiguous bit loss due to damaged or dropped packets, this paper presents a code packetization and image reconstruction scheme. The packetization method distributes the loss in both frequency and spatial domains to reduce the chance that adjacent DCT blocks lose the same frequency components. The image reconstruction takes into consideration the spatial characteristics represented by the frequency components. Combining these two approaches one can reconstruct the damaged images more accurately, even under very high loss rates. In addition, since the reconstruction technique is computational efficient, it conserves system resources and power consumption, which are restrictive in mobile computers.

Keywords: multimedia, compression, mobile computing.

1 Introduction

Many studies have proposed image and video data delivery schemes over wired channels. Since mobile computing has gained popularity in recent years, it is important also to devise robust techniques that work in a mobile environment. This paper presents image coding and reconstruction techniques that are suitable in a mobile (wireless) environment.

Wireless channels are different from wired ones in at least two respects: capacity and reliability. Regarding the first, the wireless channel's capacity is typically limited to 40 to 200 Kbps (e.g., Metropolitan Area Network) and the growth rate is slow because of inefficient FCC allocation of bandwidth and the expense of deploying new wireless routers [4]. Regarding the second, the compressed video signals delivered by wireless channels are often corrupted in transmission [4]. A compression algorithm suitable for the wireless environment needs not only to have high compression rates but also to maintain a high degree of error tolerance [11].

Some priority transmission schemes have been developed for wired channels [1]. These schemes, however, do not work in the mobile environment since signal disturbance can happen to any packet indiscriminately, despite its delivery priority. To address the problem of the lack of resiliency to channel errors, layered coding and error correction schemes such as automatic retransmission query protocols (ARQ) or forward error correction (FEC) have been proposed

[10]. However, if the network is already congested, ARQ tends to aggravate the problem by sending out retransmitted packets. Also, retransmission does not help real-time decoding schemes such as motion JPEG or MPEG. As for error correction codes, they are effective only when the loss rate is below the design threshold. Furthermore, the redundant transmissions and codes required to improve reliability decrease the effective channel capacity. For example, some low bit rate, high redundancy coding schemes (e.g., ARQ-I and ARQ-II [13]) allocate bits for FEC. This pessimistically degrades image quality (i.e., lower SNRs) for errors that may not occur.

This paper presents research on an image packetization and reconstruction scheme that works at low channel capacity and in high bursty packet loss environments. Specifically, my design objectives have aimed at 1) preventing propagation of errors, 2) smoothing out the effects of bursty loss, and 3) reconstructing damaged images accurately and efficiently. The study is based on the existing JPEG international standards. However, since standards such as H.261 and H.263 use compression schemes similar to JPEG to perform intra-frame encoding, the techniques that work for JPEG also work for video key frames.

To distribute errors, [3] proposed reordering the DCT blocks' delivery sequence. My technique takes a step further in also scrambling the coefficients in the blocks. To smooth out the bursty packet loss, the packetization scheme distributes the 64 frequency components of a DCT block to 64 different transmission units. In other words, each transmission unit contains 64 different frequency components from 64 DCT blocks. Next, these transmission units are packetized into different network packets by a carefully chosen "stride." During both steps, the packetization scheme makes sure that in the case of a bursty error, the loss is not concentrated in one area of the image. Thus, during image reconstruction, the lost frequency components have a better chance to be recovered from the neighboring blocks.

To reconstruct the image, my approach takes the spatial characteristics represented by the DCT coefficients into consideration. I show that interpolating the high frequency components in the horizontal direction by using only the top and bottom blocks, and in the vertical direction by using only the left and right blocks, repairs the damaged images more accurately than a scheme that takes an average over all neighboring blocks. (For instance, to reconstruct a standing tree in an image, the relevant information is in the DCT blocks above and below the damaged block. The information in the blocks left and right of the damaged block is irrelevant to reconstructing the standing tree.) Moreover, the reconstruction scheme, since is not computing intensive, conserves battery power for mobile computers.

The rest of this paper is organized as follows. Section 2 offers a brief overview of JPEG standards. Section 3 describes the error characteristics of the wireless network and related work to improve its transmission resiliency. Section 4 details the packetization and image reconstruction schemes proposed to combat the bursty packet loss problem. Section 5 presents the evaluation of the proposed schemes by demonstrating that the damaged images can be better reconstructed with these techniques than with others even under high loss rates.

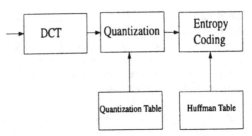

Fig. 1. JPEG Encoding Procedure

2 A Brief Overview of JPEG

To assist understanding of the techniques proposed in this paper, this section gives a brief overview of JPEG [12]. JPEG encoding procedure consists of three steps: DCT (Discrete Cosine Transform), quantization, and entropy coding. JPEG decoding, conversely, consists of entropy decoding, dequantization, and IDCT (Inverse Discrete Cosine Transform). Figure 1 depicts the encoding steps; the decoding steps are executed in the opposite direction. The following describes the encoding steps only.

JPEG deals with colors in the YUV (one luminance and two chrominances) space. For each separate color component, the image is broken into 8 by 8 pixel blocks of picture elements, which join end to end across the image. JPEG transforms each block into a two-dimensional DCT matrix by performing a one-dimensional DCT on the columns and on the rows. Figure 2(a) shows an 8 by 8 coefficient matrix generated by the DCT step. The arrows link the frequency components from DC to the highest. Note that at this point the information about the original image is mostly preserved, except for the rounding errors of the DCT coefficients.

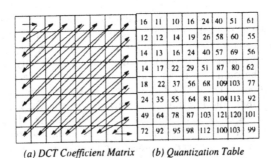

(a) DCT Coefficient Matrix   *(b) Quantization Table*

Fig. 2. DCT Coefficients

The coefficients of the DCT are quantized to reduce their magnitude, to increase the number of zero value coefficients, and to reduce the bit rate. Figure 2(b) shows the uniform midstep quantizer that is used for the JPEG baseline method, where the stepsize varies according to the coefficient location in the DCT matrix. As one can see, the low frequency components (at the upper

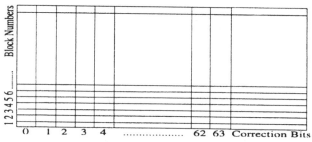

Fig. 3. Interleaved Code

left corner of the quantization matrix) have smaller steps, while the high ones have larger steps. This is because human eyes are less sensitive to high frequency components. Quantization is the lossy stage in the JPEG coding scheme. If we quantize too coarsely, we achieve a higher compression rate with poorer image quality. On the other hand, if we quantize too finely, we may spend extra bits on coding noise.

The final step is entropy coding. JPEG uses the Huffman or arithmetic coding scheme to compress the quantized Discrete Cosine Transform (DCT) coefficients to approach the entropy rate. Since both the Huffman and the arithmetic codes are variable-rate, any bit errors or loss in the transmission propagates and destroys the entire image. One remedy to this problem is to introduce resynchronization points in the code to limit the effect of the loss. Another way is to use fixed-rate coding schemes [11] that trade bit rates for error containment. With minimum changes to the current JPEG baseline, I use resynchronization bits to contain the loss effect. The proposed packetization and reconstruction schemes work orthogonally with variable or fixed-rate codes.

3 Wireless Network Error Characteristics

The transmission errors in a wireless channel may not occur independently of digit positions. Rather, the electrical disturbance of interfering radiation sources and of attenuation due to distance and obstacles frequently affects adjacent transmitted packets [7]. The packets that are damaged beyond repair are discarded and considered a loss by the network. According to the statistics collected by the Stanford University Wireless Computing Group [2], the average packet loss rate is about 3.6% in a wireless environment and occurs in a bursty fashion. According to the study conducted by the Stanford Multimedia Network Group for a teleconferencing application [5, 6], the duration of a burst, or the number of successive packets lost, ranges from one to seven packets. In terms of an ATM network, since each packet contains 56 bytes or 448 bits of data, each burst of loss translates to a loss of 448 to more than 3,000 consecutive bits, which can be a significant chunk of an image.

One approach to recover loss is introducing redundancy to correct errors. Figure 3 shows the DCT blocks in an image organized into a two-dimensional array. Each row represents a DCT block with 64 frequency components (from 0 to 63), and the number of rows represents the number of DCT blocks in an image. For each DCT block the Hamming code for instance can be used to correct its

Table 1. Bit Efficiency for Interleaved Code

Total Bits	Information Bits	Maximum Correction Bits	Overhead %
127	113	2	10%
127	106	3	12%
127	99	4	29%
127	92	5	40%
127	64	10	100%
255	107	22	150%
255	99	23	170%

bit errors. The number of bit errors the Hamming code is able to correct depends on the number of parity bits (the shaded area in the figure) added to the code. Now, in order to deal with bursty errors, the data are sent out by the columns of Figure 3. The data transmission starts from the first bit (the first column), second bit (the second column), and so on of each block. If one ATM packet (448 bits) is lost, one may lose only one to two bits in each row (DCT block). The loss can be corrected by the Hamming code. This interleaved code effectly uses a scheme that is efficient at correcting random bit errors.

However, the overhead of this interleaved code can be high. Assuming that each DCT block takes up about 100 bits (since the Huffman code is a variable-rate code, the actual bit number may vary), Table 1 lists the number of parity bits needed to correct different number of errors. The number of additional bits needed to cover additional errors grows super-linearly. The effectiveness of this interleaved code depends on the degree of redundancy, listed in Table 1. For example, the fifth and the sixth rows in Table 1 show that correcting a 20% loss rate (20 bits for each 100 bits block) doubles the code length (the total bits over the information bits). If a code is designed for up to 20% loss rate and the actual error rate is higher than 20%, the scheme breaks down. In an environment where loss is infrequent and the increasing bit rate is not a concern, the interleaved code may be a better choice. However, because of the channel capacity constraint and high error rates, the smart packetization and heuristic reconstruction techniques proposed below may be better alternatives for the wireless network.

4 Packetization and Reconstruction

My proposed scheme to combat contiguous bit loss consists of two parts: packetization and reconstruction. The objective of the packetization step is to scatter the bursty loss in the spatial domain so that adjacent DCT blocks do not lose the same frequency components. This aids to the reconstruction quality since 1) a block does not lose all its coefficients and 2) most lost frequency components can be recovered from adjacent blocks. In the reconstruction step, I also take spatial characteristics of the frequency components into consideration to repair the damaged image more accurately.

4.1 Packetization

To minimize the effect of bursty packet loss on an image, the packetization scheme must achieve two goals in the spatial domain. First, for each burst of

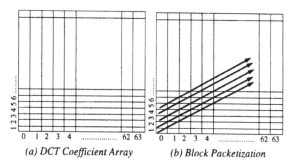

(a) DCT Coefficient Array   (b) Block Packetization

Fig. 4. DCT Coefficient Packetization

error, the lost information must not be clustered on the image. Second, the spatially adjacent 8 by 8 blocks of the image must not lose the same frequency components. If both objectives are met, each block will lose only a small number of coefficients, and the lost frequency components will have high chance of being recovered from the neighboring blocks (which do not lose the same frequency components).

Without loss of generality, one can assume that each frame is divided into an H (horizontal) times V (vertical) number of 8 by 8 blocks. Designating the code of each block as $C(h,v)$, one can construct the H times V code array shown in Figure 4(a). The horizontal axis in Figure 4(a) represents the frequency components of each block from 0 to 63. The vertical axis of the figure represents the blocks ordered by their spatial locations from the top left-handed corner ($h = 0$ and $v = 0$) of the image to the bottom right-handed ($h = H$ and $v = V$).

To make sure that the lost coefficients are shared by as many blocks as possible, each transmission unit (the new block constructed from the DCT blocks) includes frequency components from 64 blocks. Figure 4(b) illustrates a simple way to achieve this objective by packing frequency components diagonally. Note that entropy coding is performed after this packetization step, and hence the packetization scheme is not affected by whether the resulting code is fixed or variable-rate.

Packing coefficients from different blocks achieves only part of the objective. Next, one wants to ensure that the spatially adjacent blocks do not lose the same frequency components when packets are dropped. Let T (top), B (bottom), L (left), and R (right) denote the spatial adjacent DCT blocks, as depicted in Figure 5. Section 4.2 will show that the lost coefficients can be reconstructed from a block's four neighboring blocks (except for the blocks on the edges). However, to ensure that the neighboring blocks do not lose the same frequency components, i.e., to optimize the reconstruction, I propose packetizing these transmission units in "strides."

A stride is the number of blocks skipped between packing blocks. For instance, if the stride is 2, we packetize blocks in the order of 1, 3, 5, 7, . . . and then 2, 4, 6, 8, . . ., etc. This way, for example, if blocks 3, 5 and 7 are lost in a burst, the DC components of the lost blocks can be reconstructed from blocks 2 and 4 for 3, 4 and 6 for 5, and so forth in the horizontal direction of the image. To make sure that in the vertical direction no spatially adjacent blocks lose the same coefficients, one must shift the starting point of the stride from row to row. For instance, one can let the stride on the odd rows start from the first image

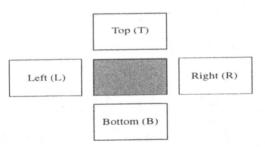

Fig. 5. Spatial Adjacent Blocks

column while that on the even rows starts from the second column. This way, even if the contiguous loss is as high as 50%, the neighbors of a lost block are still intact for reconstruction. In an environment where the loss rate is much lower, one can choose a larger stride to disperse the artifacts as long as the stride is prime to the width (in blocks) of the image.

To summarize, the coding scheme first packetizes the blocks diagonally to spread the frequency components to 64 transmission units. Then, it uses a stride method to pack these transmission units in such a way as to turn the potential consecutive block loss into a pseudo-random loss. To invert the packetization, the only information the decoder needs is the stride. This number can be sent with every packet with a negligible overhead (less than 4 bits) compared to the size of a compressed image.

4.2 Reconstruction

The studies of [8,9] show two typical approaches to reconstruct a damaged image. The first approach, introduced in [9] is a decoder side reconstruction that interpolates the T, B, L, and R blocks to reconstruct the lost block. The technique used by [9] adds only 20% in computational overhead to the decoder, and the reconstruction is of higher quality than that achieved in the previous attempts. The reconstruction formula can be depicted as follow:

$$C_z = C_z + W_t \times C_t + W_b \times C_b + W_l \times C_l + W_r \times C_r \qquad (1)$$

where the weights, W_t, W_b, W_l, and W_r, are the weighting factors for averaging the neighboring blocks' coefficients to reconstruct coefficient C_z.

In a later study [8], Hemami proposes an encoder side approach in which the "optimal" weight vectors are computed for each DCT block based on 15 different combinations of available adjacent blocks (none available, one available, etc.). During the reconstruction step, for each block lost, the proper weighted vector is selected to perform linear interpolation. These vectors, since they take up large space ($200 - 600\%$ of the image data), are compressed using a vector quantizer before the image is shipped to the clients. The resulting space overhead, as reported, is reduced to about 10% of the image size. The drawback of this approach is that either the disk space requirement at the server side increases by 110% (to keep two different compressed images), or the bit rate decreases by 10% (the inflated version is transmitted regardless of the channel's characteristics). Another concern is that this approach greatly increases encoding time. Moreover, the scheme, although achieving better reconstruction quality, may not be optimal

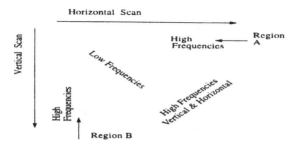

Fig. 6. Frequency Component Characteristics

after all. I argue that the optimal weight set must be at the frequency component level rather than the block level. Since the optimal weight set is computational intensive and takes up large space, it may not be practical to expect an optimal reconstruction, especially in a mobile computing environment where the system resources and power supply are restrictive. Consequently, I suggest a simple and intuitive method to set the weight factors.

The following presents a much simpler heuristic approach that incurs no extra bit rate or computational overhead (crucial for mobile computing) for image reconstruction. Figure 6 shows the 8 by 8 DCT coefficient matrix by its spatial characteristics. The high frequency components corresponding to the horizontal DCT scan (region A in the figure) represent the vertical edges in the image (e.g., a tree), and the high frequency components corresponding to the vertical DCT scan (region B in the figure) represent the horizontal edges (e.g., a roof top). To take advantage of this relationship, the interpolation function (Eq. 1) should assign different weights for different frequency components. The higher the frequencies in the vertical scan (representing horizontal lines), the smaller the weight one should assign to the top and bottom blocks. On the other hand, the higher the frequencies in the horizontal scan (representing vertical lines), the smaller the weight one should assign to the left and right blocks. For example, for reconstructing a vertical line (e.g., a tree), only the top (T) and bottom (B) blocks of the missing block are relevant. The left (L) and right (R) blocks of the missing block do not have the same tree! If one added left and right blocks into the computation for reconstructing the vertical line, one would dilute the recovered coefficients. Of course, one cannot know whether a DTC block contains a tree or not. However, if a tree passes through the missing block, the high frequencies of the horizontal scan must not be zero, and this value can be recovered from the blocks above and below. On the other hand, if no tree passes through the missing block (in other words if the high frequency components in the horizontal scan are zero), there is a high probability that the same high frequency components in the blocks above and below are also zero. Therefore, the reconstruction scheme works accurately without the content of the image being known. Based on this heuristic, the weights of the reconstruction function

$$C_z = C_z + W_t \times C_t + W_b \times C_b + W_l \times C_l + W_r \times C_r$$

can be assigned based on which portion of the DCT block is being reconstructed:

- For the high frequency components in the horizontal scan (region A in Figure 6): $W_t = W_b = \frac{1}{2}$ and $W_l = W_r = 0$.

- For the high frequency components in the vertical scan (region B in Figure 6): $W_t = W_b = 0$ and $W_l = W_r = \frac{1}{2}$.
- For the rest of the coefficients: $W_t = W_b = W_l = W_r = \frac{1}{4}$.

Again, the advantage of this technique is its simplicity. The examples in Section 5 shows its effectiveness.

Also note that, after the packetization scheme, not only does a block not lose all coefficients, but its neighboring blocks do not lose the same frequency components. This minimizes 1) the number of coefficients that need to be reconstructed in each block, and 2) the chance that consecutive blocks lose the same frequency components. Without this packetization scheme, reconstruction may interpolate using blocks many (e.g., 16 or 24) pixels away, blocks that may have no spatial correlation whatsoever.

5   Experimental Results

In my experiment, I first compare a damaged image that does not distribute the loss of the frequency components to other blocks (Figure 7) with one that uses my packetization scheme (Figure 8). Both images were generated under a loss rate of 20%. The major difference is that in the blocks where DC is lost, one can still see high frequency components in Figure 8. Although both images are damaged badly, Figure 8 looks slightly better. (The submitted images are colored.)

Next, I compared the reconstructed images from the first set of damaged images using our reconstruction technique, which takes spatial characteristics into consideration. Figure 9 is the image reconstructed from Figure 7, and Figure 10 is that reconstructed from Figure 8. It is clear that Figure 10 has better visual quality. The distant trees and lamps in Figure 10 are almost lossless as seen when Figure 10 is compared with the original image in Figure 11. The flower bed of the image in Figure 10 has much better continuity than that of Figure 9, which suffers from severe blocking effects. The distribution of the loss by the proposed packetization scheme significantly reduces the blocking effects for which DCT has often been criticized.

5.1   Limitations

This technique is effective as long as there is only one burst of errors and the duration of the burst is smaller than half the image size. If the duration of the error burst is larger than half the image size, the lost coefficients may not be recovered from the neighboring blocks, in which case the image quality degrades severely. In addition, when there are multiple bursts of errors, the chance that they cluster on the image is increased, and subsequently the reconstruction technique can perform less well. However, I argue that these above conditions are rare, and other schemes may also be less effective under such hazardous conditions.

5.2   A Note on SNR

The signal to noise ratio has been used to measure the image quality. The SNR has been shown not necessarily to reflect the quality of an image [6]. In the proposed packetization scheme, since the errors that are supposed to concentrate in one DCT block are distributed to 64 DCT blocks, the noise affects 64 blocks, rather than just one single block, after the inverse DCT is performed. Thus, the SNR is always slightly lower in the proposed packetization scheme (by less than one *db* in PSNR). But human eyes are less sensitive to errors that are diluted and spread out than discernible errors concentrated on a few spots. Therefore, the slightly lower signal to noise ratio should not be a concern in this case.

6   Conclusion

This paper shows an alternative to the ARQ and FEC schemes for low capacity mobile channels. A packetization approach is recommended to transform bursty errors into pseudo-random errors. Since each DCT block loses only a limited number of frequency components, which are preserved in its neighboring blocks, the image can in this way be reconstructed to be closer to the original one. Moreover, the approach takes advantage of the spatial characteristics of the DCT coefficients to reconstruct the lost blocks. The scheme is simple and efficient to implement, compatible with the current JPEG standards, and achieves satisfactory results. The techniques proposed in this study are applicable to other DCT-based standards such as H261 and H263 for video conferencing, and H262 for motion pictures. (Evaluating the effectiveness of this approach on various video coding schemes is a part of my on-going work.) Finally, since the scheme does not increase bit rate and reconstructs damaged images efficiently (hence keeps power consumption low), it is attractive for use in mobile computing environments.

Acknowledgement

I would like to thank professors Robert Gray and Hector Garcia-Molina at Stanford and professor Sheila Hemami at Cornell for their comments on the early draft. I would also like to thank Ken Lin for his help with the experiment.

References

1. A. Albanese, J. Bloemer, J. Edmonds, M. Luby, and M. Sudan. Priority encoding transmission. Proc. 35th Annual Symposium on Foundations of Computer Science, pages 604–612, 1994.
2. M. Baker. Wireless network characteristics. Stanford Technical Report, 1997.
3. P.-C. Chang. Interleaving and error concealment for mpeg video over atm networks. SPIE, Issue 1898, pages 271–282, 1996.
4. S. Cheshire and M. Baker. A wireless network in mosquitonet. IEEE Micro, February 1996.
5. I. Dalgic and F. Tobagi. Characterization of quality and traffic for various video encoding schemes and various encoder control schemes. Stanford Technical Report CSL-TR-96-701, August 1996.
6. I. Dalgic and F. Tobagi. Performance evaluation of ethernets and atm networks carrying video traffic. Stanford Technical Report CSL-TR-96-702, August 1996.

7. D. Eckhardt and P. Steenkiste. Measurement and analysis of an in-building wireless network. Computer Communication Review, pages 243–43, August 1996.

8. S. Hemami and R. Gray. Reconstruction-optimized lapped orthogonal transforms. IEEE International Conf. on Acoustics Speech and Signal Processing, 3:1542–45, 1996.

9. S. Hemami and T. Meng. Transform coded image reconstruction exploiting interblock correlation. IEEE Transaction on Imagine Processing, 4(7):1023–27, July 1995.

10. S. Lin and D. Costello. Error Control Coding: Fundamentals and Applications. Prentice-Hall, 1983.

11. T. Meng. Portable video-on-demand in wireless communication. Proceedings of the IEEE, 83(4), April 1997.

12. K. Sayood. Introduction to Data Compression. Morgan Kaufmann, 1996.

13. S. B. Wicker and M. J. Bartz. The design and implementation of type-i and type-ii hybrid-arq protocols based on first-order reed-muller codes. IEEE Transaction on Communications, 42(2/3/4), 1994.

Fig. 7. 20% Damaged Image Without Coefficients Spread Out

Fig. 8. 20% Damaged Image With Coefficients Spread Out

Fig. 9. Image Reconstructed from Figure 7

Fig. 10. Image Reconstructed from Figure 8

Fig. 11. Original Undamaged Image

Network-Conscious Compressed Images over Wireless Networks*

Sami Iren, Paul D. Amer and Phillip T. Conrad

Computer and Information Sciences Department
University of Delaware, Newark, DE 19716 USA
Email: {iren,amer,pconrad}@cis.udel.edu
Phone: (302) 831-1944   Fax: (302) 831-8458

Abstract. We apply the concept of *network-consciousness* to *image compression*, an approach that does not simply optimize compression, but which optimizes overall performance when compressed images are transmitted over a lossy packet-switched network such as the Internet. Using an Application Level Framing philosophy, an image is compressed into path MTU-size Application Data Units (ADUs) at the application layer. Each ADU carries its semantics, that is, it contains enough information to be processed independently of all other ADUs. Therefore each ADU can be delivered to the receiving application out-of-order, thereby enabling faster progressive display of images. We explain why this approach is useful in general and specifically for wireless/heterogeneous environments.

1 Introduction

For many years, developments in image compression had one primary objective: obtaining the minimum image size. We argue that image compression algorithms should take into account that those images are likely to be transmitted over networks that will lose and reorder packets. Therefore, compression algorithms should not focus solely on achieving minimum image size; algorithms should be optimized to give the best performance when images are transmitted over such networks.

We apply the concept of *network-consciousness* [6] to *image compression*, an approach that takes network Quality of Service (QoS) into consideration when designing image compression. Network-conscious image compression is an application of the Application Level Framing (ALF) [3] principle. An image is divided into path MTU-size[1] pieces, called *Application Data Units* (ADUs), at the application layer, so that each piece carries its semantics, that is, it contains enough

---

* Prepared through collaborative participation in the Advanced Telecommunications/Info Distribution Research Program (ATIRP) Consortium sponsored by the U. S. Army Research Laboratory under the Fed Lab Program, Agreement DAAL01-96-2-0002. This work also supported, in part, by ARO (DAAH04-94-G-0093).

[1] MTU (Maximum Transmission Unit) is the maximum frame size that a link layer can carry. A path MTU-size ADU is one that can be transmitted end to end without the need for IP layer fragmentation and reassembly.

information to be processed independently of all other ADUs. As a result, each ADU can be delivered to the receiving application immediately upon arrival at the receiver, without regard to order, thereby potentially enabling faster progressive display of images.

Our research demonstrates that with a combination of innovative transport protocols and only a small penalty in compression ratio, today's standard compression algorithms can be modified to provide significantly better overall display of images, and hence performance, in the Internet and wireless environments.

Section 2 further motivates network-conscious image compression and defines what a network-conscious compressed image is. Section 3 explains why network-conscious image compression is well suited for wireless/heterogeneous environments. Section 4 summarizes a prototype implementation of our approach: network-conscious GIF. Section 5 concludes the paper with a summary.

2 Motivation — Network-Conscious Compressed Images

Historically, images are compressed and either stored locally (e.g., on a hard disk or CD-ROM) and accessed via high-speed error-free channels, or they are stored remotely and accessed via a relatively error-free, low-bandwidth circuit-switched network, (i.e., a phone line). In the latter case, the low bandwidth causes an increase in the time between requesting an image and seeing the image displayed (that is, the *response time*). As the response time increases, so does the appeal of compression methods that allow for *progressive display*. Applications using progressive display present an initial approximate image and refine it as more image data arrives, thereby allowing the user to begin comprehending the image sooner.

In both of these past environments, the channel between the stored compressed image and the client is essentially *reliable*. All pieces of image data are delivered without loss and in the precise order they were transmitted. Today's Internet introduces a new and different channel. As depicted in Figure 1, images are often transmitted over the intrinsically lossy, variable speed, order-changing Internet. The Internet's unreliable IP network layer protocol regularly loses and reorders pieces of image data during transmission. Furthermore, sometimes the last hop of the channel is a wireless link which is inherently unreliable because of bit errors and hand-off problems.

On top of IP, the Internet offers two transport protocols: UDP and TCP. UDP is simple but does little to enhance IP's service. Together UDP/IP provide an unordered/unreliable[2] transport service. Pieces of image data or the entire image can be lost, reordered, or duplicated. This environment is generally unacceptable for image retrieval.

TCP enhances IP's service to provide an ordered/reliable transport service. Image delivery is error-free and ordered, with no loss and no duplicates. However,

---

[2] "Reliable" refers to a "no-loss" service. Likewise, "unreliable" refers to a "lossy" service.

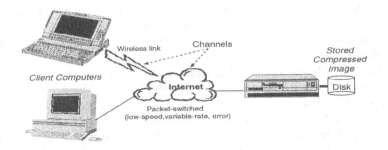

Fig. 1. Image Retrieval over Packet-switched/Wireless Internet

the overall end-to-end channel speed slows down because of TCP's retransmissions. While an image does arrive fully intact at the client, we argue that TCP service is *too* good, and that Web users are paying an unnecessary performance penalty by using it. Depending on the Internet's loss and delay characteristics, the cost of using more service than is needed can be significant [13].

Consider the following TCP-based scenario: a client Web browser retrieves a progressive image from a remote HTTP server over the Internet. After connection establishment, the client sends a request message and the server starts submitting chunks of image data to the transport sender. At the server, the transport sender segments these chunks of data and transmits individual Transport Protocol Data Units (TPDUs) over the Internet. As long as TPDUs arrive at the transport receiver in order, each TPDU is immediately delivered to the client application. On arrival, the client decompresses the data and progressively refines the display.

Figure 2a depicts the timing of such a scenario but assumes the network loses the original transmission of $TPDU_2$. Refinement of the progressive image at the client application is delayed until this lost TPDU is retransmitted and received at the transport receiver. At time $T2$, the user sees the first partial image on the display. Not until $T7$ when $TPDU_2$'s retransmission arrives are TPDUs 2, 3, 4 delivered to the client so that the decompressed complete image can be seen at $T8$.

Between times $T3$ and $T7$, the client application was unable to use $TPDU_3$ and $TPDU_4$ for two reasons: (1) TCP cannot deliver these TPDUs to the application because they are out-of-order, and (2) even if TCP could, the application (decompressor) would not be able to process these TPDUs because in general, today's decompression algorithms cannot process out-of-order data. For the time period $T4$ - $T8$, the user sees no progression in the displayed image.

In an ideal case (Figure 2b), a client application would be able to process and display all TPDUs as soon as they arrive at the transport receiver regardless of their order. When $TPDU_3$ arrives at the transport receiver, it is immediately delivered to the application. The application decompresses the TPDU and refines the image *(T4)*. At $T4$ the user sees a better image than in the previous scenario at the same point in time. Similarly, $TPDU_4$ arrives at the transport receiver

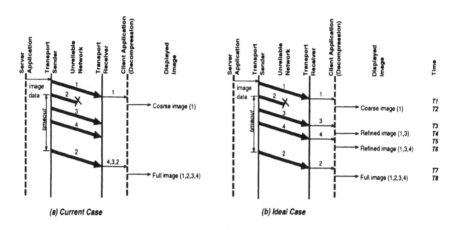

Fig. 2. Progressive Image Transmission over a Lossy Network (2 Cases)

(T5) and is decompressed and displayed by the application *(T6)*. At *T6*, the user sees yet again a better image than at the analogous point in time with TCP.

In Figure 2b, there is better progressive display for two reasons:

- the transport protocol delivers TPDUs *3* and *4* to the application sooner, and,
- the application can perform their decompression even though $TPDU_2$ is missing.

There are two basic requirements for the ideal case to work: (1) An alternative transport protocol must be available to provide an *unordered*, no-loss service. TRUMP [9] and POCv2 [4, 5] are two such transport protocols under development. (2) The receiving application must be able to decompress and display TPDUs independent of each other. That is, the image compression algorithm should allow out-of-order processing of incoming image data.

Definition 1. A network-conscious compressed image is one that is encoded *not* simply to give the *smallest size* for a specified image quality, but to give the *best (i.e., smallest) response time - image quality* combination to an end user retrieving the image over a packet-switched network.

As described in Section 1, the key feature of network-conscious image compression is that it produces path MTU-size, self-contained *blocks* (ADUs) that can be decompressed independent of each other. The basic characteristics of a network-conscious compressed image are: (1) application level framing, (2) progressive display (preferably multi-layered), and (3) robustness and adaptiveness to different user needs, and various networking conditions.

3   Wireless Networks and Network-Conscious Compressed Images

A challenging task for both transport protocol and application developers is to develop a protocol or an application that performs well over a heterogeneous network. Wireless networks have at least two inherent differences from wired networks that require special attention.

The first difference is that wireless networks suffer from high bit error rates and hand-off problems resulting in more TPDU losses than a wired network [2]. This implies that more out-of-sequence arrivals at the transport receiver can be expected. If an application cannot decompress these out-of-sequence data, they have to be buffered delaying the processing and painting of these data on the screen. Network-conscious image compression solves this problem by eliminating the in-sequence processing requirement.

The second inherent difference is that wireless devices are constrained in both their computing and communication power due to limited power supply [10]. Therefore, the transport protocols used on these devices should be less complex to allow efficient battery usage. With network-conscious image compression, a more efficient and simple transport protocol that needs not preserve order can be used. The expected buffer requirements at the transport receiver for an unordered protocol are always less than the buffer requirements for ordered protocols assuming a lossy network [13]. Ordered transport protocols require more computation to reorder ADUs before delivering them to the application thereby delaying the delivery of ADUs and resulting in a longer occupancy of the transport receiver's buffers. Furthermore the nature of the delivery is bursty and results in higher jitter. This burstiness may result in bottlenecks at the receiving application [7].

In a heterogeneous network that consists of variable speed wired and wireless links, we hypothesize that network-conscious compressed images will perform well because they adapt to different network conditions. In the heterogeneous and unstable Internet, one can expect applications which gracefully adapt to changing congestion levels to outlive those which cannot. Adaptability guarantees that applications will use all available resources and make efficient usage of these resources. This is especially important for multicast communication where each participant has different requirements. One research team argues that "network-consciousness" should be adopted as a design principle for many future applications [8].

Another advantage of using network-conscious image compression is that transmission control can be tailored to the characteristics of each ADU [7]. Not all parts of image data are uniform and require the same QoS. If the image compression algorithm provides layering of information, different layers of image data require different reliabilities and priorities. In a network-conscious compressed image, each block (i.e., ADU) can be associated with a set of QoS parameters and can be transmitted according to those parameters.

4 Experiments and Results

Our approach to testing the network-conscious image compression hypothesis consists of two phases. In phase one, we developed the Network-Conscious Image Compression and Transmission System (NETCICATS) [12] to observe the relation between compression algorithms and transport protocols over different network characteristics. We want to see how different compression techniques, when combined with different transport QoS, behave at different network loss rates. In phase two, we modified two popular image compression techniques, namely GIF89a[3] and SPIHT [14] (wavelet zerotree encoding), to make them network-conscious.

Because of lack of space, we will summarize only the network-conscious GIF algorithm. Interested readers may refer to the references [1, 11, 12] for more information on NETCICATS and algorithms.

4.1 Network-Conscious GIF

We modified the GIF89a standard to make it network-conscious. The result, called GIFNCa [1], removes the ordered delivery requirement (and for some applications the reliability requirement) of GIF89a by framing image data at the compression phase (i.e., application level).

The tradeoff between GIFNCa and GIF89a is one of compression vs. progressive display performance. GIF89a's advantage is its expected better compression. GIFNCa's advantage is its expected *faster progressive display* at the receiver when transmitted over an unreliable packet-switched network.

We ran a set of experiments comparing (1) GIF89a over a reliable, ordered transport protocol called *Sequenced Protocol (SP)* vs. (2) GIFNCa over a reliable unordered protocol called *Xport Protocol (XP)*. Both SP and XP are implemented at the user-level over UDP, and use the same code for all functions (including connection establishment/tear-down, round-trip-time estimation, retransmission timeout, acknowledgments, etc.); the only difference is that SP provides packet resequencing (i.e., ordered service) at the receiver, while XP does not.

Each experiment downloads a compressed image from server to client using an interface similar to familiar web browsers (see Figure 3). Packets are routed through a *Lossy Router*, a modified IP router that can simulate three loss models (Bernoulli, burst (2-Step Markov), or deterministic), and a *Reflector* that delays forwarding of IP packets to simulate a lower bandwidth link (28.8 Kbps for these experiments).

Due to space limitations, we provide only a portion of the results in this paper. Interested readers may refer to [1] for more information and results.

The average percentages of image data being displayed at various points in time for 0%, 5%, 10%, and 15% IP packet loss rates are graphed in Figure 4. At 0% loss rate, GIF89a performs better due to its higher compression ratio. As

---

[3] GIF89a is a Service Mark of CompuServe, Inc., Columbus, OH.

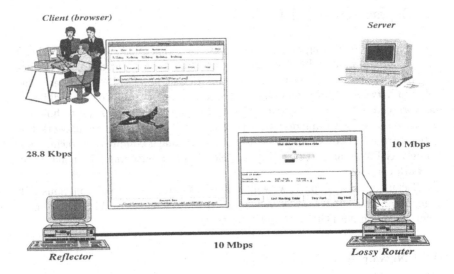

Fig. 3. Network-Conscious GIF Testing Environment

the loss rate increases, both GIFNCa and GIF89a take longer to display but the GIFNCa performance does not degrade as quickly, i.e., it improves *relative to* GIF89a.

To appreciate the significance of these numbers, Figure 5 illustrates the progressive display of an aircraft image using both GIF89a and GIFNCa, in the left and right columns, respectively. The figure shows the image that the application displayed at 5, 10, 15 and 20 seconds for the most "typical" run at a 10% loss rate; This run is closest in mean-squared distance to the average over all experiments for 10% loss rate. In all intermediate times, GIFNCa progressive image is better.

While more serious and exhaustive emprical study is currently underway, these initial results highlight the potential benefit of using GIFNCa over GIF89a under lossy network conditions.

5 Conclusion and Future Work

Traditional image compression algorithms are not designed for lossy packet-switched networks and heterogeneous environments with wired and wireless links. They are optimized to minimize image size only. However, minimum image size does not necessarily provide the best performance when those images are transmitted over lossy networks. The ordered-delivery requirement of traditional compression algorithms cause unnecessary delays at the receiving end.

We apply network-consciousness to image compression so that the compression algorithms will not be optimized only to give the minimum image size;

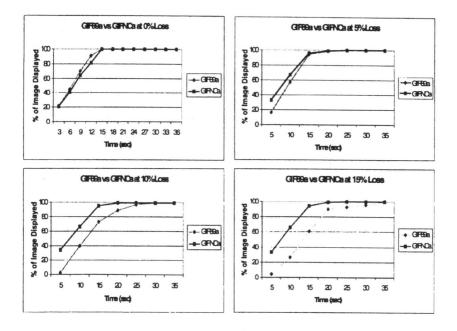

Fig. 4. Comparison of GIF89a and GIFNCa at Various Loss Rates

they will be optimized to give the best performance when transmitted over lossy networks. Network-conscious image compression is especially useful for wireless environments because (1) wireless networks inherently suffer from high bit errors and hand-off problems resulting in more TPDU losses, and (2) limited power problem of wireless devices can be addressed by using simpler transport protocols which do not have to buffer and reorder missing TPDUs.

We have developed two compression algorithms that utilize this approach: network-conscious GIF and network-conscious wavelet zerotree encoding. Initial experiments for network-conscious image transmission are promising.

References

1. P. Amer, S. Iren, G. Sezen, P. Conrad, M. Taube, and A. Caro. Network-conscious GIF image transmission over the Internet. In *4th International Workshop on High Performance Protocol Architectures (HIPPARCH'98)*, June 1998. (To appear).
2. H. Balakrishnan, V. Padmanabhan, S. Seshan, and R. Katz. A comparison of mechanisms for improving TCP performance over wireless links. In *ACM SIGCOMM '96*, Stanford, CA, August 1996.
3. D. Clark and D. Tennenhouse. Architectural considerations for a new generation of protocols. In *ACM SIGCOMM '90*, pages 200–208, Philadelphia, PA, September 1990.

4. P. Conrad. Order, reliability, and synchronization in transport layer protocols for multimedia document retrieval. PhD Dissertation, CIS Dept. University of Delaware, (in progress).

5. P. Conrad, E. Golden, P. Amer, and R. Marasli. A multimedia document retrieval system using partially-ordered/partially-reliable transport service. In *Multimedia Computing and Networking 1996*, San Jose, CA, January 1996. www.eecis.udel.edu/~amer/PEL/poc/postscript/mmcn96full.ps.

6. W. Dabbous and C. Diot. High performance protocol architecture. In *IFIP Performance of Computer Networks Conference (PCN '95)*, Istanbul, Turkey, October 1995. IFIP.

7. C. Diot and F. Gagnon. Impact of out-of-sequence processing on data transmission performance. Technical Report Project RODEO RR-3216, INRIA - Sophia Antipolis, France, July 1997. ftp://www.inria.fr/rodeo/diot/rr-oos.ps.gz.

8. C. Diot, C. Huitema, and T. Turletti. Multimedia applications should be adaptive. In *HPCS Workshop*, Mystic (CN), August 1995. IFIP.

9. E. Golden. TRUMP: Timed-reliability unordered message protocol, December 1997. MS Thesis, CIS Dept., University of Delaware.

10. Z. Haas and P. Agrawal. Mobile-TCP: an asymmetric transport protocol design for mobile systems. In *International Conference on Communications*, Montreal, Quebec, Canada, June 1997. IEEE.

11. S. Iren. Network-conscious image compression. PhD Dissertation, CIS Dept., University of Delaware, (in progress).

12. S. Iren, P. Amer, and P. Conrad. NETCICATS: network-conscious image compression and transmission system. (Submitted for publication).

13. R. Marasli, P. Amer, and P. Conrad. An analytic model of partially ordered transport service. *Computer Networks and ISDN Systems*, 29(6):675–699, May 1997. www.eecis.udel.edu/~amer/PEL/poc/postscript/cn-isdn96.ps.

14. A. Said and W.A. Pearlman. A new, fast, and efficient image codec based on set partitioning in hierarchical trees. In *IEEE Transactions on Circuits and Systems for Video Technology*, volume 6. IEEE, June 1996.

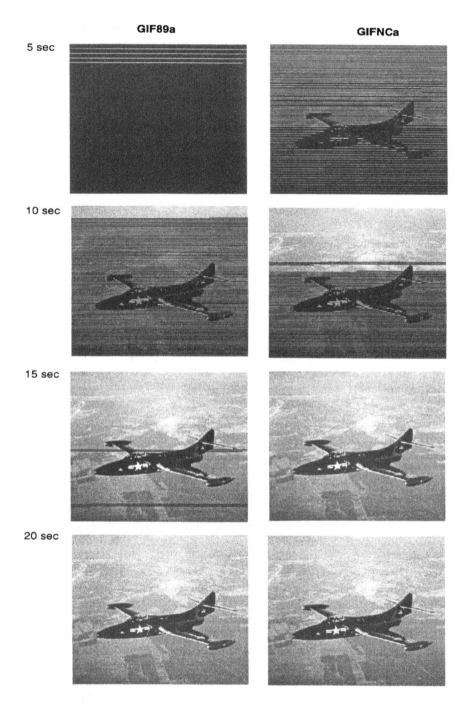

Fig. 5. Sequence of GIF89a and GIFNCa Images at 10% Loss

A Study of Delay Factors in CSCW Applications and Their Importance

Tone Ingvaldsen, Espen Klovning, and Miles Wilkins

Telenor Research and Development, P.O. Box 83, N-2007 Kjeller, Norway
{Tone.Ingvaldsen, Espen.Klovning}@fou.telenor.no
Broadband and Data Networks, BT Labs, Ipswich, IP5 3RE, UK
miles@msn.bt.co.uk

Abstract. Multimedia CSCW applications are rapidly becoming mainstream business tools. If users are to be able to perform useful tasks with these tools the acceptability of the subjective quality of the service must be adequate. This acceptability is affected by many factors, including the user interface, the task undertaken, the audio and video coding, the connection speed and the network performance. The end-to-end delay has been identified as a significant parameter affecting the user's satisfaction with the service. Earlier work identified the delay bounds for which the quality of the CSCW service was acceptable to users performing real tasks. These limits formed the basis for an investigation to identify which system components contribute most to this delay. The components contributing to the delay of audio and video have been measured and the major sources identified.

1 Introduction

Although initially targeted at home users, multimedia products are now increasingly being used by the business community. A growing market is the use of computer supported collaborative work (CSCW) tools instead of time consuming travel. With high quality audio and video streams and application sharing, CSCW applications can replace traditional meetings with several participants. Many vendors are implementing solutions with different characteristics based on ITU (H.320, H.323) and IETF standards for both personal and business use. The service quality requirements for business use are likely to be higher due to the importance of the communication or collaboration.

Service quality includes numerous different quality aspects from network loss to end-system delay and the functionality of the user interface. Current research aimed at an integrated service model for networked user applications combines work with application design, media coding, operating systems, network adapters, scheduling, protocols and network technologies. In the Internet community, the integrated service model, [1], defines three services that can be used to provide IP traffic flows with the quality of service required by CSCW applications. These are the Guaranteed Service, designed for time-critical applications; the Controlled Load service, designed for applications expecting a lightly loaded network; and the Best Effort service, which offers no guarantees. To fulfil these requirements, advanced network services are necessary. One possible solution would be to use the Resource Reservation Setup Protocol (RSVP) to signal resource reservation requests through the IP network. RSVP is especially designed for multimedia conferencing with several participants, but is criticised for its limited scalability and inherent complexity. Although this situation will probably change, the only applicable standardised solutions available today to guarantee network service quality are ATM or an over-dimensioned Intranet.

This paper focuses on the importance of user acceptance by combining user acceptance trials with experimental evaluation of important service quality factors. It has been found that even limited reductions in quality will usually be noticed but this does not necessarily mean that the user will not accept the quality for a given task. Users will accept quality deterioration up to a certain point. It is therefore important to find the user acceptable thresholds for delay, error rate and throughput. The motivation for this work is that knowledge about these service quality boundaries will enable service providers to make sure that a specific CSCW service will meet users' expectations/requirements. Service providers can then create networks with an adequate quality of service, yet at the same time making maximum use of the network resources.

The rest of the paper is outlined as follows. Chapter 2 discusses different factors with an impact on user acceptance. An experimental evaluation of some of these factors is presented in Chapter 3. The paper closes with some concluding remarks in Chapter 4.

2 CSCW Applications and User Acceptance

The single most important issue for users of CSCW applications is that the service quality of its components (i.e. audio, video, application sharing) is good enough. Service quality implies both that the graphical user interface is functional and easy to use, and that the network conditions and end-system architecture and performance provide an acceptable data transfer service. Thus, both these requirements are necessary to achieve user acceptance.

While usability issues are normally addressed during application development, the network and end-system requirements are often neglected. In [2], the most important network parameters for networked multimedia applications have been identified as throughput, transit delay, delay variation and error rate. These parameters are a result of the end-system and network architecture and performance. The results in [3] indicated that the delay is the most important parameter for ATM networks. Cell loss is less important, and the level of cell loss found in commercial ATM networks and well-engineered Intranets is too low to degrade the service beyond acceptable limits. In the Internet however, loss will also be an important issue due to the higher probability of packet loss. Loss of data and delay are in some ways related. Real-time multimedia applications use playout buffers to smooth out delay variation. However, if the delay is too large and the playout buffer is already drained when the data arrive, it can no longer be used and is in practice lost.

The required network service quality does not necessarily coincide with the conditions at which the effects of delay, error rate and low throughput are perceivable. Previous results ([3]) have shown that users can accept both loss and delay up to a certain point. For larger values the users will not use these applications. It has also been shown that the user acceptance also depends on the user task being performed. Highly interactive tasks tend to require better service quality than those with more limited interaction. The differences between CSCW solutions (platform, application, coding standards, access technology) also make a difference. Finding the boundaries for acceptable delay and loss for different tasks and for different CSCW platforms is therefore important.

Table 1. Overview of the two test application used in subsequent measurements

Application	Video coding/ Audio coding	Operating System	Protocol stack	Application sharing
Application A	H.261/G.711	Windows 95/NT	LAN Emulation	All windows applications
Application B	M-JPEG/G.711	Solaris/SPARC	1) UDP/Classical IP over AAL5 2) ATM API over AAL5	Limited set of applications

Two applications (described in Table 1) were used to determine the relationship between user acceptance and end-to-end delay. The results are presented in Table 2. These measurements were done for a highly interactive teaching session with Application A and for a session with less interactive sales negotiation using Application B. An ATM LAN environment was used, without any bandwidth limitations on the applications. Additional delay was introduced artificially between the two communicating end-systems, e.g. 0, 10, and 45 ms for Application A. As illustrated in the Table 2, the acceptance values are different for the two applications and the two tasks. However, they identify an important issue for professional use of CSCW applications: End-to-end delay is very important for user acceptance.

Table 2. User acceptance for two different task using two different application. The user rating should be interpreted as very good/ good/ acceptable/ disturbing /impossible. The inherent delay of the two applications differ

Application A	Delay value	0ms	10ms	45ms
high interaction	User rating	4/ 58/ 38/ 0/ 0	4/ 69/ 27/ 0/ 0	0/ 57/ 43/ 0/ 0
Application B	Delay value	300ms	600ms	900ms
low interaction	User rating	52/ 48/ 0/ 0/ 0	40/ 39/ 21/ 0/ 0	20/ 43/ 37/ 0/ 0

With similar levels of loss, the quality of different media streams will be perceived differently. Since the application-sharing component uses a reliable data transfer protocol, users will perceive loss of data as delay in the information transfer. Users tend to accept larger error rates for the video component than for the audio component. This may in some cases be due to the components' relative importance in the task the user is performing. For instance when two users electronically share a document, the most important components are the document window and the audio stream. Whether users accept larger error rates for video, will also depend on the video coding that is used and on the size of the video frames produced. Some applications use coding algorithms with dependencies between consecutive frames to reduce the necessary bandwidth. Other algorithms like Motion-JPEG (M-JPEG) transfer complete frames each time and can suffer less visual degradation during periods of loss. With a given bit error rate, the video quality will generally deteriorate with increasing video frame sizes, since loss probability for each frame/packet will increase. The actual effect loss of information will have on the video quality will also depend on the packet loss probability and behavior.

The total end-to-end delay perceived by the users can be separated into the application's inherent delay and additional delay incurred by throughput limitations and network latency. The latter will be denoted communication path delay. The inherent application delay is the time taken to compress, decompress, transmit and display information. This is dependent on the available throughput and the processing capacity of the end-systems, and varies between applications. Applications with a large inherent delay will require that other delay components are minimised for users to accept the total service. Communication path delay includes the delay due to throughput limitations in the access network and delay in the operating system due to concurrent tasks. Depending on the distance between the communicating end-systems, the delay through the network may also be a major delay component.

For CSCW service providers, it will be important to compare the total end-to-end delay and error rates with the boundaries for acceptable service quality, to determine if users will accept the service. If necessary the end-to-end delay and loss must be decreased by identifying, and if possible minimising, the components contributing the most to the end-to-end values. Since end-to-end delay has been identified in [3] as the most important parameter for user satisfaction with CSCW applications over ATM networks, the work described here has focused on this parameter.

3 Experimental Evaluation

The previous chapter identified how important the end-to-end delay is for interactive multimedia applications such as CSCW applications. This chapter presents an experimental evaluation of the total end-to-end delay and some of the important delay components. The goal is to provide some insight into the delay issue for CSCW applications based on detailed measurements. Knowledge about the end-to-end delay for CSCW applications is necessary for all user tasks. Characteristics of the studied applications are shown in Table 1.

3.1 End-to-End Delay

Measuring the end-to-end delay in an application is impossible without synchronising the timing equipment at both end-systems. The methods used here are tailored to the specific applications tested. Both the outgoing and incoming AV-streams of Application A were recorded by one end-system with an external VCR with a 20 ms frame interval. The end-to-end delay could therefore be found by counting the number of frames between a synchronised event in these streams. For Application B, the NTP protocol [5] was used to synchronise the end-system clocks.

Table 3. End-to-end delay of Application A video component

Delay	440 ms	460 ms	480 ms	500 ms	520 ms	540 ms
PDF	0.04	0.18	0.20	0.16	0.38	0.04

Table 3 shows the probability density function (PDF) of the total end-to-end delay of the video stream from Application A using a CIF configuration. Due to lip synchronisation in the audio/video conferencing system, the audio delay will be similar to the end-to-end delay of the video stream. Fifty independent measurements were done in a LAN setting with a negligible propagation delay. These end-to-end delay values indicate that the 20 ms granularity of the delay measurements is accurate enough.

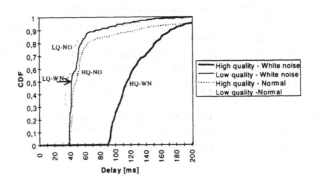

Fig. 1. Cumulative distribution function of video end-to-end delay in Application B
(UDP/CLIP version)

The gross bit rate used by the video stream is 580 kbit/s. According to the ITU-T H.261 recommendation, a single picture can not exceed 256 kbits for CIF coding. Thus, the serialisation delay will never exceed 440 ms. The remaining delay components of the total end-to-end delay includes the compression/decompression, the protocol stack, the network latency and application delays.

Figure 1 shows the cumulative distribution function of the end-to-end delay for Application B (UDP/CLIP version) for four different video streams. The legends indicate the video quality and whether the video image content was white noise or normal office background. End-to-end delay is defined as the time from when the video frame is captured in the sending end-system until it is displayed on the receiving end-system. These measurements were done with Sun SPARCstation 10/51 workstations running Solaris 2.4 connected over a 155 Mbit/s local area ATM network where network propagation delay should be negligible. The peak cell rate was set to 4 Mbit/s.

As illustrated by the figure, the video quality used by the Parallax video board has a direct impact on the delay. For a white noise image, the delay increases by nearly 60 ms when the video quality is increased. The reason is the relationship between the video quality and the video frame size. An increase in the video frame size will necessarily mean more processing to distribute the video. The white noise image represents an upper delay bound of the video component. Another important observation is that there is significant variation in end-to-end delay possibly due to overload in the end-system.

Audio end-to-end delay is lower than the video delay due to the limited packet sizes of the audio stream. Our audio measurements indicated that the audio delay is similar for the two protocol stacks, and more than 90 % of the audio packets experience less than 6 ms delay. The maximum delay was measured to approximately 20 ms for both protocol stacks.

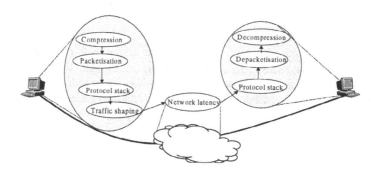

Fig. 2. Delay components of CSCW applications

3.2 End-to-End Delay Components

Some of the most important components of the end-to-end delay apart from the end-system load are illustrated in Figure 2. Whilst the end-system load cannot be controlled, values for the delay components in the figure can be found. Unfortunately, only the influence of the delay components for Application B could be measured due to source code limitations. However, the numbers presented here provide some general information about the relative importance of different delay components in other operating system environments as well. Both the application and the two communication paths used by Application B under the Solaris 2.5.1 operating system were instrumented to measure these components. Delay values for other optimised protocol stacks should be similar. The measurements were done on two dual-processor Sun workstations running Solaris connected by a 155 Mbit/s ATM LAN.

Video Compression and Decompression Delay

The video component of Application B uses the M-JPEG based Parallax video card. It offloads the CPU by doing compression and decompression on an embedded video card processor. Table 4 illustrates the CDF for the compression and decompression. It shows that the bulk of the compression and decompression operations have roughly the same delay. More than 90 % of the video frames are compressed in less than 16.3 ms. Similarly, more than 90% of the video frames are decompressed in less than 3.5 ms. These measurements were done with a white noise video image at a high video quality. Measurements with other images and quality factors gave similar results indicating that the complexity of the image has little effect on these delay components. Other video compression solutions will have different results.

Table 4. CDF table for compression and decompression delay (ms)

CDF	0.1	0.2	0.3	0.4	0.5	0.6	0.7	0.8	0.9	1.0
Compr.	12.5	13.12	13.78	13.81	13.82	13.86	14.0	14.21	16.38	31.24
Decompr.	0.25	0.28	0.29	2.31	3.04	3.06	3.09	3.14	3.50	4.71

Packetisation and Depacketisation

The application protocol for audio and video transfer needs to encapsulate the video frames and audio samples in a simple format to be able to interpret received information correctly. The processing cost of these operations is not significant compared to the other delay components. Thus, the processing cost was therefore included in the compression/decompression measurements.

Protocol Stack in the Sender

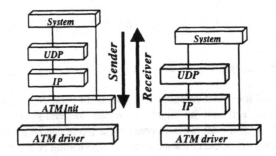

Fig. 3. Delay components in protocol stacks

The delay measurements were done with two different protocol stacks paths as illustrated in Figure 3, and two different Parallax Video card compression qualities, and two different video images giving the video frame sizes shown in Table 5. The audio component bit rate was constant during these measurements with a fixed packet size of 1356 bytes, which means that the audio delay will be significantly lower for byte dependent delay factors.

Table 5. Overview of video frame sizes for the different configurations

Image type/video quality	Low quality	High quality
White noise image	16600 byte	54500 byte
Normal office background	6000 byte	19800 byte

Figure 4 shows the delay components of the sending end-system of both communication paths for the four different video frame sizes. Scenarios with the same parameter set except for the protocol stack are grouped together in pairs. For each delay component, the low quality (LQ) normal office background (NOB) video frame size over UDP/CLIP is the leftmost, while the high quality (HQ) white noise image (WNI) over API/AAL5 is the rightmost bar as indicated by the legends. The numbers presented here are mean values. Only the System and ATM init components suffer from any significant delay variation, i.e. 2-20 ms delay.

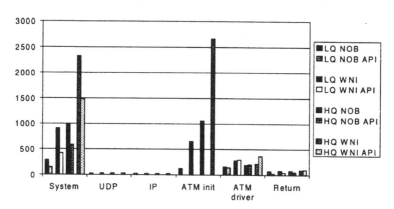

Fig. 4. Sending side delay components

The figure illustrates that for the UDP/CLIP communication path, the System and ATM init delays are the most important delay components. These components are significantly higher for the UDP/CLIP communication path than for the API/AAL5 communication path. The UDP and IP processing is minimal reflecting the limited functionality and optimisation of these protocols. For the API/AAL5 communication path, the most time-consuming operations are the initialisation of the system calls and the ATM driver operation. It should be noted that the components of the different communication paths are not 100% comparable since the differences in the instrumented paths will skew the results. However, the overall delays are comparable.

Traffic Shaping

The protocol stack delay shown in Figure 4 does not include the delay to shape the ATM traffic. This delay component is similar to the serialisation delay of Application A. Due to the DMA capabilities of advanced ATM adapters, the traffic shaping delay can not be measured in the end-system. The reason is that the device driver will return after the DMA operation is set up properly, and not after the last ATM cell has been transmitted. This is done to utilise concurrent operation of the DMA engine and the host CPU. Assuming CBR contracts, the delay can be modeled with sufficient accuracy based on the link speed and the bit rate used by the ATM connection:

$$T_{shape} = (n-1)(t_c + t_s) + t_c. \qquad (1)$$

where n is the number of cells in the packets, and t_c and t_s are the time needed to send one cell and the necessary spacing between two cells respectively. Figure 5 shows T_{shape} on a 155 Mbit/s link for the different video frame sizes as a function of the bit rate of the ATM connection. It is clear that unless the bit rate is sufficiently high for the largest video frame size, the T_{shape} component can be more than 100 ms. Given a particular T_{shape}, the frame rate must be adjusted to avoid buffer overflow in the protocol stack. For instance, with 20 fps, the delay per video frame must be below 50 ms. Or if a certain video frame rate is required and the image contents are given, the traffic contract peak rate should be adjusted.

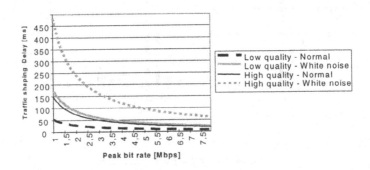

Fig. 5. T_{shape} on a 155 Mbit/s link (ms)

Protocol Stack in the Receiver

Figure 6 shows the delay components of the receiving end-system. It illustrates that the difference between the UDP/CLIP and API/AAL5 communication path costs, are less for the receiver than for the sender. Unlike the sending side, the delay of the

API/AAL5 path on the receiving side will increase significantly with larger frame sizes. However, the overall delay of the UDP/IP protocol stack is still higher than the API delay.

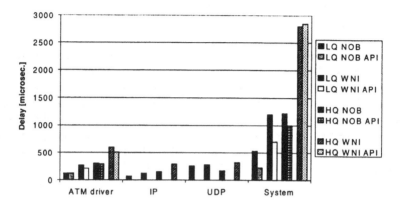

Fig. 6. Receiving side protocol delay

Combining the results in Figure 4 and Figure 6 indicates that the overall delay through the protocol stacks in the sender and the receiver varies from 0.5 ms to 9.5 ms depending on the protocol stack and the size of the video frame. These measurements have shown that the processing cost of the UDP/CLIP path is at least 75% higher than for the ATM API path. However, comparing the overall protocol delay with T_{shape} indicates that the protocol stack delay is of little importance. This is especially true when the protocol processing of a packet can be done in parallel with the traffic shaping of earlier packets belonging to the same video frame.

3.3 Application Sharing Delay

The traffic generated by shared applications is typically random bursts of short packets. Network traffic is only generated as the result of a user action (such as moving the mouse or typing). Larger bursts of longer packets may be generated when the application is first shared or a large bitmap image is exchanged.

While audio/video normally runs over UDP/IP, most application sharing solutions are based on TCP/IP for reliability. Due to the complex behaviour of TCP, the application sharing delay is too complex to measure satisfactory, but can be predicted based on the functionality of the protocol. It is clear that applications using the reliable Internet transport protocol TCP will experience more delay than applications using UDP, and thus, the application-sharing component will experience more delay than indicated in the previous audio/video delay results. The reason for this increase in delay is the TCP functionality and features, including the use of Nagle's algorithm, delayed acknowledgements, slow start mechanisms, duplicate acknowledgement thresholds, coarse retransmission timeouts, and limitations in the window size with large bandwidth-delay product. These issues are described in detail in [6], [7], [8], [9], and [10].

3.4 Summary

As illustrated in these measurements, the main delay factors for the dominant video delay of the CSCW applications are the video compression, the traffic shaping (serialisation) and potentially the network latency. These conclusions are illustrated in Figure 7, which shows a bar graph of the delay both for low and high video quality for different images. In these measurements (i.e. Application B with the UDP/CLIP protocol stack) a 50 ms propagation delay has been added. It is comparable to the propagation delay across Europe. The overall end-to-end delay can vary between 85 ms and 189 ms in such a wide area network configuration.

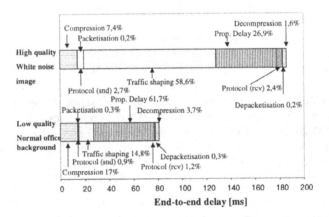

Fig. 7. Sum of end-to-end delay components

The delay percentages of each component relative to the overall delay are also indicated in the figure. The high quality video component generates larger video frames, increasing the traffic shaping delay and hence the end-to-end delay.

4 Concluding Remarks

It has been shown that the end-to-end delay experienced by CSCW applications has a significant impact on the users' acceptance of the service. This applies to both ATM and non-ATM networks. The amount of delay will depend on a number of factors, some of which are specific to certain CSCW applications. Additionally, the amount of delay that will be tolerated by users will depend on the task being undertaken. The significant variation in the inherent delay of CSCW applications makes it necessary for the application to be thoroughly evaluated for the intended task before using it. These performance issues are usually not part of the marketing for a particular application although its importance is unquestionable.

Much of the delay is due to either the coding standard or network technology used. Applications used across a network supporting low data-rates will experience a much higher inherent delay then those running over faster networks. This is due to the serialisation delay, as identified by this paper. The protocol stack and operating system have limited impact on the delay, probably due to the significant developments of these components over the past decade.

The results presented in this paper clearly demonstrate that it will not necessarily be possible to satisfactorily use CSCW applications across the WAN unless the network quality of service is adequate.

References

1. Braden, R., Clark, D., Shenker, S.: Integrated Services in the Internet Architecture: an Overview, Internet Engineering Task Force, Request For Comment 1633 (1994)
2. Fluckiger, Understanding networked multimedia, London, Prentice Hall.
3. Ranta-aho, M et al: Task-dependent User Requirements for Quality of Service of Videoconferencing-CSCW services, Proc. of Human Factors in Telecommunication'97 (1997) 251 - 254
4. Laubach M.: Classical IP and ARP over ATM, Internet Engineering Task Force, Request For Comment 1577, (1994)
5. Mills, D. L.: Network Time Protocol (Version 3) Specification, Implementation, Internet Engineering Task Force, Request For Comment 1305, (1992)
6. Moldeklev, K.: Performance Issues of Internet End Systems, Telektronikk, Vol. 93. No. 2 (1997) 33-45
7. Mathis, M., et al: TCP Selective Acknowledgement Options, Internet Engineering task Force, Request For Comment 2018 (1996)
8. Jacobson, V., et al: TCP Extensions for High Performance, Internet Engineering Task Force, Request For Comments 1323 (1992)
9. Romanow, A., Floyd, S.: Dynamics of TCP Traffic over ATM Networks, IEEE JSAC Vol. 13. No. 4 (1995) 633-641
10. Stallings, W. R.: TCP/IP illustrated Volume 1 - the Protocols, Reading, Mass., Addison-Wesley (1994)

Dynamic QoS Renegotiation in the PNSVS Videoconferencing Application

Marc Boyer[1], Philippe Owezarski[1], and Michel Diaz[1]

LAAS-CNRS, 7 avenue du Colonel Roche,
31077 Toulouse Cedex 4, France
{boyer,owe,diaz}@laas.fr

Abstract. This paper aims to study the dynamic QoS renegotiation in a particular case, a videoconferencing application: PNSVS (Petri Net Synchronized Videoconferencing System). In the paper, we present first the QoS model (TSPN), the architecture and mechanisms used to achieve this QoS. Then we study how to handle with a synchronized switching of QoS. This leads us to a switching framework (an architecture and its protocol). Finally, we present measures proving that the architecture does not penalize the application and makes a graceful switching of QoS.

Keywords: multimedia, dynamic QoS renegotiation, QoS switching, synchronization, conferencing.

1 Introduction

Current videoconferencing applications that begin to run on desktop workstations, have high throughput and new synchronization requirements.

Nevertheless, their limitation is that they have a poor underlying model (if any) and offers either no controlled quality of service (QoS), but adaptive mechanisms, or a fixed QoS for each session. These applications usually run on networks that do not provide any guaranteed QoS in terms of jitter, end to end delay, etc. Very few attempts have been done to implement and guarantee, at the user level, a given quality of service [13, 12, 4]. First of all, guaranteeing a given QoS means to define it in a precise way. It has been shown previously that temporal extensions of Petri net model are able to model the synchronization and time requirements of multimedia systems [1, 19] and that these Petri nets can be used to model the behavior of each component of a software architecture and to implement videoconferencing applications having static QoS requirements.

This paper will show that a guaranteed QoS can also be renegotiated during the normal behavior of the application, because of a decrease of the amount of available resources or because of user wish. Reducing or increasing the QoS have to be integrated in the application design. It will also be shown that negotiating and switching the QoS is equivalent to modifying the synchronization model of the application.

This approach is applied to the videoconferencing application, PNSVS (Petri Net Synchronized Videoconferencing System), and allows to change the application QoS without any discontinuity in the presentation.

Although looking simple, advanced videoconferencing applications have hard requirements, that appear in many multimedia applications, and that are the following:

- temporal synchronization requirements (intra- and inter-stream temporal constraints),
- needs of local resources (memory, CPU and I/O),
- distributed aspect (at least two computers communicating), including bandwidth and isosynchrony constraints,
- non deterministic interactions with users, introduced by the possibility of changing the QoS.

We expect that solving the QoS renegotiation and switching problem in this particular case will provide a good insight of the general case.

Section 2 presents the PNSVS application including its basic TSPN model and its architecture.

The constraints of a synchronized QoS switching and the architecture derived from these constraints will be given in section 3. The switching implementation and experimental measurements, that show efficiency of proposed protocol and architecture, are also given.

2 PNSVS

This section presents the architecture of a high-quality synchronized videoconferencing application called PNSVS. As PNSVS is based on a formal model, we will first present its multimedia synchronization model, based on temporal extensions of Petri Nets and called Time Stream Petri Net (TSPN). Then the user oriented QoS and the PNSVS architecture that is able to guarantee it will be described.

2.1 The TSPN Model

TSPN ([19]) is a Petri Nets based model for modeling synchronization constraints in multimedia applications.

One strength of Petri net models is there graphical features that allows one to extract synchronization constraints from the model in a glance.

In addition, TSPN model has a high modeling power (it is very easy to model complex inter-stream synchronization scenarios by just merging transitions), a high expressive power (all kind of synchronization scenarios can be modeled using TSPN: [18] proves that TSPN is Turing - complete), and analysis methods ([1]).

In TSPN, temporal constraints are located on edges leaving places. This allows to express the behavior of each flow, independently from other flows.

This temporal constraints take the shape of a temporal interval with 3 values: minimal, nominal and maximal, that takes into account the asynchronous system characteristics, and the acceptable jitter on multimedia objects.

Different synchronization semantics are offered to the author for firing transitions. Three main strategies are provided that favor the earliest stream, the latest stream or a master stream statically chosen. By combining these three strategies, nine different firing rules are obtained.

The semantic of the model is as follow: (1) when a token arrives in a place, the associated presentation begins; (2) its life time belongs to a validity time of an outgoing arc; (3) the firing instant is chosen in respect with the temporal validity interval and the selected semantic of the transition.

2.2 QoS in PNSVS

A video conferencing system is an application which captures live video and audio, transmits and replays them remotely in a synchronized way. Synchronization has two aspects: (1) intra-media synchronization, defining presentation flow rate, its nominal value as well as the maximum jitter that can appear in each object presentation, and (2) inter-media synchronization, as the *lip-synchronization problem* for example, that defines the temporal relationships between the two streams, and their maximum temporal drift.

Let us emphasize that those synchronizations must be guaranteed depending on the user requirements. Like [5, 22, 12, 9], we assume that QoS must be defined as user and application oriented, because the user is the only judge of the needed quality. This assumption shows that multimedia data tolerate jitter: it is useless to achieve a very high synchronization when a lower one is undetectable by the user, and it will cost for no improvement a lot of resources in asynchronous systems. By example, [7, 20] show that for video, a 10ms jitter is imperceptible to a human.

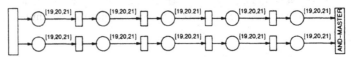

Fig. 1. videoconferencing TSPN
Times are expressed in 10^{-2} seconds.

The TSPN of Figure 1 expresses such a good synchronization scheme. It presents 5 pictures and 5 audio packets per second with an intra-media jitter bounded by 10ms and an inter-media drift bounded by 100ms[1]. In the "AND-MASTER" inter-media transition, the audio is the master and the video the slave. This means that the firing time of this transition will be chosen by first respecting the audio constraints (the "MASTER" part of the synchronization)

---

[1] In the worst case, if one flow accumulates at each data its minimal negative jitter, 10ms, and the other one accumulates its maximal positive jitter, 10ms, the drift between both will be 5*10ms positive jitter minus 5*10 negative jitter, that represents a drift of 100ms.

but also enforcing the "AND" part of this rule (that aims to favor the latest stream), in order to respect the video nominal rate (waiting the video presentation completion), as far as possible[2].

Thus, the TSPN model of Figure 1 expresses all user QoS synchronization needs. So it becomes the synchronization constraints of the application.

Another more subtle aspect of QoS management is loss recovery. In PNSVS, a data is waited until it becomes obsolete. If this occurs, a substitution data is presented in time and place of the other one: doing so, synchronization constraints are always globally fulfilled.

2.3 PNSVS Architecture

On the one hand, as in [14, 9], synchronization operations have to be run at the highest level of the software, *i.e.* inside the application layer of the receiver[3], and with a "real-time class" priority. On the other hand presentation processes make a lot of system calls and an important use of CPU. They cannot be run in "real-time class" for two reasons. The first is that a "real-time class" process that makes a system call runs into the "system class" for the system call duration, and loses its priority. The second is that the "real-time class" has the highest priority, even higher than the system, and important use of CPU in "real-time" leads to penalize or to lock the system [11, 13]. So presentation processes that perform system calls must run in "time-sharing class", managed by an orchestrator running in "real-time class".

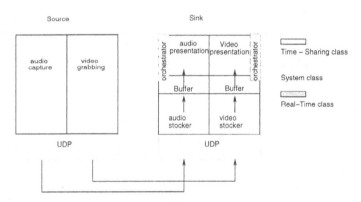

Fig. 2. PNSVS architecture

Moreover, for absorbing network jitter, and increasing the quality of the presentation by decreasing the number of discontinuities, data have to be buffered[4]. This leads to the architecture of Figure 2.

---

[2] Even if video is not the master of the transition, the "AND" aspect of the "AND-MASTER" synchronization rule (that tries to wait as much as possible the later stream) allows to reduce the number of discontinuity in the video.

[3] Because all components of distributed systems are asynchronous, temporal synchronizations done in low layers will be lost at presentation time.

[4] Buffer depth is function of the required end-to-end delay.

3   Dynamic QoS Renegotiation

A general multimedia application is not a static QoS application. As in [17], we distinguish multimedia from continuous media. A continuous media is a simple periodic (or almost periodic) function (like a MJPEG or MPEG presentation). Multimedia or more precisely hypermedia applications imply user interactions and as a consequence when new presentations are requested, their scenarios and scenes can be very different from the previous one.

For example, the presentation of a physical phenomenon could be introduced by a page of static text and pictures, followed by the video of an experiment, etc. This dynamic behavior can be seen as a dynamic renegotiation of the QoS triggered by the user.

Even for a continuous media, a network overload or more simply a request of the user could lead to a dynamic renegotiation of the QoS.

Many papers put forward the lack of dynamic QoS renegotiation [2, 10, 12, 21, 22, 5, 16, 8], but only very few propose solutions.

This dynamic QoS renegotiation problem is decomposed into two sub-problems: (1) negotiating the resources required to implement the new QoS[5] and, (2) switching from the old configuration to the new one without interrupting the application.

Solutions for end to end resources negotiation protocol, taking into account the required resources[6], can be found in [5, 16].

Let us consider there the design of the switching aspect.

Our goal is to change the QoS during the presentation without any discontinuity in the presentation. The data with the new QoS will be presented exactly in sequence after those of the old QoS, and every data is presented with its own QoS.

From a modeling point of view, a continuous media can be seen as a periodic function, *i.e.* a repetition of a simple TSPN (Video-on-demand is a good example of a continuous media application) and it will be shown that changing the QoS of a continuous media is equivalent to changing its TSPN model.

No paper has already presented a formal way to handle the switching, and we will use TSPN to model continuous media and multimedia renegotiation.

The remainder of this paper also shows how to extract from the application (or more precisely from the TSPN model as the one presented in 2.3) an adequate dynamic QoS renegotiation architecture, and implement it.

---

[5] In case of resource shortage, the request can be rejected, or a lower quality can be chosen.

[6] It exists a lot of solutions in the transport layer, but they are single connection oriented and not global application oriented, and a multimedia application can use many flows and many connections.

3.1 Constraints and Choices

As already said, the purpose of the guaranteed switching is to respect the QoS of each data, without stopping the continuous stream, and to implement the corresponding mechanisms.

What are the requirements of such an architecture ?

- Must the negotiation be made by a new entity or must it be done by the already existing threads (like stocker threads)? The architecture incites to create a new one: a Protocol Agent like [16] or QoS Agent like [5]. This is possible without system overhead by implementing this agent with a new thread (thread context switching and communications are "light").
- The dialog between the source and sink QoS agents must be reliable: we choose to open a TCP connection.
- The choice of the switching instant is critical. A data must be presented with the knowledge of the QoS it was produced with[7]. The data have all a sequence number, so the simplest solution for selecting the instant of commutation should be reduced to the choice of an index.

  A study of the *out-of-band* mechanisms (in the TCP connection for example) shows that it is impossible to assure that this index will arrive before the data depending on it[8]. *In-band* solution has to be used[9] and leads to introduce another function in the flow management: the switching detection. It leads to introduce in the architecture a switching agent into the stocker and presentation processes[10].
- Moreover, the view of a unique switching point is very inadequate: switching must be atomic from the user point of view, but can be multiple inside the system. The different sub-layers of the application do not compute the same data at the same time: if a layer works on a data number n, the underlying layer will handle following data $n + p$ $(p > 0)$. But n and $n + p$ can have different QoS. So, every layer must have its own switching instant.

  Also, inside the same layer, because different types of data are processed by different threads, and that the synchronization is made just once per TSPN period in the presentation layer, at the same moment, an audio thread can be presenting data number n while the video thread is ending the $n - 1$. So, every stack must have its own switching instant.

  As a conclusion, the switching architecture must be integrated in and complement the static application architecture (by layer and by media stack).

---

[7] Otherwise, it could introduce global inconsistency.

[8] The source and the sink must make the choice of a time $T_{switching}$ for switching and share this choice before this dead-line without any guaranteed end to end delay in the network. It is impossible. . .

[9] This index is send through the data flow, in the data UDP connections: so it will arrive with the data. More details will be given in 3.2.

[10] The switching agent is an architecture object, but in the implementation, it has not to be implemented by a parallel thread: it can just be a part of code in the main management loop activated by a boolean if renegotiation is asked and else idle.

– The switching itself must be invisible for the users: it must take place between two data and not delay the presentation. What is difficult is that the new QoS can need resources that are different from the old ones, and the time for granting a needed resource (like an X-Window) is not null. So, resources must be, as much as possible, reserved before the switching moment[11].

3.2 Renegotiation Architecture

General presentation From the constraints presented in 3.1, one can derive the architecture presented in Figure 3.

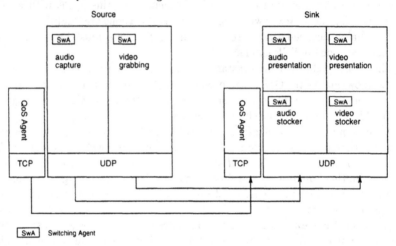

Fig. 3. Renegotiation architecture

The matching between the static and the renegotiation architecture is not an equivalence. For each media, the orchestrator thread and the presentation thread are always sharing the same QoS parameters. So, they are grouped into the same QoS component, and are driven by the same switching agent.

The global behavior of the architecture is as follows:

Negotiation and resources reservation The two QoS agents negotiate the new TSPN (*i.e.* the TSPN representing the new QoS), check that their resources are able to implement it, reserve those resources, and signal the future QoS switching to other threads. The system is ready to switch.

Switching thread by thread the master capture thread selects the commutation index, signals it to others threads. Each thread switches at its switching instant.

Switching Protocol This chapter presents the QoS switching protocol in detail, and focuses on the synchronization of the switching.

---

[11] This constraint is not of prime importance for our application PNSVS, but will be in a more general context.

Note that we do not study neither the negotiation[12], nor the origin of the QoS renegotiation request: in our implementation, the user asks it by pushing a button, but some other events could trigger it[13].

The switching period is divided into two phases: (1) the negotiation and reservation of resources, and (2) the switching itself, thread by thread.

Negotiation and resources reservation The protocol is described in Figure 4.

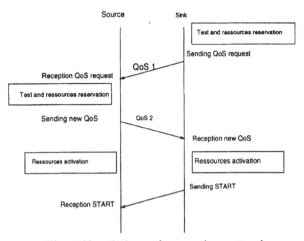

Fig. 4. Negotiation and reservation protocol

The only important point is that, when the sink send the START message, all its resources are ready: when the source has completed its resources activation and has received the START message, it knows that all resources are ready and it is allowed to switch[14].

Switching thread by thread The switching behavior is presented on Figure 5. It starts when the source receives the START message:

1. the QoS agent reads the current sequence index of the master flow, and compute the commutation index;
2. the QoS agent codes the commutation index and signals it to the capture threads;
3. the commutation index is added to every packet header;
4. the first sink thread which receives a packet with the new commutation index signals its value to all other threads;
5. finally, every switching agent tests the equality of the current sequence index of its thread and the commutation index, and switches when they are equal (or when the sequence number is greater, in case of losses).

---

[12] For such protocols, please refer to [16].
[13] such as a QoS renegotiation after network parameters violations
[14] The message is send on the reliable TCP connection.

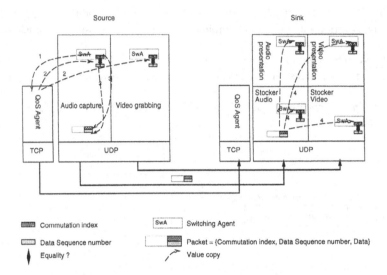

Commutation index   SwA   Switching Agent

Data Sequence number   Packet = {Commutation index, Data Sequence number, Data}

Equality ?   Value copy

Fig. 5. Switching architecture

A question appears: why coding the commutation index *in-band* and not just tagging the packets with a "new QoS" flag?

We will describe a header sequence in one flow. The notation is *Sequence Number / QoS origin*. The first packets sent are $1/1; 2/1; 3/1; \ldots$ until a QoS renegotiation request is sent. At time T, the source receives the START message, and its sequence number is 500. It chooses to switch at index 510, so it will send $500/1; 501/510; 502/510; \ldots; 509/510$ with the old QoS, and the first data with the new QoS is $510/510$.

With this "as early as possible" transmission of the QoS commutation index, there is a high probability of receiving the index in time, even in the presence of losses (in this example 9 of 10 packets can be lost without any problem[15]).

3.3 Implementation and Performances

This application has been implemented on Solaris 2.4 between 2 Sparc stations - 10, with a bi-processor sink. Both workstations have Parallax video board (with MJPEG hard compression / decompression).

Performances have been obtained by putting inside the source code, just before the image display call, some instructions, that get the local clock, and write it into specific files.

This section presents an experiment, that begins with 10 frames per second, changes the QoS to 15, then to 20 and finally to 25 frames per second.

---

[15] Event in case of a long sequence of losses, they are "recoverable". From the *in-band* coding, we assume that if the index is lost, that implies that the data are lost too, no data is presented with a bad QoS. When the first data with the new QoS arrives, then the commutation index arrives too, and the system is able to recover.

The expected behavior Before giving figures, let us define the ideal behavior. In fact, a perfectly synchronized video conferencing system must display audio and video data with a constant rate: so, the curves of the presentation moments have to be linear functions. When the number of data per second changes, the rate of presentation must change too, and the slope of the function has to change, leading to a piecewise linear function.

As we want the presentation not to be interrupted, the function has to be continuous.

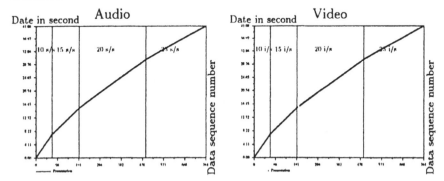

Fig. 6. Audio and Video presentation curves

Figure 6 presents the presentations dates of the audio and video data: it shows the observed behavior, but not the jitters, because the jitter values (in millisecond) are too small with respect to the experiment time scale (in second).

Experimental jitters The intra-media jitter in the TSPN model is defined as the difference between the real data duration and its nominal value. Such a definition, data per data, does not permit to have a global view of the system, as it cannot represent jitter accumulation from one data to another.

We define here the jitter as the difference between the data presentation date in the real system and the data presentation date in the perfectly synchronized video conferencing system.

Intra-media jitters are presented in Figure 7: the jitter remains very low, and in fact, it is in general less than ±3ms. Because the precision of the system clock[16] is in average 3ms, the sum of the measured value and the measured error is 6ms, and stays smaller than the 10ms required by the QoS (expressed by the temporal interval of the TSPN).

For the part of the experiment with a rate of 15 frames per second, the jitter seems to increase and to reduce periodicly. This behavior respects the requested QoS too. The jitter between two data stays under than 10ms. The drift[17] increases at the beginning of the TSPN up to the synchronization transition (but

---

[16] Given by [15].

[17] The sum of the jitters observed on all objects.

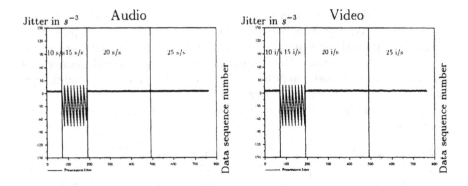

Fig. 7. Audio and Video Intra-media jitters

remains smaller than $100ms$). When resynchronization occurs, the drift value is reduced.

This is due to the fact that the scheduling period is $10ms$, and for 10, 20, 25 frames per second, it defines a entire number of periods, and that for 15, it must be rounded.

This dynamic QoS renegotiation does not penalize the application as, from the user point of view, it does not imply any discontinuity in the presentation.

The perfect continuous aspect of the jitter curves (the jitter does not increase during the switching period) shows that this requirement is perfectly achieved.

4 Conclusion and Future Works

This QoS architecture has been defined for a particular case of dynamic QoS renegotiation, going from one TSPN to another without flow interruption and without QoS violation.

After describing the requirements underlying the architecture, a solution has been implemented and measured, and shows that the goals are perfectly fulfilled.

This practical case prove relevance as insight in multimedia QoS switching: the switching framework (in-band coding, per-layer and per-stack switching, etc.) can be extended to many multimedia applications.

This experiment is being extended within a more general context $i.e.$ navigating from a TSPN to another, and taking into account the problems of re-using resources as much as possible.

This work as then to be extended with more general negotiation protocols, networks and operating systems which allow all users to negotiate and renegotiate QoS parameters.

References

[1] B. Berthomieu and M. Diaz. Modeling and verification of time dependant systems using Time Petri Nets. *IEEE Transactions on Software Engineering*, 17(3):259–273, March 1991.

[2] H. Bowman, G. S. Blair, L. Blair, and A. G. Chetwynd. Formal description of distributed multimedia systems: an assessment of potential techniques. *Computer communications*, 18(12):964–977, december 1995.

[3] J. Courtiat, M. Diaz, and P. Sénac, editors. *Multimedia Modeling*, Toulouse, France, July 1996. World Scientific Publishing.

[4] C. Fan. Evaluations of soft real-time handling methods in a soft real-time framwork. In Courtiat et al. [3], pages 407–421.

[5] S. Fischer, A. Hafid, G. v. Bochmann, and H. de Meer. Cooperative QoS management for multimedia applications. In MCS97 [6], pages 303–310.

[6] IEEE Computer Society Technical Comittee on Multimedia Computing. *International conference on Multimedia Computing and Systems*, Ottawa, Ontario, Canada, June 1997.

[7] K. Jeffay, D. Stone, and F. Smith. Transport and display mechanisms for multimedia conferencing across packed-swiched networks. *Computer networks and ISDN systems*, (26), 1994.

[8] W. Liao and V. O. Li. Synchronization of distributed multimedia systems with user interactions. In Courtiat et al. [3], pages 237–252.

[9] E. Moeller, A. Scheller, and G. Schürmann. Distributed multimedia information handling. *Computer communications*, 13(4):232–242, may 1990.

[10] J. Nang and S. Kang. A new multimedia Synchronisation Specification method for Temporal and Spatial events. In MCS97 [6], pages 236–243.

[11] J. Nieh, J. G. Hanko, J. D. Northcutt, and G. A. Wall. SVR4 UNIX scheduler unacceptable for multimedia applications. In *Proceedings of the Fourth international Workshop on Network and Operating System for Digital Audio and Video*, 1993.

[12] J. Nieh and M. S. Lam. SMART UNIX SVR4 support for multimedia applications. In MCS97 [6], pages 404–414.

[13] P. Owezarski and M. Diaz. Models for enforcing multimedia synchronization in visioconference applications. In Courtiat et al. [3], pages 85–100.

[14] P. Owezarski and M. Diaz. Hierarchy of time streams petri nets models in generic videoconferences. In *Proceedings of the International Conference on Application and Theory of Petri Nets (ICATPN) : Workshop on Multimedia and Concurrency*, pages 59–72, Toulouse, France, June 1997.

[15] Priest and Scottg. High resolution timers aren't (document/kernel/other/1175695). *SunSolve*, (1175695), 1994.

[16] K. Rothermel, G. Dermler, and W. Fiederer. QoS negociation and resource reservation for distributed multimedia applications. In MCS97 [6], pages 319–326.

[17] H. Schulzrinne. Operating system issues for continuous media. *Multimedia Systems*, 4:269–280, October 1996.

[18] P. Sénac. *Contribution à la modélisation des systèmes multimédias et hypermédias*. PhD thesis, Université Paul Sabatier, Juin 1996.

[19] P. Sénac, M. Diaz, A. Léger, and P. de Saqui-Sannes. Modelling logical and temporal synchronization in hypermedia systems. *IEEE Journal on Selected Areas in Communications*, 14(1):84–103, Januar 1996.

[20] R. Steinmetz and G. Engler. Human perception of media synchronization. Technical Report 43.9310, IBM Eureopean Networking center, 1993.

[21] T. Tsang and R. Lai. Time-Estelle : An extended Estelle capable of expressing multimedia QoS parameters. In MCS97 [6], pages 311–318.

[22] A. Vogel, B. Kerhervé, G. von Bochmann, and J. Gecsei. Distributed multimedia and QOS: a survey. *IEEE multimedia*, 2(2):10–19, Summer 1995.

Towards an ODP-compliant Object Definition Language with QoS-support

Jan Øyvind Aagedal

SINTEF Telecom and Informatics, P.O. Box 124 Blindern, N-0314 Oslo, Norway
Jan-Oyvind.Aagedal@informatics.sintef.no

Abstract. This paper presents ODL-Q, an object definition language with QoS support. ODL-Q is based on TINA ODL and extended with a contractual QoS approach where OCL is used to specify the QoS characteristics an object provides and requires. OCL is a formal language included in UML to express side-effect-free constraints. The QoS specification is based on an event model with a dating function used to specify timing constraints. ODL-Q is a superset of OMG IDL, and it is ODP-compliant by its possibility for objects to have multiple interfaces, object bindings as first class objects, and stream and signal interfaces. It is also possible for operations to have pre- and post-conditions, to specify incoming and outgoing operations, and to specify invariants on interfaces and objects. ODL-Q is presented using a video application example.

1 Introduction

Recently, technology for distributed objects has received wide market acceptance. Furthermore, standards to enable open distributed processing are progressing well based on the ISO/ITU-T standard for a Reference Model for Open Distributed Processing (RM-ODP) [1]. As technology matures, users increase their expectations of what can be achieved. Both the end user pull and the technology push contribute to the emergence of distributed multimedia systems.

In traditional systems, requests for services are either met or ignored, defining the success-criterion for the services. For multimedia applications the ability to maintain, configure and predict quality of service (QoS) is essential. Many isolated QoS issues have been addressed in individual architectural layers, and the focus lately has been on the end-to-end view for giving QoS guarantees. An end-to-end view means to focus on all communication aspects from information source to information sink. Database issues are however rarely discussed, even if they contribute to the perceived QoS from an end user point of view. [2] gives a review of the still somewhat immature field of QoS architectures. The work so far mainly focuses on QoS related to communication. As the importance of QoS has become evident, there has been some focus on standardised architectural support for QoS. International Organization for Standardization (ISO), Telecommunications Information Networking Architecture Consortium (TINA-C) and OMG are all working to incorporate QoS into their architectures [3-5], but there is yet no standardised Object Definition Language

(ODL) which supports precise specification of QoS. TINA ODL [6] is a superset of OMG IDL that enables the specification of operational and stream interfaces on computational objects. One of the additional features is support for QoS specification, but the particular QoS semantics to be supported has not been finalised.

In this paper we present an object definition language, ODL-Q, with support for specification of QoS. ODL-Q is based on TINA ODL and compliant with RM-ODP, extended with concepts from the real-time logic QL [7] using Object Constraint Language (OCL) [8]. The rest of this paper is structured as follows: In section 2 we describe distributed multimedia, including QoS and how it can be represented in application architectures. In section 3 we briefly present a number of relevant languages that are used as input in the design of ODL-Q. In section 4, the main body of this paper, we present ODL-Q and show through an example how to use it to include QoS issues in a computational specification. Conclusions and future work is presented in section 5.

2 Distributed Multimedia

Open distributed processing and multimedia is nicely covered in [7], here we focus on special multimedia issues, especially related to QoS. We conclude this chapter by specifying requirements for an object definition language with QoS support.

2.1 Multimedia and Quality of Service (QoS)

Multimedia applications are characterised by the capability to handle a variety of media representations in an integrated manner. In multimedia one distinguishes between discrete and continuous media. Discrete media like text and graphics do not have a temporal dimension, while continuous media like audio and video are time-dependent. Continuous media representations can be very complex, so multimedia applications must be able to reason about information with complex relationships, both temporal and non-temporal. A multimedia application normally integrates both discrete and continuous media, and there usually exist dependencies between the different media. A multimedia application often promises a certain level of quality of its services, and it requires some quality of service from its underlying infrastructure to be able to deliver that. Qualities offered both relate to individual media, for instance sound of CD-quality, and the relations between media, for instance lip synchronisation in a film.

A number of different definitions of QoS have been given. The general definition in [9] states that QoS is *"the collective effect of service performances which determine the degree of satisfaction of a user of the service"*. ISO's definition in [10], *"a set of qualities related to the collective behaviour of one or more objects"*, is related to RM-ODP which describes a distributed system as a set of objects. [11] presents a definition which talks about a distributed multimedia system: *"quality of service represents the set of those quantitative and qualitative characteristics of a distributed multimedia system that are necessary to achieve the required functionality of an application"*. Despite the different definitions, QoS is a general term that covers system performance, as opposed to system operation.

The need for QoS support varies between domains, with multimedia as the most prominent area where the need is high. QoS specifications can be divided into a set of categories, of which the most important are timeliness, volume, and reliability. Within each category a set of dimensions can be used to be able to quantify and measure QoS. Within the timeliness category, latency and jitter are key dimensions. Within the volume category throughput is a key dimension, while in the reliability category dimensions like bit error rate and frame loss are important.

QoS requirements can be specified on a scale from deterministically guaranteed where resource reservation is based on peak requirements, to best effort where one only hope for an appropriate QoS. Deterministic requirements are specified in absolute numbers, a more general approach is to use statistical specifications, where deterministic specifications are just special cases with probabilities equal 1.

The systems may implement QoS in different ways. At the one extreme, QoS requirements might be met statically during design and implementation by proper design and configuration choices (such as scheduling rules, network bandwidth, etc.). This will give well-defined behaviour, but without any flexibility. At the other end is the dynamic approach that lets the systems negotiate at run-time the QoS characteristics they need for their activities. This approach often involves an adaptive aspect by having monitors and corrective operations to take when the QoS level drops below a certain level. This approach is very flexible, the QoS policies can be changed at run-time, but the behaviour is not well defined. Most applications will need a combination of these two approaches.

Quality of service must be provided in an end-to-end basis from the information source to the information sink. The provision of the QoS may involve many components in systems involved, possibly with interdependencies. In a layered system this is obvious, QoS on a higher layer depends on QoS on the layers below. In a system of collaborating objects, the QoS interdependencies can be specified by contracts between pairs of objects.

2.2 Object Definition Language Requirements

The momentum of CORBA implies that an object definition language should be a superset of OMG IDL. Many systems exist that uses IDL, and IDL is familiar for a large number of system developers; it has become a de facto standard to express operational interface signatures. An object definition language should also be compliant to RM-ODP due to its influence on current and future standards in the area of distributed systems. IDL is already adopted in RM-ODP, but in addition to what IDL already provides, it should also be possible to specify stream interfaces and multiple interfaces on objects as specified in RM-ODP. RM-ODP also treats the bindings in object communications as first class objects. Another important requirement is the expression of behaviour. Behaviour must be expressible in a language that allows the complete external description of an object. Behaviour can, for instance, be specified using constraints as invariants on objects or interfaces, or pre- and post-conditions on individual operations. Also, the possibility to express both incoming and outgoing interactions is important to fully specify behaviour. In addition, an object definition language should be able to be a target language for a transformation of design models from Unified Modeling Language (UML) [12]. To fully comply with OMG, analysis and design models are expressed in UML. UML is a graphical language consisting of a set of modelling elements suited to express all aspects of a design, so a transformation without loss of information from UML to the object definition language should be supported.

The object definition language should be able to support multimedia systems. This means it should be able to represent information with complex temporal and non-temporal relationships. The real-time nature of many multimedia applications implies that the object definition language should support the notion of time. To be able to manage timing constraints, some objects should be synchronous. The synchrony hypothesis [13] states that reactions on a synchronous object should be instantaneous, meaning that reactions to incoming signals and subsequent generation of outgoing signals take zero time. Using this, we can create QoS specifications and manage these through synchronous objects. The synchronous objects can undertake QoS management without themselves being subject to such management. If this had been the case, we would have introduced an endless recursive structure to control the controllers, obviously not fruitful. Multimedia also makes demands regarding QoS specifications. It should be possible to state QoS annotations with interfaces and objects. QoS annotations usually involve quantification of some characteristics; hence the possibility to analyse and formally check consistency are important requirements. Finally, multimedia applications often involve communication between many parties. The possibility to specify multiparty communication is, therefore, essential.

3 Existing Languages

OMG IDL is the de facto language for specification of operational interfaces on possibly remote objects. The specification of the interfaces is independent of the implementation language. IDL supports multiple inheritance and exceptions, and has as default at-most-once semantics on operations that can be overridden to best-effort. Interfaces consist of attributes and operations, and these may be grouped in modules.

TINA ODL is a language to specify applications in the computational viewpoint of TINA. TINA ODL is for standardisation by ITU-T SG10/Q2. It is a superset of OMG IDL and supports both operational and stream interfaces, and allows multiple interfaces to objects. Aggregation of objects into object groups is also supported. TINA ODL supports QoS specification as service attributes on operations or streams.

OCL is an informally defined, typed formal language to express side-effect-free constraints. OCL is designed to be easy to read and write, and to be able to express unambiguous constraints. OCL is a pure expression language, not a definition language. OCL constraints are boolean expressions on model elements and their relationships.

4 ODL-Q

The need for expressing non-functional behaviour in terms of QoS specifications is evident. QoS is pervasive and should be considered throughout the lifecycle. In [14] we discussed the suitability of UML for the description of QoS from requirements analysis through to system design, and we concluded that OCL is one possible component in UML that can help to express QoS requirements and capabilities. A major limitation is the lack of a suitable target language for such a design that is expressive enough to cover the needs of multimedia applications. Multimedia applications require support for continuous media, QoS, real-time synchronisation and multiparty communication, all of which plain IDL does not support. In [7] these issues are discussed, and an extended programming model presented. Extensions include the support for signal interfaces that corresponds to real-time events. These provide the necessary support for real-time synchronisation and QoS management. Another extension is to include bindings as first-class objects, hereby considerable flexibility is achieved. This is also compliant with RM-ODP computational viewpoint. Finally, reactive objects are introduced to handle real-time requirements. Reactive objects are objects of which reactions to events take zero time, i.e. they adhere to the synchrony hypothesis. These extensions result in a hybrid object model that includes support for both synchronous and asynchronous interactions.

TINA ODL adds the support for continuous media through stream interfaces and multiple interface objects in compliance with RM-ODP. TINA ODL also specifies hooks to describe behaviour, although the actual behaviour specification is left for further study. Next we merge these ideas with the formality of OCL into ODL-Q, and add support for specification of behaviour. We introduce the concepts of ODL-Q by a modified video camera example from [7].

4.1 Stream Interfaces

The interface for the output of a video camera can be specified as:

```
interface videoCameraOut {
        source video videoOut;
};
```

Here we use the keyword source that means that this is an outgoing stream interface, in a similar fashion an incoming stream would be specified as sink. This is how streams are specified in TINA ODL. The type of the stream in the example is video, and the name of the actual stream is videoOut. video is not a predefined stream type, but it must have certain properties that can be defined in a type hierarchy like the one defined by Interactive Multimedia Association [15].

The video camera should also have some controlling operations. It should be possible to start and stop the camera, and perform a number of manipulative operations like pan, tilt and zoom:

```
interface cameraControl {
   void start();
   void stop();
   void pan(in short panDegrees)
        pre : (panDegrees < 180);
   void tilt(in short tiltDegrees)
        pre : (tiltDegrees <= 45 and tiltDegrees >= -45);
   void zoom(in short zoomFactor)
        pre : (zoomFactor <= 16);
};
```

This is a normal operational interface with extensions for operational preconditions. The preconditions are boolean OCL-expressions. Pre-condition specifications start with the keyword pre followed by a colon and the condition in OCL. In the example we state that the camera should not be panned more than 180 degrees and tilted more than 45 degrees in either direction, and maximum zoom is 16 times. Post-conditions would be specified using the keyword post.

4.2 Object Definitions and QoS Contracts

We have until now specified two interfaces, both of which relate to video camera. Unlike IDL, ODL-Q also includes the possibility to specify object templates:

```
object videoCamera {
  supports cameraControl, videoCameraOut;
  provides (videoCameraOut.videoOut.SE->forAll(
    signalEmission : Event | time(signalEmission + 24) <=
      (time(signalEmission) + 1000)) )
  and (time(videoCameraOut.videoOut.
    SE->firstSinceStop()) <=
  (time(cameraControl.start.SR->first()) + 10) );
  invariant cameraControl.start.SR->isEmpty() implies
          videoCameraOut.videoOut.SE->isEmpty();
};
```

The syntax of object template specifications is as far as possible based on TINA ODL. The object template is specified using the keyword object. An object supports a number of interfaces, specified after the keyword supports (similar to the implements-construct in Java). To be able to specify the QoS capabilities an object provides, ODL-Q introduces a new keyword provides. Here we also introduce a predefined sequence SR as used in [7]. SR is a sequence of signal reception events. A request from client to server followed by a response from the server to the client (interrogation) consists of four events: client signal emission, server signal reception, server signal emission, and finally client signal reception. All these events are accumulated in SR and SE sequences on the respective objects or operations constituting the history of events. The underlying event model and a formalisation of it is presented in [7], here we introduce the concepts as needed.

The first specification in the provides-clause states that the camera sends at least 25 frames in any given second. Using OCL we address the stream (videoOut) and specify that for each element in the history sequence of signal emissions, the moment in time the 24th frame after the current frame is emitted, will at most be 1000 ms after current time. The plus operator between the event signalEmission and 24 returns the event 24 places after signalEmission in the SE-sequence. We also specify that it takes at most 10 ms between a start operation is received and the camera starts to send frames. Using OCL, we again address the stream and specify that the time of the first element in the history sequence of signal emissions is less than 10 ms after the time the camera first received a start operation not having a subsequent stop-operation. Due to limited space, we have used a function (firstSinceStop()) to extract this particular event from the histories. (This is not legal OCL, cf. discussion in Section 5.) Finally, we have included an invariant specifying that if nobody has pressed start, the video camera has not sent any frames.

We use a special interpretation function time to specify timing constraints. This takes an event as argument and returns the time of the event. The timing information returned is relative to the event context (e.g. object), so timing information from one object cannot be compared with timing information from another object. The events are accumulated in SR and SE, and individual events are extracted using special predefined operations in OCL. SR and SE are OCL sequences that are special collections. OCL has a number of predefined operations on collections and sequences, here we have used forAll(), isEmpty() and first(). Other useful operations include exists, iterate, and select, see [8] for details.

For the model to be complete, a camera operator should operate the video camera. An operator is an active object that initiates activities through the control interface on the video camera. Introducing the keyword out, the purely outgoing operational interface of the operator can be specified as:

```
interface cameraController {
    out void start();
    out void stop();
    out void pan(in short panDegrees);
    out void tilt(in short tiltDegrees);
    out void zoom(in short zoomFactor);
};
```

Then the template of the operator that can actually operate the camera is simply specified as:

```
object operator {
    supports cameraController;
};
```

4.3 QoS Contracts

The video camera specified above delivers a service and provides some characteristics independent of the underlying infrastructure. In order for a video camera to be useful, for instance in a surveillance application, the video flow must be displayed. A video display window can be specified as follows:

```
interface videoWindowIn {
  sink video videoIn;
};

interface videoWindowStatus {
  signalOut videoPresented();
};

object videoWindow {
  supports videoWindowIn, videoWindowStatus;
  provides (videoWindowStatus.
    videoPresented.SE->forAll(
      signalEmission : Event |
        time(signalEmission + 24) <=
      (time(signalEmission) + 1000) ))
    and ( (videoWindowStatus.
    videoPresented.SE->forAll(
      signalEmission : Event | time(signalEmission) <=
      time((videoWindowIn.videoIn.SR->select(
    e : Event | e = signalEmission))->first()) + 10));
  requires videoWindowIn.videoIn.SR->forAll(
    signalReception : Event | time(signalReception + 24)
    <= (time(signalReception) + 1000) );
};
```

The video window supports two interfaces; one for display of the stream (videoWindowIn) and a signal interface indicating when a frame has been presented (videoWindowStatus). The videoWindowIn interface specifies an incoming stream (using the keyword sink) of type video. The videoWindowStatus interface specifies a signalling operation that sends out an event when a frame has been presented. Note that this is an outgoing operation, the signal is sent whenever a frame is presented.

The video is presented in a window, and the object template is defined by name videoWindow. The window provides some properties; it will present at least 25 frames per second and the first frame is presented within 10 ms from the arrival of the first frame. The comparison operation between the signalEmission event (from the videoPresented signal) and the signal reception event e on the video stream videoIn evaluates to true if the events belong to the same signal. These properties are however only provided if someone provides the requirements specified after the keyword requires. Here we state that the video stream must receive at least 25 frames per second.

4.4 Bindings

We have now specified a producer and a consumer with some requirements. The consumer delivers some characteristics provided its requirements are met. We must therefore specify the binding between the consumer and the producer, which acts as a contract between them. We treat bindings that require complex binding actions as first class objects, and can therefore simply specify the binding as:

```
typedef integer timestamp;

interface videoBindingIn {
  sink video videoIn;
};

interface videoBindingOut {
  source video videoOut;
};

interface qosControl {
  signalOut videoSent(out timestamp t);
  signalOut videoDelivered(out timestamp t);
};

object videoBinding {
  supports videoBindingIn, videoBindingOut, qosControl;
  provides -- complex OCL-expression left out
};
```

We first specify interfaces for the incoming and outgoing part of the binding through the interfaces videoBindingIn and videoBindingOut, having incoming and outgoing streams, respectively. We also specify an interface called qosControl that enables the monitoring of QoS through the signals it consists of. Finally we specify the actual binding object videoBinding. It supports the aforementioned interfaces and provides a rather complex QoS description that is left out for brevity. It states the binding should deliver 25 frames per second with a delay between 40 and 60 ms, and that proper signals are emitted through qosControl. These characteristics are supported, provided the binding receives 25 frames per second. It may seem like we now have only moved the problem of frame deliverance from between consumer and producer to between binding and producer as the binding has the same requirement on frame deliverance as the consumer. We have however introduced qosControl that can be used to monitor the QoS on the binding.

4.5 Reactive Objects

In order to manage timing constraints, we must end up in synchronous objects, or reactive objects. Due to the deterministic nature of reactive objects (they respond instantaneously), we can use reactive objects to anchor the timing dependencies down to deterministic behaviour, and thereby use these as managers without themselves having to be managed. Here we specify a reactive object with two signal interfaces, one for signals into the object and the other for emitting exceptions.

```
typedef integer violationType;

interface reactIn {
  signalIn videoSent(in timestamp t);
  signalIn videoDelivered(in timestamp t);
};

interface reactOut {
  signalOut qosViolation(out violationType v);
};

object qosManager {
  supports reactIn, reactOut;
};
```

Please note that the reactive object qosManager supports only signal interfaces and has no QoS specifications attached. Since it is a reactive object, its execution should be instantaneous.

4.6 QoS Binding

We have now specified a stream producer and consumer, and the binding between them. We have also specified a reactive object to be used as QoS manager. The missing specification is the binding between the video binding and the QoS manager:

```
interface qosBindingIn {
  signalIn videoSentIn(in timestamp t);
  signalIn videoDeliveredIn(in timestamp t);
};

interface qosBindingOut {
  signalOut videoSentOut(out timestamp t);
  signalOut videoDeliveredOut(out timestamp t);
};

interface qosControl {
  signalIn qosPoll();
  signalOut qosAverageDelay(out integer d);
};

object qosBind {
  supports qosBindingIn, qosBindingOut, qosControl;
  provides (self.qosBindingOut.videoSentOut.SE->forAll(
    signalEmission : Event | time(signalEmission) <=
    (time(self.qosBindingIn.videoSentIn.SR->select(
```

```
    e : Event | e = signalEmission) )->first()) +5) )
 and (self.qosBindingOut.videoDeliveredOut.SE->forAll(
    signalEmission : Event | time(signalEmission) <=
    (time(self.qosBindingIn.videoDeliveredIn.SR->select(
       e : Event | e = signalEmission) )->first()) +5) );
};
```

The specification states that the QoS binding should not take more than 5 ms to deliver the signals between the video binding and the QoS manager. The average delay can be polled using the `qosControl` interface, a `qosPoll` request initiates a `qosAverageDelay` operation.

We have now specified a system with QoS constraints. The constraints are specified as contracts, ending up at the reactive object `qosManager`. The QoS binding delivers the `videoSent` and `videoDelivered` signals from the video binding to the `qosManager`, and these can be used for QoS monitoring.

5 Conclusions and Future Work

We have through an example presented ODL-Q. ODL-Q is an object definition language with QoS support. The motivation for ODL-Q is to form parts of the computational specification of a distributed multimedia system. ODL-Q focuses on the type specifications of application components, and their run-time relationships, including QoS contracts through `requires` and `provides` clauses. We have introduced specification of outgoing operations, pre- and postconditions on operations, and invariants on objects and interfaces. ODL-Q is RM-ODP compliant; it can be used for specifications in the computational viewpoint. ODL-Q is also compliant with the object analysis and design meta-model standardisation from OMG [12]. In [14] we discussed how UML can be used to support QoS specifications, and we concluded that OCL is a useful tool in that respect, hence the usage of OCL in ODL-Q. In TINA ODL also initialisation and configuration is discussed, and the issues of security, transactions and trading are mentioned as areas of extension, all areas not yet considered in ODL-Q. In TINA ODL behaviour can be specified, although still only informally. Inclusion of outgoing interfaces, pre/post-conditions and invariants as we have shown is a step towards complete external formal specification of behaviour. A possible extension is to include state machine concepts as presented in [16]. An additional possible extension is to use it as a lexical specification in the information viewpoint. EXPRESS [17] is one candidate to include as basis for information modelling language. Extensions must be made to model complex multimedia information with temporal relationships. Finally, we hope to develop a compiler for ODL-Q that targets a real-time ORB like COOL or Sumo-ORB, and which generates code for a multimedia database. We realise that the usage of OCL can be tedious. The example showed that even quite simple designs could soon include large and repetitive OCL expressions, cf. the use of `firstSinceStop()`. More powerful function definition abilities are needed to collect complex OCL expressions into denotable entities. In an earlier version [18], it was possible to define parameterised constraints in OCL, making it more tractable and permitting recursive constraints. If ODL-Q were generated from an UML model (which would be the ideal solution), the tractability would be less of a problem.

This work is carried out in the context of OMODIS, a five-year project funded by the Norwegian Research Council (NFR). Main challenges in OMODIS are the development of an object-oriented modelling methodology and a QoS management that cover all elements of distributed multimedia systems.

References

[1]   ISO/IEC JTC1/SC21, "Basic reference model of open distributed processing, part 1: Overview," ITU-T X.901 - ISO/IEC 10746-1, August 1995.

[2]   C. Aurrecoechea, A. Campell, and L. Hauw, "Survey of QoS Architectures," Center for Telecommunication Research, Columbia University MPG-95-18, 1997.

[3]   ISO/IEC JTC1/SC21/WG7, "Working document on QoS in ODP," ISO 6-10 Jan. 97.

[4]   TINA-C, "Quality of Service Framework," TINA-C TP_MRK.001_1.0_94, Jan. 94.

[5]   C. Sluman, J. Tucker, J. P. LeBlanc, and B. Wood, "Quality of Service (QoS) OMG Green Paper," OMG, Green Paper om/97-06-04, 12/6/97 1997.

[6]   TINA-C, "TINA Object Definition Language Manual," TINA-C TP_NM.002_2.2_96, 22 July 1996.

[7]   G. Blair and J.-B. Stefani, Open Distributed Processing and Multimedia: Addison-Wesley, 1997.

[8]   UML Consortium, "Object Constraint Language Specification," Object Management Group Version 1.1, 1 September 1997.

[9]   F. Fluckiger, in Understanding Networked Multimedia, ITU, Ed.: Prentice Hall, 1995, pp. 338.

[10]   ISO/IEC JTC1/SC21, "QoS - Basic Framework," ISO ISO/IEC JTC1/SC 21 N9309, January 1995.

[11]   A. Vogel, B. Kerhervé, G. v. Bochmann, and J. Gecsei, "Distributed Multimedia and QoS - A Survey," IEEE Multimedia, vol. 2, pp. 10-19, 1995.

[12]   UML Consortium, "UML Semantics," Rational Software Corporation Version 1.1, 1 September 1997.

[13]   G. Berry and G. Gonthier, "The ESTEREL synchronous programming language: design, semantics, implementation," INRIA 842, 1988.

[14]   J. Ø. Aagedal and A.-J. Berre, "ODP-based QoS-support in UML," presented at First International Enterprise Distributed Object Computing Workshop (EDOC '97), Gold Coast, Australia, 1997.

[15]   Interactive Multimedia Association, "Multimedia system services - Part 1: Functional specification," IMA, 2nd Draft 1994.

[16]   D. Harel and A. Naamad, "The STATEMATE Semantics of Statecharts," Transactions on Software Engineering and Methodology, vol. 5, pp. 293-333, 1996.

[17]   J. D. Valois, "EXPRESS-X - A Proposal for a declarative EXPRESS mapping language," ISO ISO TC184/SC4/WG11 NO27, 1997.

[18]   J. Warmer, J. Hogg, S. Cook, and B. Selic, "Experience with Formal Specification of CMM and UML," presented at ECOOP'97, Jyväskylä, Finland, 1997.

DAVIC Goes to Internet:
Multimedia Service Interworking over
Heterogeneous Networking Environment

Sehyeong Cho, Youngmee Shin
{shcho,ymshin}@etri.re.kr

Intelligent Network Service Section
Electronics and Telecommunications Research Institute (ETRI)
161 Ka Jung Dong, Yu Song Gu, Taejon, Republic of Korea
Tel: +82-42-860-6121, Fax: +82-42-861-2932

Abstract. This paper describes the design and implementation of an experimental system for multimedia service interworking over heterogeneous network environment. The system, called MIDDLEMEN (MIDDLEmen for Multimedia ENvironment), consists of the interworking unit and the service broker, which cooperate to provide seamless multimedia service across different types of networks. The broker subsystem acts as a guide to multimedia services spanning possibly many networks. The interworking subsystem performs various interworking or translation functions under the control of the broker subsystem. In this paper, we mainly discuss the design of the interworking unit of the MIDDLEMEN. For real-time delivery of multimedia services across different networks, the interworking unit performs various functions, including protocol conversion, traffic monitoring and bit-rate control, service gateway conversion, and stream control conversion. Current implementation supports delivery of DAVIC-compliant VOD services to the Internet. We discuss various interworking issues, mainly at service level.

1. Introduction

Modern networking environment is characterized by the variety of networks and services. PSTN, ISDN, packet switched networks, Frame relay, internet, and ATM are such household names. All networks are different, and they serve their own purposes. Take, for example, two of the greatest phenomena - possibly hypes - in the last decade of the 20th century: the ATM network and the Internet. The ATM network promised a whole new kind of broadband network with full control of quality of service. Multimedia services seemed to have met the ideal network. Internet, or the IP network, is rather a poor choice – quite possibly the worst choice – for multimedia. These two networks are extremely different, at least technically. Another difference is that the Internet is exploding, while the ATM is still not penetrating the market as fast as many people expected a few years back. Here, we see a few differences in these networks. We have witnessed the proliferation of networks of varied types. It is not the case that one network is better than others in every respect, but different networks serve different purposes, and most of them have their own reason to exist. However, users are not willing to accept the heterogeneity of the networks; they simply want the same kind of perception, same kind of interface and the same way of using the services.

Two approaches are possible for satisfying the users. One is to provide a globally homogeneous network environment. If this happened, all network protocols shall disappear but one winner. Some people seem to believe that IP network, or the Internet will be such a network. While the authors admit that it is one possibility, and that the Internet will grow bigger, it is hard for the IP network to satisfy so many kinds of - possibly conflicting - requirements all by itself. Even if IP were the only networking protocol, Internet will hardly have a single standard for, say, Video-On-Demand. The other way of doing things is to provide service level bilateral interworking between one network and another. While this is not a "once-and-for-all" solution for every kind of networks, we believe it is one possibility, if we follow the GII's scenario-based approach[1]. In other words, while it is necessary to have $O(N^2)$ interworking devices for N networks theoretically, we can choose a few representative networks according to their commercial importance. This paper explores the second possibility.

The rest of the paper will be devoted to describing the design of the MIDDLEMEN, its broker and interworking subsystems. The first target of the experiment is the DAVIC-compliant VOD service[2] in an ATM environment delivered to the internet. Section 2 examines the difference between the ATM network and the internet. Section 3 describes the network architecture for MIDDLEMEN and a little detail inside the MIDDLEMEN. Section 4 explains various interworking functions: stream interworking, format and rate conversion, stream control interworking, and service gateway interworking. Section 5 concludes the paper with discussion of issues relating to practicality and future directions.

2. ATM Network and Internet

Although slower than many people hoped for a few years ago, ATM technology has been gaining increasing industry support, and maturing to become a dominant networking technology that will support various services requiring different quality of service. Meanwhile, the Internet, especially the World Wide Web service, has grown explosively due to the ease of navigation and abundance of information. We regarded the ATM network and the internet as two of the most important networks, as far as multimedia services are concerned

To identify the necessary interworking functions between the ATM network and the Internet, we enumerate important differences of the ATM network and the Internet that must be resolved in order to provide services across these networks in a seamless fashion.

● Difference in the transport protocols: The ATM network and the Internet use different protocol for real-time multimedia delivery. Thus the interworking unit should convert protocols between the ATM network and the Internet.

● Difference in the bandwidth: the ATM network can provide sufficient bandwidth for most real-time multimedia services; the internet is practically quite limited in the bandwidth. Thus the interworking unit must help overcome the bandwidth difference between two networks.

● Difference in QoS (Quality of Service) guarantee: The ATM network basically guarantees QoS. But Internet is a best-effort network, thus does not guarantee QoS. Thus the interworking unit must help overcome the difference in QoS guarantee.

- Difference in the way users navigate the cyberspace: DAVIC specification, for instance, is designed to fit ATM networks while internet community is standardizing their own way of doing basically the same thing. Specifically, DAVIC uses MHEG-5 [3] as the standard for service gateway (L2GW), while in the internet community HTML and Java seem to be becoming the *de facto* standard.
- Difference in the stream control methods and protocols: DSM-CC UU and RTSP are representative examples of stream control protocols, in ATM and internet, respectively.

These differences require interworking at various levels. In particular, in DAVIC terminology, differences in S1 through S5 information flows need to be resolved. They include network level interworking and service level interworking. Service interworking results in:

- Seamless service provision to the internet users by integrating with the ATM network,
- Simplified service provision that allows service providers to customize their service by interacting with MIDDLEMEN,
- And global service provision through virtual integration of service providers.

3. MIDDLEMEN in the Networking Environment

The definition of the MIDDLEMEN derives from the concept of Level 1 gateway and service gateway. Level 1 gateway (L1GW) enables the user to select the service provider. Level 2 gateway provides guidance for the user to select the content. MIDDLEMEN is the first point of contact for the users to the networked multimedia services. In other words, it acts as a level 1 gateway. MIDDLEMEN is not only a gateway for DAVIC domain, but also a gateway for the Internet users to DAVIC service providers. It conforms to the ATM protocol specifications in network aspects, and the DAVIC (Digital Audio-Visual Council) specification in terms of service. A MIDDLEMEN system consists of a service broker and an interworking unit(s) as shown in Figure 1 to provide seamless multimedia service between the ATM network and internet.

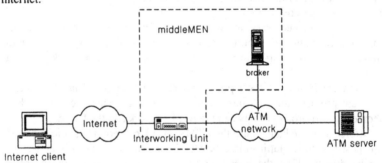

Figure 1. Physical configuration of MIDDLEMEN

MIDDLEMEN is a platform supporting control and management of communication capabilities between service providers and clients, and brokerage capabilities that are offered by the network to user applications. MIDDLEMEN can also provide various ability and functionality to applications. It represents the first contact point for the users to the service environment.

To support the service interworking in various networks, the MIDDLEMEN has to provide authentication and authorization function, the profile management for the users, terminals, and the servers regrading their home network, its QoS characteristics, the functional capabilities, personal preferences, and the servers's billing requirements and the like. Upon the first contact of the user to the MIDDLEMEN broker, the broker conducts user authentication, subsription, and preference management. It calculates an acceptable QoS, sends the negotiated QoS with user identification to the client and with server identification to the server. It also detects the differences between different service capabilities of clients and the server, selects the associated interworking assistant function supporting to the server or clients. It has limited capabilities to play and control the service, and performs the interworking service functions for the server and clients.

The service guide and navigation support helps users interact with the MIDDLEMEN for the purpose of selecting a service provider. Using this capability, the MIDDLEMEN provides the user's initial entry point to the service and it guides the user in service selection, thus users can search different program titles or previews of the program titles simultaneously. Also, MIDDLEMEN performs various functions on behalf of the server in case the server does not provide all necessary functions such as program guidance. Content-only servers are good examples. MIDDLEMEN, in that case can act as a virtual server with the service gateway capability in the distributed server environment[2]. Figure 2 depicts the services and functions of MIDDLEMEN. The circles represent the services in the picture. Only "ATM to internet multimedia" is described in detail in this paper. Rectangles represent functions. Shaded rectangles are implemented in the interworking unit and white rectangles are in the broker subsystem.

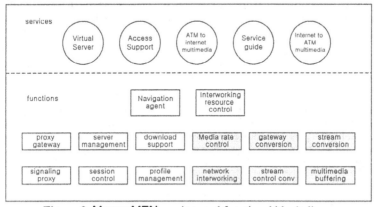

Figure 2. MIDDLEMEN services and functional block diagram.

This paper describes the design of the interworking unit of the MIDDLEMEN that provides the service interworking between the ATM network and the Internet. As previously mentioned, we must overcome the differences of protocol and bandwidth for the real-time transfer of multimedia service between the ATM network and Internet. Thus the interworking unit of the MIDDLEMEN does following functions.

- transport protocol conversion: It converts protocol of the ATM network and Internet to overcome protocol difference between the ATM network and Internet.
- Traffic monitoring and bit-rate control: It is a method to adapt bandwidth when the traffic of the Internet is increased highly during specific time.
- stream control protocol conversion: It converts the protocol for controlling the multimedia stream.
- service gateway conversion: Service gateway provides the function for guiding the user for navigating and selecting the content he/she desires. Different networks use different methods, therefore need conversion.

4. The Interworking Unit

The interworking unit contains functionality that is to be supported at the boundary between two network - in this case, the ATM network and the internet. Because the ATM network and Internet use different protocol for real-time multimedia service, the interworking unit of the MIDDLEMEN converts protocol between the ATM network and Internet. Stream conversion function denotes transport protocol conversion for video stream. Gateway conversion function converts level 2 gateway and stream control conversion converts stream control protocols. Other functions are not in the focus of this paper, but depicted in the figure for the sake of consistency.

4.1 Stream transport conversion

A DAVIC-compliant system uses MPEG-2 TS (MPEG-2 Transport Stream)[4] over AAL5 (ATM Adaptation Layer 5) to transport real-time multimedia stream. On the other hand, RTP (Real-time Transport Protocol)[5] over UDP/IP is widely used for transport of real-time multimedia stream in the Internet, although it is not exactly a formal standard. We therefore selected RTP as the representative (or at least a typical) protocol for stream transport in the Internet. In order for delivering the multimedia stream from the DAVIC domain to the internet, the interworking unit of the MIDDLEMEN converts MPEG-2 TS over AAL5 protocol to RTP over UDP/IP protocol to transfer multimedia stream of the ATM network to Internet users. In the actual implementation, MPEG1 streams are used instead of MPEG-2 streams, considering that current internet hardly provides the bandwidth for MPEG-2 streams, which usually requires 3 to 10 Mbps. Figure 3 shows the protocol conversion stack for the transfer of real-time multimedia stream. The original functional capabilities of MIDDLEMEN included multimedia format conversion to cope with the different audio-visual qualities. This would mean, for instance, converting MPEG-2 stream into MPEG-1 or H.261. Current implementation, however, does not include the format conversion functions.

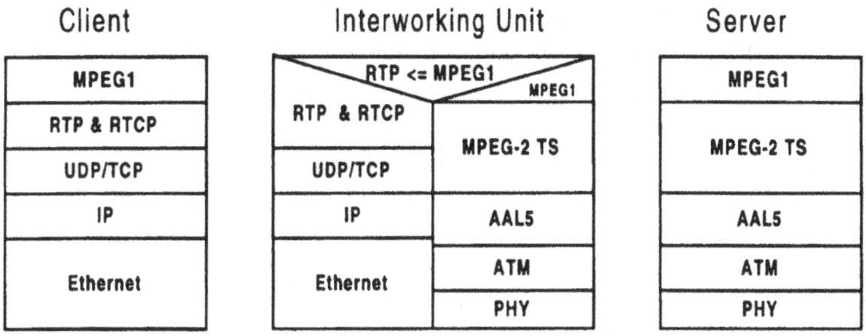

Client	Interworking Unit		Server	
MPEG1	RTP <= MPEG1	MPEG1	MPEG1	
RTP & RTCP	RTP & RTCP	MPEG-2 TS	MPEG-2 TS	
UDP/TCP	UDP/TCP			
IP	IP	AAL5	AAL5	
Ethernet	Ethernet	ATM	ATM	
		PHY	PHY	

Figure 3. Protocol conversion stack for stream transfer

4.2 Traffic monitoring and bit-rate control

Since the Internet is a best-effort network and does not guarantee QoS, the traffic situation will greatly affect the quality of real-time multimedia services. Unlike ordinary data services, multimedia service is extremely sensitive to delays and jitter, which in turn are affected by the amount of traffic and its pattern. A TCP-based stream transport will, in the case of increased traffic and increased packet loss, get even worse, due to the retransmit feature. RTP is a UDP based protocol, and therefore is better than TCP in that respect. However, traffic situation will, from time to time, make it impossible to deliver all the packets in time, even if they were sent by the server. In that case, it is better to send only part of those packets such that packets losses and delays are minimized, resulting in a uniformly degraded quality video, instead of highly jittered video. The interworking unit of the MIDDLEMEN, informed by the client about the traffic situation, controls the amount of packets.

RTCP, the companion protocol to RTP, provides mechanisms for data distribution monitoring, cross media synchronization, and sender identification[5,6]. The sender transfers multimedia data by using RTP packets. Then the receiver periodically sends RTCP packets that have information about the received RTP packets. Then the server (sender of the RTP packets and receiver of RTCP packets) calculates the traffic state of the network from the information it receives from the clients.

If the traffic on Internet increases, then the number of lost packets and untimely packets will increase. This triggers media bit-rate control to adjust the bit-rate by selectively discarding the packets. Thus we can minimize the degradation of resulting video quality, or at least give graceful degradation.

To show how the bit-rate control works, Figure 4 depicts the pictures in an MPEG video. An MPEG video consists of I-pictures, P-pictures, and B-pictures, as defined by ISO/IEC 11172-2 and 11172-3[7]. The encoded data are packetized in consideration of synchronization of audio and video. They are then stored as a stream. This structure is adequate for CD-ROM, but not for selective packet dropping, since dropping one packet to discard, say, a B-picture, may cause part of another I-picture. We therefore packetize the stream such that one packet contains information for one picture type. Therefore even if we drop a packet containing a B-picture, next GOP will be displayed normally.

With this packet structure, assuming there are 1 I-picture, 3 P-pictures, and 8 B-pictures in a GOP of 1.2Mbps video and 192Kbps audio stream, the priority of packet types (the reverse of the order of packets to drop first) are: I_1, P_1, P_2, P_3, B_8, B_7, B_6, B_5, B_4, B_3, B_2, B_1. This is because I-pictures are stand-alone pictures, whereas P pictures are dependent on preceding I picture or P-picture, and B-pictures depend both on preceding and following I or P pictures. In a normal state, all pictures are delivered to the Internet client in sequence. When the traffic on the Internet increases, the interworking unit begins discarding B-pictures, which are received on the ATM network from the DAVIC-compliant server. Table 1 shows the necessary bit rate of the stream when packets (pictures) are discarded according to the priority. The quality of the video of course degrades, but the client would be better off seeing the low jitter movie than nominally "high" quality movie which are devastated by jitters, delays and irregular packet losses. For many movies, the quality degradation was not very noticeable.

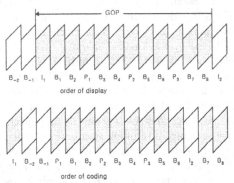

Figure 4. Pictures of MPEG video

Table 1. Necessary bit rate when certain packets are discarded
(200K/I-picture, 120K/P, 80K/B assumed)

packets discarded up to:	resulting bit rate (Kbps)
none	1392
B_1	1312
B_2	1232
B_3	1152
B_4	1072
B_5	992
B_6	912
B_7	832
B_8	752
P_3	632
P_2	512
P_1	392
I_1	192 (audio only)

4.3 Stream control interworking

Internet Real-time Stream Control

RTSP [8] is an internet real-time stream control protocol proposed in IETF, and currently is in the process of standardization. RTSP is the application level protocol for controlling the real-time featured data transport, and is able to control the multiple data transport channels. RTSP also supports the method for choosing the transport channel such as UDP, multicast UDP, and TCP, and supports the transport mechanism based on the RTP. RTSP messages consist of the request messages and the reply messages. Normally the user sends the request message and the server sends the reply message, but in some cases the server may send the request message. RTSP request message consists of the session setup or release type, stream control type such as play or stop, the request type of the specific stream information, setting or obtaining the type of the value of the specific parameter, and so on. Both the RTSP user and the server manage the state machine separately, and make transitions among the states according to the reply or request messages received. RTSP messages are summarized in Table 2.

Table 2. RTSP messages

Message type	Request message	Reply message

Request for the stream informatio n	DESCRIBE
	rtsp://host_addr/stream_name Version
	seq_no
		Version Status_code seq_no
		Reason_phrase
		Date : dd mm yyyy hh:mm:ss
		Content_Type : applicatin/x-rtsp-des
		Begin
		    title_name =
		    ...
		end

Sesion setup	SETUP rtsp://host_addr/stream_name Version seq_no Transport : tcp/rtp ; port=xx	Version Status_code seq_no Reason_phrase Session : xxxx
Stream play	PLAY rtsp://host_addr/stream_name Version seq_no Session : xxxx Range : npt = xx – xx Scale : xxxx	Version Status_code seq_no Reason_phrase
Stream pause	PAUSE rtsp://host_addr/stream_name Version seq_no Session : xxxx Range : npt = xx -	Version Status_code seq_no Reason_phrase
Session release	TEARDOWN rtsp://host_addr /stream_name Version seq_no Session : xxxx	Version Status_code seq_no Reason_phrase

ATM network real time stream control

ISO/IEC 13818 proposed the DSM-CC protocol for the purpose of the managing and controlling the MPEG-1 and MPEG-2 bit streams. Initially, DSM-CC aimed at the digital storage media(e.g., CD-ROM) application program of a single user, but later extended for networked applications, such as video on demand or interactive multimedia. Incidentally, the standardization has been accelerated because DAVIC chose the DSM-CC as the stream control protocol, and ISO/IEC 13818 finished standardization in 1996. DSM-CC considers three logical entities: the client, the server, and the SRM(Session and Resource Manager). DSM-CC message consists of UU(User-to-User) message, which is exchanged between the client and the server , and UN(User-to-Network) message, which is used between the client and SRM or the server and SRM. This paper focuses on DSM-CC UU part only. DSM-CC UU message is executed on the CORBA(Common Object Request Broker Architecture) environment, and the API of the DSM-CC UU message is described by using IDL(Interface Definition Language), and this API is called the DSM-CC UU interface. DSM-CC UU interface is classified into the core interface and extended interface. Core interface includes Base, Access, Directory, File, Session, Service Gateway, and Stream. Table 3 shows relevant DSM-CC UU interfaces and primitives.

Table 3. DSM-CC UU interfaces

interface	primitive
Base	Close(), Destroy()
Session	Attach(in serveID, in objName, out objRef) Detach()
Stream	Pause(in rStop) Resume(in rStart, in rScale) Status(in rAppStatus, out rActStatus) Reset() Jump(in rStart, in rStop, in rScale) Play(in rStart, in rStop, in rScale)

Stream Control Interworking

The stream control interworking enables the user to control the stream served from the heterogeneous network service provider, just like one controls one's VCR. In this section, we describe the translation of RTSP, internet stream control protocol, into the DSM-CC UU, ATM network stream control, for the interworking between internet client and ATM service provider. Figure 5 shows the structure of the stream control interworking.

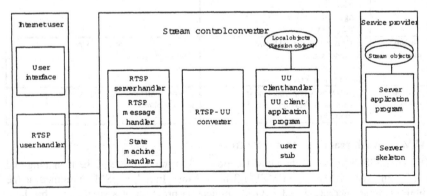

Figure 5. The structure of stream control interworking.

Internet client is endowed with RTSP user handler and user interface such as stream player. The service provider is endowed with server skeleton, server application program and stream type objects, which is created and freed dynamically by the server application program. The stream control converter located at the interworking unit of MIDDLEMEN is composed of three entities: the RTSP server handler, the RTSP-UU converter and the UU client handler. The RTSP server handler receives the RTSP request message from the internet client, and analyzes the syntax of the received RTSP message. Then the RTSP handler requests for translation of the received RTSP message into corresponding DSM-CC UU message, and generates and sends the reply RTSP message to the internet client. The RTSP-UU converter performs the translation from the RTSP message to DSM-CC UU message. The UU client handler receives the translated DSM-CC UU message, and then performs the proper actions relevant to the message type of the translated DSM-CC UU message. For example, if the translated message is a primitive of the session interface, then the UU client handler invokes the DSM-CC UN(user-network) function, and requests to the service provider for the creation or removal of a stream object, and then receives the reference to the created object. If the translated message is a primitive of stream interface, then the UU client handler sends the translated message to the service provider. Table 4 shows the mapping between RTSP messages and DSM-CC messages.

Table 4. Mapping between RTSP messages and translated DSM-CC messages.

RTSP message	DSM-CC UU message
SETUP	Attach
PLAY Scale : zz	resume(NULL, zz)
PLAY Range : npt = xx - Scale : zz	resume(xx, zz)
PLAY Range : npt = xx – yy Scale : zz	play(xx, yy, zz)
PAUSE	pause(NULL)
PAUSE Range : npt = xx -	pause(xx)
TEARDOWN	Detach

4.4 Service Gateway Interworking

Service navigation process is guided by MHEG-5 objects in DAVIC-compliant systems. MHEG-5[3] is a specification from the Multimedia-Hypermedia Experts Group. In the Internet world, HTML[9] is the *de facto* standard for hypermedia markup and navigation.   While HTML gained more popularity than MHEG, MHEG is richer in features. See Table 5 for comparison of MHEG-5 and HTML.   For the purpose of giving the internet users the freedom of using HTML-based browsing, the interworking unit translates the MHEG-5 objects on the fly. This also eliminates the need of CORBA in the client terminal.

Table 5. Comparison of MHEG-5 and HTML.

comparison items	MHEG-5	HTML
spatial dimension	3-dimensions	2-dimensions
temporal dimension	supported	not supported
location	absolute location supported	absolute not supported
reference to objects	Group ID, inclusion possible	URL, only reference
dynamic behavior	supported	not supported
events	supported	not supported

Since MHEG-5 is richer in features compared to HTML, it is not possible to translate all MHEG-5 objects into HTML documents. However, for practical purposes, such as VOD control, most objects are translatable. What is not supported in HTML is simply ignored by the translator. The service gateway conversion function is tightly coupled to stream control interworking function. For instance, the button objects for play or stop is translated into html, the user clicks at the "play" or "stop" button shown in the web browser, then the action is conveyed as an RTSP message, and then the RTSP message is translated to a DSM-CC UU message. Figure 6 depicts an example interworking scenario. Figure 7 shows MHEG-5 object displayed by an MHEG broswer and the translated html in a Web browser.

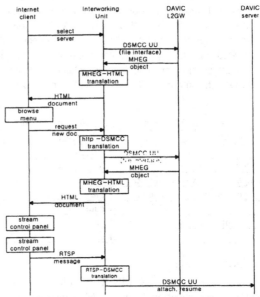

Figure 6. Example interworking scenario for level 2 gateway interworking.

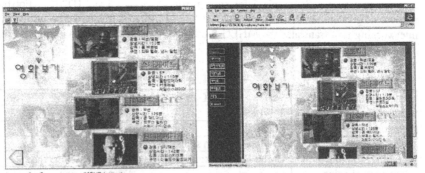

Figure 7. Objects in an MHEG-5 browser(left, courtesy Kwangwoon University) and translated html document displayed in a web browser.

5. Concluding Remarks

In this paper, we explained one of the MIDDLEMEN services, which is delivery of DAVIC VOD service to internet users. The prototype consists of a Solaris workstation that accommodates the MIDDLEMEN broker, a Pentium PC that translates MPEG-2 TS into RTP and MHEG into HTML and so on. Current configuration was not aimed at powerful multi-stream interworking for commercial use, but is able to provide only one stream. The net result of interworking by MIDDLEMEN is that the end users need not be aware that they are accessing service offered from a different network. Their terminal equipment need not have the DAVIC protocols and ATM interfaces either. The internet users might well believe that it is a service offered by an internet site. This is what we call a "seamless service interworking." Telephone users today are using telephone sets manufactured by a number of vendors. They talk to each other without any problems. They are served by a number of network operators, local or long-distance. They do not want to know how many network operators are involved in their calls and they do not wish to know the technical details such as A-law or μ-law. Multimedia service users basically want the same level of homogeneity. They just want to see what they want to see, without the details of networking protocols, streaming protocols, and the like. What is important to users is the content, but not the technologies or standards. MIDDLEMEN offers one way of fulfilling this requirement. The difficulty is, it is hard to provide $O(N^2)$ interworking functions for N different networks or services. In that case, we can take the GII's scenario-based approach, and select only a few that are most popular. It is yet too early to assess the commercial viability of MIDDLEMEN and the interworking approach. We will have to wait and see for the moment how networked multimedia services make their way in the market, from expectations and hypes to commercial reality. In the mean time, we plan to explore the possibility of creating a common middleware architecture for interworking, in order to accommodate interworking functions for various networks and services with more ease.

References

1. K. Knightson, "Scenario methodology and examples of use," proc. International workshop on Global Information Infrastructure (GII), Seoul, Korea, (Feb. 1997)
2. Digital Audio-Visual Council, "DAVIC 1.0 Specifications," (Dec. 1995)
3. ISO/IEC 13522-5 Information Tecnology – Coding of Multimedia and Hypermedia Information – part 5: Support for Base level Interactive Applications.
4. ISO/IEC International Standard 13818; "Generic coding of moving pictures and associated audio information", (Nov 1994)
5. 5.H. Schulzrinne, S. Casner, R. Frederick, V. Jacobson, "RTP: A Transport Protocol for Real-Time Applications", RFC 1889, (Jan 1996)
6. Busse, I., Deffner, B., Schulzrinne, H., "Dynamic QoS control of multimedia applications based on RTP," Computer Communications, Vol. 19, pp49-58, (1996)
7. ISO/IEC International Standard 11172; "Coding of moving pictures and associated audio for digital storage media up to about 1.5 Mbits/s", (Nov 1993)
8. 8.H. Schulzrinne, A. Rao, R. Lanphier: Real Time Streaming Protocol (RTSP), http://ds.internic.net/internet-drafts/draft-ietf-mmusic-rtsp-03.txt (135617 bytes, 7/30/97)
9. 9.T. Berners-Lee, D. Connolly , "Hypertext Markup Language 2.0," RFC 1866, (Nov. 1995)

A Temporal-Spatial Flow Control Protocol for ABR in Integrated Networks

Wei Kang Tsai, Lee Chuan Hu, and Yuseok Kim

Department of Electrical and Computer Engineering
University of California-Irvine, Irvine, CA 92697, USA
email: {wtsai,lhu,ykim}@ece.uci.edu

Abstract. Many end-to-end feedback flow control protocols experience the rate oscillations caused by latency phase shift (LPS). This problem comes from time-varying bandwidth and non-zero feedback latency. A temporal flow control (TFC) protocol called MTS (Multiple-Time-Scale) was proposed to significantly reduce the oscillations in our earlier publication [2]. In this paper, the class of temporal flow control is further studied and a fundamental theorem relating LPS rate oscillations to the ratio of feedback latency to available bandwidth window duration is proved. The MTS protocol is generalized and two propositions showing the advantages of the generic MTS protocol is proved. Simulation results show MTS significantly improves network performance in terms of stability, throughput and cell loss. In particular, MTS smoothens the output traffic very effectively, thus further reducing the traffic fluctuations.

1 Introduction

Rate-based end-to-end feedback flow control (FC) protocols in integrated networks such as ATM networks often exhibit oscillations in the link flow rates. Rate oscillations can occur for a number of reasons [9], but the type of oscillations caused by latency phase shift (LPS) has been a major concern. Such oscillations will occur at a link when the changes of the available bandwidth (AB) and the data arrival rate are out of phase: either the input rate is higher than the AB (overshoot), or the input rate is lower than the AB (undershoot). The out-of-phase phenomenon is caused by feedback latencies being large relative to the AB window duration. An overshoot will occur at a link if a switch informs the sources to increase their rates when it detects an increase in the AB of the link, but by the time when the data associated with the increased rates arrive, the AB window has disappeared. An undershoot will occur if the sources are requested to reduce their rates in response to a sudden reduction in a link's AB, but by the time the rates are reduced, additional bandwidth has reappeared.

Theoretically, LPS oscillations can be solved completely by decreasing the latencies to zero, which is impossible. While other methods are possible, our earlier paper [2] proposed a temporal flow control (TFC) approach which focuses on exploiting latency disparity among the sources. In [2], a new protocol called MTS (multiple-Time-Scale) was proposed. The fundamental idea is based on the observation that among all the sources crossing a link, some have short latencies and others have long latencies. The short latency sources will be able to respond to fast changes in AB while the long latency sources will only be able to respond to slow changes in AB. As long as a link has a healthy mix of short and long latency sources, the link controller can direct short latency (SL) sources to react to fast changes in AB, and direct both short and long latency (LL) sources to react to slow changes in AB, causing rate oscillations to be significantly reduced. This idea is the foundation of the present paper.

In [2,11], the concept of *integrated networks* was introduced. The word "integrated" is used in several perspectives: service, network geography and architecture. A distinguishing feature of integrated networks is that, both available bandwidths and sources have a very large range of variation. For example, cyclic video VBR traffic typically has periods of about 30 ms and has a ratio of peak to valley bandwidth of 2:1-7:1 [8]. The latencies in WAN and GAN range from a few milliseconds to hundreds of milliseconds. These large variations in latencies can cause the phase shifts to be very large and the oscillation problems to be very severe. For different integrated networks, the rate oscillation problems impose different degrees of difficulty. The problem is very hard if the connections have long latencies relative to the duration of the AB windows. Due to historical reasons, most current ATM flow controls attempt to solve the oscillation problem by forcing connections to slow down their response. Such an approach could make things worse as it introduces additional latencies [1, 3-5]. This feedback action may actually cause more burstiness or even oscillations in the face of dynamic background.

In this paper, the class of temporal flow control is further studied and a fundamental theorem relating LPS rate oscillations to the ratio of feedback latency to available bandwidth window duration is proved. The original MTS protocol proposed in [2] is generalized into a generic MTS protocol. Two propositions showing the advantages of the generic MTS protocol are proved.

For general temporal flow control, there are two dimensions in which the performance needs to be optimized: space and time. The space dimension refers to the use of physical bandwidth in the physical network, while the temporal dimension refers to the temporal variation in the bandwidth allocation. The generic MTS protocol presented in this paper focuses on the temporal dimension and does not optimize over the space dimension. The reason for the focus on the temporal dimension is that an integrated design for both the space and temporal dimensions turns out to be a major task and there is no way to address both dimensions in a short paper such as this one.

Given the emphasis on the temporal issue, there is no need to perform a simulation study with more than one link. (A simulation study with more than one link requires fundamentally the spatial considerations such as global fairness and global throughput maximization.) Therefore, in this paper we summarize the results of our previous simulation study on a single-link network from [2], showing that MTS significantly improves the network performance in many aspects, and highlight a number of technical issues.

In particular, we would like to draw the reader's attention to an added bonus of MTS. The generic MTS protocol with a simple queue control can smooth the output traffic very effectively, thus further reducing the traffic fluctuations. Recently, researchers (for example, [10]) have recognized the importance of queue control to keep the output queue at a nonzero threshold. The non-empty queue is used to reduce the fluctuations of the output traffic. However, a simple queue control does not work very well if the input traffic is a mixture of data cells from long and short latency connections. The response to the queue control from the long latency connections is too slow and this causes the queue control to lose its effectiveness. This problem is simply solved by using the MTS approach in which the short latency connections play the role of *virtual buffer* by fast charging and discharging the actual reservoir queues according to the short-term AB changes. Using MTS with simple queue control, the traffic output from any link can be smoothed very effectively; the effect of smoothing is directly proportional to the availability of short latency connections. Without MTS, such smoothing is practically impossible to achieve.

The rest of the paper is organized as follows: In section 2, the space-time fairness of temporal flow control is further discussed and the LPS theorem is proved. Section 3 summarizes the generic version of the MTS protocol while Section 4 analyzes the performance of the generic MTS protocol. Section 5 gives simulation results with additional discussions and conclusions in Section 6.

2 Temporal-Spatial Flow Control and LPS Oscillation

In an integrated network, even though not all applications are real-time in nature, the flow control has to address the temporal issues. This is because applications interact with one another and real-time applications are typically present in most integrated networks. To achieve high utilization and QoS goals, available bandwidth window allocations must match connection latencies. Therefore, temporal flow control, which is defined to be the group of protocols which generate control commands as explicit functions of time, is perhaps the best flow control class to provide QoS in the integrated network.

In the second half of this section, we shall prove a theorem relating LPS oscillations to the ratio of feedback latency to the AB window duration.

2.1 Space-Time Joint Optimization

One key feature of Temporal Flow Control is that there exist two dimensions of optimization: *space* and *time*. In the space dimension, independent variables are the bandwidth allocation at the physical links; in the time dimension, the independent variables are the temporal variations of the bandwidth allocation. Most existing flow control protocols are one-dimensional: space or time dimension optimization only.

However, in most integrated networks, there are strong time-varying interactions between the network (space) components. For example, in many integrated networks, the time-critical VBR traffic share the same links with non-time-critical ABR traffic. In each link, the available bandwidth to the lower priority ABR traffic is the bandwidth left-over after VBR and other higher priority traffic has been assigned their bandwidth. Therefore, the best form of temporal flow control is one that jointly optimizes both the VBR and ABR bandwidth assignment.

Given constant feedback latency (time), the well-known max-min fairness generates a fair allocation of rates while maximizing the link utilization. However, given constant space (for example, all connections are unconstrained at each link or all connections are able to follow the advertised rate at each link), a fair allocation of rate should depend on the feedback latency. Most works on fairness (such as max-min fairness) do not consider the time dimension, and they can be considered to be works on spatial fairness; the implicit assumption is that the network is operating at a steady state. However, if the available bandwidth changes continually, then the fair allocation of rates should be time-dependent.

In this paper, we focus on the time dimension and ignore the max-min issues. A complete space-time temporal flow control will be reported in a separate paper [6]. Notice that the class of credit-based flow control can be considered to be time-dependent flow control in the sense that the rates vary according to the dynamic changes (in time) of the available buffer size and bandwidth. Therefore, with the concepts of temporal flow control and space-time fairness, it is possible to study both rate-based and credit-based flow controls in a unified framework.

2.2 LPS Oscillations and Temporal Flow Control

To establish a theorem on LPS oscillations, we need to establish the notation and the formulation. We shall focus on a generic link j, and a generic left-over AB (the AB minus the total input traffic) window of duration T and bandwidth size AB_j. We shall consider the case where there is only one ABR connection with T_{ij} feedback latency (or response time) between source i and link j. Let C_j be the total capacity at link j. For link j, the CBR and other traffic will be ignored and the average VBR traffic is denoted by VBR_j.

Proposition 1. (The LPS Theorem) Assume that at time $t = 0$, the AB for link j is zero, and a left-over AB window with duration T and size $AB_j > 0$ is generated, and the flow control calls for the source i to use that left-over bandwidth of size AB_j. Then, there will be an undershoot, to be followed by a full utilization of the AB, which is to be followed by an overshoot. The average link utilization over the period $[0, T]$ is given by:

$$\overline{U}_j = \frac{VBR_j}{C_j} + \frac{AB_j}{C_j}\left[1 - \frac{T_{ij}}{T}\right],$$

and the buffer size needed to store the data during the overshoot period is given by:

$$S_j = AB_j T_{ij}.$$

Proof. The proof is straightforward and is omitted.

Notice that a similar theorem can be stated and proved for the case of a negative left-over AB window. In that case, the LPS oscillation is consisted of an overshoot followed by a full utilization and again followed by an undershoot. The buffer size needed to store the excess data during the overshoot transient period remains the same. It is obvious to see that as the ratio $T_{ij}/T \to 0$, the LPS oscillation disappears and the utilization improves to the ideal value; as $T_{ij}/T \to 1$, the LPS oscillation reaches its peak. The above theorem, even though is straightforward to show, is the foundation of all LPS oscillations and the foundation of the MTS protocol proposed in [2].

3 Generic Multi-Time-Scale (MTS) Protocol

The original MTS protocol was proposed in [2], which is a particular realization of the broader class of temporal flow control protocols. In this paper, we shall strip down all the less essential details and state only the basic features. The result is the generic MTS protocol. The MTS protocol is based on three key observations: First, the background traffic is time-varying and AB exists only in the form of time windows. Second, oscillations are caused by the slow response (relative to the fast speed of AB change). Third, there exist fast and slow responding connections in integrated networks. Therefore, if all of the AB is assigned to the fast responding connections, the oscillation problem is essentially solved. But the scheme is not fair to the slow responding connections. The fairness issue is a separate topic of research, for the generic MTS, the fairness doctrine is not specified.

Connection Classification: The connection classification is determined based on the latency of a connection from a switch. The connections passing a switch node is grouped into at least two classes: short latency and long latency. The Feedback latency between a switch node and a source is defined to be the round trip time between the switch node and the source. For simplicity, the round trip time can be approximated by the propagation delay. A connection can be considered as a SL connection at a node close to source and a LL one at a down stream node far away from the source. This means the classification is a local concept.

Left-over AB Window Estimation: In the generic MTS protocol, it is assumed that the protocol uses a reasonable estimation method to estimate the left-over AB window in term of duration and size. Left-over AB windows will be classified into at least two classes: short life (SL) windows and long life (LL) windows.

Left-over AB Allocation: For the two-class case, 100% of the short-life windows will be equally allocated to the short latency connections. The long-life windows are distributed to both short and long latency connections. The shares of the SL and LL connections in the LL windows depend on the fairness doctrine adopted by the protocol. For the case with more than two classes, each latency class has the priority to get most (or all, for the shortest latency class) of the bandwidth for the matching left-over AB window class.

Optional Queue Control: A simple queue control, which is designed to implement a reservoir buffer to reserve data cells for very short-term need to use (or un-use negative) left-over bandwidth can be attached. Whenever a queue is below a pre-specified threshold, it will be recharged to reserve some data cells.

4 Performance Analysis of the Generic MTS

First, we shall expand the notation and the formulation given in Section 2.2. In this section, only two classes will be considered: the short latency (SL) class and the long latency (LL) class. Let N_j be the number of ABR connections at link j. Let N_{SL} (or N_{LL}) denote the number of short latency (or long latency) connections, and P_L (or P_S) denote the proportion of the LL (or SL) connections at link j: N_{LL} / N_j (or N_{SL} / N_j). Let T_{SL} (or T_{LL}) denote the feedback latency of the short latency (or the long latency) connections. Again, assume that at time $t = 0$, a left-over AB window with duration T and size $AB_j > 0$ is generated. In this analysis, the non-MTS protocol is assumed to assign all the AB to all the ABR connections equally, while the generic MTS protocol will assign all the left-over bandwidth AB_j to the SL connections during the initial period $[0, T_{SL}]$, and during the rest of the period (i.e., during the period $[T_{SL}, T]$, the left-over bandwidth is equally assigned to all the connections.

Proposition 2. Assume that at time $t = 0$, the AB for link j is zero, and a left-over AB window with duration T and size $AB_j > 0$ is generated. Then the following is true:

(a) The link utilization for link j for the AB window under the non-MTS protocol, denoted by $\overline{U}_j^n$, is given by

$$\overline{U}_j^n = \frac{VBR_j}{C_j} + \frac{AB_j}{C_j}\left[(1-P_L)(1-\frac{T_{SL}}{T}) + P_L(1-\frac{T_{LL}}{T})\right], \qquad (1)$$

and the buffer size required for no cell loss is given by:

$$S_j^n = AB_j\left[(1-P_L)T_{SL} + P_L T_{LL}\right]. \qquad (2)$$

(b) The average link utilization for link j at time t for the MTS protocol, denoted by $\overline{U}_j^m$, is given by

$$\overline{U}_j^m = \frac{VBR_j}{C_j} + \frac{AB_j}{C_j}\left[(1-\frac{T_{SL}}{T}) + P_L(1-\frac{T_{LL}}{T})\right], \qquad (3)$$

and the buffer size required for no cell loss is given by:

$$S_j^m = AB_j[T_{SL} + (T_{LL} - T_{SL})\max\{0, P_L - P_S\}]. \qquad (4)$$

Proof. For any source i crossing link j, it takes T_{ij} to reset the ABR to the advertised rate, the effective link utilization contributed by source i is given by

$$\overline{U}_{ij} = \frac{(T - T_{ij})AB_j}{TN_jC_j}.$$

Summing over all the connections through the node j plus the VBR background:

$$\overline{U}_j = \frac{VBR_j}{C_j} + \sum_{i=1}^{N_j} \frac{(T - T_{ij})AB_j}{TN_jC_j}. \tag{5}$$

Equations (1) and (3) can be obtained by simply applying equation (5). Equations (2) and (4) take a little more thinking but the derivation is still straightforward. Q.E.D.

Assuming $T_{SL} = 1$ ms, $T_{LL} = 33$ ms (~3300 km), the AB window duration to be $T = 33$ ms (for VBR video traffic), and $P_L = 0.5$, (1) suggests that 50% of AB_j is wasted or is to be buffered. This is a very significant percentage and is highly undesirable. On the other hand, for the MTS protocol, the unused left-over bandwidth accounts for only about 3%.

Note that in equation (4), the second term is due to the fast response of short latency connections which function like a *virtual buffer* by yielding their bandwidth to long latency connections. If $P_S \geq P_L$, then a buffer of $(T_{LL} - T_{SL})P_LAB_j$ can be saved. Since $T_{LL} \gg T_{SL}$, the buffer reduction could be very significant.

In what follows, we shall show that the MTS protocol has a faster convergence than the non-MTS protocol to the maximum link utilization under a mixture of persistent and non-persistent sources. Let f_p (or f_{np}) denote the proportion of persistent (or non-persistent) sources. Obviously, $f_p = 1 - f_{np}$. A non-persistent source is assumed to send out no data cells for the period of time under study. Again, we focus on the time in the period $[0, T]$.

Proposition 3. Let average $U_j^n(t)$ (or $U_j^m(t)$) denote the link utilization for the non-MTS (or MTS) protocol at time t. Assume that SL connections are capable of utilizing the entire left-over bandwidth, then

$$U_j^n(t + qT_{LL}) = \{[1 - (1 - f_p)^{\lfloor (q+1)T_{LL}/T_{SL} \rfloor}]P_S + [1 - (1 - f_p)^{q+1}]P_L\}AB_j, \tag{6}$$

$$U_j^m(t + kT_{SL}) = [1 - (1 - f_p)^{k+1}]AB_j. \tag{7}$$

Proof. Let $U_S^n(t)$ denote the average link utilization contributed by the SL sources for the non-MTS protocol at time t. Then, $U_S^n(t) = f_p(1 - P_L)AB_j$. By straightforward induction, it is easy to show that

$$U_j^n(t + kT_{SL}) = [1 - (1 - f_p)^{k+1}]P_SAB_j,$$

$$U_j^n(t + kT_{LL}) = [1 - (1 - f_p)^{k+1}]P_LAB_j.$$

Equation (7) is the result of combining the above equations. For the MTS protocol, every incremental unused left-over bandwidth will be assigned to SL connections, thus, it is straightforward to use induction to show equation (7). Q.E.D.

If $T_{LL}/T_{SL} \gg 1$ and f_p is significant, we can approximate

$$U_j^n(t + qT_{LL}) \approx \{1 - P_L + [1 - (1 - f_p)^{q+1}]P_L\}AB_j = \{1 - (1 - f_p)^{q+1}P_L\}AB_j.$$

Thus to achieve 90% of AB_j, $\lceil q \rceil = \lceil \log \frac{0.1}{P_L}/\log(1 - f_p) - 1 \rceil$. Assuming $P_L = 0.5$ and $f_{np} = 0.5$, then $\lceil q \rceil = 2$, indicating that after $2T_{LL}$, 90% of AB_j is used. But, for the

MTS protocol, the number of iterations required is $\lceil k \rceil = \lceil \log 0.1/\log(1 - f_p) - 1 \rceil = 3$, indicating that after $3T_{SL}$, 90% of $AB_j(t)$ is used. If we assume $T_{LL} = 10$ *ms* and $T_{SL} = 0.5$ *ms*, the non-MTS protocol takes more than 12 times the time needed by the MTS protocol to achieve 90% use of the left-over AB.

5 Simulations

This section summarizes the results presented in our previous paper [2]. The MTS protocol was simulated using the NIST ATM Network Simulator package [7]. The network configuration is shown in Fig. 1. In order to demonstrate the performance improvement purely made by the MTS protocol, we used a simple configuration with one common link shared by all the VC's in the simulation and the buffer size is infinite. Host 1s - Host 4s are the sources of ABR VC's. In order to simulate dynamically-changing background traffic, a VBR VC is added, whose random peaks are at 78-102 Mbps and valleys are at 30 Mbps. It has a cycle time of 33 msec with 11 msec ON (peak) and 22 ms OFF (valley).

In these simulations, we used 1 msec of feedback latency as the boundary to classify between short latency (SL) and long latency (LL) VC's. Note that Host 1s and Host 2s are the sources of SL VC's and Host 3s and Host 4s are the sources of LL VC's. The performance of MTS protocol is compared with that of EPRCA. The parameters used in the simulations are as follows:

Common parameters: ICR = 7.75 Mbps, PCR = 155 Mbps, MCR = 0.2 Mbps, T_{RM} = 100 μsec, and N_{RM} = 31.

EPRCA parameters: AIR = 0.053 Mbps, DQT = 50 cells, MACR (init) = 1.492 Mbps, ERF = 0.9375, MRF = 0.95, and AV = 0.0625.

We ran the simulations for 300 msec. According to the simulation results shown in Table 1, MTS shows significant improvement over EPRCA in all cases. Note that queue size, delay, and jitter reductions are more important improvement than utilization or total cells received since the use of infinite buffer mitigates the utilization drop in EPRCA. Fig. 2 and Fig. 3 show the utilization of both protocols at the link between SW 1 and SW 2. Note that MTS maintains 100% utilization after about 1

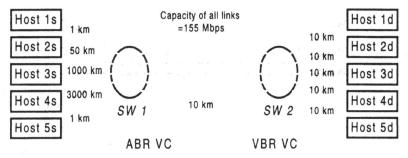

Fig. 1. Simulation configuration

Table 1. Simulation results of MTS and EPRCA

Performance	Persistent sources			Non-persistent source		
	MTS	EPRCA	Improv.	MTS	EPRCA	Improv.
Utilization	≈ 100%	< 100%		≈ 100%	< 100%	
Total Cells Received	75,458	68,138	10.7%	74,648	68,137	9.6%
Max. Queue Size at SW 1	453	1,094	58.6%	378	1,800	79%
Mean Queuing Delay (ms)	0.862	1.20	28.2%	0.705	2.80	74.8%
Queuing Delay (Std. Dev.)	0.715	1.268	43.6%	0.456	3.31	86.2%
Jitters (ms)	3	5	40%	2	6	66.7%

msec. Since the SL traffic can quickly fill up the available bandwidth, MTS was able to keep a small queue while achieving a high utilization as shown in Fig. 4 and Fig. 5. On the other hand, since EPRCA uses a slow start and very large buffer averaging under dynamic background, it was difficult for EPRCA to strike a balance between utilization and queue size. Even with a much larger queue, EPRCA's utilization frequently drops to a very low level.

The most significant advantage of MTS is that quick response nature changes the buffer requirement and SL connections function as if a virtual queue dynamically adjusts to the background traffic changes. From the simulations, the maximum queue size of EPRCA is almost 2.5 times that of MTS. Upon AB reduction, SL traffic yields its bandwidth to LL traffic and buffers the impact of high priority background changes from LL connections. Furthermore, the variation in queueing delay is smaller in MTS than in EPRCA as shown in Fig. 6. Note that MTS has a short tail comparing with EPRCA, which means that a shorter average delay and less jitters. Again, a smaller queue contributes to this better QoS performance.

Fig. 7 shows the total cells received (or total throughput) for both MTS and EPRCA. The MTS protocol produces about 10% improvement. One can see the major difference in the accumulative effects of the two algorithms. Since MTS almost always has a higher utilization, it has a better total throughput over EPRCA even for an infinite buffer size which helps EPRCA averaging the traffic in dynamic load. If we limit the queue size to be less than 1,100 cells, the total throughput of EPRCA would be worse.

To slow response LL traffic, the SL traffic compensates the background and makes the VBR and SL traffic combination less fluctuation so LL connections do not have to adjust as much (they can not adjust themselves to follow background changes effectively anyway). This virtual buffering nature of SL class is an important part of MTS flow control. On the other hand, without classification, EPRCA simply forces both long and short latency connections to respond the same way (with extra delay) and as a result it performs poorly in dynamic environment. Figure 6 shows a simulation result with a non-persistent source (Host 4s), which starts transmitting 1 Mbits of data at 100 ms to simulate web browsing. In this case, MTS shows a very stable performance and keeps the similar queue pattern as in the case of persistent sources while the peak queue size of EPRCA grows up to about 4.5 times that of MTS. It also takes 32 ms longer for EPRCA to transmit the data.

6 Conclusions

The fundamental idea behind the MTS protocol is the principle that *dynamically-changing available bandwidth should be allocated only to those sources that can use it timely*. According to this principle, connections are to be separated into feedback latency classes and the left-over AB windows are to be similarly classified. The left-over AB windows are to be allocated only to the proper classes that can utilize the windows in a timely manner. The number of classes should depend on the existing disparity in the feedback latencies in the network and the need to fine-tune the flow control.

The MTS approach has an added bonus of smoothing output traffic. With MTS, the short latency connections crossing a link act as a *virtual buffer*, and the reservoir queue can be controlled effectively and timely. This smoothing effect makes MTS to be an ideal protocol to be used at the edge of a backbone network, even if the backbone does not use MTS.

The broader class of temporal flow control is further studied in this paper. A theorem relating LPS oscillations and the ratio of the feedback latency to the left-over AB window duration is proved and two propositions on the performance of the generic MTS protocol are proved in this paper.

The current paper has focused on the time dimension, a forthcoming paper [6] will report a temporal flow control which treats both space and time dimensions in a unified framework.

References

1. The ATM Forum, "The ATM Forum Traffic Management Specification", v.4.0, 1996.
2. L. Hu, Y. Kim, and W. Tsai, "An Oscillation Reducing Rate-based Protocol based on Multiple Time Scale for ABR Flow Control", IEEE SICON '98, Singapore, July 1998. Also available from http://www.eng.uci.edu/~netrol.
3. A. Arulambalam, X. Chen, and N. Ansari, "Allocating Fair Rates for Available Bit Rate Service in ATM Networks", IEEE Comm. Mag., Nov. 1996.
4. K. Siu and H. Tzeng, "Intelligent Congestion Control for ABR Service in ATM Networks", ACM SIGCOMM, Comp. Commun. Rev., Oct. 1996, pp.81-106.
5. L. Roberts, "Enhanced PRCA (Proportional Rate-Control Algorithm)", ATMF 94-0735R1, Aug. 1994.
6. L. C. Hu, Y. Kim, and W. Tsai, "A Space-Time Fair Temporal Flow Control for Integrated Networks", To be submitted to IEEE Infocom'99.
7. N. Golmie, A. Koenig, and D. Su, 'The NIST ATM Network Simulator Operation and Programming', NISTIR 5703, Version 1.0, August 1995.
8. L.C. Hu and K-J. Lin, "A Forward Error Control Scheme for Real-Time VBR Traffic in ATM", Proc. Pacific Rim Int'l Symp. on Fault-Tolerant Systems, 1995, Newport Beach, Calif., Dec. 1995.
9. W. Tsai, Y. Kim, and C.-K. Toh, "A Stability and Sensitivity Theory for Rate-based Max-Min Flow Control for ABR Service", Invited Paper, IEEE SICON '98, Singapore, 1998. Also available from http://www.eng.uci.edu/~netrol.

10. S. Kalyanaraman, R. Jain, S. Fahmy, R. Goyal, and B. Vandalore, "The ERICA Switch Algorithm for ABR Traffic Management in ATM Networks", Submitted to IEEE/ACM Transactions on Networking, November 1997.

11. L. Hu, Y. Kim, and W. Tsai, "A Temporal Flow Control Protocol for Best-Effort Service in Integrated Networks", UCI ECE Tech. Report 97-12-01, University of California, Irvine, 1997.

Appendix: The Original MTS Pseudo-code

Parameters:

N_W - *window size, in unit of 10 ms.* ($N_W = 5$ for 50 ms).

$B[N_W]$ - *bandwidth window array.*

BL, BS - *long term and short bandwidth allocations, respectively.*

ns, nl - *number of short and long latency connections, respectively.*

P - *ratio of total number of long latency VC's to total number of VC's.*

C_L - *link capacity.*

Q - *current input queue size.*

Q_T - *queue threshold for rapid reduction.* ($Q_T = 400$)

Q_r - *reservoir buffer size.*

F - *additive fairness adjustment.*

IS - *SL allocation integrator.*

η - *multiplicative fairness threshold to avoid too high LL traffic mix* (= 1.2).

BRM - *backward RM cell.*

Switch algorithm:

```
1      IS = 0;  F = 0; //additive fairness F is reset every FW (=500 ms).
2      every T_MS (=1 ms)
3             ABR = total input traffic rate measured for ABR;
4             VBR = total input traffic rate measured for VBR;
5             TAB = C_L - VBR - ABR;
6             BS = max (min (BS + TAB, C_L), 0)
7             if (Q > Q_T) BS = 0;  //rapid reduction to avoid overflow
8             IS = IS + BS;  //recording the allocation for SL
9      every T_ML (=10 ms)
10            B[t mod N_w] = CL - VBR;
11            BL = min(min_{k∈N_w} B[k], P * B[t mod N_w] + F, η * P * B[t mod N_w]);
12            if (BL = P * B[t mod N_w] + F) F = 0;
13                 else if(BL = min_{k∈N_w} B[k]) F = F + P * B[t mod N_w] - min_{k∈N_w} B[k];
14                 else F = F - (η - 1)P * B[t mod N_w]);
15            F = F - (BL / (BL + IS) - P) * B[t mod N_w];  //unfair allocation
16            IS = 0;
17            if (Q > Q_T) BL = max(BL - (Q - Q_r)/T_ML, 0);
```

18   *else if* $(Q < Q_T)\, BL = BL + (Q_r - Q)\, /\, T_{ML}$; // *recharge the queue*

19   *if (BRM cell is for SL connection)* $BRM.ER = \min(BRM.ER, BS\,/\,ns)$;

20   *else* $BRM.ER = \min(BRM.ER, BL\,/\,nl)$;

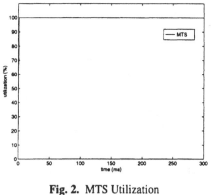

Fig. 2. MTS Utilization   **Fig. 3.** EPRCA Utilization

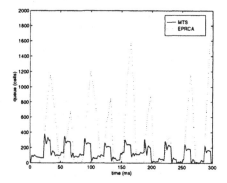

Fig. 4. Queue lengths for MTS and EPRCA   **Fig. 5.** Queue lengths for MTS and EPRCA
                                                     (Host 4s is Non-persistent source)

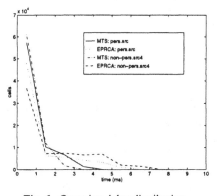
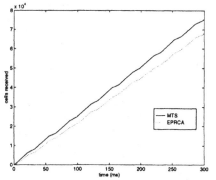

Fig. 6. Queueing delay distribution   **Fig. 7.** Cells received for MTS and EPRCA

A Low Complexity Congestion Control Algorithm for the ABR Class of Service

Jorge Martínez, José R. Vidal, and Luis Guijarro *

Departamento de Comunicaciones.
Universidad Politcnica de Valencia. Spain.
jmartinez@upvnet.upv.es

Abstract A new generation of systems called Networked Multimedia Systems are currently being the subject of intense study. These systems require a high throughput and QoS guarantees. The Broadband Integrated Service Digital Network (B-ISDN) based on the Asynchronous Transfer Mode (ATM) provides these requirements in an efficient manner. A new ATM service category, the Available Bit Rate (ABR) service, will systematically and dynamically allocate available bandwidth to users by controlling the flow of traffic with a closed-loop feedback mechanism. The ABR service was initially design to support data traffic but recently there has been much interest in using ABR to support voice and video applications [9]. In this scenario, the voice and video connections, which may require small delays, and the bursty data connections are multiplexed on different queues at the switches. An admission control policy over the real-time connections is usually required to guarantee that the end to end delay is kept below a target. With explicit rate feedback the sources can adapt faster to the new network conditions achieving in this way less queueing delays and cell-loss rates.

The CAPC algorithm was suggested by the ATM Forum as an explicit rate feedback squeme with low implementation complexity. It has received little attention in the literature because the value of its parameters must be tuned carefully to avoid oscillations. We propose a new algorithm called CAPAC that achieves an oscillations free behaviour and at the same time obtains good performance.

1   Introduction

The Asynchronous Transfer Mode (ATM) is the multiplexing and switching technique that supports the Broadband Integrated Services Digital Network (B-ISDN). The B-ISDN has been designed with the objective of supporting applications that require a guarantee for the Quality of Service (QoS) that they will get from the network. The network is able to guarantee the QoS that the applications request by providing different time and space priorities to each connection.

---

* This work was supported by the Spanish Science and Technology Commission (CI-CYT) under Grant TIC96-0680.

Both the ATM Forum [5] and the International Telecommunications Union –
Telecommunications Sector (UIT-T) [6] define a set of service classes that can be
used by applications according to their QoS requirements. These classes of service
can be classified into three groups: those that provide quantitative assurances,
those that provide qualitative assurances and those that provide no assurances.
The first group is commonly used by the so called "real time" applications, while
the other two are used by data applications.

The ABR class of service was initially conceived to support data traffic. Its
service model is based on the *best-effort* paradigm but enhanced by some specific characteristics. First, its ability to provide *fair sharing* of the available resources among the contending ABR connections. Second, a closed-loop feedback
mechanism that allows the network to send personalised signals to the sources[1].
The sources use this information to adjust their transmission rate in accordance
with the congestion state of the network, achieving in this way minimum losses.
This is the so called "reactive congestion control mechanism", that is orders
of magnitude faster, and therefore more efficient, than the reactive congestion
mechanisms provided by conventional data networks like the Internet [11].

Real-time applications that do not require strict QoS bounds and that can
adapt with changing network conditions have been called quasi-real-time by
some authors [3]. These applications can obtain substantial benefits by using
ABR connections. These benefits can be summarised in the following three aspects. First, quasi-real-time applications typically require some guarantee on
bandwidth, for example a minimum encoding rate for a video stream, but can
take advantage of spare bandwidth. This can be supported by an ABR connection defining a Minimum Cell Rate (MCR) at connection set up. Second,
when explicit rate feedback is used and the ABR connections supporting quasi-
real-time applications are multiplexed on a dedicated queue at the switches, the
cell transfer delay is more predictable because the congestion control mechanism
keeps the queues almost empty, as it will be shown later. And third, the feedback
mechanism keeps the sources informed of the available bandwidth they have at
their disposal. This information can be used by the quantization logic to adapt
quickly to new network conditions.

This paper focuses on the study of the congestion control mechanism proposed by the ATM Forum for the ABR class of service [5]. The ATM Forum
has standardised the source behaviour, e.g. the way the sources react to the
congestion control signals sent by the network. But, to allow for some degree of
product differentiation, it has left unspecified the algorithm used by switches to
estimate the available bandwidth share (*fair share*) that should be allocated to
each ABR connection.

---

[1] In this case, the term "source" instead of "application" has been used because the
congestion control mechanism that we are referring to is located at the ATM layer,
and its interface is not accessible to the application. Nevertheless, the application
could have an indirect perception of it by the backpressure signals sent by the ATM
layer as a consequence of buffer shortage.

In particular, this paper proposes a new low complexity switch algorithm called CAPAC (Congestion Avoidance with Proportional *Adaptive* Control) that substantially improves the performance of a previous proposal made by Barhart in [1] called CAPC (Congestion Avoidance with Proportional Control) algorithm. The new CAPAC algorithm is much more robust and its parameters are independent of the network configuration, eliminating the need to perform a fine tuning of the parameters required by the CAPC algorithm.

The rest of the paper is structured as follows. In section 2 we describe the elements that compose the ABR class of service. In particular, we focus on the feedback mechanism and on the reaction of the Source End Systems (SESs) to feedback signals. In section 3 we present the simulation model used to evaluate the new algorithm proposed. In section 4 we characterise the ABR switch algorithms according to their implementation complexity. In section 5 we describe the CAPC algorithm and provide some simulation results. In section 6 we define the new CAPAC algorithm and we show simulation results that substantiate our claims. In section 7 we state the conclusions.

2 Elements of the ABR Class of Service

The elements that compose the ABR class of service are: i) the Source and Destination end Systems (SES and DES) protocols; ii) the switches; iii) the feedback mechanism; iv) the virtual source/virtual destination systems; and v) the Usage Parameter Control/Network Parameter Control (UPC/NPC) mechanisms. A detailed description of these elements can be found in [3]. Here, we would like to briefly review both the feedback mechanism and the actions taken by SESs and DESs when feedback signals are received. A detailed description of the SES and DES behaviour can be found in [8].

The SES must perform two distinctive actions during its operation. First, it has to insert special Resource Management (RM) cells into the normal flow of data cells. These RM cells go all the way to the DES, where they will be sent back to the SES crossing the same switches. The RM cells support the feedback signals from the network towards the SES. Second, it must adapt its transmission rate according to the feedback signals received from the network. The format of the RM cells has been defined in [5]. Here we would like to describe only the most relevant fields:

- Direction (DIR) (1 bit). Shows if the RM cell is a forward (FRM) or a backward (BRM) cell. The RM cells transmitted by the source are FRM cells. When they are received by the DES its DIR bit is changed and retransmitted as BRM cells.
- Congestion Indication (CI) (1 bit). It is set by a switch when it experiences congestion.
- No Increase (NI) (1 bit). It is set by a switch to prevent the SES from increasing its transmission rate.
- Explicit Rate (ER). It is initialised by the SES to the Peak Cell Rate (PCR). The PCR is defined during the connection set up phase and establishes the

maximum cell rate that the SES wishes to transmit to. The switch algorithms compare the value of the ER field to their own estimation of the fair share and overwrite the former with its own estimation when the value of the ER field is greater. Many switch algorithms perform these actions only upon the BRM cells, but other also upon the FRM cells.

The SES behaviour is determined by a set of parameters, like the PCR and the values of some internal variables like the Allowed Cell Rate (ACR). The value of the ACR defines the maximum rate a SES is allowed to transmit to at a given time. When a SES receives a BRM cell it compares its ER field to the ACR, if ER is smaller it overwrites ACR with ER. If ER is greater and the NI field is not set, the SES can increase its ACR using the following additive process:

$$ACR = ACR + RIF \times PCR \tag{1}$$

where RIF is the Rate Increase Factor, a parameter defined at connection set up. The new ACR value should never be greater than ER.

3 Performance Evaluation and Simulation Model

Some of the objectives that must be met by the ABR switch algorithms are: i) maximise the utilisation of the available bandwidth; ii) minimise the cell loss; iii) allocate shares of the available bandwidth to the contending connections according to the fairness criteria chosen by the network operator[2]; and iv) converge as fast as possible to a stable situation when the available bandwidth changes its value. A fast convergence to the new situation will help to achieve less losses and better link utilisation.

The parameters that have been selected to evaluate the performance of the ABR switch algorithms are: i) The instantaneous value of the ACR of the SESs, which will help us to measure the degree of fairness that can be obtained; ii) the instantaneous occupation of the queues in the switches; and iii) the instantaneous link utilisation. In this work we have chosen a switch architecture with queues only at the output ports. At each queue, the cells are served using a FIFO discipline. The queues have been dimensioned generously to avoid losses.

The performance evaluation study has been done by simulation due to the limitations imposed by the analytical models. The ATM Forum has defined a set of test configurations, each of them designed to represent real scenarios of different complexity. The configurations that have been selected in this work are the Parking Lot and the Generic Fairness Configuration 1 (GFC1), the later proposed by Simcoe in [12]. We will only show simulation results using the Parking Lot because is this configuration which creates a more demanding scenario. This configuration is shown in Fig.1. For the simulations we use MAN distances, that

---

[2] Different fairness criteria are possible, see for example [14]. In this work we have chosen the Max-Min criteria [2].

is, the backbone links are 50 Km long and the access links 0.2 Km long. The propagation delay is 5 μs/Km.

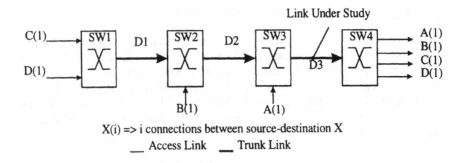

X(i) => i connections between source-destination X
___ Access Link   ___ Trunk Link

Figure1. The Parking Lot Configuration

Two scenarios have been considered to evaluate the transient behaviour of the switch algorithm. The first one evaluates how fast a new connection obtains its own share of bandwidth when others already share all the available bandwidth and how fair is the allocation. The second one evaluates how fast the algorithm handles changes in the available bandwidth due to the existence of higher priority "background traffic". In both cases we use persistent sources because they provide us with results that are easier to interpret.

The first scenario will be simulated by delaying the instant at which the sources start transmitting. Thus, in the Parking Lot configuration the source A starts transmitting at 0 ms., sources B and C start at 20 ms. and source D starts at 30 ms. The second scenario will be simulated by forcing step changes in the available bandwidth of the backbone link labelled as "link under study" in Fig.1. The first step change occurs at 50 ms. and halves the available bandwidth, that is, it reduces it from 150 Mbit/s to 75 Mbit/s. The second step change occurs at 100 ms. and restores the available bandwidth to its original value, that is, it increases it from 75 Mbit/s to 150 Mbit/s.

The value of the SES parameters that have been used for all the simulations are shown in Tab.1. As it can be observed, the use-it-or-loose-it (UILI) mechanism has been switched off by initialising ADTF to a big enough value. The ACR reduction mechanism that is activated when no BRM cells are been received has also been switched off by initialising Crm and CDF conveniently. The PCR value that has been chosen corresponds to 150 Mbit/s and emulates the capacity of a STM-1 link without overhead.

Table1. SES parameter definition.

PCR	354 cells/ms	Nrm	32	Crm	1000
MCR	PCR/1000	Mrm	2	CDF	0
ICR	PCR/100	Trm	10 ms	TCR	10 cells/s
TBE	-	ADTF	10 s	RIF	1/16
FRTT	-			RDF	1/16

4 Classification of ABR Switch Algorithms

Different criteria have been proposed to characterise an ABR switch algorithm based on its implementation complexity. One of them focuses on its storage requirements while another focuses on the number of computations.

Some algorithms require to store a reduced set of variables that define the state of the aggregated traffic while others require a set of variables per connection. Examples of the first group of algorithms are the EPRCA (Enhanced Proportional rate Control Algorithm) algorithm proposed by Roberts in [10] and the CAPC. One example of the second group of algorithms is the ERICA (Explicit Rate Indication for Congestion Avoidance) algorithm proposed by Jain in [7].

The number of computations required by different algorithms can vary enormously from one algorithm to another. Most of them require to perform a small number of computations when a BRM cell is received. For example, comparisons, computing the result of an equation that includes additions, multiplications and divisions, and writing into a few registers. On the other hand, when a BRM cell is received some algorithms require to access the state variables of each connection and to perform the computations described before for each connection, for example the algorithm described in [4].

Another interesting classification criteria focuses on the technique used to detect congestion. The algorithms that where initially proposed, like the EPRCA, detected congestion when the number of cells at the queue was beyond a predefined threshold. A later enhancement proposed by Siu and Tzeng in [13] suggested to detect congestion when the derivative of the $Q(t)$ function were positive, being $Q(t)$ the instantaneous queue length. In general, $Q(t)$ in these algorithms tend to oscillate even in the absence of external perturbations, this tends to increase the convergence time of the algorithms and increases the cost of the switches because more memory is required to obtain a low loss rate.

A later generation of algorithms detected congestion by measuring a parameter called Load Factor (LF). The LF is the ratio between the Input Rate (IR), that is, the aggregated cell rate at the entrance of the output port queue and the available bandwidth given as a cell rate. In this algorithms the congestion is detected when LF>1. This technique is used for example with the CAPC or the ERICA algorithms. To estimate IR, the algorithm adds up the number of cells received during a measurement interval and divides it by the duration of the interval. A measurement interval ends when N cells have been received or when a timer elapses.

The algorithms that use the value of LF as a congestion indication make also use of a technique called congestion avoidance. This technique is based on using the Target Rate (TR) instead of the available bandwidth to compute LF, where the Target Rate is a percentage, say 95%, of the available bandwidth given as a cell rate. Using this technique the queues remain empty once the algorithm has converged to a steady state situation.

5 The CAPC Algorithm

At the end of each measurement interval the CAPC algorithm computes the Load Factor and estimates the Fair Share (FS) that corresponds to each connection using the following expression:

$$FS_n = FS_{n-1} \times ERX_n \tag{2}$$

where FS_{n-1} is the last estimation of the FS and ERX_n is a variable that is computed each measurement interval by the following expressions:

$$ERX_n = \begin{cases} \min\{ERU, 1 + (1 - LF_n) \times Rup\} & \text{if } LF_n \leq 1 \\ \max\{ERF, 1 + (1 - LF_n) \times Rdn\} & \text{if } LF_n > 1 \end{cases} \tag{3}$$

As it can be observed, at each measurement interval the value of ERX is adapted following a linear function to keep complexity small. The adaptation functions are controlled by four constants. Rup and Rdn define how fast the adaptation process takes place, while ERU and ERF define an upper and a lower bound for ERX respectively.

Table2. CAPC algorithm parameter definition as suggested by Barnhart in [1].

Utilisation Factor = 95 %	ERU = 1.5
Qthreshold = 20 cells	ERF = 0.5
N = 100 cells	Rup = 0.1
T = 1 ms	Rdn = 0.8

The algorithm only processes the BRM cells. When a BRM cell is received if its ER field is bigger than FS then the ER field is overwritten with FS. Additionally, while the queue length is beyond a threshold (Qthres) the algorithm sets the NI bit of all the BRM cells.

The value of the adaptation constants must be chosen carefully to avoid oscillations. Tab.2 displays the values of the algorithm parameter as suggested by Barnhart in [1]. With these values for the adaptation constants, the CAPC algorithm performs poorly because it adapts too slowly to step bandwidth changes, as it shown in Fig.2.

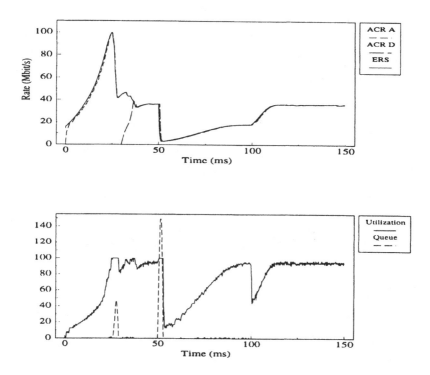

Figure2. Instantaneous Values (SESs ACRs and Link Utilisation and Port Queue) for the CAPC Algorithm with Rup=0.1 and Rdn=0.8

A faster response is achieved using Rup=0.5 and Rdn=1.0, but unfortunately with these new higher values the algorithm oscillates, as can be seen in Fig.3.

6   The CAPAC Algorithm

The CAPAC algorithm suggests a new technique to solve the problem of finding the proper definition for Rup and Rdn for each network configuration and set of connections.

As we said before, the CAPC algorithm achieves a faster response when high values for Rup and Rdn are chosen but this advantage comes at the expense of a higher probability of instabilities. What it would be needed is another degree of adaptation by which the value of the constants would change with LF as well. That is, it would be desirable that the adaptation constants would have high values when LF is far from LF=1. At the same time, as LF gets close to its optimum, the constants should decrease their value to obtain a smooth convergence.

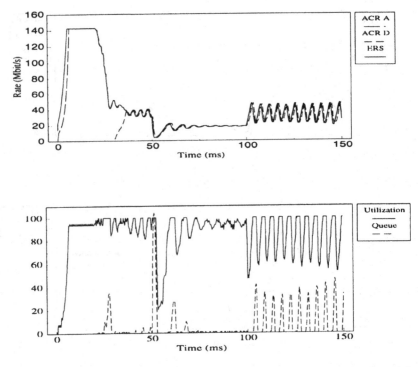

Figure3. Instantaneous Values (SESs ACRs and Link Utilisation and Port Queue) for the CAPC Algorithm with Rup=0.5 and Rdn=1.0

In the CAPAC algorithm the value of Rup and Rdn adapt with LF following a linear function to minimise the implementation complexity. The new adaptation function is:

$$
\begin{aligned}
\text{Rup}_n &= \min\{\text{MaxRup}, \text{MinRup} + (1 - \text{LF}_n) \times \text{KRup}\} && \text{if } \text{LF}_n \leq 1 \\
\text{Rdn}_n &= \max\{\text{MaxRdn}, \text{MinRdn} + (\text{LF}_n - 1) \times \text{KRdn}\} && \text{if } \text{LF}_n > 1
\end{aligned}
\tag{4}
$$

The values chosen for the constants are: MinRup=0.1, KRup=1.0, MaxRup = 0.5, MinRdn=0.8, KRdn=0.5, MaxRdn=1.0 . It has been demonstrated by simulation that the convergence of the algorithm is independent of them, at least, when they take reasonable values, say ±50% of the given values.

Fig.4 displays the results of a simulation in the same scenario as before, that is, the Parking Lot configuration with step changes in the available bandwidth. As can be seen, the peak values of the Q(t) function are lower. This occurs at the expense of a small reduction of the link utilisation at the time the available bandwidth changes take place.

The CAPAC algorithm is characterised by an overreaction during congestion periods. This overreaction is in general desirable because it helps to empty the

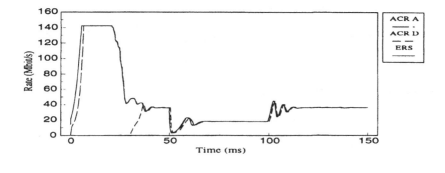

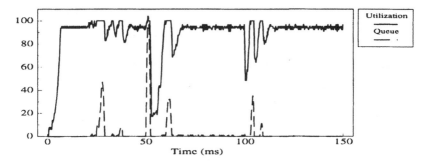

Figure4. Instantaneous Values (SESs ACRs and Link Utilisation and Port Queue) for the CAPAC Algorithm with Rup=0.5 and Rdn=1.0

queues rapidly and therefore it reduces the transfer delay and the loss rate. This behaviour is not shown by other ABR algorithms, like for example the ERICA. This algorithm adjust the ACRs of the SESs to make IR equal to TR very quickly. In this scenario, when congestion vanishes the link has almost no spare capacity to empty the queue.

For example, when TR is set to 95% of the link capacity then only 5% of the link capacity can be dedicated to empty the queue.

Fig.5 shows the results of a simulation in the same scenario as before but using the ERICA algorithm with a measurement interval of 60 cells. As can be seen, the time it takes to empty the queue is now considerably longer.

The new CAPAC algorithm is specially suited for MAN scenarios. The participation of connections with larger Fixed Round Trip Times (FRTT) does not represent a limitation in many practical configurations because their slow response is compensated by the faster reaction of other sources closer to the switch. Nevertheless, it is convenient to limit the speed with which the sources with long FRTTs occupy bandwidth by setting their RIF to a small value. As stated in [5], the network knows the value of the FRTT for each connection because it must be supplied to the SES at connection set up.

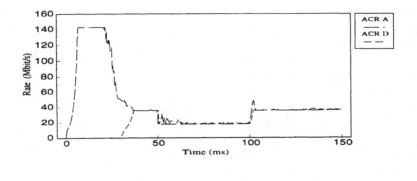

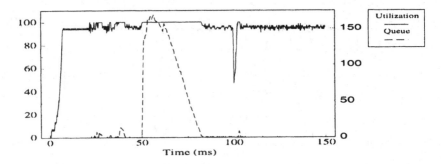

Figure5. Instantaneous Values (SESs ACRs and Link Utilisation and Port Queue) for the ERICA Algorithm.

7 Conclusions

In this paper we have proposed a new switch algorithm for the ABR class of service that adapts by it self to the network configuration and eliminates the need to perform a fine tuning of the parameters required by the CAPC algorithm. The algorithm reacts aggressively to changes in the available bandwidth achieving good link utilisation and very low peaks in the queue occupancy. Additionally, the algorithm incorporates a congestion avoidance technique that keeps the queue almost empty in steady state regime.

Quasi-real-time applications can obtain substantial benefits when they are supported by ABR connections. Switch algorithms like the CAPAC, which react quickly to changing network conditions, will help to achieve consistently small transfer delays, improving in this way the QoS perceived by the users.

References

1. Barnhart, A. W.: Explicit Rate Performance Evaluations. ATM Forum Technical Committee, Traffic Management Working Group, Contribution ATM Forum/94-0983 (October 1994)

2. Bertsekas, D., Gallager, R.: Data Communications, second edition. Prentice Hall (1992)
3. Bonomi, F., Fendick, K.W.: The Rate-Based Control Framework for the Available Bit Rate ATM Service. IEEE Network, (March/April 1995) 25-39
4. Charny, A., Clarck, D., Jain R.: Congestion Control with Explicit Rate Indication. ATM Forum Technical Committee, Traffic Management Working Group, Contribution ATM Forum/94-0692 (July 1994)
5. The ATM Forum Technical Committee, Traffic Management Working Group: Traffic Management Specification, Version 4.0. Contribution ATM Forum/95-0013R11 (March 1996)
6. ITU-T Draft Recommendation I.371: Traffic Control and Congestion Control in B-ISDN (May 1996)
7. Jain, R., et al.: ERICA Switch Algorithm: A Complete Description. ATM Forum Technical Committee, Traffic Management Working Group, Contribution ATM Forum/96-1172 (August 1996)
8. Jain R., et al.: Source Behaviour for ATM ABR Traffic Management. IEEE Communications Magazine, vol. 34, no. 11 (November 1996) 50-57
9. Lakshman, T. V., Mishra, P. P., Ramakrishnan, K. K.: Transporting Compressed Video Over ATM Networks with ABR Feedback Control. ATM Forum Technical Committee, Traffic Management Working Group, Contribution ATM Forum/97-0652 (July 1997)
10. Roberts, L.: Enhanced PRCA (Proportional Rate-Control Algorithm). ATM Forum Technical Committee, Traffic Management Working Group, Contribution ATM Forum/94-0735R1 (August 1994)
11. Roberts, L.: Explicit Rate Flow Control. A 100 Fold Improvement over TCP. http://www.ziplink.net/~lroberts (April, 1997)
12. Simcoe, R. J.: Test Configurations for Fairness and Other Tests. ATM Forum Technical Committee, Traffic Management Working Group, Contribution ATM Forum/94-0557 (July 1994)
13. Siu K. Y., Tzeng H. Y.: Adaptive Proportional Rate Control with Intelligent Congestion Indication. ATM Forum Technical Committee, Traffic Management Working Group, Contribution ATM Forum/94-0888 (September 1994)
14. Yin, N.: Fairness Definition in ABR Service Mode. ATM Forum Technical Committee, Traffic Management Working Group, Contribution ATM Forum/94-0928R2 (1994)

Protocol for Browsing in Continuous Data for Cooperative Multi-server and Multi-client Applications

Tobias Helbig, Oliver Schreyer
Philips Research Laboratories
Weißhausstr. 2
D-52066 Aachen, Germany
Email: {helbig, schreyer}@pfa.research.philips.com

Abstract: The paper describes a flow control and synchronization protocol for interactive cooperative browsing in stored continuous data, such as audio and video. The protocol is targeted at controlling the playback of digitally stored continuous data flows which are delivered by one or more servers and consumed on one or more client workstations with or without synchronization. It allows for continuous streaming and single-step browsing in audio/video data for individual and cooperating users as needed, for example, for producing TV news broadcasts.

1 Overview: Browsing in Digitally Stored Continuous Data

Applications of digital multimedia technology can be found in academia and consumer markets for quite some time. They are entering the high-end professional markets, too. The transition into the professional domain goes along with a jump of the requirements in terms of reliability, quality of service, and interactively with regard to handling data. This is mainly due to the fact that digital multimedia technology must compete with sophisticated analog technology (high quality) and digital technology that is not based on off-the-shelf computers (high reliability). Furthermore, replacing sophisticated but expensive professional solutions requires features (e.g., jog/shuttle, very low command latencies, cooperative control of contents) not yet offered by available approaches (e.g., RTSP [9], DSM-CC [2]). Consequently, new advanced algorithms and protocols are needed to meet the challenges of professional applications.

Browsing is a highly interactive activity in these applications. It covers continuously viewing with very high quality and interactively viewing by single-stepping. Consequently, an application supporting browsing needs to offer two modes. In the *streaming mode* a sequence of data units is presented after a user's request to start the presentation. The timing of the data streaming is known in advance. In the *single step mode*, an individual data unit is presented due to a user's request. Both modes of operation in combination pose very high requirements on the underlying infrastructure. This is mainly due to the fact that fulfilling the requirements of both the activities requires system designs that are in contradiction to each other. While streaming requires to set up tight schedules in advance to make sure data units are ready for delivery on time, single-stepping does not allow for planning at all since it purely depends on a non-deterministic request of a user. In contrast, setting up schedules for streaming data delays quick interactive responses which are essential for single-stepping.

The paper is structured as follows. In Sec. 2, we analyze flow-control schemes for professional interactive browsing. Some background about modeling temporal properties of continuous streams is given in Sec. 3. Our protocol for flow-control in multi-server and multi-client browsing application is described in Sec. 4. The protocol is evaluated in Sec. 5. Finally, we discuss conclusions.

2 Flow-Control Schemes for Real-Time Audio/Video Transfers

A number of different approaches for controlling the data flow of real-time audio/video data are on the market. This section gives a rough overview of the different schemes to argue for the scheme chosen in the protocol described in Sec. 3.

The general system model for this kind of applications consists of one or more servers and one or more clients. The client has a bi-directional communication channel to the server to send control messages. Audio and video data are transferred from the server to the client via one or more uni-directional communication channels.

For the single-stepping, the requests of a client are answered by a server with the requested data unit. For the streaming, a number of different schemes exist:

In the *Passive Client Approach*, the client is driven by server streaming. On the server, the time-critical decisions are made to determine when a data unit is delivered. The temporal properties of each delivered data unit needs to be kept up during transfer in the network so that it can be played out directly as soon as it arrives at the client site. This approach usually is found in video-on-demand settings (e.g., [7, 10]). This approach is expensive since it poses stringent real-time requirements on servers and networks to keep up the temporal properties of data units (isochronous transfer). It furthermore is insufficient to support fast interactions on single-stepping requests, since there are long set-up times for real-time streams in the (video) server. The interactive requests are in contradiction to the tight scheduling. Moreover, it is difficult to realize more complex scenarios (e.g. the synchronous play-out to multiple clients or seamless branching between different servers as needed in multi-server applications).

In the *Active Client Approach*, the server is driven by client requests. This approach corresponds to all settings where a client reads data from a remote server via some form of networked file system. All time-critical decisions are performed by the client leading to a very short real-time critical data path. Server and network only need to provide sufficient performance (bandwidth) but no real-time capabilities (e.g., local play-out engines such [8], [6], [1]). This approach is very simple to implement since it mainly requires to access a remote (file) server via network file system. However, it does not scale since an increased number of clients will overload the server with their continuous requests for data. The major disadvantage is that each individual data unit needs to be requested from the server.

In the *Active Client and Server Approach*, both the server and client execute timed operations. This approach is expected to be the most efficient one. For the Active Client and Server Approach, the protocol is described in Sec. 4 (e.g., [5], [3], [11]).

This approach leads to reduced requirements on the real-time features of the server and network since the real-time critical data path is only in the client. The requirements on the features of network and servers with regard to their real-time capabilities may be traded off against the size of buffer on the client site. Hence, the usage of a (less expensive) file server instead of video server becomes feasible. The approach offers an easy migration path to scenarios with multiple servers (seamless branching between different servers) and multiple clients (interstream synchronization among clients).

3 Modelling Temporal Properties for Browsing in Continuous Data[1]

A stored data flow is associated with a set of attributes that describes its *temporal properties* independently of its actual presentation. Each data unit is associated with a timestamp which defines its positioning at a time axis. The succession of timestamps describe the *stream time*. For periodic streams (which are treated here) the *difference between succeeding timestamps (ΔST)* is fixed. For each stream a "normalized" presentation rate is defined which has a meaning to a user. The normalized presentation rate corresponds to the presentation of the data flow with a speed of 1. The specification is given by the *real-time duration ΔRT* of the data units.

When *presenting* a continuous data flow, the time axis of a stream time and the time axis of global real-time are related to each other. The speed of playback may be different to the normalized real-time duration ΔRT. The *speed factor S* of a presentation describes the mapping between the normalized real-time duration ΔRT as described above and the global real-time during presentation. Starting a presentation with a data unit having *timestamp M* defines the alignment of this data unit to a certain point *T in real-time*.

Synchronization relationships describe the relation between stream times of multiple data flows. This is achieved by correlating the stream times of data flows by so-called reference points. A *reference point $RP = [ST_1 : P_1, ST_2 : P_2]$* defines that timestamp P_1 in stream time ST_1 corresponds to timestamp P_2 in stream time ST_2.

4 Protocol for Multi-server and Multi-client Browsing

The section describes a data flow control protocol for browsing in continuous data such as video and audio. It supports single-stepping and streaming of data. It uses the approach of active clients and servers. Data streams may originate from multiple servers and may be played out to multiple clients synchronously.

The implementation model underlying the protocol is the following: A user requests control operations from a controller. The controller may be located anywhere in the system. It instructs entities called agents that are located on the same end-system as the sources and sinks of data units. The agents are responsible for controlling the fine-granular timing of sources and sinks. Interaction among controller and agents is according to the control protocol described below.

---

1. More details about the modelling of continuous data may be found in [4].

4.1 Protocol for Single-Step Playback Mode

The following is the sequence of operations to perform a single step in a data flow: The user requests to perform a single step with a relative or absolute position parameter. The request is given to the controller that instructs the agent of the sink to flush the local buffer and instructs the agent of the source to activate the source functional node to generate the correct data unit. The source functional node reads the correct data unit and delivers it. It is transferred to the sink where it presented immediately.

In case of multiple synchronized data streams, these steps are performed in parallel for each stream. Note that this may require to transform the positioning parameter according to the synchronization relationships defined by reference points.

4.2 Protocol for Streaming Playback Mode

The presentation of a data flow may be separated into a number of intervals in which data units are streamed from source to sink with an a priori known timing. For each interval: the temporal parameters are defined, the data flow is started and runs for a time and later is stopped again. For browsing, an arbitrary number of such intervals having different temporal parameters may be concatenated.

4.2.1 Preparation of the Presentation

All attributes of streams are made available to the stream control protocol. It is beyond the scope of this description how this is achieved. Hence, the stream control protocol knows in advance the attributes ΔST, ΔRT, and S for each data flow before any start command is given. The synchronization relationships between all grouped data flows are known according to the defined reference points. The attributes M and T are derived during start-up. Another parameter known in advance is the internal delay of each of the sink functional nodes. This parameter is needed to correctly equalize different internal delays for inter-stream synchronization.

4.2.2 Start-up Protocol for a Single Data Flow

To start up a data flow, the following operations are executed: The user requests to start a data flow with a given timestamp M. The start operation is to be executed immediately by the controller executing the start-up protocol with "on-the-fly" preload.

The controller instructs the agent of the sink to flush the local playout buffer and the agent of the source to start the data delivery of the source at real-time t_0, with the data unit having timestamp M, a data rate $1/\Delta RT$, and a speed S. The source generates data units with a fixed rate $1/\Delta RT$. Speeds other than 1 are achieved by dropping every S-th data unit (if $|S| > 1$) or duplicating every S-th data unit (if $|S| < 1$). Each data unit is timestamped with a sequence number. Sequence numbers start with 0.

The controller instructs the agent of the sink to start playout at time $t_0+\Delta-d_{sink}$. t_0 is the same real-time as for the source agent, Δ is an offset determined by the sum of transfer delays and the preload buffer level, d_{sink} is the internal delay of the sink. The sink's playout is started with a base rate $1/\Delta RT$ independently of the speed factor S.

At the end of the presentation the activation of source and sink simply is blocked to stop the generation and playout of data units. Stopping is caused implicitly at the boundaries of the medium or on explicit request.

Due to space limitations, further subprotocols are not described in detail. They cover fast preloading, start-up protocol for synchronized data flows for local playout as well as for distributed storage and playout, and, finally, zombie detection.

5   Evaluation and Conclusions

The major achievements of a stream control and synchronization protocol according to the Active Client and Server approach are:

- The protocol *reduces the number of requests for data* that are sent to (performance-critical) servers since clients and servers are active during streaming of continuous data (less expensive servers, increased number of clients).

- The protocol *reduces the length of the (expensive) real-time critical data path* to inside the client. This allows to use servers and networks that deliver sufficient bandwidth but do not need to provide expensive isochronous real-time capabilities.

- The protocol *allows to trade-off the real-time capabilities* with the amount of data buffered in the client.

In addition to the performance achievements, the protocol directly supports a number of new features that are of relevance for future browsing and editing applications: The protocol directly supports the *synchronous* play-out of data at different client workstations. Further, the protocol directly *supports the storage of continuous data on different servers* even if the data need to be synchronized.

The protocol was integrated into a prototypical implementation of an audio/video browsing and editing testbed. The testbed consisted of a number of Multimedia PCs (Pentium 166 MHz, 64 MB RAM, Targa Video Board, ATM Adapter Board 155 MBit/s, WindowsNT) interconnected among each other and a server by an ATM Switch (Fore ASX 200, 155 MBit/s). The server was a DEC Alpha 2100 A (WindowsNT, 500 MByte RAM, disk array with NT striping, disk array with hardware striping). As video format we used Motion JPEG compressed video, 640x480 pixel, 30 frames per second leading to data rates of about 2.3 MByte/s depending on the compression quality.

A first, early evaluation of our system dealt with the questions: What are the bottlenecks in the system and where are the limits? In all our experiments, the multimedia PCs were at the limits of their CPU performance (load between 70 and 100%). Since decompression of video was performed in hardware, the load was mainly due to I/O-handling. A single client caused a server CPU load of about 10%. The server CPU load did not increase linearly with the number of streams served concurrently. With 4 high-data rate streams the server reached its limits, i.e. video quality started to decrease.

Concerning our protocol the first impression was that even with high data rates at the client sites video quality was good and stable (as long as the server could work with medium load). Interstream synchronization (for a cooperative work scenario) between multiple clients provided very satisfying results.

References

[1]   D. P. Anderson and G. Homsy. Synchronization Policies and Mechanisms in a Continuous Media I/O Server. Report No. UCB/CSD 91/617, Computer Science Division (EECS), University of California, Berkeley, CA, 2 1991.

[2]   V. Balabanian, L. Casey, N. Greene, and C. Adams, An introduction to digital storage media - command and control, IEEE Communications Magazine, vol. 34, pp. 122-127, Nov. 1996.

[3]   T. Helbig. Timing Control of Stream Handlers in a Distributed Multi-Threaded Environment, 6th International Workshop on Network and Operating System Support for Digital Audio and Video, Zushi, Japan, April 1996

[4]   Tobias Helbig, "Communication and Synchronization of Multimedia Data Streams in Distributed Systems" (in German), PhD thesis, Verlag Dr. Kovacs, Hamburg. 1996.

[5]   T. Helbig and K. Rothermel. An Architecture for a Distributed Stream Synchronization Service. European Workshop on Interactive Distributed Multimedia Systems and Services, Berlin, Germany, 1996.

[6]   T. Käppner, F. Henkel, M. Müller, and A. Schröer. Synchronisation in einer verteilten Entwicklungs- und Laufzeitumgebung für multimediale Anwendungen. Innovationen bei Rechen- und Kommunikationssystemen, S. 157–164, 1994.

[7]   S. W. Lau and J. C. S. Lui. A novel video-on-demand storage architecture for supporting constant frame rate with variable bit rate retrieval. International Workshop on Network and Operating System Support for Digital Audio and Video, Durham, New Hampshire, pp. 315-326, Springer, Apr. 1995.

[8]   Microsoft Corporation. Online Documentation for Media Player. 1995.

[9]   A. Rao and R. Lanphier, Real time streaming protocol (RTSP.). Internet Draft, Internet Engineering Task Force, Nov. 1996.

[10]   S. Ramanathan and P. V. Rangan. Continuous Media Synchronization in Distributed Multimedia Systems. 3rd International Workshop on Network and Operating System Support for Digital Audio and Video, S. 289–296, 11 1992.

[11]   K. Rothermel and T. Helbig. An Adaptive Protocol for Synchronizing Media Streams, ACM Multimedia System Journal, Vol. 5. 1997

Implementation of a DSM-CC-Server
for a DAVIC-Terminal

Reinhard Baier

GMD FOKUS, Berlin, Germany
baier@fokus.gmd.de

Abstract. This paper describes a multimedia information server which has been developed by GMD FOKUS and Deutsche Telekom Berkom for multimedia terminals based on DAVIC specifications. It also gives a survey of the current status of multimedia networking focused on Internet and DAVIC technology.

Keywords. DAVIC, digital TV broadcast, Internet, ATM, CORBA, DSM-CC, Video Pump.

1   Introduction

The Digital Audio-Visual Council (DAVIC) [2] is a non-profit industry consortium exploring the potential of digital technologies applied to audio and video services. DAVIC has adopted standards and specifications from several standardization bodies which include the ATM Forum Audiovisual Multimedia Services (AMS) specifications [12], the Multimedia and Hypermedia Experts Groups (MHEG) standards [3], and the Digital Storage Media Command and Control (DSM-CC) specifications [5] from the Moving Picture Experts Group (MPEG). AMS defines the MPEG to ATM mapping, while DSM-CC includes functions to retrieve MHEG-5 objects and control a video server. The DSM-CC architecture uses the Common Object Request Broker Architecture (CORBA) [8] as defined by the Object Management Group (OMG) to implement the interaction between objects in distributed systems.

The first set of specifications (DAVIC 1.0) was released in December 1995. It concentrates on TV distribution, New Video on Demand (NVoD) and Video on Demand (VoD) addressing residential users with Set Top Unit (STU) access, while the next version (DAVIC 1.1) addresses additional applications and Internet access. After the establishment of the consortium in August 1994 the first DAVIC-based implementations have begun to appear.

In parallel to DAVIC activities, the Internet has been expanding exponentially, mainly driven by the popularity of the World Wide Web (WWW). Internet and WWW based paradigms are evidently of growing interest to the Telecoms, but high quality multimedia delivery is not feasible with current technology, and thus the best-effort Internet of today is not suitable for providing high-quality services. To the contrary the DAVIC approach has focused on the quality of service, but cannot ignore the importance of the Internet. This led to new guidelines (DAVIC 1.3 and DAVIC 1.4) which are centered around Internet technology.

Although Internet services and digital TV broadcast services have been marketed successfully, the multimedia market is far from being stable. The DAVIC approach can be criticized in comparison to others, but no solid technology has appeared able to dictate the rules for the whole multimedia market. Internet services offer a huge variety of information to be accessed as interactive applications on a PC, while digital TV broadcast focuses on distribution in the digital domain of traditional television services consisting of associated real-time audio and video.

Internet and digital TV broadcast technologies are still evolving. Transmission of real-time media is supported by the Internet, while digital TV broadcast services describe methods for data transmission largely based on MPEG-2 technology which will be used to enhance the more traditional television services by interactive applications. It is expected that Internet services will migrate to digital TV services and vice versa. In this process DAVIC plays a key role by defining tools based on standards in both worlds.

This paper starts with a survey of the current status of multimedia networking focused on Internet and DAVIC technology. Section 3 describes a implementation of a multimedia server and a video server developed by GMD FOKUS in a project funded by Deutsche Telekom Berkom based on DAVIC specifications. It also outlines results of interworking experiments. Section 4 gives a summary and an outlook for future work.

2 Multimedia Networking

Until very recently, digital multimedia information was available for playback only from a local storage, a hard disk or a CD-ROM. The Internet is changing all of that. Multimedia is now available on remote servers residing in a network. Clients connect to servers across a network, and receive multimedia content as multimedia data streams. Besides computer data, networks are also used with varying qualities of service for Internet telephony, multimedia conferencing, transmission of lectures and meetings, distributed simulations, network games and other real-time applications. In this network scenario, standards are needed for a number of steps from data creation up to delivery and presentation on a client's display.

Multimedia networking faces many technical challenges like real-time data over packet-based networks, high data rate over limited network bandwidth, and the unpredictable availability of network bandwidth. High bandwidth network protocols such as Gigabit Ethernet, Fiber Distributed Data Interface (FDDI), and Asynchronous Transfer Mode (ATM) make the networking of digital audio and video practical. Almost all multimedia applications require real-time traffic which is very different from non-real-time data traffic. If the network is congested, the only effect on non-real-time traffic is that the transfer takes longer to complete. In contrast, real-time data becomes obsolete if it does not arrive in time. As a consequence, real-time applications deliver poor quality during periods of congestion. On the other hand, the receiver has a limited buffer and if the data arrives too fast, the buffer can be overflowed and some data would also be lost, resulting in poor quality.

2.1 Multimedia over Internet

Internet pages contain information in the form of text, images, interactive forms, animation, audio, and video, coming from two different kinds of servers: Web servers and media servers. The predominant types of information delivered by Web servers are text and graphics. Media servers, on the other hand, stream multimedia content, such as audio and video. They are necessary due to the bandwidth wasting and real-time nature of such content.

Media servers and Web servers are different not only in terms of power and function, but also in terms of standards. Formats and protocols for Web servers are fairly well established: the HyperText Markup Language (HTML) and the HyperText Transfer Protocol (HTTP) which is based on TCP/IP. The emergence of multimedia content on the WWW has followed a much different path. Although datagram networks do not seem suitable for real-time traffic, in the last couple of years, a number of new, wild, and incompatible multimedia presentations have flooded the WWW, since the infrastructure is often already in place saving expensive software development.

Working groups in the Internet Engineering Task Force (IETF) are developing an enhanced Internet service model that includes best-effort service and real-time service. The Resource ReSerVation Protocol (RSVP) together with Real-time Transport Protocol (RTP), Real-Time Control Protocol (RTCP), and Real-Time Streaming Protocol (RTSP) provide a working foundation for this architecture, which is a comprehensive approach to provide applications with the type of service they need in the quality they choose [10, 11]. Examples of applications that use RTP are Netscape's LiveMedia and Microsoft's NetMeeting, Voice over IP, and H.323 based conferencing systems.

2.2 DAVIC Approach

Interactive digital TV systems use a low-cost Set Top Unit (STU) that can be configured remotely to connect to the outside world. They also use new high bandwidth network architectures like ATM, Hybrid Fiber/Coax (HFC), and Asymmetric Digital Subscriber Line (ADSL) to provide the necessary higher bandwidth to the consumer.

In the future many consumers will have access to high bandwidth information services through an Interactive TV provider such as cable TV or telephone service. Consequently, DAVIC specifications are likely to be important for developing web clients and server standards which support real-time video and audio delivery. Similarly, MHEG-5 which provides both a time-composition model and an object-oriented framework for incremental delivery of content, may also be relevant for future extensions of HTML which currently lacks these key features as shown in the following table.

Table 1. Comparison between Internet and DAVIC

Feature	Internet	DAVIC
Document encoding	primarily HTML	primarily MHEG-5
Multimedia delivery	primarily download	real-time
Stream interface	RTSP	DSM-CC U-U
Session interface	none	DSM-CC U-N
Inter media synchronization	none	MHEG-5 links

DAVIC requires MHEG-5 as a run-time environment for STUs, but not necessarily as a complete MHEG-5 implementation. It identifies all required MHEG-5 specifications, a standard set of user input events, connection management, a standard set of RPC interfaces, persistent name spaces, and standard encoding of content data. Conformance is achieved defining all these requirements.

3   Digital Storage Media - Command and Control

DSM-CC is a set of protocol specifications for managing and controlling multimedia data such as MPEG-2 Transport Streams (MPEG-2 TS). These protocols are intended e.g. for MHEG-5 and MHEG-6 applications to set-up and tear-down network connections using DSM-CC User-to-Network (U-N) primitives and for communicating to a server across a network using DSM-CC User-to-User (U-U) primitives. U-N primitives are defined as a series of messages to be exchanged among the client, the network, and the server, while U-U primitives use a RPC-type protocol. MPEG-2 TS are intended to be transported via ATM Adaptation Layer 5 (AAL5) but may also be carried by other lower level protocols.

DSM-CC U-U defines library sets in order to facilitate inter-operation. The DSM-CC U-U *Core Interfaces* represent the most fundamental DSM-CC U-U interfaces. These interfaces serve as a basis for *Core Client* configurations: The *Stream* interface provides VCR-like control to the client, the *File* interface allows clients to read and write files stored on a server, the *Directory* interface provides navigational facilities, and the *Session* interface allows attachment to and detachment from service-gateways. The standard defines the *Core Consumer* as a client with access role READER and with limited capabilities for saving application states, i.e. the ability to write files. The European Telecommunications Standards Intitute (ETSI) for example has defined the *org.etsi.dsmccuu* package to give Java Virtual Machines access to the *Core Consumer Client Application Portability Interface* [16].

DAVIC systems are (partially) defined in terms of information flows. Information flow S1 is responsible for transfer of MPEG-2 TS unidirectional from servers to clients, while S2 controls the content flow with DSM-CC U-U commands and is also responsible for transferring MHEG-5 objects and other non-real-time content. Information flows S3, S4, and S5 deal mainly with User-to-Network related issues such as session and resource management.

As part of the GLUE project [7], funded by Deutsche Telekom Berkom, GMD FOKUS has implemented a DSM-CC Server and a number of DAVIC-Terminals using different hardware and software components. Additional DAVIC-Terminals have been implemented by GMD FOKUS in ACTS IMMP [6]. The term DAVIC-Terminal throughout this paper is used as a synonym for end consumer devices which are compliant to DAVIC Specifications, primarily Set Top Units but also PC desktops and other clients. The first prototype of a DSM-CC Server and a DAVIC-Terminal was demonstrated at the 13. DAVIC Interoperability event, at Columbia University, New York City, USA, in June 1996. Other important interoperability demonstrations followed: Cebit 97, Hannover, Germany, March 1997, Internationale Funkausstellung 97, Berlin, Germany, August 1997, and Telecom Inter@ctive 97, Geneva, Switzerland, September 1997.

3.1 Implementation of a DSM-CC Server

The DSM-CC Server developed within the GLUE project [7] is implemented on a Sun Workstation with 32 megabytes memory running Solaris 2.5. It requires several gigabytes of disk space, depending on the amount of video material available. The CORBA 2.0 compliant protocol stack is implemented using Orbix from IONA Technologies Ltd. The DSM-CC Server has been successfully tested with Orbix releases 2.0.1, 2.1, and 2.2 in single-threaded and multi-threaded versions. ATM connectivity is achieved by a FORE SBA-200 adapter (driver version 4.0.2). The DSM-CC Server can handle an arbitrary number of clients simultaneously, limited only by available memory resources.

Since DAVIC-Terminals are classified as *Core Consumers*, the DSM-CC Server supports all interfaces of a *Core Consumer*, i.e. all operations with access role READER for attaching to or detaching from a service domain, navigating through directory hierarchies, resolving names to object references, controlling MPEG-2 TS, and reading and writing files. All these operations belong to S2 information flow.

Due to the real-time capabilities for audio and video data a Video Pump has been implemented as a separate process which is responsible for delivering the MPEG-2 TS through a high bandwidth network. Normally both processes reside on a single workstation, but the distributed Video Pump architecture enables the use of a heterogeneous set of UNIX-based workstations to deliver MPEG data to DAVIC-Terminals. The DSM-CC Server does not deal with S1 directly, therefore it does not need access to ATM networks, as shown in figure 1.

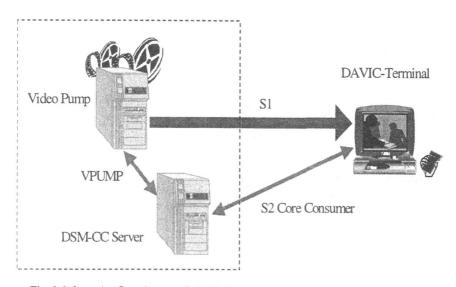

Fig. 1. Information flows between DAVIC-Terminal, DSM-CC Server, and Video Pump

To enable the DSM-CC Server to control the Video Pump an additional *VPUMP* Interface has been defined similar to *DSM::Stream*. If the DAVIC-Terminal opens a stream the DSM-CC Server instructs the Video Pump to create a new S1 flow with *VPUMP::StreamFactory::newStream()*. This flow is controlled by *DSM::Stream* operations called by the DAVIC-Terminal and mapped one-to-one by the DSM-CC Server to corresponding *VPUMP::Stream* operations. The following table summarizes all the implemented interfaces.

Table 2. DSM-CC U-U Core Consumer and VPUMP interfaces

DSM-CC U-U interface	Core Consumer operation *(DSM::...)*	Video Pump operation *(VPUMP::...)*
		StreamFactory::newStream()
Stream	*Stream::resume()*	*Stream::resume()*
	Stream::pause()	*Stream::pause()*
	Stream::status()	*Stream::status()*
	Stream::reset()	*Stream::reset()*
	Stream::play()	*Stream::play()*
	Stream::jump()	*Stream::jump()*
	Stream::_get_Info()	*Stream::_get_Info()*

DSM-CC U-U interface	Core Consumer operation (DSM::....)	Video Pump operation (VPUMP::....)
File	File::read() File::write()	
BindingIterator	BindingIterator::next_one() BindingIterator::next_n() BindingIterator::destroy()	
Directory	Directory::list() Directory::resolve() Directory::open() Directory::close() Directory::get()	
Session	Session::attach() Session::detach()	
ServiceGateway	Directory and Session operations	

The DSM-CC Server has been developed to fulfill the requirements of a DAVIC-Terminal, i.e. all *Core Consumer* interfaces have been implemented. Uploading new applications to the server would require the interface set of a *Core Producer Client* with OWNER privileges to perform the create, write, bind and destroy functions. Although these functions are not implemented, it is very simple to put new applications on the server since the DSM-CC Server uses the UNIX-filesystem directly for storing files and streams. The DSM-CC hierarchical name space is mapped to UNIX-directory trees and the DSM-CC access role READER or WRITER is mapped to the UNIX-permission to read or write a file.

3.2   Implementation of a Video Pump

On selection of a movie with *DSM::Directory::resolve()* or *DSM::Directory::open()* a DAVIC-Terminal indirectly establishes with *VPUMP::StreamFactory::newStream()* a new S1 information flow for carrying MPEG-2 TS from the Video Pump to the DAVIC-Terminal with constant bit rate Quality of Service (CBR QoS). After initializing the S1 flow the transmission of the video can be controlled using *play()*, *pause()*, *resume()*, *reset()*, or *jump()* of the *DSM::Stream* interface on S2. As mentioned above the DSM-CC Server maps these operations to the corresponding *VPUMP::Stream* operations.

The S1 flow can be based on a pre-established Permanent Virtual Channel (PVC) or a Switched Virtual Channel (SVC). The former eliminates the need for an interoperable signaling stack. Beyond DAVIC specifications the Video Pump also allows S1 to run on Internet protocols such as TCP/IP and UDP/IP on top of ATM, Ethernet or other networks. Since U-N signaling is currently not supported, a configuration file is used to select protocol stacks, ports, and the S1 bit rates for each individual DAVIC-Terminal. The following Video Pump configuration file gives some examples.

```
# Video Pump configuration file.
# Each line should consist of 4 or 5 entries:
# CLIENT       name or IP address of the client
# DEVICE       e.g. /dev/qaa0 (ATM), tcp or udp
# PORT         VPI,VCI (permanent virtual channel)
#              ASAP    (switched virtual channel)
#              port    (TCP and UDP)
# TPP          number of transport packets per PDU
# BITRATE      number of bits per second,
#              optional, default is 6000000
# If more than one entry for a client is given, the
# first match is taken. If a file XX.bitrate for a
# given transport stream XX exists, the bitrate value
# in XX.bitrate is used.
#####################################################
# CLIENT           DEVICE   PORT/PVC/ASAP TPP BITRATE
#####################################################

### SVC example with ASAP 5400
phobos.mars.org    /dev/qaa0   5400          2 2000000

### PVC example with VPI=0 and VCI=200
deimos.mars.org    /dev/qaa0   0,200        14 6000000

### TCP/IP example with port 5369
sagan.mars.org     tcp         5369         10

## UDP/IP example with port 5370
sojourner.mars.org udp         5370         10
```

The Video Pump is implemented as a multi-threaded program using Solaris threads. For each *VPUMP::StreamFactory::newStream()* call the main thread creates a new thread which initializes a new S1 flow. Each *VPUMP::Stream* operation is then distributed by the main thread to the corresponding S1 flow handling thread using shared variables. The Video Pump can handle an arbitrary number of S1 flows in parallel, limited only by available memory and network resources.

Due to the CBR QoS of MPEG-TS the Video Pump does not need to recalculate the bit rate from the Program Clock References (PCRs) fields inside the stream. Instead, a global default bit rate of 6000000 bits per second is assumed, which can be redefined for each individual client or TS. This method is simple and robust for CBR

QoS, but requires the maintenance of additional configuration files. To avoid overflow and underflow of buffers in the DAVIC-Terminal it is important that the actual average bit rate is as constant as possible. Measurements have shown that UNIX library functions like *usleep(3)* and system calls such as *setitimer(2)* are not able to guarantee the needed time granularity in scale of microseconds. Therefore, the Video Pump uses the high resolution timer operations of the POSIX.4 Realtime library of Solaris for a finer resolution in time.

Another precaution for constant bit rate transmission is to minimize the delay for copying from disk into memory, i.e. reading the next PDU must not exceed the time available for each transmission cycle. This is achieved with file-to-memory mapping functions and hints to the virtual memory system for intended sequential read operations on that memory. Within each cycle the consumption of time for reading and sending is measured. The delay is used to calibrate the available time for the next cycle and gain average constant bit rate over several cycles.

3.3 DAVIC-Terminals and other DSM-CC Clients

DAVIC focuses primarily but not exclusively on STUs as low-cost end consumer devices. A key component of a DAVIC-Terminal is the MHEG-5 engine [9] which has been implemented by GMD FOKUS for different hardware platforms using different operating systems and software components [6, 7], as shown in the following table. An STU running an MHEG-5 engine is currently under development.

Table 3. DAVIC-Terminals developed by GMD FOKUS

DAVIC-Terminal	Operating System	DSM-CC interface	ATM board	MPEG-2 decoder
PC desktop	Windows 95	Orbix 2.2cMT (IONA)	SBA-200 (FORE)	VideoPlex (Optibase)
TV/PC (Loewe Opta)	Windows 95	Orbix 2.2cMT (IONA)	SBA-200 (FORE)	VideoPlex (Optibase)
Sun Workstation	Solaris 2.5	Orbix 2.0.1, 2.1, 2.2 MT or ST (IONA)	SBA-200c (FORE)	MpegTV Player Software, MPEG-1
JAVA [1,13]	Netscape Navigator (Windows 95, Solaris 2.5, Linux)	Visibroker (Visigenic)	No ATM Adapter	Netscape plugin, MPEG-1

Although the DSM-CC Server has been developed for use by DAVIC-Terminals it could also be attached by other DSM-CC clients for general purposes. For example, in the JUPITER project [14] the ARMIDA™ system [15], from Centro Studi e Laboratori Telecomunicazioni (CSELT), Telecom Italia Group, has successfully used the DSM-CC Server for retrieving images and controlling multimedia streams.

Another example from that project is a JAVA-based browser from Centro de Estudos de Telecomunicações (CET), Portugal Telecom, which is able to navigate through files and directory hierarchies of the attached DSM-CC Server.

Accompanying the implementation phase of the DSM-CC Server, the verification tools *dsmcntl* and *vcntl* developed by GMD FOKUS were used to evaluate individual functions of the DSM-CC Server and the Video Pump. Sequences of DSM-CC U-U operations are verified by a set of *test-tools* developed in the JUPITER project. Due to the complexity of the DSM-CC standard these tools were very helpful during our early successful work on interoperating with foreign clients.

4 Summary and Future Work

In a local scenario it is simple, useful, and DAVIC-compliant to configure a client, server, and network according to some kind of configuration file, but in a wide area network this approach is not reasonable and must be automated. The U-N part of DSM-CC defines messages and behavior for such a dynamic and automatic configuration. It assumes that a Session and Resource Manager (SRM) resides somewhere within the network which is able to allocate and manage resources by exchanging U-N messages. There are plans to enhance the implementation of the DSM-CC Server and the DAVIC-Terminals with a minimal set of U-N messages to fulfill this requirement. Such a set will include U-N Configuration messages to provide clients and servers with configuration parameters such as *primary Server ID* and *device ID*. U-N *SessionSetup* and *SessionRelease* as well as the U-N *AddResource* and *DeleteResource* messages will also be implemented to support DAVIC information flow S3.

The Video Pump uses stored MPEG-2 TS files with CBR QoS for delivery. Although the bit rate of a MPEG-2 TS could be reconstructed from the Program Clock References (PCRs) from inside the stream, the exact bit rate value is currently gained by other means, i.e. an additional bit rate file, a per-client default value, or a global default value. This simple and robust method has the disadvantage of maintaining additional bit rate and configuration files. Reconstructing the bit rate from PCRs inside the stream itself is more flexible and more complex, but it is the only way for TS containing multiple programs with independent time bases and separate PCR fields for each program. Although currently TS with CBR QoS are used, there are plans to implement the second method as well and compare it with the former.

The ability of IP to solve many problems faced by other network architectures has helped foster significant growth of the Internet. But recent strong demands for real-time applications from traditionally non-computer fields are stretching the Internet's capacity. In practice it is an extremely inefficient way to supply huge data requirement of 6 Mbps of MPEG-2 TS. On the other hand DAVIC has adopted the very flexible DSM-CC standard. A network supporting DSM-CC can offer a wide range of broadband applications. Each protocol area can be implemented separately thus aiding in the integration of the DSM-CC standard with other standards. Digital

Video Broadcast (DVB) for example makes use of a subset of U-N and U-U messages, but not the rest of DSM-CC. The set of DSM-CC protocols could enhance the Internet protocols and make the mutual approach between digital TV and Internet easier.

Acknowledgments

I would like to thank all my colleagues in the GLUE project and the IMMP project for their encouraging enthusiasm implementing MHEG-5 engines, especially Christian Gran for adapting the DSM-CC client interfaces to a non-UNIX platform and Andreas Zisowsky for inter-ORB tests with a non-Orbix ORB. Special thanks to Klaus Hofrichter and Eckhard Moeller for their comments on this paper.

References

1. Sun Microsystems, Inc., Java Home Page, http://java.sun.com/
2. DAVIC Consortium, DAVIC Home Page, http://www.davic.org/
3. ISO/IEC IS 13522-5, Information technology — Coding of Multimedia and Hypermedia information — Part 5: MHEG Subset for Base Level Implementation.
4. K. Hofrichter: MHEG 5 - Standardized Presentation Objects for the Set Top Unit Environment, in Proceedings of the European Workshop on Interactive Distributed Multimedia Systems and Services, Berlin, Germany, 4-6 March 1996, Springer Lecture Notes in Computer Science, 1996
5. ISO/IEC IS 13818-6, Information technology — Generic Coding of Moving Pictures and Associated Audio - Part 6: Digital Storage Media Command and Control (DSM-CC), 1996
6. IMMP Home Page, http://www.nokia.com/projects/IMMP/ and http://www.fokus.gmd.de/ovma/immp/
7. GLUE Home Page, http://www.fokus.gmd.de/ovma/glue/
8. OMG: CORBA 2.0/IIOP Specification, OMG Technical Document PTC/96-03-04, http://www.omg.org/corba/corbiiop.htm
9. R. Baier, C. Gran, P. Hoepner, K, Hofrichter, A. Scheller: PENGUIN: DAVIC and the WWW in Coexistence in Proceedings of the European Workshop on Interactive Distributed Multimedia Systems and Telecommunication Services, Darmstadt, 10-12 September 1997, Springer Lecture Notes in Computer Science, 1997
10. RFC 1889: RTP: A Transport Protocol for Real-Time Applications
11. RFC 1890: RTP Profile for Audio and Video Conferences with Minimal Control.
12. ATM Forum, Audiovisual Multimedia Services: Video on Demand Specifications 1.0, ATM Forum, January 1996
13. MAJA Home Page: http://www.fokus.gmd.de/ovma/maja/
14. Joint Usability, Performability and Interoperability Trials in Europe (JUPITER), Eurescom Project P 605
15. ARMIDA Multimedia Services, http://drogo.cselt.stet.it/ufv/
16. European Telecommunications Standards Institute (ETSI): ETS 300 777-2

A Client-Server Design for Interactive Multimedia Documents Based on Java

D. Tsirikos[1], T. Markousis[1], Y. Mouroulis[1], M. Hatzopoulos[1], M. Vazirgiannis[2], and Y. Stavrakas[3]

[1] Dept. of Informatics, University of Athens, HELLAS
[2] Dept. of Informatics, Athens Economic & Business University, HELLAS
[3] Dept of El. & Comp. Engineering, National Technical University of Athens, HELLAS

Abstract. In this paper we present the design and implementation of a client-server system for Interactive Multimedia Documents (IMDs). IMDs are based on a well-founded theoretical model that covers the issues of interaction and spatiotemporal synchronization of multimedia objects that are presented according to an IMD scenario. The scenaria reside on a server, while the media objects are distributed over the Internet. The client retrieves a scenario from the server, requests the appropriate media from the corresponding http servers and subsequently resents the scenario according to the specifications it defines. In this respect the client uses events (simple and complex) to track the state of each media object and manipulate it. The whole framework has been implemented in Java using the RMI (Remote Method Invocation) client server communication protocol and the JMF (Java Media Framework) for handling multimedia objects. The system presents a promising approach for distributed interactive multimedia on the Internet and intranets.

Keywords. Interactive Distributed Multimedia Applications, Interactive Scenario Rendering, Multimedia Synchronization, Java.

1. Introduction

Multimedia technology has greatly affected the way we interact with computers. But although multimedia capabilities have become something we expect—and get—from most software applications, the exponential growth of the Internet is bearing a second wave of change, in the form of distributed multimedia. The media objects do not have to be replicated locally in order to be presented; they can be viewed on demand directly from the site where they reside. The issue of distributed Interactive Multimedia Documents (IMDs) and, specifically, their retrieval and execution, is an issue of current research [9,4]. However, most of the proposed systems suffer from limited interaction support, both at the modelling and at the implementation level.

In order to create and present an IMD we have defined a strong theoretical model. An IMD is defined in terms of *actors*, *events* and *scenario tuples*. The actors represent the participating media objects and their spatiotemporal transformations. An actor does not contain the media to be presented; instead it uses a pointer to the location of the media. Events are the interaction primitives and they may be atomic or complex. They are generated by user actions, actor state changes or by the system. In [18] the reader may find details about a rich model for events in IMDs. The primary constituent of an IMD is the scenario (i.e. a set of scenario tuples). A tuple is an autonomous entity of functionality in the scenario, conveying information about which event(s) start (or stop) an instruction stream. The latter is a set of synchronised media presentations, i.e. an expression that involves Temporal Access Control (TAC) actions on actors, such as *start, stop, pause,* and *resume*. In [19] a set of operators has been defined for the TAC actions and for the corresponding events.

The rest of the paper is organised as follows: in section two we refer to the technical choices we did in terms of software tools and platforms, while in sections three and four we elaborate on the design and implementation of the server and the client respectively. In section five we refer to related work and in the last section we summarise our contribution and indicate directions for further research.

2. The Implementation Framework

The system implementation is based on Java and other accompanying technologies due to its appealing features, such as built-in multi-thread support and cross-platform compatibility. The advantages that arise by that choice are:

- *Platform independence:* The server is written in 100% Java and will run on any environment that supports Java. The client is also written in Java, but makes extensive use of the JMF API. This API uses native (platform dependent) methods and it is currently available for Windows/Intel, Solaris/Sun, IRIX/SGI and MacOS/Macintosh machines. We tested our implementation with Intel's API for Windows, which was the first to be made available.
- *Internet use:* Most current browsers support Java. Shortly the client will run as an applet, it can be downloaded by the browser and used to present scenaria on a separate window. This eliminates the need to install and customise the client, and enables its automatic upgrade without user intervention.
- *Built-in multi-thread support:* With Java it is easy to create multi-threaded programs. The theoretical model we exploited is oriented to concurrent media presentations that interact with each other. Thus implementing each object as a thread, comes quite naturally. Moreover, using separate threads improves robustness since if one of them crashes the rest of the application will continue. This improves the fault tolerance, a necessary measure considering the number of potential pitfalls in a network application.

The communication between the client and the server is performed exclusively using the RMI (Remote Method Invocation) protocol [6], a technology used to seamlessly distribute Java objects (in our case IMDs) across the Internet and intranets. The choice of RMI instead of CORBA for the communication protocol is based on the following reasons:

- RMI allows Java objects to call methods of other Java objects running in different virtual machines. These methods can return primitive types and object references, but they can also return objects by-value unlike CORBA and DCOM.
- RMI has a very flexible way of providing support for persistent objects (the IMDs in our case) as it uses Java serialisation to store and retrieve objects. Serialisation is efficient and easy to use and suits well our case as we only need to store scenaria without any need for complex operations on objects, relations

between them or transaction processing. Furthermore RMI does not require the use of extra software as ORBs and is more efficient than CORBA.

When it comes to presenting media objects we make a distinction between continuous (video and sound) and static (all other kinds of) media. The former are presented using the JMF [7], which specifies a unified architecture, messaging protocol and programming interface for playing and capturing media. Streaming media is supported, where video and sound are reproduced while being downloaded without being stored locally, a feature we exploit extensively. For static media we use the standard Java classes as defined in the Java language without any need for the JMF.

An important architectural choice in our system is the *logical* and *physical* separation of the content (media data) and structure of a scenario. The advantages of the logical separation are well known and are explained in many approaches (such as [5,19]). The physical separation may contribute to significant enhancement of Quality of Service (QoS). As the media data can reside in different servers, we should be able to dynamically select the server with the least workload and the best network connection in order to minimise the presentation delay of the scenario. This can prove extremely helpful when dealing with scenaria that contain a large amount of video and sound data (the most demanding media types in terms of network bandwidth). Concerning the implementation status of the proposed architecture, we have a fully functional server and client that have been successfully used to view example scenaria that range from a few buttons to a full-fledged presentation with lots of sound and images and about 20MB of video. All scenaria were tested over Ethernet LAN's and over a WAN. Areas not yet covered are spatial synchronization relationships and QoS issues.

3. The Server and the Communication Architecture

The servers' task is to provide the client with the scenaria it requests, together with all the media they use. In order to minimise download latency and space requirements at the client side, the media are requested by the client only at the moment they are to be presented. This depends on user interactions and on the scenario itself (for example if the user presses ButtonA then he will see Image1 whereas if he presses ButtonB he will see Video2).

The server system carries out two tasks:
- *The storage of scenaria.* This is handled by the IMD server which is responsible for publishing a list of the scenaria it can provide. At this level, all communication with the client is performed by remote method calls, through the Java RMI registry. All scenaria are implemented as serializable Java objects, stored in a file at the server side.
- *The distribution of media*, which is handled by a set of http servers. The client downloads a scenario, parses and executes it. When some media should be displayed, the client communicates directly with the corresponding http server and retrieves it. In case of static media, these are *first* downloaded and *then* presented according to the scenario specifications. However, when continuous media are to be shown, they are played directly from their site of origin without

being locally stored, using the JMF. The decisive factor on the selection of JMF was that it needs to be present only at the client side; while on the server side, any http server can be used without any special configuration. This allows the massive distribution and replication of media to any number of http servers, thereby reducing the load on any individual server; whereas the scenaria (usually only a few kilobytes in size), can all be served by one machine. Another interesting option, is the ability to use http servers owned and administered outside the scenario creation team.

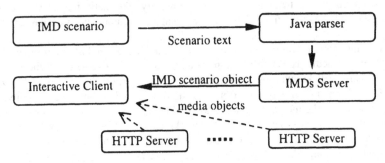

Figure 1. An IMD lifecycle

4. The Client

The client retrieves scenaria from the server, media objects from the appropriate http servers, and presents them according to scenario and interaction. An IMD scenario execution scheme must primarily be able to detect and evaluate events generated by the system, the user or the actors. Other important features are asynchronous activation of tuples, concurrent execution of all instruction streams and synchronised presentation actions according to the scenario tuples' specifications.

Each element of a scenario (i.e. tuples, events and actors) has been implemented as a different Java class. Therefore, we have a *ScenarioPlayer* class and a *TuplePlayer* class that are capable of handling an IMD scenario and a scenario tuple respectively. Each actor is an instance of the *Actor* class that serves as the super-class of *Video*, *Image*, *Sound*, *Text*, *Button*, *Label* and *Timer*. The class *InstructionStreamPlayer* is responsible for synchronised presentation of media objects, while the listeners are in charge of the presentation of a single media object and also of detecting all events related to the object presented. Another fundamental class of our client design is the *EventEvaluator* class, which is in charge of evaluating the start and stop events of all tuples each time a simple event occurs and then send messages to the *ScenarioPlayer* indicating which tuples should start or stop.

The outline of the IMD client architecture is shown in Figure 2. When an IMD session starts, a *ScenarioPlayer* and an *EventEvaluator* object are created and the "StartApp" (start application) event is generated. This event is sent to the *EventEvaluator* , which determines which tuple(s) are to be started. *ScenarioPlayer* then creates the corresponding *TuplePlayer* objects that create as many *InstructionStreamPlayer* objects as necessary (remember, a tuple is a set of instruction streams). Each *InstructionStreamPlayer* contains some actors, each actor holding the presentation specifications for the media object it points to. For each actor an appropriate listener is created. Each object created corresponds to a new thread. During scenario execution, all events generated that are of some interest to the IMD are sent to the *EventEvaluator*, which evaluates them and notifies the *ScenarioPlayer* for changes in tuples' states. Then the *ScenarioPlayer* starts/stops the appropriate tuples either by creating new *TuplePlayer* objects or by destroying the ones that should stop. When a tuple must be interrupted, all the participating actors are interrupted (if they are active) and the corresponding event is sent to the *EventEvaluator*. The client performs two main tasks: starting and interrupting scenario tuples on the basis of occurring events and presenting media objects according to the specifications of the actors. In the following subsections we present these tasks in detail.

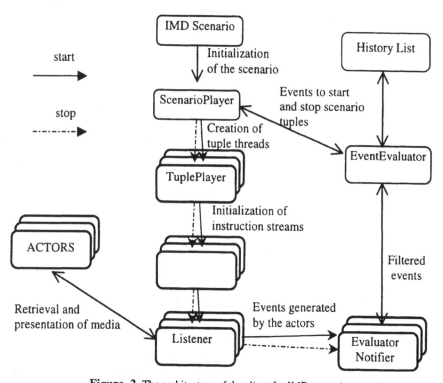

Figure 2. The architecture of the client for IMD scenario execution

4.1 Starting and Interrupting Scenario Tuples

Before proceeding we must distinguish between simple and complex events. Simple events refer to an actor changing state, to events caused by the system or to events originating from the user. Complex events are combinations of simple events, using a set of operators (e.g. "event e1 AND (event e2 before event e3)"). The only complex events in our design are the start/stop events of the tuples.

For the client application to present a scenario it must detect and evaluate the events that occur in an IMD session and match them against the events included in the "start event" / "stop event" attributes of the scenario tuples. A tuple is considered *active* when the start event of that tuple is evaluated as *true*. At this point all instruction streams of the tuple start executing. Once a tuple has been initiated, it may end in *natural* or *forced* way. In the first case, the tuple falls into the idle state when all instruction streams have finished. An instruction stream is considered as finished, when all the involved actors have stopped. In the second case, the tuple stops when its stop event becomes true. In order to avoid confusion, we explain hereby what are the semantics of interrupting an actor. For this purpose we distinguish between actors with inherent temporal features (sound or video) and actors without such features. An actor of the first category falls in the idle state either when its natural end comes (there is no more data to be presented) or when it is stopped using the stop operator "!" [19]. Actors of the second category (e.g. an image) stop only when we apply the stop operator to them. Hereafter we will examine the classes that are related to management of scenario tuples, namely the *ScenarioPlayer*, the *TuplePlayer*, the *EventEvaluator*, and the *HistoryList* classes.

The *ScenarioPlayer* class is responsible for the execution of an IMD. Initially it constructs the window where the media are to be presented and receives all input events (keyboard or mouse generated) as well as all application timer events. This class is also responsible for starting and interrupting tuples. The *TuplePlayer* class is in charge of starting and interrupting a scenario tuple. In other words, it starts the instruction streams of the scenario tuple with no further effect on them. The *TuplePlayer* must detect the termination of the instruction streams that it contains. When all instruction streams have finished, the *TuplePlayer* informs the *ScenarioPlayer* and then it stops. The *EventEvaluator* class evaluates simple events, and the start and stop events of all the scenario tuples. This means that on arrival of a new event, the start events of all idle tuples and the stop events of all active tuples are evaluated, and those that are found to be true trigger the appropriate action(s). The *EventEvaluator* additionally controls the synchronization of all threads that send messages to it about events that occurred. This function is further explained in the *EvaluatorNotifier* class presented in the next subsection. The *HistoryList* class is contained as an attribute in the *EventEvaluator*. There is only one instance of this class in each IMD session; it keeps information on the events that have occurred in an IMD session from the start to the current time, which is defined as the time (in seconds) elapsed since the start of the session. For each event we keep all the timestamps of its occurrences. It is important to clarify that in the *HistoryList* only simple events are stored.

4.2 Presenting the Media

In this section we present the classes of the client that are in charge of presenting the media objects according to the synchronization relationships that are included in the instruction streams. As mentioned above, each scenario tuple consists of a set of instruction streams. Since not all instruction streams have the same effect on the actor states, we distinguish two categories of instruction streams. The first one includes instruction streams that begin with an actor followed by the start operator (>) and remain active until *all* participating actors stop. The second category includes instruction streams that contain the synchronization operator "∧" and remain active until the temporally shorter of the involved actors finishes executing. If an instruction stream contains the synchronization operator "∧", it cannot contain any other operator (i.e. >, !, ||, |>). The role of an instruction stream is to translate the synchronization relationships between actors into actual operations on them.

A listener is responsible for presenting a single media object. For that purpose a set of six classes (each for a different kind of actor) were created and all have the suffix "Listener". These classes do not only present actors, but also detect ("listen to") any events concerning the actor they are controlling (i.e. media state changes etc.). For instance, the *VideoListener* class can start, stop, pause and resume a video clip; it can also detect all kinds of events that are related to the particular video. A *VideoListener* must receive appropriate messages from the *InstructionStreamPlayer* to start, pause, resume and stop the video it is currently playing. The class is also in charge of presenting the video according to the specifications in the corresponding actor. The same applies to the other listeners.

Each listener occurrence is paired with an occurrence of the *EvaluatorNotifier* class. This class serves as a filtering mechanism that sends to the *EventEvaluator* only the events of interest to the IMD (i.e. the ones that the author of the scenario has already defined and are stored in an auxiliary list). The *EvaluatorNotifier* receives messages denoting actor state change, checks whether there is a related event defined by the scenario author and, if such an event exists, sends it to the *EventEvaluator*. For example, if the *ButtonListener* for button A detects that the button has been pressed, it will send a "ButtonDown" event to the *EvaluatorNotifier*. The *EvaluatorNotifier* checks if an event "ButtonDown" related to button A is defined by the author. If such an event exists, it will be sent to the *EventEvaluator* together with its occurrence time (timestamp). The *EvaluatorNotifier* class is responsible for performing the filtering of events so that the *EventEvaluator* does not have to process redundant events.

4.3 Event Evaluation

As already mentioned, the interaction in our system is handled in terms of simple and complex events occurring in the IMD context, generated by the user or the actors. Hereafter, we describe the event evaluation process during which a simple event that occurs in the IMD session is compared to the events that start/stop each tuple or denote that the IMD session must stop. The evaluation process is carried out as follows. At first, we are interested in the evaluation of a simple occurring event. This task is accomplished by the function `evaluate_simple_event(simple event e)`, that does not actually receive the event, but is called after the event has been received. The method follows:

```
eventEvaluator "locks" itself after receiving an event
evaluate_simple_event(simple event e) {
EventEvaluator receives e and writes it to HistoryList
for each tuple t
        if t is idle
        then evaluate (t.start_event, e)
                if t.start_event is true
                then add t in tuples_to_start array.
        else
        if t is active
        then evaluate (t.stop_event, e)
                if t.stop_event is true
                then add t in tuples_to_stop array
end for
start_tuples(tuples_to_start)
stop_tuples(tuples_to_stop)
}
eventEvaluator "unlocks" itself
```

It is important to stress that during the period of event processing (*EventEvaluator* in locked state) the occurring events are not lost, but are maintained in the respective *EvaluatorNotifiers*. When the *EventEvaluator* is again available, it receives another event and goes one more time into the locked state and processes it.

The function evaluate(t.start_event, e) carries out the evaluation of the event e against the event expression stored in the start/stop event of each tuple. The resulting value (true or false) will determine whether tuple t should start/stop. When the start/stop event is a simple event, the evaluation is limited to searching in the *HistoryList* for an occurrence of such an event. In case the start/stop event is complex, it may contain expressions including operators and functions that are defined in the framework presented in [19]. Our system implements the following subset of operators: AND, OR, NOT, and of functions: ANY, ANYNEW, IN, TIMES, SEQ and (event1: time_indication : event2).

For complex events the evaluation process is carried out in three distinct steps. The first step is the transformation of the event expression into postfix form resulting in an expression without brackets. The second step is the evaluation of each function appearing in the expression, and replacing the function with the token "true" or "false" according to the result of each function. The last step is to evaluate the result that now consists of the tokens "true" or "false" combined with the Boolean operators.

An IMD session is an environment that involves concurrent execution of several tasks, such as event detection and evaluation, starting, interrupting and monitoring scenario tuples, presenting media objects according to synchronization specifications, etc. As already mentioned, we have used Java's support for threads. Thus, each instance of the classes *Listener, EvaluatorNotifier, InstructionStreamPlayer, TuplePlayer* are served by the corresponding Java thread.

5. Related Work

Regarding Multimedia Document Standards, there have been mainly two efforts: HyTime and MHEG. HyTime [2] provides a rich specification of a spatiotemporal scheme with the FCS (Finite Coordinate Space). HyTime is not an efficient solution for IMD development since "there are significant representational limitations with regard to interactive behaviour, support for scripting language integration, and presentation aspects" [2]. MHEG [5] allows for user interaction between the selection of one or more choices out of some user-defined alternatives. The actual selection by a user determines how a presentation continues. Another interaction type is the modification interaction, which is used to process user input. Object Composition Petri Nets (OCPN) [10] do not allow modelling of interaction.

As mentioned in [1], event based representation of a multimedia scenario is one of the four categories for modelling a multimedia presentation. There it is mentioned that events are modelled in HyTime and HyperODA. Events in HyTime are defined as presentations of media objects along with its playout specifications and its FCS coordinates. All these approaches suffer from poor semantics conveyed by the events and, moreover, they do not provide any scheme for event composition and detection. There has been substantial research in the field of multimedia storage servers, especially video servers. For real-time applications, there is a strong need for streaming media. Most of the work in this field has been carried out by the industry. Some related efforts are the following:

- RTSP, developed by Progressive Networks and Netscape Communications [15] to cover the need of transferring multimedia through IP networks. RTSP offers an extensible framework for transferring real-time data such as audio and video. It has been designed to work with established protocols such as RTP and HTTP, and constitutes a complete system for the transmission of streaming media through the Internet.
- Microsoft Netshow. It is a product of Microsoft for the transmission of streaming multimedia through intranets, LANs and the Internet. It supports multicasting and unicasting and it can broadcast stored data as well as live feed. NetShow is related to ActiveMovie technology, which is used by the Intel implementation of the JMF.
- Berkeley Continuous Media Toolkit (CMT) [16]. It is a framework that consists of a suite of customisable applications that handle streaming multimedia data. It requires significant programming to support each medium. On this toolkit, cmplayer [14] was built, an application that is used to present remote continuous media in conjunction with a web browser. It supports the synchronised reproduction of multiple media and is available for most platforms.

All the above projects concentrate on how media are transferred and displayed. On the other hand, the context in which the media are to be presented is not considered.

This is the field of distributed multimedia applications, which has received less attention by researchers. Some of the most interesting efforts are:

- NetMedia. A client-server architecture that can be used for the development of multimedia applications. It is described in [8], where algorithms are described for the effective synchronization between media and the maintenance of a QoS.
- CHIMP. Here the definition of multimedia document is broader than in other efforts, since such a document "consists of different media objects that are to be sequenced and presented according to temporal and spatial specifications" [3].
- The system proposed in [12] involves more user participation, since it is the user who controls the course of the presentation. A framework for link management within hypermedia documents is described, which supports embedding dynamic links within continuous media such as video, as well making queries to a database.
- A similar architecture is presented in [11], which suggests the use of video-based hypermedia to support education on demand. The system is based on URLs, which are embedded in QuickTime movies. There is no notion of time or events, and the systems bias towards applications such as video-based lectures could be the reason for the limited interaction it offers.
- The time factor is systematically considered in [13], where temporal as well as spatial events between multiple media are defined. A prototype scenario-authoring tool based on Windows 95 is described, while the scenaria it produces can also be reproduced in different platforms.

To summarise, there is an extensive coverage of topics such as streaming video, as well as multimedia presentations. However, the merging of the two areas combined with substantial user interaction, has received little attention by researchers and is still an open issue.

6. Conclusions

In this paper we have presented a Java-based client-server system for IMDs, supporting a high level of interactivity and distribution of scenario and media. The architecture of the implemented system consists of the IMD scenario server, the media servers and the client module. The IMD scenario server provides the scenaria, while the media objects are distributed in any http server. The client retrieves a scenario from the server and requests the appropriate media from the corresponding http servers. The client design covers widely the issue of interaction with external and internal entities in terms of simple and complex events. Moreover, it maintains the high-level spatial and temporal synchronization requirements of each scenario. The system has been implemented in Java using the RMI client server communication protocol and the JMF for handling multimedia objects.

The salient features of the system presented are:

- *Support for highly interactive presentations*, due to the model exploited in [18, 19]. This model covers internal and external interaction in terms of events.

Complex interaction may be covered by composite events using the appropriate composition operators.

- *Platform independence*: platform independent design of a client server system for IMDs. The physical separation of IMD structure (scenario) and content (media), i.e. media to be presented may reside at any http server, allows the usage of external resources for storage and presentation on the IMD content, and reduces the workload and maintenance for the server. The choice of Java (along with accompanying technologies like RMI and JMF) as the implementation platform and the storage of media objects in http servers, makes the design appealing for wide Internet usage. The clients are capable of presenting multiple scenaria simultaneously. The ability to view IMDs using Java applets makes the application available to anyone with a WWW browser.

- *Generic multi-threaded approach for rendering interactive scenaria*. Based on a rich IMD model [18, 19], we have developed a robust mechanism for detection and evaluation of events as carriers of interaction, and the corresponding synchronized media presentation algorithms. This approach is generic and may be considered as rendering architecture in other emerging application domains like synthetic 3D worlds etc.

Due to the feasibility of running the client module in any WWW browser, the system presents a promising approach for distributed interactive multimedia on the Internet and intranets.

The architecture presented here may be extended towards the following directions:

- *Provision of QoS*. Provisions could be made to ensure the QoS.
- *Database support at the server side*. Another extension would be the storage of IMDs in a database system. This will make the server capable to serve large quantities of IMDs and requests, as well as handling queries related to the structure of the scenario. Such queries might me: "give me the IMDs that include video1" or "give me the IMDs which include the word "vacation" in at least one of the texts that they present".
- *"Import" other document formats*. Extend the parser module so that documents resulting from popular authoring tools or other Multimedia Document Standards (Hytime, MHEG) may be stored in our system. This procedure would involve development of translators of such documents to the IMD model that serves as the basis of our system.

References

1. Blakowski, G., Steinmetz, R., "A Media Synchronization Survey: Reference Model, Specification, and Case Studies", IEEE Journal on Selected Areas in Communications, vol 14, No. 1, (Jan. 1996), 5-35

2. Buford, J., "Evaluating HyTime: An Examination and Implementation Experience", Proceedings of the ACM Hypertext '96 Conference, (1996)

3. Candan, K., Prabhakaran, B., Subrahmanian, V., "CHIMP: A Framework for Supporting Distributed Multimedia Document Authoring and Presentation", Proceedings of the fourth ACM international multimedia conference, Boston, (1996), 329-340

4. Huang, C.-M., Wang, C., "Interactive Multimedia Communications at the Presentation Layer", in the proceedings of IMDS'97 workshop, Darmstadt, Germany, (1997), LNCS 1309, 410-419

5. ISO/IEC, Information Technology - Coded representation of Multimedia and Hyper-media Information Objects (MHEG), (1993)

6. Java-Remote Method Invocation, available at:
http://java.sun.com:81/marketing/collateral/rmi_ds.html

7. Java–Media Framework, available at: http://www.javasoft.com/products/java-media/jmf/

8. Johnson, T., Zhang, A., "A Framework for Supporting Quality-Based Presentation of Continuous Multimedia Streams", Proceedings of the IEEE International Conference on Multimedia Computing and Systems (ICMCS'97), Ottawa, Canada, (June 1997), 169-176

9. Karmouch. A., Emery J., "A playback Schedule Model for Multimedia Documents", IEEE Multimedia, v3(1), (1996), 50-63

10. Little, T., Ghafoor, A., "Interval-Based Conceptual Models for Time-Dependent Multimedia Data", IEEE Transactions on Data and Knowledge Engineering, Vol. 5, No. 4, (August 1993), 551-563

11. Ma, W., Lee, Y., Du, D., McCahill, M., "Video-based Hypermedia for Education-On-Demand", Proceedings of the fourth ACM international multimedia conference, Boston, (1996), 449-450

12. Manolescu, D., Nahrstedt, K., "Link Management Framework for Hypermedia Documents", Proceedings of the IEEE International Conference on Multimedia Computing and Systems (ICMCS'97), Ottawa, Canada, (June 1997), 549-556

13. Nang, J., Kang, S., "A New Multimedia Synchronization Specification Method for Temporal and Spatial Events", Proceedings of the IEEE International Conference on Multimedia Computing and Systems (ICMCS'97), Ottawa, Canada, (June 1997), 236-243

14. Patel, K., Simpson, D., Wu, D., Rowe, L., "Synchronized Continuous Media Playback Through the World Wide Web", Proceedings of the fourth ACM international multimedia conference, Boston, (1996)

15. Schulzrinne, H., Rao, A., Lanphier, R., "Real Time Streaming Protocol (RTSP)", ftp://ftp.isi.edu/in-notes/rfc2326.txt, (1997)

16. Smith, B., Rowe, L., Konstan, J., Patel, K., "The Berkeley Continuous Media Toolkit", Proceedings of the fourth ACM international multimedia conference, Boston, (1996), 451-452

17. Stamati, I., Trafalis, M., Vazirgiannis, M., Hatzopoulos, M., "Event Detection and Evaluation in Interactive Multimedia Scenaria - Modeling And Implementation", Technical Report, Dept of Informatics, University of Athens, Hellas, (1997)

18. Vazirgiannis, M., Boll, S., "Events In Interactive Multimedia Applications: Modeling And Implementation Design", in the proceedings of the IEEE - ICMCS'97, (June 1997), Ottawa, Canada

19. Vazirgiannis, M., Theodoridis, Y., Sellis, T., "Spatio-Temporal Composition and Indexing for Large Multimedia Applications", to appear in ACM/Springer Verlag Multimedia Systems Journal, September 1998.

Asynchronously Replicated Shared Workspaces for a Multi-media Annotation Service over Internet

Hartmut Benz[1], Maria Eva Lijding[2]*

[1] University of Stuttgart, Institute of Parallel and Distributed High-Performance Systems (IPVR), Breitwiesenstraße 20–22, 70565 Stuttgart, Germany, benzht@informatik.uni-stuttgart.de

[2] Technical University of Catalonia, Department of Computer Architecture (DAC), Campus Nord D6-008, Jordi Girona 1–3, 08034 Barcelona, Spain, mariaeva@ac.upc.es

Abstract. This paper describes a world wide collaboration system through multimedia Post-its (user generated annotations). DIANE is a service to create multimedia annotations to every application output on the computer, as well as to existing multimedia annotations. Users collaborate by registering multimedia documents and user generated annotation in shared workspaces. However, DIANE only allows effective participation in a shared workspace over a high performance network (ATM, fast Ethernet) since it deals with large multimedia object. When only slow or unreliable connections are available between a DIANE terminal and server, useful work becomes impossible. To overcome these restrictions we need to replicate DIANE servers so that users do not suffer degradation in the quality of service. We use the asynchronous replication service ODIN to replicate the shared workspaces to every interested site in a transparent way to users. ODIN provides a cost-effective object replication by building a dynamic virtual network over Internet. The topology of this virtual network optimizes the use of network resources while it satisfies the changing requirements of the users.

1 Introduction

DIANE (Design, Implementation and Operation of a Distributed Annotation Environment) is a service to create multimedia annotations to every application output on the computer, as well as existing multimedia annotations. DIANE is suitable for every field of application since it is not restricted to be used only with certain programs or application areas. In contrast to normal multimedia authoring tools, DIANE provides authoring on the fly capability to users. It thereby satisfies the users need to efficiently and effectively create short, precise multimedia annotations to every object of day to day use (on the computer). Field tests of DIANE indicate that multimedia annotations are an ideal service to support collaborative work in a wide variety of application areas.

DIANE is a European Union funded ACTS project near its completion. During the project, the service has been extensively tested by users in the areas of medical diagnosis, computer based training, and industrial research collaboration. During the project,

---

* Working on a grant of Fundación Estenssoro, Argentina.

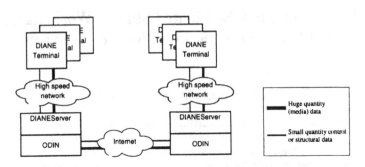

Fig. 1. Principle architecture of connected DIANE sites.

doctors from the pathology department of a hospital evaluated DIANE doing diagnoses, asking colleagues for second opinions, and training students.

However, DIANE requires a high performance network (ATM, fast - dedicated - Ethernet) between the DIANE server and its DIANE clients since it deals with large multimedia object. When only slow or unreliable connections are available between a DIANE terminal and server, useful work becomes impossible. Accessing a DIANE server via Internet on the other side of the globe is possible, but results in poor performance and low quality multimedia presentations.

The current task described in this paper is to overcome this restriction and enable DIANE to be usable between distant sites only connected by low-quality networks (low bandwidth, high latency, high packet loss). Following the current trend and using the available technology, we connect DIANE sites via Internet. This gives us a cheap, simple and world wide reach, but limits strongly the quality of the connection.

We achieve this by introducing *asynchronously replicated shared workspaces (ARSW)* into DIANE using the distributed replication service ODIN over the Internet. An ARSW can be seen as a special type of directory very similar to a newsgroup. It enables users worldwide to see each others documents and create annotations to them. In this paper we use the term *shared workspace* synonymous for the ARSW.

Figure 1 shows the principle architecture of two DIANE sites connected via the replication service ODIN. Each site consists of a set of DIANE client terminals which are connected via a high speed network to a DIANE server. Each connection consists of two channels, an asynchronous control channel to exchange document information and presentation schedules, and a high bandwidth channel for continuous media streams and other high volume data [1]. Two DIANE servers are connected over a low quality Internet connection.

Both DIANE and ODIN have been implemented almost completely in Java making extensive use of standard packages like RMI, SSL, JMF. Only some minor function currently not available via platform independent API like grabbing screen contents and reading the audio device have been realized in Java classes wrapping native code.

The remainder of this section presents two usage scenarios in *Medical Consultations* and *Computer Based Distributed Learning* to illustrate the application of DIANE/ODIN and replicated shared workspaces. Section 2 and 3 give short overviews of DIANE and ODIN. Section 4 describes the semantics of the replicated shared workspaces. Section 5 gives an overview of the architecture and the changes introduced by combining DIANE and ODIN. Section 6 describes the building of the communication topology and the protocols used to replicate objects. Finally, Section 7 concludes the paper and highlights some future work.

1.1 Usage Scenarios

Asynchronous medical consultations between practitioners, specialist, and students of medicine has proven to be an effective means of communication during our test experiences with DIANE. With a network infrastructure being installed in developing areas we wish to provide distant medical institutions access to the experience and technology of important medical centers and universities.

Consider a provincial hospital using software to manage the data of their patients which include images from X-ray, computer tomography, etc. A doctor who is reviewing a diagnosis with this system likes to get third-party opinions on his diagnosis. Using the annotation service DIANE, he records the X-ray image and the most recent physiological data of his patient displayed by several tools of the management software. He adds his diagnosis talking into a microphone and pointing out relevant regions on the image with the mouse. He links the resulting annotation into a shared workspace he uses to confer with a specialized colleague on the other side of the continent or the world.

The colleague may view this document at a convenient time and annotate it in a similar fashion to support or contradict the original diagnosis. These annotations may consist of parts of the original document and other media objects, e.g. images, results from current research, or references to comparable cases from the literature.

Another example is computer based distributed learning which is a cost-effective way to allow individuals, teams, and organizations to manage, share, and develop their knowledge assets and learning capabilities.

Consider a multinational company where instructors prepare a simple multimedia tutorial about the use of a graphical user interface. Using DIANE, the tutorial can be created directly by recording the correct and efficient interaction with the program. The instructor enhances this recording with spoken comments and links to related material. This tutorial is asynchronously distributed by ODIN to all sites of the company where users of the program are located. Now available locally, users can conveniently review the tutorial. Additionally, they can add their own annotations, either for private use, or as a contribution to the multimedia discussion forum of the users of the program.

The participants in each scenario may be distributed all over the world. Since the communication with multimedia annotations is asynchronous, discussions do not suffer from time differences between different parts of the world.

2 Overview of DIANE

DIANE supports various ways of making annotations. Several users can produce annotations on top of the same document. Also, users can create annotations to other annotations, reflecting in this way evolving discussions. Annotations are attachable (can be created on top of) both as discrete and continuous media objects such as images, texts, audio, and mouse pointer movement. Therefore, the annotation itself and its relation to the annotated document have a temporal dimension.

The distinction between document and annotation is primarily semantical. Both are identically structured multimedia objects internally represented by the same class. The distinction is made to highlight the special semantics assigned to the annotation by the user during creation and the fact, that an annotation always refers to the document it annotates, whereas the more general term document does not imply this.

Users of DIANE can freely organize their multimedia documents in directories. This organizational structure is independent of the implicit structure given by the annotation process itself, e.g. document A is an annotation of document B. A user interacts with DIANE by navigating through the hypermedia structure (supported by several types of visualization), selection of documents for replay, recording new documents, and linking them into the workspace document structure.

DIANE implements security with authentication, role based authorization, and encryption of communication channels. This ensures that only authenticated users can interact with DIANE and that they only access documents appropriate to the users defined rights. Normally, only the owner of a document or directory has access to its contents.

DIANE does not allow documents to be modified after creation. This very severe restriction is necessary because of the *annotates* relation. An annotation A to a document B incorporates a presentation of B. Since A is likely to refer to the contents of B (e.g. spatially by pointing to elements of B or temporally by repeatedly pressing pause, resume, fast-forward, or fast-backward on the presentation of B). Modifying the contents of B will in almost all cases render the annotation A completely useless. The problems of keeping temporally and spatially anchored annotations consistent over changing objects has been judged too complex to solve in the DIANE project.

The objects managed in DIANE (documents, annotations, and directories) are versatile large multimedia objects with a complex internal structure. The DIANE document, for example, aggregates several organizational attributes (creator, creation date, access rights, etc.) and a hierarchically aggregated multimedia content. For structural and efficiency reasons the objects, the hyperlink graph structure, and the large multimedia raw data are stored in separate specialized databases.

Figure 2 shows an example of a document structure. It shows a directory (*Dir*) containing a document (*Doc1*) annotated by another document (*Doc2*). Each document consists of several aggregated media objects. A special media object (*VCR*) is attached to the link (*Link*) which includes all manipulations made to the annotated document during recording of the annotation (e.g. pause, resume, ff, fb, scroll).

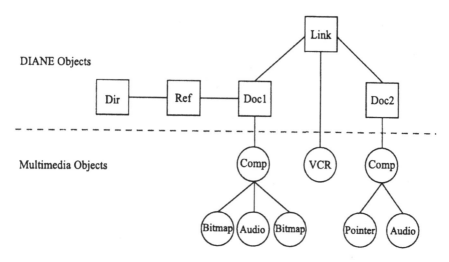

Fig. 2. The Document Model of DIANE.

3 Overview of ODIN

ODIN (Object Distribution Intelligent Network) is a service to replicate arbitrary objects over the Internet in a cost effective way. ODIN, thereby, provides a virtual network over Internet. Many virtual networks can be set up and managed independently from each other. The membership of sites to a network can be controlled to keep it private if desired. Once a site belongs to a network it can access all objects distributed in that network. ODIN is a refinement of ODS presented in a previous paper [4].

Each virtual network can contain several disjunct distribution chains. A distribution chain provides an optimal path for the replication of objects in a shared workspace. It minimizes the use of network resources based on the subscription matrix between users and shared workspaces, the preferred replication schedule of each distribution chain and site. It also adapts to the state of the underlying network. Distribution chains ensure that every object generated in a shared workspace is replicated to all sites subscribing to it. The replication process is transparent to the users which gain a service with high availability of the replicated objects and - except from replication delay - short response times, because objects can be accessed at their local servers.

ODIN follows the replication model from USENET, providing replication of objects with high read/write ratio. As in USENET objects are read-only, but in ODIN they can be updated (creating a new version) on the site the object has been created at. However, the main difference between ODIN and USENET is that USENET uses a static distribution topology where each link must be configured by a system administrator. Therefore, this topology is primarily governed by administrative forces. Mailing list, on the other hand, do not use distribution topologies at all but use random flooding when distributing objects.

The replication process in ODIN is asynchronous and can therefore easily cope with a wide range quality of network links, varying load situations, and interrupted transport connections. Replication is performed by a connection-oriented application layer protocol named *Data Forwarding Protocol (DFP)*. DFP uses UDP for its control channel and TCP to distribute the data objects itself. The TCP connection is enhanced with transaction control allowing to detect communication failures and interrupted connection and restart transmission from the last byte transfered correctly whenever the network allows. DFP is described in Sect. 6.2 in more detail.

4 Asynchronously Replicated Shared Workspaces

In DIANE, a *shared workspace* is a set of documents and directories which are known to and accessible by more than one person. Each shared workspace has a base directory which is a regular DIANE directory to which documents, annotations, and subdirectories are added explicitly by the users. All objects in the base directory and its subdirectories belong to the shared workspace (transitive closure of the *part of* relation). Additionally, all documents annotated by objects of the shared workspace also belong to it (transitive closure over the *annotates* relation).

Compared to existing CSCW systems like [3, 5, 2] we use a very simple model for shared workspaces that does not realize any of the advanced features like event recording and notification services. It was considered to be sufficient within the DIANE project following the requirements analysis of our users. Nevertheless, system design and implementation are prepared to easily incorporate these features.

A directory becomes a shared workspace when its owner sets the access rights of the directory and its recursive contents to allow access to other users and makes the directory known to the future participants (e.g. by mailing a reference to it or publishing it in an agreed upon public directory).

Figure 3 shows an example shared workspace with its base directory (*WS-Base*) and some documents (*D1, D2, D3*) shared by two users A and B. Objects accessible by both users are shaded. The left side shows the integration of the workspace in user As private directory structure. The right side shows this view for user B. Note, that document *D2* is not a member of the base directory but is part of the shared workspace since it is annotated by *D3* and, therefore, is necessary for the presentation of *D3*. Documents *D4* and *D6* are private to the users A and B respectively, since they are not part of (the presentation of) any shared document.

Participation in a shared workspace described so far (and implemented in the DIANE project) is restricted to the DIANE server the workspace has been created on. In order to access it, a user has to connect to the correct server. Effective participation in a shared workspace, though, is only possible using a high performance network (ATM, fast Ethernet) since DIANE deals with large multimedia objects and continuous stream based presentations. When only slow or unreliable connections are available between a user's DIANE terminal and server, useful work becomes impossible.

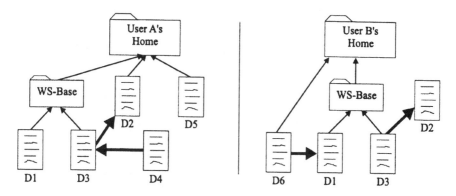

Fig. 3. Example (asynchronously) shared workspace of users A and B. Grey objects are part of the shared workspace and are accessible by both users, white objects are private. Thick arrows represent the *annotates* relation, thin arrows the *part of* relation. Left and Right side shown may be on a single DIANE server or replicated on several DIANE/ODIN connected sites.

To overcome this restriction *asynchronously replicated shared workspaces (ARSW)* are introduced which allow the objects of a shared workspace created on one server to be accessible on other servers. A user may now use or install a DIANE server in a local, sufficiently fast environment. Since the replicated documents are available locally, the access quality a user experiences is now the same as using a non-replicated DIANE service over a high bandwidth connection.

Asynchronous replication between sites is transparent to the user except for the replication delay. This is similar to the semantics used in USENET where each user just sees the documents at the local site. Therefore, the two user directories shown in Fig. 3 can as well be on different DIANE sites. In contrast to USENET, a DIANE user will never encounter a (temporal) inconsistency in the available documents, as regularly happens in USENET when a reply becomes available at a site prior to its source. The replication service ensures that an annotation only becomes available simultaneously to or after the annotated document is available.

The users ability to remove objects from a shared workspace or later restrict its access rights follows the newspaper paradigm: once you have shared an object and someone actually is interested in it (e.g. annotates it, links it to a private directory), you cannot delete it any more. A user can attempt to remove an object from a shared workspace at any time but this will fail as long as other people still reference it. Only if no more references exist the object is actually removed from the shared workspace. Restricting the access rights of a shared object is not allowed at all.

5 Architecture

The architecture of DIANE can roughly be divided into four quadrants (Fig. 4). The vertical separation follows the classical client/server paradigm. The horizontal separa-

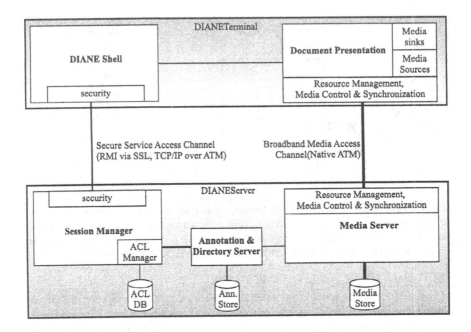

Fig. 4. DIANE annotation system architectural blocks (without ARSW extension).

tion distinguishes between broadband multimedia transport using streams (multimedia access channel) and narrowband object transport using RMI (service access channel). This distinction reflects the documents model which also separates between DIANE object structure (documents, annotations, and directories) and its multimedia contents.

The raw media data are stored on the MediaServer via direct broadband stream connections between the media sources and sinks (right half of Fig. 4). The document, link and directory objects and their hypermedia graph structure are stored in the Annotation&DirectoryServer. The login, session management, navigation, security, object relocation and loading functionality are realized in the DIANEShell in the client and the SessionManager as its counterpart on the server.

The architectural changes resulting from the introduction of ARSWs are restricted to the DIANEServer (Fig. 5) which is extended by two components of the ODIN replication system: NetworkRouter and ObjectReplicator. The existing DIANE components remain unchanged because the new components can use their interfaces as they are. The replicated objects (documents, directories, media data) remain unchanged since ODIN treats them as unqualified objects (binary large objects, BLOB).

On each site, two special system directories /Available and /Subscribed list the available ARSW in the network and those the site has subscribed to. The operations to create, subscribe, unsubscribe, and remove shared workspaces have been mapped to existing operations of manipulating directories. To subscribe to an available ARSW a

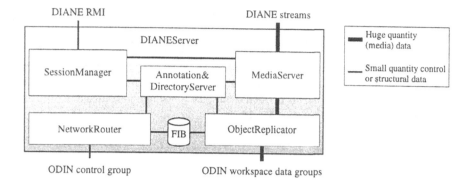

Fig. 5. Principle architecture of the extended DIANEServer.

user links it into /Subscribed. To create a new ARSW a user creates a new directory in /Subscribed which automatically becomes visible in /Available. A site administrator can easily restrict usage of ARSWs by setting the access rights of these system directories appropriately. To selectively prevent the import of undesired ARSWs the system administrator can adjust the read access rights of the unwanted ARSWs in the /Available.

The NetworkRouter monitors operations on shared workspaces by observing the contents of the directory /Subscribed. In this way it knows which shared workspaces the site participates in and forwards this information to other NetworkRouters (cf. Sect. 6.1). It, furthermore, learns about new shared workspaces created at its site, shares this information with its peers and publishes the complete list in /Available. It also builds the *Forwarding Information Database (FIB)* which is used by the ObjectReplicator and contains the sites it must exchange objects with for each of the shared workspaces the site participates in.

The ObjectReplicator collects DIANE objects, raw media data, and relevant hypermedia graph structure and aggregates them into a uniform ODIN objects. These are distributed according to the information provided in the FIB. Likewise, the ObjectReplicator inserts the objects received from other servers into the respective databases. The complexity of DIANE's objects is hidden from the replication service by the ObjectReplicator. Raw media data collected from DIANE already is compressed according to data type. In addition, the ObjectReplicator allows the transparent incorporation of compression schemes.

6   Inter-site Communication

The communication model used between sites is *group multicast*. Each shared workspace is associated to a process group called *workspace data group* which acts as the logical destination for multicast messages. ObjectReplicators belong to the process groups corresponding to the shared workspaces indicated in /Subscribed. There is also a special process group called *control group* to distribute control information over the network. All NetworkRouters communicate through this process group.

We implement group multicast in each process group by store-and-forward of objects between neighbouring sites in the distribution chain of the group. The next section describes the building of the distribution chains, the following subsection describes the object distribution inside a workspace data group.

6.1 Distribution Chains

The NetworkRouters build a distribution chain for each workspace data group in order to implement group multicast communication with optimal communication cost. A distribution chain guarantees that every object generated in the respective ARSW reaches all sites in the workspace data group.

To build distribution chains we use routing mechanisms that can adapt to the traffic's service requirements and the network's service restrictions. Network routing, as a basis, ensures that packages take the best path between a given source-destination pair. In addition, our routing decides on the optimal source-destination pairs to build a distribution chain. This routing mechanism uses the same principles as network routing. All communication networks share a core of three basic routing functionalities [7]: assemble and distribute network and user traffic state information, generate and select routes, and forward user traffic along the routes selected.

To aggregate the network state information and obtain the communication topology of the control group we selected topology-d [6]. Topology-d is a service for applications that require knowledge of the underlying communication and computing infrastructure in order to deliver adequate performance. It estimates the state of the network and networked resources for a group of given sites. To join a group, a machine sends a request to a master. With these estimates it computes a fault tolerant, high bandwidth, low delay topology connecting participating sites. This topology is to be used by the control group for assembling user state information.

The functionality of generating and selecting routes is replicated in each site. Given the network and user state information each NetworkRouter computes the distribution chains independently for the shared workspaces the site belongs to. As a mechanism to provide stronger consistency of these computations, only important changes in the network state information must be taken into account.

The algorithm to compute a distribution chain is very simple. A minimum spanning tree is generated with all the sites in the workspace data group. Since sites have unique identifiers that can be ordered with lexicographic order, whenever there are two nodes that may be incorporated to the minimum spanning tree, we choose the one with lower identifier.

The last routing functionality, forwarding of user traffic, is carried out by the ObjectReplicators using DFP in each site. This protocol is described in the next subsection.

6.2 Data Forwarding Protocol

The *Data Forwarding Protocol (DFP)* is the connection-oriented application layer protocol used between adjacent sites in a distribution chain. DFP is optimized to transport large objects over unreliable low bandwidth connections.

The protocol consists of the notification of available objects and the actual transfer of objects. A site with a new object - either from the distribution chain or created locally - immediately notifies its neighbours in the distribution chain using an acknowledged UDP message. Neighbours later request the objects to be transferred at a convenient time (e.g. low traffic hours, low workload, fixed time, more than N objects to transfer) When an object is announced by several neighbours simultaneously the site chooses the one with the best connection. Objects successfully received are treated as new objects.

The object transfer is realized as a transaction over a TCP connection that deals with communication failures, interrupted connection, and restarts transmission from the last byte transfered correctly whenever the network allows.

Each site keeps a database with information about the protocol-state of its neighbours which consists of the objects the neighbour has and the announcements made to it. When a site is assigned a new neighbour in a distribution chain, it starts a synchronization phase by sending it announcements for every object in the workspace data group.

7 Conclusions and Future Work

The paper describes a simple and effective way to extend the distributed annotation environment DIANE with asynchronous replicated shared workspaces to enable collaborative work with DIANE over low quality networks.

DIANE has proved to be an ideal service to provide support for collaborative work through the use of multimedia post-its. Due to its network requirements effective collaboration is limited to high performance networks, even though the collaboration paradigm is asynchronous. Recently, users extended their requirements in order to be able to collaborate beyond the local networks using DIANE over Internet.

ODIN, also based on the paradigm of asynchronous collaboration proved to be the ideal extension to DIANE to satisfy the new user requirements. Another very important benefit is that both systems are almost completely implemented in Java which eases integration very much.

In the future, we will analyze the introduction of semi-public shared workspaces, where subscription is restricted to a subset of sites, and the security issues this will raise. It will, furthermore, deal with managing uniform access rights over multiple DIANE sites.

Work continues on improving the procedure for building distribution chains for better scaling capability. We are looking into other publishing paradigms and their consequences which, for example, allow users to 'take back' (delete) or modify documents and annotations they made.

References

1. H. Benz, S. Fischer, and R. Mecklenburg. Architecture and implementation of a distributed multimedia annotation environment: Practical experiences using java. In H. König, K. Geihs, and T. Preuß, editors, *Distributed Applications and Interoperable Systems*, pages 49–59. Chapman & Hall, Oct. 1997.
2. L. Fuchs, U. Pankoke-Babatz, and W. Prinz. Supporting cooperative awareness with local event mechanisms: The groupdesk syste. In H. Marmolin, Y. Sundblad, and K. Schmidt, editors, *Proceedings of the 4th European Conference on Computer-Supported Work, ECSCW'95, Stockholm, Sweden*, pages 247–262. Kluwer Academic Publishers, Sept. 10–14 1995.
3. A. Gisberg and S. Ahuja. Automatic envisionment of virtual meetin room histories. In *Proceedings ACM Multimedia '95*, pages 65–75, San Francisco, CA, USA, Nov. 1995. ACM Press, ACM Press.
4. M. E. Lijding, L. Navarro Moldes, and C. Righetti. A new large scale distributed system: Object distribution. In *Proceedings of the Thirteenth International Conference on Computer Communications - ICCC'97, Cannes, France*. International Council for Computer Communication, Institut National de Recherche en Informatique et en Automatique, INRIA, Nov. 1997. Annex.
5. S. Minneman, S. Harrison, B. Janssen, G. Kurtenbach, T. Moran, I. Smith, and B. van Melle. A confederation of tools for capturing and accessing collaborative activity. In *Proceedings ACM Multimedia '95*, pages 523–534. ACM, ACM Press, Nov. 1995.
6. K. Obraczka and G. Gheorgiu. The performance of a service for network-aware applications. Technical Report 97-660, Computer Science Department - University of Southern California, Oct. 1997.
7. M. Steenstrup, editor. *Routing in Communication Networks*. Addison-Wesley, 1995.

Object Graphs as a Pivotal Representation for Hypermedia

M. Brelot, G. Privat

France Telecom, Centre National d'Etudes des Télécommunications[1]
CNET/DTL/ASR/Grenoble
Distributed Systems Architecture Department
Gilles.privat@cnet.francetelecom.fr

Abstract. This position paper advocates a possible bridging of multiple heterogeneous formats and interfaces for hypermedia data and metadata. Rather than one more text, bit-stream or procedural script format, a language-neutral graph of linked objects is proposed as a high-level pivotal representation model. A suitable distributed object platform provides the underlying implementation and communication medium for node objects. Different projections of the global object graph may be mapped to different representation domains, while node objects of different granularities may implement all related, semantic, structural or programmatic information. Bulk media content itself may be conveyed separately under standard stream/file formats, for which higher-level objects act as proxies. This proposal has been validated by implementing, on top of the Java® platform, this graph-based representation as an interface to a prototype MPEG-4 visual composition engine.

1 Hypermedia Application Spectrum

The hypermedia model expands and unifies traditional audiovisual applications, opening up a wide spectrum of interactive communication architectures, from user-centric (authoring, pull-based retrieval) to server-centric (push/broadcast-based delivery). Beyond linear monolithic media, hypermedia break up all modalities of information into a versatile network of interrelated data units, across the semantic, syntactic and presentation layers.

Vertical integration of dedicated resources throughout the communication chain is no longer required : the envisioned ubiquitous distributed computing milieu provides, instead, the breeding ground for hypermedia objects to travel and thrive, consuming communication and computing resources through neatly standardized horizontal interfaces.

This rosy picture is currently marred, however, by a mind-numbing proliferation of multimedia representation formats and programmatic interfaces. Among those, so-called exchange formats are merely lowest common denominators.

From a brief overview of current interfaces to the hypermedia galaxy, we try to lay down the specifications for what could be a pivotal format acting as a highest-common-denominator intermediary.

---

[1] Work sponsored by the EU ACTS programme under the Emphasis ("MPEG4-systems") AC 105 project

These ideas have been put to test with the structured representation of hybrid natural/synthetic visual scenes, with individual image regions singled out for manipulation within what is usually handled as a "black box" media stream. The proposed pivotal representation was first mapped to a spatio-temporal composition engine handling these contents. As such, this work originated from early contributions to the MPEG-4 [1] standardization process, under its "systems" (formerly MSDL) part [2,3,4].What we present here is currently more in line with the ongoing development of a Java-based version 2 (MPEG-J) of the MPEG-4 standard [5].

2   Hypermedia Representation Domains

A sample of the different categories of APIs and languages to and from which hypermedia content has to be mapped is given below :

Languages

- Stream-based binary or text formats for individual media (e.g. JFIF, G728…)
- Synchronized stream/file/multiplex formats for composite media (e.g. MPEG-2 systems mux)
- parametric formats for audiovisual scene description (VRML/ MPEG-4 BIFS)
- native formats of multimedia authoring environments (e.g. Shockwave®)
- hypertext formats and markup languages (e.g. XML)
- Metadata description languages (e.g. MCF, RDF)
- multimedia/hypermedia "container" description formats (such as MHEG, HyTime, XML/SMIL, etc.)
- scripting languages (e.g. ECMAScript, Perl, TCl/Tk, etc)
- interpretable/executable code for individual components

Programmatic Interfaces

- process/task/thread dependency (OS scheduler interface)
- external asynchronous events (user interface, system or network events)
- database engines
- spatial (2D or 3D) and temporal composition engine
- Web/VRML brows

Mapping each of these formats to one another by developing as many conversion utilities is clearly hopeless. The obvious benefit of a pivotal representation is to avoid this by developing only conversions to and from the intermediate format. This trivial idea is certainly not enough to specify a good intermediate format, as there are already too many such candidate intermediaries which only add to the overall proliferation.

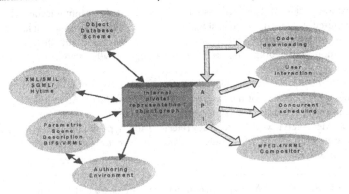

Fig. 1. Hypermedia representation languages and interfaces

3 Requirements for a Pivotal Hypermedia Representation

Existing exchange formats tend to correspond to lowest rather than highest common denominators, e.g. vector graphics and text being bridged by a common flattening to bitmap. These mappings are usually one-way, essential structural information being lost in the process. A pivotal representation should be able to retain all structural and semantic information that can be natively present or associated with external formats. A generalized syntactic level [6], integrating hyperlinks and semantic metadata, is the best-adapted common denominator format for various types of hypermedia data. This level may be obtained; in a more or less automated way, as a result of analyzing or parsing an external representation.

The coding proper of this abstract data model has to match the same requirements of universality, which usually mandated some kind of ASCII textual form. Objects, not ASCII text, are now the high-level common denominator between computing systems making it possible to describe the proposed data model at a much more abstract level, unencumbered by coding peculiarities.

4 Object-Oriented Graph Models

A graph is in itself an extremely versatile and expressive representation, with inherent compositional and hierarchical properties. It is ideally suited to embody the generalized syntactic level outlined above. Contrary to a linear textual language, a graph need not be parsed to extract relevant information, provided its coding makes this direct access possible.

There are numerous ways to efficiently represent graphs in classical programming lore. Using a linked list in object-oriented formalism, with each node or edge typed as a self-contained object may seem gross overkill by comparison. It is however, the most flexible solution as the data structure is entirely dynamic, and consistent with the idea of using objects as an atomic representation entity[2].

To emphasize the language-neutral nature of this data model, it will be described using UML [7] with a few variants of primitive graph data structures, which could be enriched and composed at will.

4.1 Directed Acyclic Graph

In this case each node[3] comprises a vector of arcs[4] linking it to children nodes, with possibly one backward link to its parent for fast traversal :

4.2 Non-directed Graph/Hypergraph

A generalization of arc typing leads to the separate object encapsulation of arcs/edges themselves. This will more naturally represent a non-directed graph : an edge object points to the two nodes which it links together, the nodes themselves having pointers to the edge objects to which they are linked. This generalizes naturally to the representation of hypergraphs [8, where "edges" link more than 2 nodes

---

[2] Such representations have long been used by object database models

[3] In proper graph-theoretic parlance, a node is a vertex. We don't use it to avoid confusion with geometric interpretations (as in VRML)

[4] "Arc" is a directed notion, while "edges" are non-directed

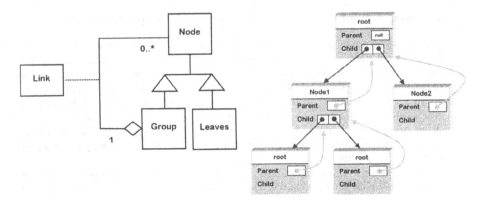

Fig. 2. Directed acyclic graph representation model and example

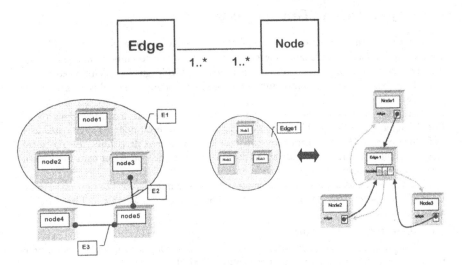

Fig. 3. Hypergraph representation model and examples

5 Object-Oriented Media Models: Migrating Across Language and OS Boundaries

The simple idea of using an object graph representation to retain structural information from all different media formats is seductive, yet it is all too clear why it couldn't be put in practice so far :

- internal object-based representations could not, almost by definition, migrate outside language and OS boundaries
- stringent constraints imposed by real-time handling of classical continuous media and low-level network interfaces mandated the use of low-level stream formats which matched these very constraints.
- the overhead of such a representation may seem unreasonable

Taking advantage of such evolutions as :

- "object bus" paradigms hiding system and language boundaries beneath high-level protocol abstractions (IIOP, Java RMI...)
- decomposition of traditional continuous media into finer grain temporal/spatial entities
- increased availability of bandwidth and computational capacity
- availability of standard object persistency APIs

makes it possible to leverage the power of object-based representations :

- high-level media objects travel transparently above these generic ORB layers, enabling a direct implementation of all the functionalities attached to them without explicit back and forth conversion to and from low level stream/file formats
- heretofore stringent "real-time" constraints can be handled as a generic scalable QoS constraint in a more flexible content-related and user-directed way.
- Links which make up the graph may transparently be local to a given system or cross system boundaries
- Linked nodes may be instantiated or uninstantiated if stored in a database
- Proxy objects can make it possible to manipulate stream-based content from the object layer

The latter combination is crucial to most real-world multimedia applications, where media cannot be decomposed, scaled, and customized at will : continuous-time media with strict throughput, synchronization and rendering constraints still have to be handled appropriately, and present mux/stream/file formats, (such as e.g. the MPEG2 systems mux [9], the MPEG-4 Flexmux [10] or, in a less rigid way, the Advanced Streaming Format) are still the best for this. In the proposed framework, low-level real-time streams can be opened from a higher level ORB environment and bound to objects acting as proxies for the streams in the object domain. This adaptation of a generic ORB kernel to real-time multimedia communication through object-stream binding has been worked out by the EU ACTS ReTINA project [11].

The resulting hybrid architecture is illustrated below

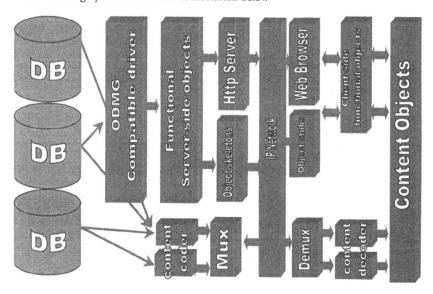

Fig. 4. Hybrid architecture with binding of synchronous media streams into an object middleware

6   Conclusion

The proposed representation is truly language-neutral, as it uses a particular language only for the implementation of node objects. Though the example implementation which we have developed for an MPEG-4 visual scene composition engine was based on Java®, it did not use any special property of the Java *language* as a programming language, but used all properties of the Java *platform* as a powerful distributed object milieu. The vast body of shared knowledge between both ends of the communication chain (virtual machine +APIs implementation) is what makes such a format efficient in terms of information coding. Apart from the possible use of specific stream/file formats for bulk data, the entire set of classes necessary for this representation to be used could, in theory, be downloaded before setting up a communication session. The only assumed pre-standardization is an entirely generic one: the specification of the distributed object platform used. This is ultimate compliance with a minimal specification principle.

We have shown how the proposed object-graph-based representation can be implemented and used as a pivotal format: it has been specified by external mappings from composition representations and to composition, user-interface and scheduling APIs.

It remains to be shown how such a pivotal format would lend itself to similar mappings in other representations languages and APIs. Mapping to and from object database engines/database schemes is clearly a key issue to manage object persistence. From there will new hypermedia retrieval and navigation applications come to fruition.

References

1. ISO-IEC JTC1/SC29/WG11 Document N2078, "MPEG-4 Version 1 Overview", February 1998; http://drogo.cselt.it/mpeg/standards/mpeg-4.htm
2. G. PRIVAT, M. BRELOT : "A Flex-1 compliant object compositing representation, ", ISO/IEC JTC1/SC29/WG11 document M1025, contribution to the 35th MPEG meeting, Tampere, July 1996
3. G. PRIVAT, M. BRELOT, "An implementation of compositing API for 2.5D image representation", ISO/IEC JTC1/SC29/WG11 document M1289, contribution to the 36th MPEG meeting, Chicago, September 1996 (http://www.chips.ibm.com/.mpeg/mhtml/m1289.html)
4. M. BRELOT, G. PRIVAT, "Using a generic object-oriented metadata representation as the MPEG4 scene description format", ISO/IEC JTC1/SC29/WG11/MPEG97/ M2000, contribution to the 39th MPEG meeting, Bristol, April 1997
5. ISO-IEC JTC1/SC29/WG11 Document N2049, "MPEG-4 systems version 2, Working draft 1.0", J. Courtney, editor, February 1998.
6. R. Gonzalez, "Hypermedia Data Modeling, Coding, and Semiotics", *Proceedings of the IEEE*, vol. 85 n°7, July 1997.
7. UML version 1.1 (September 1, 1997) Rational Software Corporation, Santa Clara, Ca., http://www.rational.com/uml/documentation.html
8. Claude Berge, *Hypergraphs, Combinatorics of finite sets*, North-Holland Mathematical library, vol.45, 1989 Hypergraph is not a fancy use of the "hyper" prefix! It is a well defined mathematical concept which predates hypermedia!
9. ISO/IEC International Standard 13818-1 (MPEG-2 Systems), 1994
10. ISO-IEC/JTC1/SC29/WG11 Final Committee Draft 14496-1, MPEG-4 systems Document N2201, May 1998.
11. F. Dang Tran, V. Perebaskine, J.B. Stefani, "Binding and streams, the ReTINA approach", *TINA'96 Conference*.

A New Real-Time Disk Scheduling Algorithm and Its Application to Distributed Multimedia Storage Systems

Ray-I Chang[1], Wei-Kuan Shih[2], and Ruei-Chuan Chang[3]

[1] Institute of Information Science, Academia Sinica
Taipei, Taiwan, ROC
william@iis.sinica.edu.tw
[2] Department of Computer Science, National Tsing Hua University
Hsinchu, Taiwan, ROC
wshih@cs.nthu.edu.tw
[3] Department of Computer & Information Science, National Chiao Tung University
Hsinchu, Taiwan, ROC
rc@cis.nctu.edu.tw

Abstract. In this paper, a new real-time disk scheduling algorithm called *BFI* (*best-fit-insertion*) is proposed. Notably, different from the conventional real-time problem, the service time of a disk request depends on its schedule result. As the service time is not a constant value, it is time-consuming to verify the feasibility of a schedule. In this paper, we introduce a temporal parameter called *maximum tardiness*. With the help of *maximum tardiness*, we can verify the improvement of an insertion test within a constant time. We have evaluated and implemented our proposed algorithm on operating systems. Experiments show that the proposed algorithm can support more requests and can achieve higher disk throughput than that of the conventional approach.

1 Introduction

In traditional computer applications, the number of disk request is less than that of the CPU requests and the disk data size is usually very small. Thus, the designs of operating systems usually base on the philosophy that the applications are processor-demand rather than disk-demand. However, this situation is dramatically changed because multimedia applications are becoming more popular [23-24,31-35]. Media data are usually in large volume and have strict timing requirements. Thus, the performance of a multimedia system would heavily depend on the design of a good real-time disk system to increase the number of requests that can be supported in a constant time interval [18]. In this paper, we focus on the real-time disk scheduling problem. Some results on the data placement problem and the real-time network transmission scheduling problem are shown in [31-32]. Considering the disk scheduling problem, SCAN is the best known algorithm by which we minimize the seek-time in serving disk I/O [18]. SCAN can utilize the disk head efficiently. However, it may not be suitable for real-time disk scheduling problems with additional timing constraint [10]. Different from the conventional disk schedule problem, the timing constraints in data storing and retrieving are more crucial for multimedia applications [1-3]. The retrieved data would become meaningless if the timing requirements are not satisfied. To support these real-time disk requests, a storage system needs to provide new disk scheduling policies to maximize the I/O throughput and guarantee the timing requirements simultaneously [4-7].

The real-time scheduling problem is important, and is also a challenging issue in designing operating systems [8-9,11-17]. Assume that the earliest time at which a request can start is call the *release time*, and the latest time at which a request must be completed is called the *deadline*. Define the *start-time* and the *fulfill-time* to denote the actual times at which a request is started and completed, respectively. To meeting the timing constraints, the start-time of the request should not be larger than its release time and the fulfill-time of the request should not be later than its deadlines. The values of release time and deadline are given by the network transmission schedule. The earliest-deadline-first (EDF) algorithm is the best-known scheme applied for scheduling these real-time tasks [22]. However, different from the conventional real-time problems, the required service time of a disk request is not pre-specified. The service time of disk request is highly dependent on the required *seek-time* of the disk head. It is related to the distance (from the current position of the disk head to the relative data position) specified by the new request. Due to the overheads of unknown service time, strict real-time scheduling may result in excessive disk head seeking and lead to the poor utilization of disk resource. The combination of the seek-optimization technique and the good real-time scheduling policy is considered to be a good solution for providing real-time disk services. In 1993, Reddy and Wyllie [15] have presented a method called *SCAN-EDF* that combines SCAN and EDF to incorporate the real-time and seek-optimization aspects. They sort requests by EDF first and simply reschedule the requests with the same deadlines by SCAN. It can be found that the performance of SCAN-EDF will depend on the probability of requests that have the same deadlines. If no requests have the same deadlines (that always happens in real-world applications), this method is the same as EDF. This combination is so crude, such that the improvement is very little. Although the requests with the similar deadlines are also suggested to be able to reschedule by SCAN, there is no precise definition about what kinds of requests are considered to have similar deadlines. If a non-proper request is selected for rescheduling, the real-time requirements may be violated.

In this paper, a new real-time disk schedule algorithm is proposed to utilize the seek-optimization strategy to support real-time disk requests. Our approach applies a more refined combination of SCAN and real-time EDF scheduling to guarantee deadline constraints with high I/O throughput. We at first employ EDF to guarantee the correctness of real-time requirements. Then, we try to insert each request into the related best-fit position in the schedule to reduce the schedule fulfill-time. An insertion test is accepted if and only if the schedule fulfill-time is not deferred. This schedule-refinement scheme is called *best-fit-insertion (BFI)*. For the comparisons, we have also tested the *first-fit-insertion (FFI)* approach and the *last-fit-insertion (LFI)* approach. Our experiments show that BFI is better than FFI and LFI. To speedup the BFI algorithm, a temporal parameter called *maximum tardiness* is introduced. By applying *maximum tardiness*, the improvement of an insertion test would be easily computed by a constant time. In this paper, both the I/O throughput and the number of supported requests are investigated. All the simulation and the implementation experiments show that the proposed BFI approach is significantly better than the conventional approaches.

2 Disk Scheduling for Real-Time Multimedia Applications

A disk request, said T_i, generally specifies a pair (a_i, b_i) with the track location a_i and the amount of transferred data b_i. To serve this request, the disk arm must be moved to the appropriate cylinder a_i by a *seek-time*. After that, the system must wait until the desired block rotates under its read-write head and switches the controller's attention from one disk head to the other within the same cylinder. Finally, the amount b_i of data actually transferred between the disk and buffer. In a disk service, the seek-time usually stands for the major part of the total service time. The rest part of this service can then be represented by a small constant, called the *rotation time*. Generally, a real-time request T_i can be denoted by three parameters [19]: the release time r_i, the deadline d_i, and the service time c_i. A simple example to demonstrate the used terminology is shown in Fig. 1 where e_i is the start-time and f_i is the fulfill-time. Notably, the start-time of a request should not be larger than its release time and its fulfill-time should not be later than its deadlines. The start-time e_i is only available for a pre-specified time range $[r_i, (d_i-c_i)]$ where (d_i-c_i) is the slack time [19]. Different from the conventional real-time scheduling problem, the service time c_i relies on the random components of seek-time and rotation time [18]. It depends not only on the data capacity b_i but also on the address a_i of the presented request and the current location of the disk head. The actual service time is determined only when the schedule is determined. However, a good schedule is determined only when the service time is determined. In this paper, we will focus on this difficult issue.

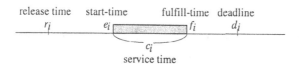

Fig. 1. A simple example to demonstrate the terminologies used and their relations. Notably, the start-time of a request should not be larger than its release time and its fulfill-time should not be later than its deadlines.

In a real-time disk scheduling problem, there are a set of requests $T = \{T_0, T_1, T_2, ..., T_n\}$ where n is the number of disk requests and T_0 is a special request to represent the initial condition of disk arm. A request T_i can be simply denoted by four parameters (r_i, d_i, a_i, b_i). The release time r_i and the deadline d_i are provided from real-time requirements. The track location a_i and the data capacity b_i are used to represent the disk service. The disk arm is usually assumed to be at the outermost track (track 0) and let T_0

= (0, 0, 0, 0). Assume that $S = T_0 T_1 T_2 ... T_n$ is a schedule of T. The start-time e_i and the fulfill-time f_i of request T_i are defined as follows:

$$e_i = \begin{cases} 0 & \text{if } (i = 0) \\ \max\{r_i, f_{i-1}\} & \text{otherwise} \end{cases}$$

$$f_i = e_i + c_i \tag{1}$$

The service time $c_i = S_{i-1,i} + R_i$ and $c_0 = 0$. The variable $S_{i-1,i} = S(a_{i-1}, a_i)$ is the seek-time between request T_{i-1} and request T_i, and $R_i = R(b_i)$ is the rotation time for reading request T_i. In a HP 97560 disk device, the seek-time (ms) from request T_i to T_j can be modeled as follows [20].

$$S_{i,j} = \begin{cases} 3.24 + 0.400\sqrt{D_{i,j}} & \text{if } (D_{i,j} \le 383) \\ 8.00 + 0.008 D_{i,j} & \text{otherwise} \end{cases} \tag{2}$$

$D_{i,j} = |a_j - a_i|$ is the seek distance. Notably, conventional approaches commonly use the average seek-time or the maximum seek-time as a merit [21]. These assumptions are simple, but will waste a lot of waiting time between the successive requests. In this paper, our considered disk model is relatively precise compared to the conventional methods.

DEFINITION: *Real-Time Disk Scheduling*

Given a set of tasks T, find a schedule $S = T_0 T_1 T_2 ... T_n$ that solves $\min\{ f_n \}$, where f_n is the schedule fulfill-time and S is feasible ($f_i \le d_i$ for all i).

Assume that the request data size is constant (i.e., 36 KB for a track of HP 97560), the obtained I/O throughput is defined as $(n * (36 * 8 / 1024) / (f_{Z(n)} / 1000))$. $f_{Z(n)}$ is the schedule fulfill time and n is the number of requests. As the I/O throughput is just the inverse of schedule fulfill-time, we can simply define the measurement of maximum I/O throughput as minimum schedule fulfill-time.

3 Maximize Disk Throughput with Guaranteed Requirements

This real-time disk scheduling problem can be modeled by a complete graph $G = (V, E)$ with vertices $V = T$ and edges E. The scheduling goal is to start a tour from the vertex 0 and visiting each vertex exactly once to minimize the tour cost. In this graph, there is a cost bound d_i on each vertex i and a transition cost $C_{i,j} = S_{i,j} + R_j$ on each edge from vertex i to vertex j. The tour cost on each vertex is defined as the sum of the individual costs along the edges of the tour. Assume that $S = T_0 T_1 T_2 ... T_n$ is a tour in this graph, the tour cost for vertex i can be defined as $f_i = e_i + C_{i-1,i}$ subject to $f_i \le d_i$ where $f_0 = 0$. We want to find a tour with minimum cost without violating the bounded cost constraints (or the deadline constraints) on each vertex. The cost of the entire schedule is defined as the tour cost at the last vertex f_n. We can easily design a simple greedy method for this tour planning. In this algorithm, the request with the smallest fulfill-time is retrieved in each processing step to maximize I/O throughput. It is easy to program but may not provide the best solution. Furthermore, as the relative deadlines and track locations are not simultaneously exploited, some requests may miss their deadlines. For example, consider a set of requests $T = \{T_0, T_1, T_2, T_3\}$ as shown in Table 1. Assume that the read-write head is initially at track 0 for request T_0. By applying this simple greedy algorithm, the read-write head will be moved from T_0 to T_3, then to T_1. At this moment the deadline d_1 is missed. This situation is illustrated in Fig. 2. The same result is obtained if we only apply SCAN to this set of disk request. To guarantee the deadlines, we need to consider both the aspects of seek optimization and the real-time timing constraints more precisely.

Table 1. Request parameters and transition costs for a simple example $T = \{T_0, T_1, T_2, T_3\}$

	Request Parameters				Transition Costs ($C_{i,j}$)			
	r_i	d_i	a_i	b_i	0	1	2	3
T_0	0	0	0	0	0	-	5	6	3
T_1	0	5	4	1	1	5	-	2	3
T_2	3	12	5	1	2	6	2	-	4
T_3	1	11	2	1	3	3	3	4	-

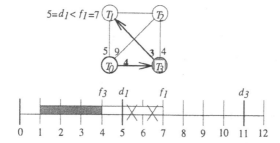

Fig. 2. From the simple test example shown in Table 2, the scheduling result of the greedy algorithm will introduce the deadline missing of d_1.

3.1 Conventional SCAN, EDF and SCAN-EDF Approaches

In the real-time disk scheduling problem, disk requests need to be scheduled to maximize the I/O throughput and to satisfy the real-time requirements. The schedule results with only the SCAN approach would not satisfy the real-time requirements. To schedule real-time requests, EDF [22] is considered as the best-known algorithm. However, due to the seek-time overheads, the I/O throughput of the pure EDF algorithm is poor. As shown in Fig. 3, the schedule results produced by EDF is $T_0T_1T_3T_2$. It is not good enough. For example, if request T_2 can be serviced before request T_3, the total disk head movement would be further reduced. The schedule fulfill-time is decreased substantially with high I/O throughput.

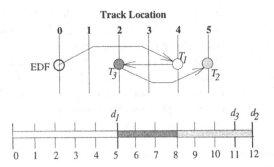

Fig. 3. From the simple test example shown in Table 2, the scheduling result of the SCAN-EDF algorithm does not optimize the seek-time cost of T_2.

A combination of SCAN and EDF is proposed in [15]. The basic idea of SCAN-EDF is to schedule the requests by real-time EDF order. After the real-time constraints are satisfied, it tries to reschedule requests to match the SCAN service order without violating the real-time timing constraints for any requests. Generally, the degree of improvements is determined by the rescheduling scheme applied. In SCAN-EDF, the rescheduling scheme is so crude. If there is no request with the same deadlines, this SCAN-EDF approach would be the same as EDF. The drawback of SCAN-EDF motivates us to find a more refined combinations of the real-time scheduling scheme and the seek-optimization scheduling scheme.

3.2 Our Proposed Best-Fit-Insertion Scheme

Given $S_{EDF} = T_{E(0)}T_{E(1)}...T_{E(n)}$ as the scheduling result of EDF, we can easily partition S_{EDF} into a number of scan lines according to requests' track locations. This partitioning process can be easily accomplished by finding the maximum set of successive requests that follow the same seek order, *e.g.*, left-to-right or right-to-left. Regarding an example with 10 requests, 5 scan lines can be obtained as shown in Fig. 4. It can be found that the overhead of disk-head seeking can be further reduced if requests can be rescheduled into better positions (*i.e.*, inserting the rescheduling request T_9 into the front of the test request T_6). Note that the redundant seek operation from T_8 to T_9 is removed by this rescheduling process. Our proposed best-fit-insertion (BFI) algorithm is based on this simple idea. BFI improves the I/O throughput of EDF schedule by trying to insert rescheduling requests into their best-fit positions. Basically, each rescheduling request $T_{E(i)}$ will be tested by inserting it into the front of different test requests $T_{E(1)}$, $T_{E(2)}, ..., T_{E(i-1)}$ to obtain the best rescheduling result. However, by analyzing the scan line structure, we can reduce the number of insertion test to some really useful insertion points. For example, a request belongs to the scan line L_i would be only tested by inserting into its related scan positions of $L_{i-1}, L_{i-2}, ..., L_1$. Considering the example of Table 1, two scan lines L_1 and L_2 are obtained as shown in Fig. 4. Applying the scan-line-based insertion, the requests T_0 and T_1 on the first scan line would not be selected for rescheduling. At the second scan line, we try to insert the request T_3 into the same track location (track 2) for L_1. In this example, T_3 is trying to reschedule into the front of T_1 and a possible solution $T_0T_3T_1T_2$ is tested. However, the schedule $T_0T_3T_1T_2$ is not valid because request T_3 would miss its deadline. We try the insertion test of the next request T_2. As shown in Fig. 5, T_2 is inserted into the front of T_3 and a new schedule $T_0T_1T_2T_3$ is built. Since the schedule $T_0T_1T_2T_3$ is valid and the obtained fulfill-time is reduced, it would be accepted as a new schedule solution.

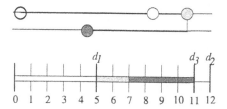

Fig. 4. From the simple test example shown in Table 2, the scheduling result of the proposed BFI algorithm can optimize the seek-time cost with guaranteed deadline.

3.3 Maximum-Tardiness Algorithm for Fast BFI

If there are m scan lines, m possible insertions should be examined. Whenever a rescheduling result is accepted, all the real-time requirements should be guaranteed. Furthermore, the rest parts of the schedule should not be deferred. Since we should verify each insertion tests one by one, the total algorithm will take $O(k*mn)$ if the test procedure for one specified insertion is $O(k)$. Generally, m is much smaller than n. In this paper, we introduce the *maximum-tardiness* concept for each request to speedup the insertion test procedure to a constant time routine. Let $S(t) = T_{A(0)}T_{A(1)}...T_{A(n)}$ as the obtained schedule at iteration t and $S(0) = S_{EDF}$. For each request $T_{A(i)}$ selected for the rescheduling, the maximum-tardiness $D_{A(k)}$ is defined as "the maximum possible defer of request $T_{A(k)}$", where $k = 1$ to i-1. Even if the request $T_{A(k)}$ is started at $(e_{A(k)} + D_{A(k)})$ with $D_{A(k)}$ tardiness, the starting time of next rescheduling request $A(i+1)$ would not be gotten latter than that of the original schedule. Thus, the rest parts of the schedule would not be delayed. The request $T_{A(i)}$ can be successfully inserted into the front of $T_{A(k)}$ to obtain a *valid* solution. At the next step, we also want to compute the obtained improvement to select the best insertion points. By using the above concept, we at first compute $f_{A(j)} = \min\{ d_{A(j)}, e_{A(j+1)} \}$ and $e_{A(j)} = f_{A(j)} - C_{A(j-1),A(j)}$, where $j = i+2$ to n-1, with the maximum-tardiness. We also compute $f_{A(i+1)} = \min\{ d_{A(i+1)}, e_{A(i+2)} \}$ and $e_{A(i+1)} = f_{A(i+1)} - C_{A(i-1),A(i+1)}$. Given $D_{A(i-1)} = \min\{ d_{A(i-1)} - f_{A(i-1)}, e_{A(i+1)} - f_{A(i-1)} \}$, as show in Fig. 5, the maximum-tardiness $D_{A(k)}$ for rescheduling $T_{A(i)}$ can be defined as follows.

$$D_{A(k)} = \min\{ DD_{A(k)}, RD_{A(k+1)} + D_{A(k+1)} \}$$
$$DD_{A(k)} = d_{A(k)} - f_{A(k)} \text{ and } RD_{A(k)} = e_{A(k)} - f_{A(k-1)} \tag{3}$$

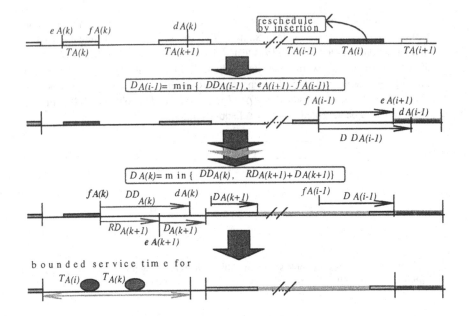

Fig. 5. Descriptions of the release-tardiness, the deadline-tardiness, and the maximum-tardiness.

$DD_{A(k)}$ and $RD_{A(k)}$ are called the *deadline-tardiness* and the *release-tardiness* of request $T_{A(k)}$, respectively. At the boundary cases, we can define that $e_{A(n+1)} = f_{A(n)}$ and $f_{A(-1)} = r_{A(0)}$. The request $T_{A(i)}$ can be successfully inserted into the front of $T_{A(k)}$ to obtain a valid solution. Define the *test start-time* $e^k_{A(i)}$ and the *test fulfill-time* $f^k_{A(i)}$ for inserting request $T_{A(i)}$ before request $T_{A(k)}$ as follows.

$$e^k_{A(i)} = \max\{ r_{A(i)} - f_{A(k-1)}, 0 \}$$
$$f^k_{A(i)} = e^k_{A(i)} + C_{A(k-1),A(i)} \tag{4}$$

Note that, now, the scheduling result considered is $T_{A(0)}T_{A(1)}\cdots T_{A(k-1)}T_{A(i)}$ $T_{A(k)}\cdots T_{A(i-1)}T_{A(i+1)}\cdots T_{A(n)}$. By the same way, we can also calculate $e^k_{A(k)}$ and $f^k_{A(k)}$. The time complexity is a constant term for computing these four variables: $e^k_{A(i)}, f^k_{A(i)}, e^k_{A(k)}$ and $f^k_{A(k)}$. As the real tardiness can be computed by $RT = f^k_{A(k)} - f_{A(k)}$, the obtained improvement for the schedule fulfill-time can be evaluated by

$$\text{improvement} = \min\{ (e_{A(i+1)} - f_{A(i-1)}) - RT, MIT \}$$

in $O(1)$ time complexity. The maximum improvement of the tail part, called MIT, is defined as $\min\{e_{A(j)} - r_{A(j)}\}$ where $j = i+1$ to n. We have the following property.

PROPERTY: Give the maximum-tardiness for inserting request $T_{A(i)}$. For each priori request $T_{A(k)}$, the rescheduling result for inserting $T_{A(i)}$ before $T_{A(k)}$ is a valid schedule if (1) $f^k_{A(i)} \le d_{A(i)}$ and (2) $f^k_{A(k)} \le f_{A(k)} + D_{A(k)}$.

Assume that the maximum-tardiness of each test request has been pre-determined before the insertion test of the rescheduling request. It can be found that the new test procedure will take only O(1) to know whether an insertion is valid or not. Furthermore, we can also know how many improvements it can be obtained. Thus, the time complexity for this best-fit-insertion algorithm can be reduced to O(mn). In [30], Shih and Liu use a hierarchy of priority-queues to speed up the on-line scheduling. We can apply this data structure to speedup the time complexity of BFI as O($n\log m$).

Table 2. The obtained I/O throughput for different approaches

Algorithms	I/O Throughput (Mbps)		
	minimum	maximum	average
BFI	7.10	9.97	8.60
SCAN-EDF	6.22	7.64	6.94

4 Experimental Results for Performance Evaluation

In this paper, a HP 97560 hard disk is applied for performance evaluation. We assume that the data access for each input request uses only one disk track and has constant size 36 KB as shown in [32]. Generally, the release time and the deadline are given by the network transmission schedule. In this paper, without losing the generality, the release times of all requests are assumed to be uniformly distributed from 0 to 240 ms with random arrivals. The deadline for an individual request is the summation of the release time and a random period time varied from 120 to 480 ms. We introduce two evaluation models. The first one is the I/O throughput. A good real-time disk scheduling policy would offer high I/O throughput. The second one is the maximum number of supported requests. The obtained results from different conventional approaches are presented for comparisons. To do fair comparisons with other approaches, we use the same set of I/O requests that can be successfully scheduled by the real-time EDF policy (said $\{T_{E(0)}, T_{E(1)}, ..., T_{E(n)}\}$) as the initial test input. For a valid schedule $S_Z = T_{Z(0)}T_{Z(1)}...T_{Z(n)}$ obtained by an algorithm Z, the improvement of I/O throughput of the scheduling algorithm Z can be easily computed by $(f_{E(n)} - f_{Z(n)}) / f_{E(n)} \times 100\%$. $f_{Z(n)}$ is the fulfill time of schedule S_Z. Fig. 6 shows the average I/O throughput improvements of BFI for different request arrival rates. In this figure, each point is obtained by conducting 100 experiments with different randomly generated request sets. We compute the mean values of the I/O throughput as the graphed performance improvement. Table 2 summaries the obtained I/O throughput for SCAN-EDF and the proposed BFI approach. To keep the comparison as fair as possible, all scheduling policies have the same experiment input data. Notably, periodic requests are generated for a continuous media stream. In this paper, we consider that requests are in the same schedule period. Besides, media streams are continuously placed (track by track) in the disk. Without losing the generality, we randomly generate 100 test examples. Each test example contains 10 requests. For each scheduling policy, the minimum, maximum, and average I/O throughputs are presented to do more detail comparisons. It can be found that BFI is better than SCAN-EDF in all categories.

We also study the behaviors of other disk scheduling algorithms such as SCAN, FCFS and the simple greedy algorithm proposed in this paper. As these three disk scheduling algorithms do not guarantee that all the input requests would meet their deadlines, data throughput is no longer a good measurement for these approaches. Thus, our next performance measurement is to compare the maximum number of requests supported by different real-time disk scheduling policies. The maximum number of supportable requests is obtained by "*incrementally increasing the size of the set of input requests until the real-time timing constraints can not be satisfied.*" A good real-time disk scheduling policy should have the capability to support as many requests as possible. Our experiments show that the proposed BFI algorithm is also good in the number of supportable requests. Table 3 shows the maximum number of real-time request that can be supported by different scheduling methods. According to our experiment, FBI has the best performance. The number of supported requests is ranging from 6 requests to 26 requests. In average, BFI can support over 15 requests and SCAN-EDF can support only 10 requests. We have implemented BFI in the kernel of UnixWare 2.01 operating systems to support distributed multimedia VOD applications. The implementation results also show that the proposed BFI approach is better than the conventional SCAN-EDF approaches in both the I/O throughput and the number of supported requests.

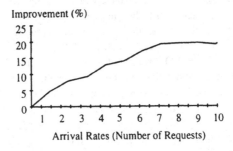

Fig. 6. The obtained improvements of our proposed BFI approach with different number of input requests (arrival rates).

Table 3. The maximum number of request supported by different scheduling policies

Algorithms	Number of Supported Requests		
	minimum	maximum	average
BFI	6	26	15.14
SCAN-EDF	4	24	10.21
EDF	3	24	9.87
Greedy	1	10	4.38

5 Conclusion

In this paper, we propose a new real-time disk scheduling algorithm, called BFI, in which the disk requests are scheduled to meet their timing constraints and to maximize the I/O throughput. Our scheduling scheme utilizes the disk characteristics to reduce the seek costs under the real-time constraints. The performance of the disks is significantly improved for supporting real-time requests. Modern disks usually apply some zoning and buffering algorithms. Besides, some distributed multimedia systems also use disk arrays [26-27] or hierarchical systems as their storage devices. The disk model would become very complex. Our proposed algorithms can be extended to these architectures by replacing the request transition cost with a generalized cost function. We can also consider the rotational latency in the cost function if it is significant for request service.

References

1. Anderson, D.P., Osawa, Y., Govindan, R.: Real-Time Disk Storage and Retrieval of Digital Audio/Video Data. Tech. Report. Univ. of California, Berkeley, CS (1991)
2. Anderson, D.P., Osawa, Y., Govindan, R.: A File System for Continuous Media. ACM Trans. Computer Systems. 4 (1992) 311-337
3. Anderson, D.P.: Metascheduling for Continuous Media. ACM Trans. Computer Systems. 3 (1993) 226-252
4. Rangan, P.V., Vin, H.M.: Designing File Systems for Digital Video and Audio. Proc. ACM Symp. Operating Systems. (1991) 81-94
5. Gemmell, D.J., Christodoulakis, S.: Principles of Delay Sensitive Multimedia Data Storage and Retrieval. ACM Trans. Information Systems. 1 (1992) 51-90
6. Gemmell, D.J., Han, J.: Multimedia Network File Servers: Multichannel Delay Sensitive Data Retrieval. Springer/ACM Multimedia Systems. 6 (1994) 240-252
7. Vin, H.M., Rangan, P.V.: Designing File Systems for Digital Video and Audio. Proc. ACM Symp. Operating System Principles. (1991) 81-94
8. Lougher, P., Shepherd, D.: The Design of a Storage Server for Continuous Media. The Computer Journal. 1 (1993) 32-42
9. Rangan, P.V., Vin, H.M.: Efficient Storage Techniques for Digital Continuous Multimedia. IEEE Trans. Knowledge and Data Eng. 4 (1993) 564-573
10. Gemmell, D.J., Vin, H.M., Kandlur, D.D., Rangan, P.V., Rowe, L.A.: Multimedia Storage Servers: a Tutorial. IEEE Computers. May. (1995) 40-49
11. Lin, T.H., Tarng, W.: Scheduling Periodic and Aperiodic Tasks in Hard Real-Time Computing Systems. Proc. SIMMetrics Conf. (1991) 31-38
12. Chen, M., Kandlur, D.D., Yu, P.S.: Optimization of the Grouped Sweeping Scheduling (GSS) with Heterogeneous Multimedia Streams. Proc. ACM Multimedia Conf. (1993) 235-242
13. Lehoczky, J.P.: Fixed Priority Scheduling of Periodic Task Sets with Arbitrary Deadlines. Proc. Real-Time Systems Symp. (1990) 201-212
14. Yee, J., Varaiya, P.: Disk Scheduling Policies for Real-Time Multimedia Applications. Tech. Report, Univ. of California, Berkeley, Dept. of Computer Science (1991)
15. Reddy, A.L.N., Wyllie, J.: Disk Scheduling in a Multimedia I/O System. Proc. ACM Multimedia Conf. (1993) 225-233

16. Reddy, A.L.N., Wyllie, J.: I/O Issues in a Multimedia System. IEEE Comp. March (1994) 69-74
17. Jeffay, K., Stanat, D.F., Martel, C.U.: On Nonpreemptive Scheduling of Periodic and Sporadic Tasks. Proc. of Real-Time Systems Symp. (1991) 129-139
18. Peterson, J.L., Silberschatz, A.: Operating System Concepts, 2nd Edition, Addison-Wesley (1985)
19. Stankovic, J.A., Buttazzo, G.C.: Implications of Classical Scheduling Results for Real-Time Systems. IEEE Computer. June (1995) 16-25
20. Ruemmler, C., Wilkes, J.: An Introduction to Disk Drive Modeling. IEEE Comp. March (1994) 16-28
21. King, R.P.: Disk Arm Movement in Anticipation of Future Requests. ACM Trans. Computer Systems. 3 (1990) 214-229
22. Liu, C.L., Layland, J.W.: Scheduling Algorithms for Multiprogramming in a Hard Real-Time Environment. Journal of ACM. (1973) 46-61
23. Dan, A., Sitaram, D., Shahabuddin, P.: Scheduling Policies for an On-Demand Video Server with Batching. Proc. ACM Multimedia Conf. (1994) 15-22
24. Terry, D.B., Swinehart, D.C.: Managing Stored Voice in the Etherphone System. ACM Trans. Computer Systems. 1 (1988) 3-27
25. Mok, A.: Fundamental Design Problems for the Hard Real-Time Environment. MIT Ph.D. Dissertation, Cambridge, MA. (1983)
26. Patterson, D.A., Gibson, G., Katz, R.H.: A Case for Redundant Arrays of Inexpensive Disks (RAID). Proc. ACM SIGMOD Conf. (1988) 109-116
27. Chen, M., Kandlur, D.D., Yu, P.S.: Support for Fully Interactive Playout in a Disk-Array-Based Video Server. Proc. ACM Multimedia Conf. (1994)
28. Shih, W.K., Liu, J.W.S., Liu, C.L.: Modified Rate Monotone Algorithm for Scheduling Periodic Jobs with Deferred Deadlines. Tech. Report, Univ. of Illinois, Urbana-Champaign, Dept. of CS. (1992)
29. Kim, M.Y.: Synchronized Disk Interleaving. IEEE Trans. Comp. 11 (1986) 978-988
30. Shih, W.K., Liu, J.W.S.: On-Line Scheduling of Imprecise Computations to Minimize Error. Proc. of Real-Time Systems Symp. (1992) 280-289
31. Chang, R.I., Chen, M., Ho, J.M., Ko, M.T.: Optimizations of Stored VBR Video Transmission on CBR Channel. Proc. SPIE Performance & Control of Network Systems. (1997) 382-392
32. Wang, Y.C., Tsao, S.L., Chang, R.I., Chen, M., Ho, J.M., Ko, M.T.: A Fast Data Placement Scheme for Video Server with Zoned-Disks. Proc. SPIE MM Storage & Archiving Systems. (1997) 92-102
33. Chang, R.I.: Real-Time Disk Scheduling in Multimedia Systems.
34. Gemmell, D.J., Beaton, R.J., Han, J., Christodoulakis, S.: Real-Time Delay Sensitive Multimedia in a Disk-Based Environment. IEEE Multimedia. Fall (1994)
35. Sahu, S., Zhang, Z., Kurose. J., Towsley, D.: On the Efficient Retrieval of VBR Video in a Multimedia Server. Proc. Intl. Conf. on Multimedia Computing Systems. (1997)

Continuous Data Management on Tape-Based Tertiary Storage Systems

Jihad Boulos and Kinji Ono

National Center for Science Information Systems
Otsuka 3-29-1, Bunkyo-Ku, Tokyo 112, Japan {boulos,ono}@rd.nacsis.ac.jp

Abstract. Video-on-Demand (VOD) servers are becoming feasible. These servers have voluminous data to store and manage. A tape-based tertiary storage system seems to be a reasonable solution to lowering the cost of storage and management of this continuous data. In this paper we address the issues of decomposing and placing continuous data blocks on tapes, and the scheduling of multiple requests for materializing objects from tapes to disks. We first study different policies for continuous object decomposition and blocks placement on tapes under different characteristics of the tertiary storage drives. Afterwards, we propose a scheduling algorithm for object materialization.

1 Introduction

Most multimedia data is currently stored on magnetic hard disks, yet the proliferation of such applications is generating massive amounts of data such that a storage subsystem based solely on hard disks will be too expensive to support and manage. The video-on-demand (VOD) server is one particular multimedia application requiring huge storage capacity.

While current issues associated with VOD servers are focusing on the physical layout on disks of continuous objects (movies) such that the number of serviced streams can be maximized the number of available on-line objects will soon become an important issue as well. The problem arising is that some objects will only be requested infrequently, while others—especially new ones—may be simultaneously requested by any number of viewers. Because the cost per gigabyte using magnetic hard disks or tertiary storage systems is different by more than an order of magnitude, it is more economical to store all objects on a tertiary storage system and to replicate only the most requested ones at a certain time on disks. This is also beneficial for fault-tolerance—as a copy of any object exists on the tertiary storage—as well as for lowering the cost and physical size of the storage system.

In the present study, we consider the issues of placing continuous objects on a tape-based tertiary storage system and also the ensuing scheduling policy. We focus on a VOD server which can *service multiple streams with a multitude of videos using a large number of hard disks and a tape-based tertiary storage system with several drives*. The size of the continuous objects is assumed to be several times larger than the secondary storage capacity. Under such conditions and in light of the potentially large capacity of currently available tapes and the high transfer bandwidth of their drives[1], a tape library is considered to be advantageous in comparison to other kinds of tertiary storage systems.

With continuous objects stored on tapes it is envisioned that when a request arrives for a partially or completely non-disk resident object, the system starts transferring non-disk resident portions from the tertiary storage system to disks, and after some described conditions are satisfied the service commences while the transfer continues. Under these "pipelined" transfers, *i.e.*, between tapes and disks on one side and disks and memory on the other side, the service can commence prior to the end of the object transfer with minimum delays incurred. The envisioned system requires that several problems be addressed, however. We consider here the following issues: 1) a placement strategy for object blocks on one or more tapes, and 2) a real-time-like scheduling algorithm for materializing continuous objects from tapes.

Section 2 briefly mentions related works and Section 3 describes the system architecture. Section 4 considers the issue of block size and placement on tapes. An adapted real-time-like scheduling algorithm for transferring object blocks from tapes to disks is described in Section 5. The results of simulations are discussed in Section 6, with concluding remarks being given in Section 7.

2 Related Works

Several studies have addressed hierarchical storage systems for continuous or conventional data, although none have considered the general framework for continuous data management on a hierarchical storage system.

[6] and [2] describe each a replacement policy between a tertiary storage system and disks. However, neither addresses the issues of object decomposition or transfer alternation. [8] presents a study on a scheduling policy for continuous data from a tape-based tertiary storage to disks; the study does not consider decomposing objects nor does it address tertiary storage systems with multiple drives or drives with higher transfer rates than the objects service rates. [4] and [10] advise a certain block placement policy on tertiary storage platters but their works need a-priory knowledge of data access patterns. This is difficult for continuous objects where access patterns change over time. Finally, [5] and [7] considered robotic storage libraries, analyzing the performance and trade-off of stripping large files on several tapes. Both studies deal with non-continuous large data files in which no transfer alternation and synchronization is necessary.

3 System Architecture

Fig. 1 shows the architecture of the envisioned system. A tape-based tertiary storage system and a multiple-disk secondary storage system are connected to a

---

[1] Tapes of more than 150 GB storage capacity and drives of 15 MBps transfer rate exist at the time of writing.

large server through a high-speed network. Transfer of an object from tapes to disks must pass through the server memory if the hardware and software connection interfaces of different storage components do not permit direct transfer from tape drives to disk drives. All considered tasks are managed by a server-based database management system.

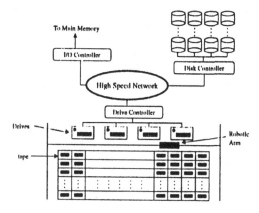

Fig. 1. System Architecture.

We consider in this paper tape-based tertiary storage system. Two different technologies exist for currently available tapes; however, we do not consider this issue here. In our simulations, we assumed that the seek time between two locations on a tape is proportional to their positions on that tape; an assumption which does not hold for serpentine tapes and therefore this is considered as the worst case seek time between two positions in the simulation configuration. As shown in Fig. 1, a robotic arm moves a requested tape to/from a drive from/to its cell in the library. We assume there is no contention for this arm, and considering the current state of robotic technology, this is a realistic assumption. Table 1 summarizes major parameters of the system architecture with their corresponding meanings.

The secondary storage system is based on an array of disks. We define the ratio between the secondary storage capacity and the data size in the tertiary storage system as STR, i.e., $STR = \frac{n_d \cdot c_d}{\sum_{i=1}^{O} L_i}$. Materializing object blocks is defined as replicating the blocks from the tertiary tapes to disks.

The number of continuous objects O stored on tapes in the tape library is large. We assume that all the objects have the same service rate, and that at a certain time a subset of popular objects must be materialized on disks because of the larger transfer rate of disks and the possibility of multiple streams of the same object. When an object is requested, if it is completely materialized on disks, then the service may start immediately if sufficient disk bandwidth is available. If, on the other hand, some fraction of the requested object is not on disks, then the non-disk resident fraction is requested from the tape library. Of

Table 1. Typical parameters used in our study.

Tertiary storage param.		Disks parameters		Database parameters	
Nb drives	k	Read rate	r_d	Init. available obj.	O
Tape exchange	t_{ex}	Seek time	t_{dseek}	Regularly added	A
Seek rate	t_{tseek}	Rotate time	t_{lat}	Object length	L_i
Read rate	r_t	Disk capacity	c_d	Display rate	D
Nb tapes	n_t	Block size	B_d	Mem. Block size	B_m
Tape capacity	c_t	Nb disks	n_d		
Block size	B_t				

interest here are such cases, *i.e.*, requested objects are either partially or fully non-disk resident.

Whenever a request arrives, sufficient disk space must be freed up to materialize the non-disk resident fraction of the requested object, and once the free space is available, the transfer from tapes to disks may start. In parallel with the transfer, the service may start in a pipelined manner although some fraction of the object must be materialized on disks before starting the service. Adopting the definition from [6], the ratio between the transfer rate per tape drive and the consumption rate of an object is termed as the Production Consumption Ratio ($PCR = \frac{r_t}{D}$). In this study we use an extension of the replacement policy advised by [6].

3.1 Object Decomposition

The continuous objects have different sizes. An object O_i is split into n_i blocks $O_{i,1}, \ldots, O_{i,n}$, which may be stored on just one tape in a contiguous manner, inter-lapped with blocks from other objects, or be distributed on more than one tape. A block is the unit of transfer from tapes to disks and of space freed up on disks.

Upon system installation, some number O of continuous objects will be placed on a particular number of tapes. At either constant or variable time intervals (*e.g.*, one week), a number of new objects A are added to the system and $O \leftarrow O + A$. These objects are initially added on tapes, and upon being requested, a new object is materialized on disks. It is expected that the request frequency of new objects will reach a peak level a short time after being added to the system.

3.2 Latency Time

The ultimate objective of the server is to minimize the latency time while guaranteeing an uninterrupted service stream. Latency time is defined as the elapsed time between request arrival and the beginning of service. For a new request of an object with non-disk resident blocks, the following conditions must be satisfied before service commencement:

- Sufficient disk space must be freed up to store non-disk resident blocks of the object.
- The scheduling algorithm of the tape library drives must guarantee the materialization on disks of any non-disk resident block before its service time.
- Some fraction of the object is disk resident.
- Sufficient disk bandwidth is available for parallel servicing the requested stream and materializing non-disk resident blocks.

Regarding the last condition, this is not an issue studied here. Hence, the latency time T_i for a request of object O_i having non-disk resident blocks is calculated as

$$T_i = L_{FreeSpace} + L_{Schedule} + M_i \qquad (1)$$

$L_{FreeSpace}$ is the time needed to free up disk space equivalent to the non-disk resident fraction of O_i. We do not consider this cost in the rest of this paper.

$L_{Schedule}$ is the time needed by the tertiary storage scheduling algorithm to place the request for O_i in a list of requests and the elapsed time between the end of the scheduling algorithm and the arrival of the list element carrying request O_i to the drive handling it. If the scheduling algorithm is FCFS or has a low complexity, then the execution time of the scheduling algorithm is insignificant, i.e., considered to be zero.

M_i is the time to materialize the $FirstSlice(O_i)$, which is the fraction of object O_i that must be materialized on disks before service commencement, being related to the value of PCR, i.e.,

$$FirstSlice(O_i) = L_i - (min(PCR, 1) \times L_i) + B_m \qquad (2)$$

where $min(PCR, 1)$ expresses the fact that when $PCR \geq 1$, the size of any $FirstSlice(O_i)$ is equal to the size of B_m, independent from L_i. Accordingly, M_i can be computed using

$$M_i = P(t_{ex}) + StartPosition(O_{i,1})/t_{tseek} + FirstSlice(O_i)/r_t \qquad (3)$$

where $P(t_{ex})$ is a function that returns the cost in seconds of a tape exchange if needed.

3.3 Multiple Drives

The tape library is comprised of k drives ($k > 1$) in which all are assumed to have the same characteristics. The transfer bandwidth of the tape library becomes $k \cdot r_t$. The following three cases apply regarding pipelining and blocks placement on tapes:

- $k \cdot PCR < 1$.
- $PCR < 1$ and $k \cdot PCR \geq 1$.
- $PCR \geq 1$.

These three cases are the initial points from which the design of a tape-based tertiary storage system for continuous data must start, the cost of which is primarily determined by the number of drives/tapes comprising it. One important question that must be addressed is: "What is the optimal number of drives in a tertiary storage subsystem such that it is nearly always available for servicing a transfer request yet at the same time economical?" The answer is heavily dependent on PCR, STR, and the object access patterns—as well as drive characteristics.

We determine the optimal number of drives, k, as follows. Let λ be the average number of requested objects to be transferred from the tertiary storage subsystem to the disks during some Δt (e.g., 30 min); n_{A_i} be the number of tapes on which the ith requested object is stored ($n_{A_i} \geq 1$); and L_i be the length in MB of object O_i. To reach equilibrium of the tertiary storage, the following formula must hold:

$$\frac{1}{k} \cdot \sum_{i=1}^{\lambda} \left(\frac{L_i}{r_t} + n_{A_i} \cdot \sum_{j=1}^{O_{i,n_j}} \left(P(t_{ex_j}) + Abs \left(SP(O_{i,n_j}) - EP(O_{i,n_{j-1}}) \right) / t_{tseek} \right) \right) \leq \Delta t$$

that gives

$$k = \lceil \frac{1}{\Delta t} \cdot \sum_{i=1}^{\lambda} \left(\frac{L_i}{r_t} + n_{A_i} \cdot \sum_{j=1}^{O_{i,n_j}} \left(P(t_{ex_j}) + Abs \left(SP(O_{i,n_j}) - EP(O_{i,n_{j-1}}) \right) / t_{tseek} \right) \right) \rceil$$

where $P(t_{ex_j})$ is the function that returns the tape exchange time when block O_{i,n_j} is the next to be transferred, SP and EP stand for $StartPosition$ and $EndPosition$ respectively, and with the other variables being self explanatory. If no transfer alternation is made between the transfers of two contiguous blocks of the same object, then $P(t_{ex_j})$ and the seek time are both equal to zero.

4 Blocks Size and Distribution

As distribution of continuous data blocks on multiple tapes can be beneficial, we evaluated several different placement strategies in simulation experiments, comparing only the most effective strategies regarding selection of block size/distribution in Section 6. From the results, we discuss the potential gains in latency time when using striping and/or overlapping.

At system installation, a number of objects O will be placed on tapes, and due to tape capacity being typically several times larger than object size, several objects will normally be placed on one tape. In an iterative manner, a small number of objects A is chosen from the initial number O to be placed on n_A tapes, where n_A is termed the stripe size. Parameters A and n_A are determined according to PCR and $\sum_{i=1}^{A} L_i \leq n_A \cdot c_t$, although a good rule-of-thumb is that $n_A \leq k$.

We define the $UtilizationFactor UF$ of a drive to be the fraction of drive time spent in transferring data, i.e., one minus the fraction of time it is idle, exchanging tapes, or seeking locations in tapes. The utilization factor of the tertiary system becomes $k \cdot UF$. One successful heuristic method is to distribute only a portion of an object blocks. That is, a $DistributionFactor DF$ gives the number of blocks from each object in A to be distributed and overlapped with other objects blocks on n_A, with the remaining blocks of an object being stored in a contiguous manner on a single tape.

4.1 $k \cdot PCR < 1$

When $k \cdot PCR < 1$, distributing blocks on $n_A = k$ tapes showed a significant improvement in latency time when the tertiary system is lightly to moderately loaded, being due to the fact that $FirstSlice(O_i)$ is very large in this case. Decomposing $FirstSlice(O_i)$ and distributing its blocks on multiple tapes allows parallel transfer of the blocks and hence lowers M_i in Eq. 3 since r_t is multiplied by k. An upper bound on the block size in this situation is $\lceil B_t \rceil = FirstSlice(O_i)/k$. No alternation of transfers is possible in this case. Fig. 2 shows an example in which three objects are distributed on two tapes in which their first blocks are overlapped in a round-robin manner. The optimal DF under $k \cdot PCR < 1$ was determined as the average size of $FirstSlice(O_i)$ divided by the size of a block, $i.e.,\ DF = \dfrac{\sum_{i=1}^{O} FirstSlice(O_i)}{O \cdot B_t}$.

Fig. 2. Distribution of three continuous objects on two tapes.

4.2 $PCR < 1$ and $k \cdot PCR \geq 1$

If $PCR < 1$ and $k \cdot PCR \geq 1$, this situation is not much different from $k \cdot PCR < 1$. The main difference being that n_A might be less than k, and in such a case, the lowest average latency occurs when 1) n_A is minimal and 2) $n_A \cdot PCR \geq 1$. In other words, a minimum number of tape exchanges and seeks is balanced against reducing the size of $FirstSlice(O_i)$ of all objects in O. Accordingly, $DiskSlice(O_i)$ of each object is no longer dependent on the particular size L_i of that object, rather it depends on the value of B_t; hence, $FirstSlice(O_i)$ becomes $FirstSlice(O_i) = B_t - (B_t \times PCR) + B_m$ which is independent from L_i and is the same for all objects. An upper bound on the size of a block in this case is $\lceil B_t \rceil = FirstSlice(O_i)/n_A$. In our results $B_t = FirstSlice(O_i)/n_A$ provided the lowest average M_i. Once again no alternation of transfers on the same drive can be performed here. The optimal DF was its minimum value, *i.e.*, $DF = n_A$, which provides a lower number of tape exchanges and seeks and prevents a request from utilizing a drive more than it needs; thereby preventing any delay in satisfying subsequent requests.

4.3 $PCR > 1$

When $PCR > 1$, striping was only advantageous when the system was lightly loaded, though it yielded bad consequences when the system was moderately to highly loaded. This outcome is due to the fact that the read rate is relatively high and the ensuing tape exchange and seek times account for a significant cost relative to the read time. Hence n_A is best when no striping is permitted, *i.e.*, $n_A = 1$. In this case $FirstSlice(O_i) = B_m$ is independent of the size of any object.

An alternative to striping large objects on multiple tapes when $PCR > 1$ is to decompose an object into several blocks and overlap different blocks from different objects on the same tape . The first blocks of all objects on one tape are placed near the head of the tape, which lowers the average seek time for the first B_t of all objects.

B_t must have a greater consumption time than the time for rewinding and switching a tape, seeking and transferring another B'_t, and again rewinding and switching a tape and seeking the start position of a third B''_t. This case can be formulated as follows

$$B_t \geq (t_{ex} + SP(B'_t)/t_{tseek} + B_t/r_t + t_{ex} + SP(B''_t)/t_{tseek}) \times D \qquad (4)$$

where the switch and seek times must be taken as the worst case. B_t may be equal to L_i, and if so, every object O_i consists of one block and no alternation is subsequently allowed, although as mentioned alternation can be beneficial.

5 Transfer Scheduling

Scheduling the transfers of continuous objects from a tertiary storage system with a pipelined service requires a different strategy from scheduling random I/Os. The issue has several similarities with real-time scheduling problems. One must take care of some differences, however. In most real-time scheduling algorithms context switching cost is assumed to be negligible or constant [9]. Under our framework tape exchange and seek costs vary widely and are important parameters as they significantly affect the utilization factor and system performance accordingly; and in fact, extensive switching between different transfers may have disastrous consequences on performance.

The two cases do have an obvious similarity in that they both impose a firm deadline constraint on completing their jobs before a certain time. However, a direct adaptation of real-time scheduling algorithms would be too restrictive for admission control of a new transfer request because exchanges and seeks must be computed as worst cases. To improve the latency time of the system under different conditions, we experimentally investigated several different heuristics; finding that some scheduling choices perform well under a particular block distribution/system workload but demonstrate catastrophic performance under other circumstances. We observed that PCR and STR are in most cases the decisive parameters when considering resultant quality of the implemented heuristic algorithm.

For admission control and transfer scheduling, the system manager processes requests as follows. At the arrival of a request, the system makes a list of the non-disk resident blocks and transmits it to the scheduler. This list consists of elements, termed as tasks, that specify each requested block, on which tape it is stored, its position on that tape, its position within the object, and several other parameters. The two following heuristics showed valuable applicability:

- Balancing workload between drives (obvious optimization practice).
- Never migrates a tape from one drive to another.

Due to space limits we could not state the algorithm here. A detailed version can be found in [1]. Its implementation counts for one-third of the simulator and it took the largest amount of work to be enhanced and verified. We present its results in the following section.

Table 2. Fixed values used in system performance simulations.

Disks parameters					
r_d	6.0 MBps	t_{lat}	8 ms	B_d	0.256 MB
t_{dseek}	15 ms	c_r	4.55 GB	B_m	0.256 MB

6 Simulation Results

The majority of the discussions and results given thus far have been based on the results taken on a simulated system. That is, to better understand tertiary storage system behavior under different workloads, we conducted extensive simulations on a model of the proposed system architecture implemented in a combination of C and C++ as part of a simulation program integrated into the CSIM18 [3] simulation package. As full control on the lists and their member entries is required, and CSIM18 does not permit such control, we implemented our own queuing system for the tape drive lists. The simulator is comprised of three components: the request generator, tertiary storage manager, and disk manager.

All the simulations were executed on a bi-processor Sun-Ultra2 workstation. Simulation results are given for 5,000 requests, although no statistics collections were taken until 1,000 requests were processed. Simulations lasted on average from 1 to 15 min.; we report this simulation time to allow an evaluation of the complexity of the scheduling algorithm. The request generator is an open system

Table 3. Summary of parameter values used in three simulated scenarios.

	First Scenario	Second Scenario	Third Scenario
t_{ex}	100 sec.	70 sec.	30 sec.
t_{tseek}	50 MBps	150 MBps	500 MBps
r_t	0.5 MBps	2.0 MBps	15.0 MBps
c_t	5 GB	50 GB	165 GB
B_t	200 MB	1.2 GB	7.5 Gb
k	4	4	4
n_d	20	100 / 200 / 400	500
D	24.0 Mbps	24.0 Mbps	48.0 Mbps
A	7	9	19
O	504	504	513
L_i/D	$6 \sim 15$ min.	$30 \sim 60$ min.	$68 \sim 84$ min.

with the inter-arrival time between requests being distributed according to an exponential time distribution with a varied mean. We made simulations using two access patterns to the objects—uniform and Zipf-like (*i.e.*, skewed). The skewed access pattern had its moving peak at the new added objects to the system.

The following subsections present simulation results and analyze system behavior under various conditions. All results were repeated and parameters were varied several times in order to ensure reproducible results and to exclude the possibility of special cases being a factor in our observations. Tables 2 and 3 respectively summarize the values of fixed parameters and those varied in four simulated scenarios. The time period for different objects is uniformly distributed between the sizes given in line L_i/D.

6.1 $k \cdot PCR < 1$

Scenario 1 considered $k \cdot PCR < 1$ and $STR \approx 0.1$ in which an object has an average size of 1.89 GB and can be transferred by one drive in 3780 s. B_t was varied, and a value of 200 MB was found to be most effective. Fig. 3 shows the results, where for both access patterns the distribution of blocks on 4 tapes ($n_A = k = 4$) with $DF = 9$ yielded lower average latency times when the system was lightly loaded. For a highly loaded system, however, increases in tape exchange/seek times overcame the gains from parallel transfers on multiple drives.

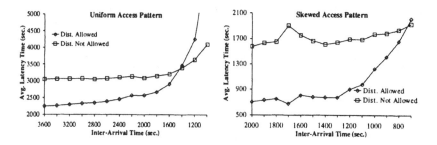

Fig. 3. Scenario 1 results: average latency times for disk space when striping was allowed (dist. allowed) versus single tape placement (dist. not allowed) with $k \cdot PCR < 1$ for a (a) uniform and (b) skewed access pattern.

6.2 $PCR < 1$ and $k \cdot PCR \geq 1$

Scenario 2 considered the case of $PCR < 1$ and $k \cdot PCR \geq 1$, with results being shown in Fig. 4. This scenario is not as simple to analyze as that of 1. Regarding both access patterns with $STR \approx 0.1$ (*i.e.*, 100 disks), note that disk capacity was smaller than the sum of all the $DiskSlise(O_i)$, such that striping on two tapes (*i.e.*, $n_A = 2$) improved the average latency time when the system was lightly loaded, although this gain was reversed by increasing exchange/seek times for a highly loaded system. However, for the uniform access pattern with $STR \approx 0.5$ (*i.e.*, 400 disks), disk capacity became greater than the sum of all the $DiskSlice(O_i)$, such that striping yielded a higher average latency time.

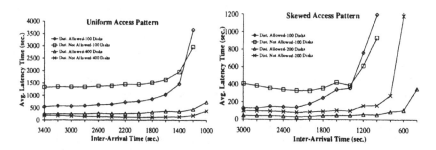

Fig. 4. Avg. latency times under different conditions when $PCR < 1$ and $k \cdot PCR \geq 1$.

For the skewed access pattern, when the number of disks was increased to 200, object striping still had an advantage over non-striping. With 400 disks, the results were similar but latency times were too small to be apparent. Such behavior is due to the fact that drive load balancing could not be achieved when a tape had a high probability of being requested several times in parallel (new films added on the same tape). With the no striping policy, this put a heavy load on one drive while other drives were idle.

Again, and due to space limites we could not include here the results for $PCR \geq 1$ (*i.e.*, Third Scenario). Interested reader is referred to [1].

7 Conclusion

We conclude that continuous object decomposition is advantageous in a lightly loaded tertiary storage subsystem, one expected to have a high hit ratio (*i.e.*, object already on disks) for most requests arriving at large VOD servers. A second conclusion is that block placement on different tapes is only effective when $PCR < 1$ and $STR \ll 1$. A third conclusion is that when $PCR \geq 1$, blocks from the same continuous object must be placed on the same tape.

References

1. Boulos, J., Ono, K.: Continuous Data Management on Tape-Based Tertiary Storage Systems. NACSIS Report, Nov. 1997. Available from http://www.rd.nacsis.ac.jp/~boulos/VOD_Paper.ps.Z
2. Brubeck, D., Rowe, L.: Hierarchical Storage Management in a Distributed VOD System. IEEE Multimedia, Vol. 3, No. 3, (1996)
3. CSIM18 Simulation Engine, Mesquite Software Inc., 3925 West Braker Lane, Austin, Texas 78759-5321, (1994)
4. Christodoulakis, S., Triantafillou, P., Zioga, F.: Principles of Optimally Placing Data in Tertiary Storage Libraries. Proc. of the 23rd VLDB Conf., Athens, Greece, August (1997)
5. Drapeau, A., Katz, R.: Striped Tape Arrays. Proc. of the 12th IEEE Symposium on Mass Storage Systems, Monterey, CA, (1993)
6. Ghandeharizadeh, S., Shahabi, C.: On Multimedia Repositories, Personal Computers, and Hierarchical Storage Systems. Proc. of the 2nd ACM Int. Conf. on Multimedia, San Francisco, CA, (1994)
7. Golubchik, L., Muntz, R., Watson, R.: Analysis of striping techniques in Robotic Storage Libraries. Proc. of the 14th IEEE Symp. on Mass Storage Systems, CA, (1995)
8. Lau, S., Lui, J., Wong, P.: A Cost-effective Near-Line Storage Server for Multimedia System. Proceedings of the 11th Int. Conf. on Data Eng., Taipei, Taiwan, (1995)
9. Liu, C., Layland, J.: Scheduling Algorithms for Multiprogramming in a Hard-Real-Time Environment. Journal of the ACM, **20**, No. 1, (1973) 46–61
10. Triantafillou, P., Papadakis, T.: On-Demand Data Elevation in a Hierarchical Multimedia Storage Server. Proc. of the 23rd VLDB Conf., Athens, Greece, (1997)

Exploiting User Behaviour in Prefetching WWW Documents

Abdulmotaleb El-Saddik[1], Carsten Griwodz[1], and Ralf Steinmetz[1,2]

1	2
Industrial Process and System Communications	GMD IPSI
Dept. of Electrical Eng. &	German National Research Center
Information Technology	for Information Technology
Darmstadt University of Technology	Dolivostr. 15 • D-64293 Darmstadt • Germany
Merckstr. 25 • D-64283 Darmstadt • Germany	

{Abdulmotaleb.El-Saddik,Carsten.Griwodz,Ralf.Steinmetz}@kom.tu-darmstadt.de

Abstract. As the popularity of the World Wide Web increases, the amount of traffic results in major congestion problems for the retrieval of data over wide distances. To react to this, users and browser builders have implemented various prefetching and parallel retrieval mechanisms, which initiate retrieval of documents that may be required later. This additional traffic is even worsening the situation. Since we believe that this will remain the general approach for quite a while, we try to make use of the general technique but try to reduce the destructive effects by retrieving less content which remains finally unread.

In our user-specific prefetch mechanism, the prefetching system gathers references by parsing the HTML pages the user browses, identifies the links to other pages, and puts the words describing the links into a keyword list. If such a word was already present in the list, its associated weight is incremented. Otherwise it is added to the table and a weighting factor allocated. We have designed and implemented a client based proxy-server with this mechanism. This paper shows the design and implementation of this prefetching proxy server, presents results and general considerations on this technique.

1 Introduction

The simplicity of access to a variety of information stored on remote locations led to the fact that World Wide Web services have grown to levels where major delays due to congestion are experienced very often. There are several factors influencing the retrieval time of a web document. These factors are network bandwidth, propagation delay, data loss, and the client and server load. Although several approaches have been implemented to reduce these delays, the problem still exists.

The latency of retrieval operations depends on the performance of servers and on the network latency. Servers may take a while to process a request or may refuse to accept it due to over-load. The network latency depends on the network congestion and the propagation delay. While the propagation delay is a constant component, which can not be reduced, the network bandwidth is steadily increased by the increase of networks' capacities and the installation of new networks.

The rest of the paper is organized as follows. Section 2 discusses related work. Section 3 describes our approach in designing a newer prefetch proxy. The description of the system architecture is followed by initial experiences in section 4, section 5 concludes the paper.

2 Related Work

Various approaches to solve the problem of retrieval delays were presented in the past. Most of them deal with caching ([5][9][10]). However, the effectiveness of caching to reduce the WWW latency is small. Several papers report that the hit-rate of the caching proxy server is under 50% ([9][10]). Actually, we observe that the hit-rate is constantly falling because the number of documents and the size of those documents grows faster than the typical proxy server.

An alternative approach to reduce delay experienced by the end user is prefetching. The majority of users browse the Web by following hyperlinks from one page to another with a general idea or topic in mind. While users read the downloaded page, there is a communication pause. Since there is a general topic that drives the user's navigation, this time can be used to prefetch pages that are likely to be accessed as a follow up to the current page. Actually, prefetching does not reduce latency, it only exploits the time the user spends reading, and thereby theoretically decreases the experienced access time. Practically, the growing number of users of this technique destroys the effects by increasing considerably the overall amount of data transfers on the networks.

Prefetching has some problems and drawbacks. One of these problems is to decide or to predict what and when to prefetch. Another problem is the large amount of traffic. Both problems can be addressed by increasing the hit-rate of the prefetching mechanism. There is a long list of references considering prefetching of WWW pages. Each of these references deals with different situations and different mechanisms. In general we can consider the following strategies:

- Non statistical prefetching
- Servers' access statistics
- Users' personal preferences

Chinen ([11]) prefetches referenced pages. The prefetching system he suggested is to prefetch all the referenced pages of an HTML document at each request of the client. This scheme reduces the relative latency experienced by the user, but it suffers from the fact that there is no speculative prediction.

Server access statistics to prefetch WWW documents is investigated by Markatos ([5]), Bestavros ([2]), Doi ([4]), and Padmanhaban ([6]). Such a strategy is based on the observation of a client's access pattern. They exploit the fact that users do generally not access files at random. Although the access pattern of a user is not deterministic, the server can obtain a good idea of the files likely to be accessed next based on the currently accessed file. In order to achieve high hit-rates, a long observation time is required. It is difficult to react to new trends in user behaviour immediately using this scheme. Padmanhaban and Mogul ([6]) propose protocol modifications on both server and clients to keep state in the server.

The use of users' personal preferences is also a way to prefetch document in the WWW. This mechanism is implemented by Microsoft's Channel Bar ([12]) and Netscape's Netcaster ([13]), which enable (so-called) push delivery of information and off-line browsing. This technology enables users to subscribe to channels, which describe an interest profile for a user. When the user starts the browser, the prefetching mechanism that is built into the browser contacts the servers specified by the channel information and retrieves all appropriate information for off-line browsing by the user. The user doesn't have to request or search manually for the information.

All of these approaches work with long-term constant interests of the users. No approach considers the appropriateness of prefetching for short-term interests of the user. We consider questions such as "where can I find information on MPEG-2 encoders?" or "how do I travel in Tibet?" short-term interests, which concern the user for some minutes up to a few days but are not worth the manual specification of a user-specific profile. Since we believe that all of these prefetching techniques are not specific enough to cover the short-term interests of a user, and thus, that too much unnecessary information is retrieved, we have designed an alternative approach to prefetching.

3 Design of a New Prefetching-Proxy Algorithm

3.1 Design considerations

The user's browsing strategy can be determined by observing the user's earlier behaviour. Most user events are of the type "select hyperlink on current document" (52%) and "browser-back-button" (41%) ([7]). For effective prefetching, a mechanism should take these events into account. In other words, many web sessions start with an idea of what to search. In general, the user detects very quickly whether a piece of information is interesting for him or not and decides to move on. Other browsing strategies are less relevant to prefetching. It is not useful to prefetch when the major user event is "goto URL". Users who demonstrate this kind of behaviour are just surfing in unpredictable ways and find information randomly. However, this is rare and additionally, those users move on slowly because they don't look for specific topics but consume all input. Models which describe and determine the different browsing strategies are investigated in [3].

We believe that very specific interests are (in the mind of the user) expressed by a keyword or set of keywords; these keywords are also the basis of any search he performs, typically by starting with a typical search engine such as Alta Vista. For such a user behaviour, the prefetching of a subset of links is viable and we have implemented a mechanism to exploit it. Our idea is to make use of the Web technology as is and to implement a mechanism that can be used with all clients without replacing servers and protocols. Our mechanism differs from those which prefetch all pages referenced by the current page, by loading only those referenced pages which are predicted to be interesting to the user and thus, probably visited.

3.2 Structure of a Web page

Usually a Web page is a simple text document with in-line images and references to other pages (links). In general, all web documents can be grouped into two categories with regard to the time at which the content of the page is determined.

The first category consists of *static* documents. The content of these is determined at creation time. Although some documents of the static category are generated dynamically by server processes, these contents are independent from user interaction and are presented in the same way whenever they are accessed. Typically, the content remains unchanged for a while, so this kind of document is very suitable for caching and prefetching.

The second category are *dynamic* documents. This group can be subdivided into a *fully dynamical* category and an *active* category. A dynamical document is created by a web server when the document is requested (e.g. CGI-scripts). Dynamic documents can not be cached or prefetched because the results of a request are entirely dependent on a specific situation. An active document includes a program that runs on the client machine, e.g. a Java applet, and which may communicate with one or more server processes. The client parts of active documents may be prefetched and cached, since they remain unchanged for longer periods and their download operation is similar to the download of a computer program.

3.3 Description of the Prefetching Algorithm

We have implemented a client side architecture that addresses the prefetching of static documents. Our approach includes criteria which are determined by observing the user behaviour. In our implementation the collection of the user-specific criteria is accomplished by a „clicked-word-list". This list is the database in which the frequencies of words extracted from the selected anchors are collected (see figure 1). As soon as an HTML-document is retrieved by the proxy, the prediction algorithm parses this document, builds a list of current links and anchor texts. The words in this list are compared to a user database of user-specific keywords. This database grows while the user is browsing. Each time a link is clicked, the words in the anchor text of the link are recorded in the database, respectively their counters are incremented. The database is kept for future sessions. The possibility of deleting this database is also given.

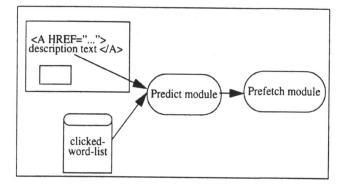

Fig. 1. The predict module compares the anchor text with the user's clicked word list

The advantages of the mechanism are:

- Web latency is reduced: The system prefetches the predicted pages until all predicted pages are retrieved or until a new request is made by the user, whichever occurs first.

- The prefetching is not a recursive copying of all references on a page but only of the relevant documents.

- Using the user's preferences: The algorithm gathers the links by parsing the HTML document and by comparing the words in the anchor text with the user's database.

- abandon the use of statistics

The disadvantages of the mechanism are:

- Synonyms, and words that contain less than 4 lowercase letters are not taken into consideration: we have to add thesauri

- the large traffic that comes generally with prefetching

3.4 Modules

This section describes the module of the prefetching proxy server called MObile proxy helPER (MOPER). Figure 2 shows the system architecture of MOPER which consists of three modules: ClickedWord module, Predict module and Prefetch module.

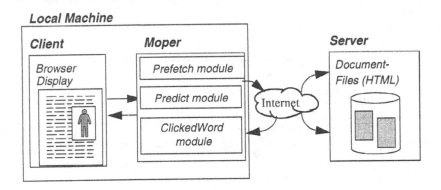

Fig. 2. System Architecture

ClickedWord module: The main task of this module is to identify the anchor associated with a click, to extract the relevant words and to put them into a list with their associated URLs. In the current version of our implementation we consider only words which consists of more than three letters, except words in capital letters. In future implementations we will incorporate thesauri to decide which words are worth considering and which are not.

The requested HTML document is parsed on the fly. The list of all included URL and their anchor text are saved until the browser sends a new request. If the new requested URL matches one of the URLs in the list, the words of the anchor text are entered in a database. The words in the database reflect the user's preferences, which are used in the predictive algorithm. Every word entered in the list has an associated counter which will be incremented when the word occurs once again. We consider case insensitive words (Java = JAVA = java)

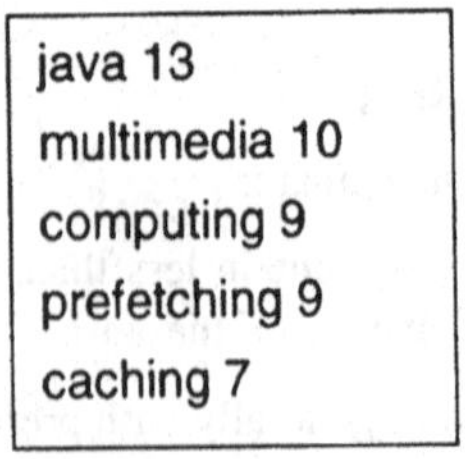

```
java 13
multimedia 10
computing 9
prefetching 9
caching 7
```

Fig. 3. Excerpt from clicked-word-list

Prediction module: This module compares the words in the clicked-word-list (Figure 3) with the words describing the links on the actual HTML page, starts the prediction algorithm, and sends the URLs to the prefetch module according to the correct order of their importance to the user. A prediction range is assigned to these URLs.

Prefetch module: The prefetch module preserves a list of URLs to load. URLs with a higher prediction range will be prefetched first. For more interactivity this module implements a stop method which enables the user to stop all on-line prefetching activities.

4 Implementation Results

Moper (MObile proxy helPER) is a WWW proxy server. Moper is installed on the local machine to support prefetching of web pages based on user preferences, thus reducing the waiting time of the user. Our application is a proxy server for the actual browser and poses as a browser for the remote server. We decided to implement our mechanism in Java ([14]) to overcome platform dependencies. We tested and evaluated our system on various platforms (Win 95, Win NT, Linux and Solaris).

To compare the efficiency of profile-dependent prefetching with the prefetching of all referenced pages, Moper is equipped with a couple of switches to make this decision. A small survey on educational web sites related to multimedia was made to inquire about relevant settings for these switches. We found that bigger cross-linking pages contain references (links) to 100 other pages and more, but we found only some pages with less than 7 links. The average number of links on the set of pages that were taken into account in our survey was 17.4. We consider it noteworthy that only 6.5% of these pages were greater than 15 kilobytes when the referenced images were not considered. Based on the results of the cross-linking survey, we chose to restrict the number of prefetched links per retrieved page to 15.

To compare our algorithm with unrestricted prefetching operations, we tested Moper in two different configurations. In the first one Moper made use of our approach and was configured to prefetch a maximum of 15 referenced pages if the words in the anchor text match the words in the clicked-word-list. The second configuration did not use the restriction and was set to prefetch any 15 referenced pages in the requested page, which reflects the approach taken by other prefetch mechanisms ([4][11]).

Using these settings, we made a couple of sample web surfing sessions without taking the download delay per page into account (all pages were loaded completely before the next request was issued). This approach does not give us any indication of the speed increase or decrease of our approach in comparison with other prefetching approaches but instead, provides us with an indication of the better efficiency of our prefetching approach in terms of transmission overhead, as well as hit-rate comparisons between ours and the simpler approach.

We defined the induced traffic as the number of prefetched pages and the hit-rate as

$$\text{Hit-rate} = \frac{\text{Responses from prefetch-proxy}}{\text{Requests}}$$

Figure 4(a) and Figure 5(a) present the results of various surfing sessions when our approach is used, Figure 4(b) and Figure 5(b) present the results of the typical approach. For each exemplary surfing sessions, a different general topic was chosen, ranging from technical issues such as Java programming to private interests such as travelling to South America.

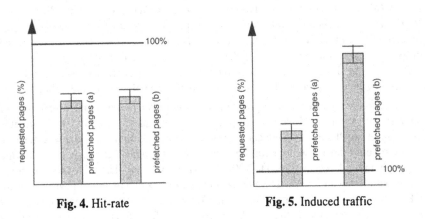

Fig. 4. Hit-rate   **Fig. 5.** Induced traffic

As shown in Figure 4, both configurations make approximately the same hit-rate (60%). While the configuration according to our idea of the user's behaviour has a hit-rate of about 61.05%, the random prefetching 15 referenced pages in the requested page achieves a slightly better hit-rate of 63.86%. Obviously, our approach will never have a better hit-rate than the trivial approach, but the difference is marginal in the experiments.

The advantage of our mechanism concerning the reduction of unnecessary traffic in the network, however, is considerable. Figure 5 shows that the overhead induced by the general prefetching technique (Figure 5(b)) is 10.04 times the amount of data compared with the pages that are actually visited by the user, our approach (Figure 5(a)) reduces this overhead to 4.29 times the number of actually visited pages.

5 Conclusion and Future Work

Prefetching is a speculative process. If the guess is wrong, a (high) price may have been paid by the community of Internet users at large for nothing. If the guess is correct, on the other hand, time is saved for the individual user. Prefetching is only sensible if the payment for the Internet connection depends on time, not on the amount of transferred data.

In this paper we have described a predictive prefetching mechanism for the World Wide Web to improve the access time without the extraneous penalty in network load that is typical for applications that prefetch speculatively. We consider that the links appropriate for prefetching come from the current user page. In our model the system guesses the next user request and prefetched those referenced pages, whose words in the anchor text are found in the user's clicked-word-list. We found out that our model reduces the bandwidth used by other prefetch systems which prefetch all referenced pages by the factor 2.34 for browsing sessions aimed at a focused information search, and that the hit-rate is approximately still the same.

We are now in the process of incorporating thesauri inside our prefetch module to increase the hit-rate, and to have better decision about words which may be entered in the user's database.

Another way of works in which we are interested is to use our proxy as a blocker, like per example, porno blocker, advertisements blocker or racism blocker. We do not need to know the IP-address or the domain name of servers related to the topic to be blocked, all we need is to define the words which should not be requested. The concept may even be extended to editing such links out of the presented pages.

6 Acknowledgments

We thank testers and users of our system. We also thank our colleagues Cornelia Seeberg, Stephan Fischer and Michael Liepert for useful comments on this paper.

References

(1) T.Berners-Lee, R. Fiedling, and H.Frystyk. "Hypertext Transfer Protocol-HTTP/1.0", RFC 1945, May, 1996.

(2) Azer Bestavros, Using Speculation to Reduce Server Load and Service Time on the WWW. Technical Report TR-95-006, CS Dept., Boston University, 1995

(3) Carlos Cuncha, Carlos Jaccoud, Determining WWW User's Next Access and its Application to prefetching, International Symposium on Computer and Communication, 1997

(4) Katsuo Doi, "WWW Access by Proactively Controlled Caching Proxy", Sharp Technical Journal, No. 66, December 1996.

(5) Evangelos Markatos, Main Memory Caching of Web Documents. In Electronic Proccedings of the fifth International World Wide Web Conferece, Paris, France, May 6-10, 1996.

(6) V.N. Padmanabhan, J.C. Mogul, "Using Predictive Prefetching to Improve World Wide Web Latency", ACM SIGCOM, Computer Communication Review, 1996.

(7) Catledge Pitkow, Characterizing Browsing Strategies in the World Wide Web, Technical Report 95-13, Graphics, Visualization and Usability Center, Georgis Tech, USA, 1995

(8) N.J. Yeager, R.E.McGrath, Web Server Technology, Morgan Kaufmann Publishers Inc., 1996.

(9) Marc Abrams et al. "Caching Proxies: Limitations and Potentials", http://ei.cs.vt.edu/~succeed/WWW4/WWW4.html

(10) Anawat Chankhunthod et al, "A Hierarchical Internet Object Cache", Usenix 1996 Technical Conference, http://excalibur.usc.edu/cache-html/cache.html

(11) Ken-ichi Chinen, "WWW Collector Home Page", http://shika.aist-nara.ac.jp/products/wcol/wcol.html

(12) Microsoft active Channel guide, http://www.iechannelguide.com/

(13) Netscape Netcaster,http://home.netscape.com

(14) Sun Microsystems Inc.: "The Java Tutorial``, http://Java.sun.com

Single Pair of Buffers: Reducing Memory Requirements in VBR Media Servers

Alberto García-Martínez[1], Jesús Fernández-Conde[2], Ángel Viña[3]

[1] Departamento Electrónica y Sistemas, Universidad Alfonso X el Sabio. Madrid, Spain
alberto@cesat.es
[2] Department of Computer Science. University of Massachussetts, Amherst, MA, USA.
jefer@cs.umass.edu
[3] Departamento de Electrónica y Sistemas, Universidade da Coruña. A Coruña, Spain
avc@des.fi.udc.es

Abstract. Most Video-on-Demand scheduling models are focused on the optimization of disk and network utilization, paying less attention to memory management. In this paper we present, analyze and evaluate a new buffering policy, namely Single Pair of Buffers, which greatly reduces Video-on-Demand server memory requirements when used in combination with any cycle-based scheduling algorithm. This technique is based on the synchronization of a single pair of buffers per storage device, as opposed to existing solutions based on per-stream buffering allocation. The influence of factors such as Variable Bit Rate streams, zoned disks, network speed and cycle length has been considered in detail. Extensive simulation results show that Single Pair of Buffers leads to more than one order of magnitude memory reduction when compared to the popular double-buffering approach, at a cost of a minor (less than 2% in the worst case) performance degradation.

1   Introduction[1]

The high rates and large quantities of data required in the service of multimedia contents are causing a growing demand for computing resources. Among these increasing requirements, we can observe the significantly large amount of memory used in Video-On-Demand (hereafter VOD) servers for scheduling and transmission purposes. Most of current cycle-based scheduling and transmission models assume the existence of an underlying *per-stream* buffering scheme, in which the number of buffers needed is proportional to the number of streams (i.e., clients) served simultaneously.

The most popular per-stream buffering implementation, Double Buffering, is based on the cooperation of two per-client buffers of identical size. While the first

---

[1] This research was supported in part by the National R&D Program of Spain, Project Number TIC97-0438.

buffer is being filled with data retrieved from the disk, a network I/O device reads the information previously retrieved from disk and stored in the second buffer. When the retrieval period ends, the two buffers interchange their roles. Double Buffering benefits from the simplicity of the shared memory paradigm to achieve a continuous flow between disk and network in a concurrent fashion. Per-stream buffering requires a substantially large amount of memory, especially in high bandwidth systems where several sessions are supported concurrently.

In this paper, we propose SPB, a buffering policy that uses a Single Pair of Buffers per storage device, as opposed to the allocation of buffers on a per-stream basis. The first buffer is receiving data from disk while the second one is delivering data that was read from disk immediately before, corresponding to the previous client. Buffers interchange roles whenever a fragment of data has been read from disk. We will see that this solution reduces server's memory usage in more than one order of magnitude, although it forces the computation of a new buffering admission test, that may slightly reduce the number of clients accepted by the server.

The definition of a global period is considered to be a convenient server's scheduling strategy [9]. The SPB buffering policy can be used in combination with any disk scheduling policy based on a global period. Two different approaches in global period disk-scheduling policies are the following:

- Round Robin (RR): all the clients are served in the same fixed order each round. In most cases this restriction is enforced by the division of a cycle into equally sized slots and the assignment of a single client to each slot. Slotted schedulers (e.g., [11]), present small latency (one cycle time in the worst case for accepted clients), but they are not bandwidth efficient, especially working with Variable Bit Rate (hereafter VBR) streams.
- SCAN: SCAN serves the clients according to their relative position in the disk, trying to minimize disk head movement. Compared to RR, disk efficiency is greatly increased, but worst case latency is doubled.

  Grouped Sweeping Scheduling (GSS, [5]) establishes a compromise between RR and SCAN. It divides a cycle into G groups. Each client is assigned to a group, and each group is served in a previously established order. The streams in each group are served in a SCAN basis.

VBR streams and zoned disks add further constraints to VOD server architectures. We take into account their influence, modifying the SPB buffering policy conveniently in order to make it effective under the conditions imposed by these two factors.

The remainder of the paper is structured as follows: in section 2, after stating some preliminary considerations, we describe the SPB buffering technique and detail the required admission test; memory consumption expressions are also provided. In Section 3 we develop an adaptation of SPB that allows its application to VBR streams stored in zoned disks. We describe our simulator in section 4, and present simulation results in section 5. Related work is summarized in section 6. Finally, section 7 is devoted to conclusions and future work.

2 The Single Pair of Buffers Policy

2.1 Preliminary Considerations

In order to analyze and evaluate the SPB scheme, it is convenient to state the following assumptions and conditions of applicability of the model:

- As pointed out in the previous section, SPB should be used in conjunction with a scheduling algorithm based on a global period. We will choose SCAN, although an analogous analysis can be developed for RR or GSS. The disk cycle time T will be selected statically and will not depend on the number of clients being served.
- SPB requires the use of *Bursty Transfer* mode [2] to deliver the data, that is, it will employ just one transfer to send to the client the amount of data read from the storage device in a cycle. Memory buffers at the client store the data until playback is required. This is opposed to *Continuous Transfer* mode, in which the client receives smaller data units with more frequency, and each unit is used to maintain playback for a small period of time (for example, a Group of Pictures for MPEG compression or a single frame for JPEG).
  Continuous Transfer, reduces client's memory requirements and allows a smoother transmission flow over the network. Its main disadvantages are that it makes data delivery scheduling more complex, and the performance may be reduced due to the inefficiency derived from processing small packets. In addition, Continuous Transfer leaves per-stream buffering as the only option. Bursty Transfer is an attractive option when a reasonable amount of memory is available at the client side, for example in personal computers interfacing Enterprise Video Servers, hierarchical architectures for multimedia distribution, interaction with powerful video-game stations, etc.
- The VOD server is disk bounded, i.e., network and bus are not bottlenecks. We will assume that enough network bandwidth is available, and that packets are never discarded. Bus influence is small because both network and disk use DMA to access main memory, and I/O operations are performed in parallel with bus transmissions, thanks to dual-ported memory buffers. In addition, bus conflicts are likely to be distributed equally between disk and network operation. Some studies based on performance monitoring analysis of data-intensive applications using network and disk on high-end UNIX stations with fast SCSI and ATM interfaces [10], confirm that I/O bus influence is a second order factor.
- Network transfers, triggered by disk interrupts, are activated after a certain delay (L_{net}), which is the sum of two components: the time taken to execute the interrupt code and issue the transference (which embodies the part of the network protocol processing that corresponds to the first fragment of data to send), and the delay the network interface may suffer when the information is transmitted (this last factor is negligible in a switched network with previously established virtual circuits).
- Client and server are loosely coupled. A server-push system model is considered, rather than a client-pull one. The synchronization of the sending cycle in the server

with the playback cycle in the client is performed in the connection phase, and network transfers are not driven by acknowledgements from clients.

- The parameters used in the analysis and evaluation of the SPB model are listed in table 1.

Table 1. Model parameters

T	Global cycle period
$n(c)$	Number of users served in cycle c
τ	Set of different cycle periods in a VOD server's run
$b(s,c)$	Number of bytes requested by stream s in cycle c
$L(s,c)$	Disk latency incurred when switching to stream s in cycle c
$R_{disk}(i,p)$	Disk transfer rate for the data requested by stream i in period p
$L_{net}(i,p)$	Sum of the time needed for in starting network processing (interrupt service, first part of the protocol processing that corresponds to the first fragment of data to send) and the maximum delay the network interface may suffer when the information is transmitted
R_{net}	Network transfer rate, including protocol processing in steady state
M	Memory required for scheduling

2.2 Model Description

SPB is based on the replacement of a set of buffers (allocated on a per-stream fashion) by a single pair of buffers per storage device. We define *storage device* as the minimum storage subsystem that can serve a single request; it could be a single disk, each disk in an interleaved disk array or the whole disk array in a spindle-disk configuration.

These two buffers are used in the following way: the first buffer (buffer a), receives data retrieved from the storage device corresponding to the stream $i+1$; at the same time, the data already stored in the second buffer (buffer b), corresponding to the stream i, is delivered to the network. These two buffers interchange their tasks whenever a whole fragment of data is read from the storage device (see Figure 1).

The admission test, needed to guarantee the proper behaviour of the system, checks two conditions every time that a new client asks for service:

- The network buffer has to be completely empty before the buffer switch occurs, otherwise some information would never be sent. A buffer switch is caused by an interrupt generated by the disk when it has finished reading a fragment of data.
- All the network transfers corresponding to a cycle have to be performed before the end of the current period. As a result, network transfer cycle and disk cycle will always stay synchronized, and therefore the clients will have a time reference to regulate their playback. Guaranteeing that the information corresponding to a cycle is delivered in the same period reduces the maximum start-up latency from two

cycles to one cycle in a SCAN-driven server. As a drawback, this condition is responsible for a short disk idle time at the end of the cycle, causing a slight performance degradation compared to normal SCAN operation. This condition is not mandatory, but is included in order to make synchronization easier and to reduce latency.

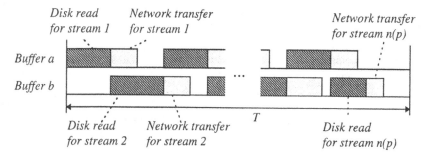

Fig. 1. Buffer Management in SPB

These two requirements can be mathematically expressed as:

$$\forall\, p \in \tau \quad \forall\, i, 2 \le i < n(p) \quad L(i+1,p) + \frac{b(i+1,p)}{R_{disk}(i+1,p)} > L_{net}(i,p) + \frac{b(i,p)}{R_{net}} , \qquad (1)$$

$$\forall\, p \in \tau \quad \sum_{j=1}^{n(p)} \left(L(j,p) + \frac{b(j,p)}{R_{disk}(j,p)} \right) + L_{net}(n(p),p) + \frac{b(n(p),p)}{R_{net}} \le T . \qquad (2)$$

Before accepting a new client into the system, these equations should be checked for all the periods that the new stream is expected to last. Note that in equation (1) buffer switching is not required to be tested for the first stream on each period, because the network is idle.

We should point out that equation (2) is sufficient to ensure that all disk operations are performed in the cycle time, and therefore no additional disk scheduling conditions are needed.

When long cycles are used to improve disk performance (large quantities of data are read contiguously), the key parameters to guarantee both conditions are the relation between disk and network speeds, and the difference in the size of the data read for consecutive streams.

2.3   Memory Utilization Analysis

Memory utilization is the primary figure of merit when comparing SPB with traditional per-stream buffering strategies. The amount of memory needed in SPB is

$$\forall\, p \in \tau \qquad M = \mathop{Max}_{i=1}^{n(p)-1} \big(b(i, p) + b(i+1, p) \big) . \tag{3}$$

An upper bound of (3) is

$$\forall\, p \in \tau \qquad M = 2\, \mathop{Max}_{i=1}^{n(p)} \left(b(i, p) \right) . \tag{4}$$

We can compare the previous amount with the memory needed when using double-buffering:

$$\forall\, p \in \tau \qquad M = Max \left(\sum_{i=1}^{n(p)} b(i, p) + \sum_{i=1}^{n(p)+1} b(i+1, p) \right) . \tag{5}$$

When memory is dynamically redistributed among all the buffers (5) is upper-bounded by

$$\forall\, p \in \tau \qquad M = 2\, Max \left(\sum_{i=1}^{n(p)} b(i, p) \right) . \tag{6}$$

3 The Influence of Zoned Disks and VBR Streams

Both zoned disks and the service of VBR streams complicate scheduling in VOD servers, compared to systems using simpler disk models and serving Constant Bit Rate streams:

- Zoned disks increase total disk capacity by placing more sectors per track as we move away from the disk axis. As a result, differences up to 80% in disk transfer rates can be observed between inner and outer disk zones.
- VBR streams allow constant picture quality at the minimum capacity cost. Factors of 3:1 are typical between peak and mean bit rates, while peak to peak divergences can exceed one order of magnitude.

Variations in disk transfer rate and stream playback rate in compromise the efficiency of *Worst Case* scheduling admission tests. *Statistical* tests provide better resource utilization, but do not guarantee jitter-free operation. *Ideal Deterministic* admission tests [4] provide full guarantee with optimal performance by estimating future service demands: the scheduler relies on a model of the underlying hardware and software to perform an admission test each time a new client asks for service, based on the pre-computed requirements for each stream in each cycle, $b(i,p)$. The model can be built over a simple average performance estimation [11], or may involve a detailed and time-consuming simulation of the whole multimedia system (disk, buses, CPU, memory, network interface, etc.). In a disk-bounded system, this simulation should focus at least on disk (paying an especial attention to disk zones, far more relevant than disk head movements or rotation times when the fragments read are large) and network simulation. Second-order effects could be included in the simulation if more computing power is available. The admission test proposed for SPB in the previous section is greatly affected by variations in the number of bytes demanded in a cycle by consecutive streams, especially when disk and network transfer rates are similar. The test is more likely to fail when a small request follows a large one. In most situations, the difference between network and disk transfer rate is unable to absorb stream rate divergences of one order of magnitude that arise in VBR contents, precluding the use of pure SPB. Variations in disk transfer rates are also important, although they are slightly concealed by SCAN ordering.

We present *Multiple Cycle Reading* (MCR), an adaptation of SPB that allows its application to a set of VBR streams played from zoned disks, when an Ideal Deterministic test is used. Basically, if the admission test fails because the network transfer for stream i takes longer than disk retrieval for stream $i+1$ (Figure 2a), we increase disk reading time adding all the data required for stream $i+1$ corresponding to the next cycle (Figure 2b). Then, client $i+1$ receives data corresponding to the current and the next cycle, (in the next cycle, this stream will be skipped). If the test still fails, subsequent cycles are grouped in a single read for client $i+1$. If the scheduling test fails on the modified schedule, the stream tested for admission is rejected. In general, the accumulation of data in some cycles will generate session rejections that will reduce performance slightly. The size of the grouped data should be limited by the amount of memory available at the client.

In the final schedule layout, data corresponding to a cycle for a given client should not be split in order to: (1) use the pre-computed information that characterize the requirements of the movie for each cycle, $b(i,p)$; and (2) reduce the number of disk head movements, since disk sectors for each cycle are stored contiguously in the disk.

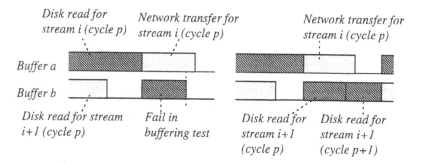

Disk read for stream i (cycle p)   Network transfer for stream i (cycle p)   Network transfer for stream i (cycle p)

Buffer a

Buffer b

Disk read for stream i+1 (cycle p)   Fail in buffering test   Disk read for stream i+1 (cycle p)   Disk read for stream i+1 (cycle p+1)

Fig. 2a. Fail in SPB Buffering Test   **Fig. 2b.** SPB - Multiple Cycle Reading

4 Simulation of the SCAN-SPB Scheduling Policy

The SPB buffering technique has been evaluated using a detailed simulator of a Seagate ST31200W zoned disk [6], including disk head movement, rotation and variable transfer speed. Disk cache and bus transferences are ignored.

The modelled network interface has an initial transfer latency of 1 millisecond, that accounts for the service of the disk interrupt, the first part of network protocol processing and the delay for accessing the network. A constant transfer rate is used, embodying steady state protocol processing and network transfer. Some measures of UDP/IP transmission over ATM OC-3 [10] yield to R_{net} values of 60 Mbit/s.

Streams (VBR-encoded MPEG-1 traces from [8] and [13]) are placed contiguously in the disk, extended along the whole disk surface, with equal spare zones among them. GOP (Group Of Pictures) units, 12 frames for the traces considered, are never broken.

The scheduler retrieves data in fragments corresponding to playback duration, using SCAN disk scheduling, and SPB including MCR. The maximum number of cycles that can be grouped for a given client is set to 300.

Client arrivals have been modelled using a time-homogeneous Poisson process, where minimum interarrival values have been established. The parameters are chosen to obtain system overload conditions. When a client is rejected, the same request is performed in subsequent cycles until it is accepted. The selection of movies is driven by a Zipfian distribution with a skew of 0.271, value observed in video rental requests. Movies that are closer to the outer edge of the disk (with higher transfer rates) are considered to be more popular.

It is important to note that the primary parameter for performance evaluation should be the *Effective Transfer Rate* (ETR), i.e., the number of bytes transferred per time unit. Disk utilization is skewed for zoned disks and the number of clients is not appropriate for heterogeneous VBR streams. We also compute the *Memory Saving Factor*, obtained dividing the amount of memory used by Double Buffering into the equivalent value for SPB. Memory usage is computed using expression (4) for SPB-MCR and (6) for Double Buffering.

5 Experimental Results

A comparison between Double Buffering and SPB (with Multiple Cycle Reading) in overload conditions is represented in Table 2. We observe a Memory Saving Factor of 38, while ETR decreases only by 1.2%. Multiple Cycle Reading is sparingly used, since we measured that only 2.6% of all the sectors read corresponded to grouped sectors.

When the system load is reduced, performance of SPB-MCR and Double Buffering are very close. Memory Saving Factors are lower with smaller loads, because memory is almost independent of the load in SPB-MCR, while Double Buffering requirements are greatly relaxed.

Table 2. Performance comparison of Double Buffering vs. SPB-MCR

Buffering Policy	Memory Usage (KBytes)	ETR (MByte/s)
Double Buffering	156994	3.48
SPB-MCR	4112	3.44

5.1   Effect of Network Transfer Speed

Network transfer speed is a key factor in our admission test. If the difference between network and disk speeds were sufficiently high, the admission test would always hold and no performance penalty would be observed. When network speed is only slightly higher than disk transfer rate, increasing buffer conflicts require more cycle grouping, degrading overall performance (Figure 3 - note that the disk maximum transfer rate is 33.4 Mbit/s).

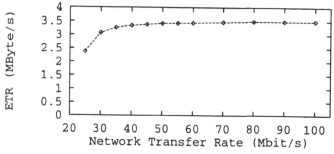

Fig. 3. Effective Transfer Rate vs. Network Transfer Rate (SPB-MCR)

The difference required between maximum disk and network speeds for acceptable performance is fairly small, and therefore the use of SPB-MCR does not add stringent network requirements to existing systems. Current computer configurations (typical disks and ATM network devices) allow the use of the SPB-MCR buffering technique proposed in this paper.

5.2   Effect of Cycle Length

Performance and latency in VOD systems largely depend on cycle length. When short cycles are used, the increased relative importance of disk seek times degrades the ETR (and consequently the number of clients served). Conversely, long periods imply higher service latency.

Effective Transfer Rates are very similar for Double Buffering and SPB-MCR (Figure 4), regardless of the cycle length. On the other hand, memory consumption in both buffering techniques is affected by cycle length (Figure 5). We can observe that, in Double Buffering systems with large cycle times, much more memory is consumed, because (1) there are more clients being served, and (2) more memory is required for each client in order to maintain playback. In SPB-MCR, only the second reason is relevant. The Memory Saving Factor is greater than 40.

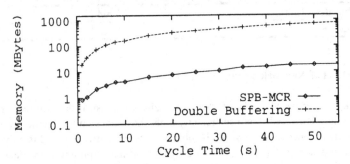

Fig. 4. Effective Transfer Rate vs. Cycle Time

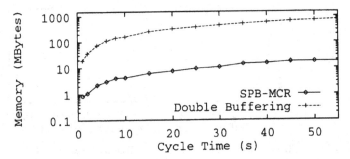

Fig. 5. Memory required vs. Cycle Time

6 Related Work

Reutilization of buffers is a known strategy in Operating System's practice. However, its application to the VOD environment, in which timely delivery of huge amounts of data is mandatory, has not been properly addressed.

Just-in-time scheduling [3] includes a per-device buffering technique for Continuous Transfer delivering in large arrays composed of independent disks. Clients are serviced in a SCAN basis, keeping the same order due to a stringent data placement strategy that forces all contents to be placed in the same zone on all the disks. There is a gap between the start of their cycles that stands for the playback time of the data sent for a client. The server delivers the data just after being read from disk, requiring three buffers per disk. However, the model considered is too simple: the time taken for reading a track is constant; seek times are accumulated in a single outermost to innermost sweep; and contents are equally demanding CBR streams. Disk and network issues are not considered to evaluate the feasibility of the solution.

The Tiger Filesystem [1] defines slots that are large enough to accommodate the largest disk transfer that may occur. Data is immediately sent at the end of each slot, but buffer reuse is not mentioned, and the applicability conditions are not stated.

Some adaptations have been proposed to per stream buffering strategies to overcome excessive memory consumption, being the most important GSS [5]. However, the total amount of memory needed still depends on the number of users served and is larger than in SPB-MCR.

Ng [12] combines buffer reuse with Double Buffering, to free up to 50% of the memory, but the scheme is difficult to implement, requiring non-contiguous buffer management.

The *Subgrouping and subcycling* scheme [14] focuses on buffer reutilization for Continuous Delivery disk array servers. G groups are formed, and the starting cycle time is shifted from group to group. Disk accesses on each cycle are also divided into G subcycles. This technique, similar to GSS, requires equally demanding CBR streams and does not consider zoned disks. Furthermore, subcycling leads to performance degradation.

7 Conclusions and Future Work

The main contribution of this paper is the presentation and validation of a new buffering technique for cycle-based VOD server schedulers, Single Pair of Buffers, suitable for working in realistic scenarios (VBR streams and zoned disks) when Multiple Cycle Reading is incorporated. SPB-MCR greatly reduces VOD server memory requirements when compared with existing per-stream buffering allocation schemes, at a negligible performance cost. Although our technique slightly increases network and computing demands, enough resources are generally available in off-the-shelf systems. The Memory Saving Factor obtained comparing SPB-MCR and other per-stream schemes, e.g., Double Buffering is greater for heavily loaded systems. To the best of our knowledge, this is the first analysis of the implications of the disk/network interface interaction in the optimal buffering of VOD streams.

SPB can be easily integrated with existent CBR homogeneous-movie-set media servers, using a worst-case based admission test. On the other hand, simulation is mandatory for performing admission tests and scheduling in deterministic VBR servers. We should point out that this is not an additional requirement of our technique, since simulation is considered as a must in high performance deterministic VBR servers.

We can increase the number of used buffers per storage device to allow more margin of operation [7]. This is an interesting option when stringent hardware parameters (such as too close network and disk transfer rates) are found, or when it is difficult to build an accurate simulation model of the underlying system.

Multiple Cycle Reading is an appropriate technique for dealing with VBR streams in zoned disks and mixed-rate streams, leading to both good performance and a simple implementation. Nevertheless, more elaborated strategies could be developed to allow the service of more clients: for example, the accumulation of information in cycles prior to the one in which the admission test failed.

In disk array based servers, SPB-MCR memory savings should outperform existing buffering techniques. SPB-MCR can be directly applied to spindle synchronized disk arrays (that constitute a single storage device), while in interleaved arrays a pair of buffers should be allocated per independent disk. This topic is addressed in detail in [7].

References

1. Bolosky. W. J. et al. The Tiger Video Fileserver. Proc. NOSSDAV. Zushi, Japan (1995).
2. Bernhardt, C., Biersack, E. The Server Array: A Scalable Video Server Architecture. Chapter 5 in "High-Speed Networking for Multimedia Applications. Eds. Kluwer. (1996).
3. Berson, S., Muntz, R. R.. Just-in-time Scheduling for Video-on-Demand Storage Servers. Technical Report, UCLA Computer Science Department. (1995).
4. Chang, E., Zakhor, A. Cost Analyses for VBR Video Servers. IEEE Multimedia, Vol. 3, n° 4. (1996) 56 - 71.
5. Chen, M.-S., Kandlur, D. D., Yu, P. S.. Optimization of the Grouped Sweeping Scheduling (GSS) with Heterogeneous Multimedia Streams. Proceedings of the ACM Multimedia Conference, Anaheim, CA (1993) 235-242.
6. Ghandeharizadeh, S., Stone, J., Zimmermann, R. Techniques to Quantify SCSI-2 Disk Subsystem Specifications for Multimedia. Technical Report TR 95-610. University of Southern California (1995).
7. García-Martínez, A., Fernández-Conde, J., Viña, A.. Efficient Memory Management in VOD Disk Array Servers Using Per-Storage-Device Buffering. To appear in Proc. of the IEEE Euromicro Workshop on Multimedia and Telecommunications (1998).
8. Garrett, M. and Willinger, W. Analysis, Modeling and Generation of Self-Similar VBR Video Traffic. Proc. ACM SIGCOMM (1994) 269-280.
9. Gemmell, J., Vin, H. M., Kandlur, D. D., Rangan, P. V. Multimedia Storage Servers: A Tutorial. IEEE Computer Magazine, Vol. 28, n° 5 (1995) 40-49.
10. Johnston, W. et al. Distributed Large Data-Object Environments: End-to-End Performance Analysis of High Speed Distributed Storage Systems in Wide Area ATM Networks. Proc. NASA/Goddard Conference on Mass Storage Systems and Technologies (1996).
11. Neufeld, G., Makaroff, D., Hutchinson, N. Design of a Variable Bit Rate Continuous Media File Server for an ATM Network. Proc. Multimedia Computing and Networking Conference, San Jose, CA (1996).
12. Ng, R. T., Yang, J. An Analysis of Buffer Sharing and Prefetching Techniques for Multimedia Systems. Multimedia Systems 4 (2). Springer-Verlag (1996) 55 - 69.
13. Rose, O. Statistical Properties of MPEG Video Traffic and Their Impact on Traffic Modelling in ATM Systems. Technical Report TR-101, Institute of Computer Science, University of Wuerzburg (1995).
14. Tobagi, F., Pang, J., Baird, R., Gang, M. Streaming RAID - A Disk Array Management System for Video Files. Proc. ACM International Conference on Multimedia. Anaheim, CA (1993) 393-400.

Author Index

Lecture Notes in Computer Science

For information about Vols. 1–1397

please contact your bookseller or Springer-Verlag